Shelter Blues

Contemporary Ethnography

Series Editors
Dan Rose
Paul Stoller

A complete list of books in the series
is available from the publisher.

Shelter Blues

Sanity and Selfhood
Among the Homeless

Robert Desjarlais

PENN

University of Pennsylvania Press

Philadelphia

Copyright © 1997 University of Pennsylvania Press
All rights reserved
Printed in the United States of America on acid-free paper

10 9 8 7 6 5 4 3 2 1

Published by
University of Pennsylvania Press
Philadelphia, Pennslyvania 19104-6097

Library of Congress Cataloging-in-Publication Data
Desjarlais, Robert R.
   Shelter blues : sanity and selfhood among the homeless / Robert Desjarlais.
      p.   cm. — (Contemporary ethnography)
   Includes bibliographical references (p.   ) and index.
   ISBN 0-8122-3407-3 (cloth : alk. paper). — ISBN 0-8122-1622-9 (pbk. : alk. paper)
   1. Homeless persons—United States.   2. Homeless persons—Mental health—United
States.   3. Homeless persons—Services for—United States.   4. Homelessness—
Psychological aspects.   5. United States—Social conditions.   I. Title.   II. Series.
HV4505.D47   1997
305.569—dc21   97-8656
                                                                                                        CIP

Contents

Illustrations

It's like the shelter blues. I feel this sometimes, when I get depressed. Others too, I think.People begin to feel worthless, as if they're not doing anything in their lives. I try to make people feel more alive by touching them, talking to them.

—Richard Groton to the author, June 1991

There I'll be, in the old shelter, alone against the silence and . . .
(*he hesitates*)
. . . the stillness. If I can hold my peace, and sit quiet, it will be all over with sound, and motion, all over and done with.

—Samuel Beckett, *Endgame*

You live on the other side of the world. You can't know what it's like to be living here.

—Eva Winfield to the author, October 1991

"Beauty and the Street"

"Fresh croissants, hot coffee, classical music, a carnation on every table," begins one journalist's account of "Compassion Fatigue" in 1991 Boston:

—the Au Bon Pain [a local cafe] on Mass Ave between Harvard and Central Squares couldn't be a more inviting place to start the day. Regulars hunker down here every morning before work or school, settling into cafe chairs, eating pastries, poring sleepily over the morning papers. Rarely does anyone look up.

But one frigid morning late in January, the peaceful civility here was rudely—and horribly—interrupted. A homeless man limped in, bleeding heavily from the nose. He wailed with pain, and screamed something about having been beaten up. His shrieks filled the cafe, and a thick mixture of blood, mucus, and tears dripped down his face. Finally, the man's "family"—other homeless people from the neighborhood who gather, usually more inconspicuously, at one side of the cafe—calmed him down. When the crying stopped, a collective sigh of relief rose up in the room. The storm had passed.

But tension lingered. Even as they returned to the safety of their newspapers, the regulars in ties, skirts, and Gap clothing remained grim-faced. The barriers that keep despair like this at bay had been challenged. It was a bitter way to start the day.[1]

The hook in this article pursues a gambit common to the beginnings of many recent newspaper stories. To grab the reader it sparks a collision of motifs, a feat uncanny or jarring in an ordinary setting: the classical stillness of a croissant breakfast is "horribly interrupted" by a bleeding, wailing vagabond. Pain shatters the beauty of order.

Other tales of homelessness open with similar themes. "Here's a museum show that'll kill you," ventures a *Washington Post* story:

As in, you lie face up on a mock morgue slab, and somebody slides you into darkness, and the first words spoken by the cassette in your Walkman are "You're going to die."

But then you get reincarnated. Into the American urban underclass. And then things get really bad.[2]

The article goes on to explain that, at the Smithsonian's Experimental Gallery, the exhibit "Etiquette of the Undercaste" enables visitors to lie on a mock morgue slab and hear first-person tales of the homeless. "The park seems suddenly alive with macabre spirits," says a writer for the *New York Times Magazine* of Washington's Lafayette Park, separated from the White House by Pennsylvania Avenue.[3] On this avenue the police gunned down Marcelino Corniel, a homeless resident of the park, in December 1994. Another article refers to the "cardboard homes and potential coffins" in which people sleep in Chicago's "gloomy underworld of pavement and loading docks."[4] "To his mother, he is a child back from the dead," writes Royal Ford of the *Boston Globe* of a Dickens-reading teen who, after sleeping in the "chilly" woods of Maine, came to live, in hiding, in the attic of the State Library.[5] "People would come up to talk just because they wanted to hear what a person like me would sound like," the boy says after being arrested for burglary. The article is similarly intent on announcing the unique find of a homeless lad who, on the edge of the wild, actually can and likes to read.

A common problematic vision is apparent in many accounts: the homeless live in an underworld; they are a ghostly, animal-like brood who threaten the peaceful, artful air of cafes, libraries, and public squares. Television shows and Hollywood movies like *The Fisher King* create pictures of ghostly, ragged vagabonds haunting the post-industrial wastelands of American cities, while newspaper accounts thrive on images of death, transgression, and grotesque bodies. Distinct themes or images are often paired: a morgue in a museum, a runaway in a library, blood and Beethoven. The homeless themselves serve to counter images of health, wealth, purity, and high culture. The imagery passes swiftly, unquestionably, as if it was in the nature of sentences, of putting words onto paper, to set pain against beauty and wretchedness against form.

The "Names and Faces" section of the *Boston Globe* personified the play between beatitude and grotesqueness on December 16, 1993, in a brief blurb entitled "Beauty and the Street," which reported on a Fruit of the Loom-sponsored visit by Kimberly Aiken, Miss America '93, to the Salvation Army church in Cambridge.[6] "Dressed in a black sweater with matching slacks set off by a Santa Claus red blazer," the article notes in a stunning mix of fashion sense and humanitarian concern, "Aiken seemed right at home with the 200 or so homeless men, women and families sheltered at the Army." The blurb ends by noting that Miss Aiken "hopes people remember not how she looked but what she did."

The homeless can also be defined by how they look. To describe someone as "homeless" announces a lasting identity. When used, the adjective is lasting and all-encompassing: journalists and others often speak of a "homeless" woman or man with the same certitude that they identify someone as a doctor, a politician, or a white man. Homelessness denotes a temporary lack of housing, but connotes a lasting moral career. Because this "identity" is deemed sufficient and interchangeable, the "homeless" usually go unnamed. The identification is typically achieved through spectral means: one knows the homeless not by talking with them but by seeing them. Such a similar logic of appearances apparently aided the New York railroad police when they arrested twenty-four people who "appeared homeless" in Grand Central Station.[7] Can one be certain of another's homelessness, short of documenting the absence of housing? In 1988, Ed Koch, then mayor of New York City, explained what he took to be the obvious to the American Institute of Architects. "These homeless people, you can tell who they are," he said. "They're sitting on the floor, occasionally defecating, urinating, talking to themselves—many, not all, but many—or panhandling."[8]

Scatologies here and elsewhere recall the "grotesque realism" that Mikhail Bakhtin finds in the sixteenth-century stories of Rabelais, who wrote animatedly of the multiple, protuberant corpulences of everyday life in France.[9] But whereas Rabelais and other writers of his day played up the carnivalesque, ambivalent, symbolically inversive, and generative sides of the "material bodily lower stratum," Koch and other contemporary authors zero in on the negative, sexless, horrific sides. For them, the homeless are those who fail to restrain their bodies from an outpouring of scat, urine, words, or outstretched arms; they offend a spectator's sensory faculties. The cafe intruder in the article on "Compassion Fatigue," for instance, is identified as "homeless" partly on the basis of the limp and wailing he bodies forth; in contrast to the hunched forms of the pastry eaters, his flesh exudes blood, mucus, and tears. What matters most are the bodily and social transgressions involved—even though in Koch's account the transgressions can just as readily be read as political economy: sitting on a floor (chairs and homes are denied them), defecating and urinating in public (due to the privation of toilet facilities), panhandling (for want of money), and talking to oneself (a result of extreme isolation).

The latter theme signals the mental deviance of some itinerants, otherwise known as the "homeless mentally ill." Here the added imagery is of disorder and irresponsibility. One journalist describes an encounter with a woman during a nighttime survey of the streets:

An old woman, her hair whipped wildly about her head, lay cocooned in an orange sleeping bag . . . shielded ever so slightly against the frigid December night. . . . "Move on, move on," she bellowed, her voice echoing against the vast brick buildings in the quiet of midnight. She mumbled something about "sick blood" and clutched her meager belongings.[10]

The unruly hair is a classical sign of madness, as are the paranoid, incomprehensible mumblings.

Another article describes a youth living in a Boston shelter for the homeless mentally ill as "a small man, 24 years old, with eyes like nails and the bones of a sparrow. . . . The hands fold and unfold on the wooden table, revealing inch-long fingernails—thin, dirty claws."[11] The piercing eyes, sparrow bones, and unkempt claws speak of animality and potential violence.

These characterizations of a mad "old woman" and a birdlike young man imply certain ideas of human personhood and agency. In a 1976 paper the philosopher Amelie Rorty argues that modern concepts of a person entail distinct strands of thought that can be traced back to societal and literary notions of "characters," "figures," "persons," "selves," "individuals," and "presences."[12] Each of these notions entails "layers and accretions of usages" that have developed through time and contribute to certain perspectives on human agency.

Characters are delineated; their traits are sketched; they are not presumed to be strictly unified. They appear in novels by Dickens, not those by Kafka. Figures appear in cautionary tales, exemplary novels and hagiography. They present narratives of types of lives to be imitated. Selves are possessors of their properties. Individuals are centers of integrity; their rights are inalienable. Presences are descendants of souls; they are evoked rather than represented, to be found in novels by Dostoyevsky, not those by Jane Austen.[13]

Many journalists, politicians, and films cast the homeless as negative "figures." Rorty notes that "Figures are defined by their place in an unfolding drama; they are not assigned roles because of their traits, but rather have the traits of their prototypes in myth or sacred script. Figures are characters writ large, become figureheads . . . their roles and their traits emerge from their place in an ancient narrative. The narration, the plot, comes first: it requires a hero, a betrayer, a lover, a messenger, a confidant."[14] Although figures are allegorical, they are also fully embodied, vivid, and realized. "But far from being individuating, these traits run true to type, even in their concreteness and specificity."[15] Figures include the biblical personages of Christian dramas—the pilgrim, the tempter, the savior, the innocent—and revolutionary heroes.[16]

Figures also include the homeless, at least as portrayed in the media. The homeless are usually characters writ large, serving as figureheads of despondency, vagrancy, insobriety, madness, or moral failure. The plot often comes first: the scene in Au Bon Pain requires a "homeless man, bleeding heavily from the nose"; a wintry survey requires "an old woman, her hair whipped wildly about her head." Such figures are at once allegorical (expressing the idea that homeless bodies transgress social orders, or that only crazy people refuse to stay in shelters) and fully embodied (a bloody nose, wildly whipped hair). The traits run true to type: the bag lady, the shopping-cart woman, the runaway youth, the homeless vet, the inebriated panhandler, and the paranoid schizophrenic are rarely individuated, even if they are endowed with two or three physical details. Yet whereas biblical and hagiographic figures are, by definition, exemplary idealizations, to be read as "inspirational models to be imitated, to guide lives and choices," homeless figures are presented negatively, as models to be avoided, and thus as illustrations of the value of other ways of being. Their roles and their traits emerge from their place in ancient narratives. They are the descendants of witches, old hags, tramps, drunks, beggars, mendicants, and madmen.

Lest anyone take these ways of making meaning to be inconsequential, without real force in the world, we need only recall the predictable fate of Mr. Corniel, who was portrayed as a leprous lunatic in the wake of his death at the hands of the police in front of the White House, or read about the man set afire in New York City in the summer of 1995, or consider the "social cleansings" (*limpieza social*) enacted by vigilantes in Colombia, who have killed hundreds of vagrants, criminals, prostitutes, street children, and drug addicts, all known as "disposables."[17] These are metaphors to kill by. In the United States, those living on the streets, in doorways, or in train stations are often forcibly removed because of the dangers and unsightliness posed by—or, more accurately, imposed on—them. Archaic themes of dirt, displaced matter, and ritual expulsion are also involved. "They look at us like we're germs, like we're dirt," said one man to director Bill Brand during the filming of *Home Less Home*.[18] Cleansing can thus be seen as necessary, and in a throw-away society this often takes the form of trash removal (a 1989 cartoon in a Brooklyn paper casts homeless people as human refuse).[19] The Grand Central Partnership apparently sought such a cleanup in 1994 when they allegedly paid "outreach workers" to beat up and displace those who slept on the sidewalks and doorways of central Manhattan.[20] Similar offenses have occurred in other urban centers in the United States. A 1996 report found that, of the country's 50 largest cities, 19 had initiated crackdowns on homeless people in the mid-1990s, and 27 had recently engaged in police "sweeps" of homeless people.[21] The spectral presence of the homeless is bad for business. Barriers are erected to keep the despair at bay, and the violence said to be integral to homelessness turns back on the homeless themselves.

Alice Weldman's Concerns

Such is the potent imagery of homelessness, to which we will soon return: that of grotesque bodies, unnamed figures, animal behaviors, incomprehensible utterances, and deathly underworlds. Yet while the images might seem accurate, natural, or inevitable, they are not intrinsic to, or necessarily representative of, the lives of those who sleep on the streets or in shelters. In *Powers of Horror* Julia Kristeva notes that, while the "intimate side" of abjection is suffering, horror is its "public feature."[1] The above accounts are concerned more with the perceived horrors and stigmata of homelessness than with its intimacies.

To counter such horrors as well as the violence and social policies they commonly spawn, this book is concerned with the intimacies of homelessness, illness, and abjection. Its methodological mandate works against the grain of most media representations of homelessness. In trying to shy away from knowing and portraying people chiefly through visual means it draws as much if not more on conversations with people as it does on observations of them. And in trying to avoid portraying the homeless as figures embodying ancient but negative themes it considers their lives in terms of complex swirls of cultural, political, economic, sensorial, psychological, and biological forces. These considerations call for a way of writing that moves nomadically from one theme to another, grounding everyday events in cultural forms and political realities, and ragpicking through a crowd of objects, surfaces, voices, bodies, images, and stances to detail their makings.

Several of these themes and forces are evident in the life of Alice Weldman, a highly intelligent and deeply religious white woman in her late thirties whom I came to know in the early 1990s while I was conducting ethnographic fieldwork in a shelter where she was staying. The shelter, for people considered both homeless and mentally ill, was set up in a defunct gym on the ground floor of a large mental health center in downtown Boston—in the same building, in fact, where the reputedly "clawed, sparrow-boned" man lived. While staying in the shelter Alice could often be found in or around the mental health center, in a social club upstairs on weekday mornings and early afternoons (when the shelter was off-limits to guests), and in the shelter itself or a "lobby" next to it evenings and on weekends. She spent much of her time by herself, reading the Bible or, when she was not doing so well, sitting curled up in a corner, nodding her head repetitively. Quite often she would approach others in order to bum cigarettes from them. She did not want to start buying packs of her own lest she pick up an expensive habit, since she had little money. The Bible helped her to reduce the noise, worries, and distractions that were an inescapable part of life in the building. "If I can just read the Bible for fifteen, sixteen hours a day," she said one day, "and just block out all the rest, then I'm okay." Given the lack of calm in the building and Alice's own troubles, the task was not an easy one.

Since I was hanging out in the same places that Alice frequented, we spoke with each other quite often in the next few months. Through what I took to be a mutual enjoyment in talking with one another, I was learning about life in the shelter while she had a chance to voice her concerns and frustrations. Through these conversations I learned a bit about her life and background. Born and raised in a Boston suburb, Alice had worked for a while as a secretary after finishing high school. She could not stand hearing about the "infidelities" of her co-workers, however, and quit a few years later. She said she had a "nervous breakdown" in her early twenties that stemmed from her parents' treatment of her and the physical and psychological abuse she suffered in life. Sometime later she had a child, which the state, deeming Alice an unfit mother, took away in the early 1980s. Since then she has considered herself "estranged from society," living principally on the streets, in shelters, or in local psychiatric hospitals. "I lived on the street for fifteen years," she said. "I was happy on the street. People gave me food. I found safe places to sleep, on doorways, and read the Bible in libraries during the day. Nobody bothered me. I told the police that I was a woman who preferred to live on the streets. . . . Out on the streets I found my sense of honor again. I couldn't take working with secretaries, hearing of all their infidelities. I'm more comfortable sitting in a lounge with a bunch of street people, with their raggy clothes, than with a bunch of secretaries or professionals. I could find more distance living in the streets than if I were to remain a secretary. . . . Now that I'm pushing forty, though, I'm starting to talk with more people."

For a long time, she said, it was as if "civilization" was "sympathetic" to her problems. But then "they"—the police, psychiatrists, social workers—started to treat her badly by forcing her to take medications, confining her in psychiatric hospitals, and heeding the edicts of psychiatric and legal institutions. She was therefore deeply ambivalent about staying in the shelter: while it provided more comfort and companionship than she found on the street, it also put her under the power and authority of the Massachusetts Department of Mental Health. "You know," she said in rushing up to greet me one day, "they put me into a hospital and forced me to take meds. They're just monsters. They won't leave me alone. They'll probably take me to court to force me to take meds, and they'll win."

"What do the meds do?" I asked.

"All they do is make me stuff myself with food. They're supposedly to heal my supposed illnesses."

She had stopped taking medications a few weeks before and soon began to spend her days in a withdrawn state, sitting with her hands curled around her knees and nodding her head repetitively. Staff members who worked in the shelter later told me that, after she "partially disrobed" in public, they sent her to a hospital where she was forced to take anti-psychotic medications. The use of pharmaceuticals was particularly troublesome for Alice because she was a faithful follower of Mary Baker Eddy's Christian Science, which prohibits the use of medications.

Around this time Alice showed me a passage from the Bible's Tenth Psalm, which, she said, fit her life to a T:

Their mouths are filled with cursing and deceit and oppression;
under their tongues are mischief and iniquity.
They sit in ambush in the villages;
in hiding places they murder the innocent.

Their eyes stealthily watch for the helpless;
they lurk in secret like a lion in its covert;
they lurk that they may seize the poor;
they seize the poor and drag them off in their net.
The hapless are crushed, sink down, and fall by their might.

Alice identified herself as one of the hapless, innocent poor—seized, caged, and crushed by the mighty. "Lower-enders like myself get the brunt of it," she once told me. Evidently Alice also thought of herself as an "individual," to use another of Amelie Rorty's terms: as a unique and autonomous individual, encroached upon by the mandates and infidelities of a corrupt society, who maintained her sense of honor and moral righteousness by resisting such encroachments.[2] She eventually left the shelter to occupy the doorfronts and side streets of Harvard Square. The last I saw her was in 1993; she was sitting in a storefront, close to a guitar-playing folk singer, nodding her head repetitively.

Although Alice's desire and ability to live alone on the streets was exceptional, many themes in her history recurred in the lives of other "lower-enders" I came to know in the shelter. The problems that came with hearing voices or acting "crazy"; the difficulties in relating to and getting along with others; the unnerving effects of pharmaceuticals; the tribulations of life "on the street"; the desire to find "safe places" in an often frightful and isolating city; the mandates, confinements, and displacements enforced by employees of the state; a constant lack of money; the pros and cons of living in a shelter; and efforts to "block out all the rest" were topics about which many had a lot to say.

These and related issues have also been on the minds of a few anthropologists. There are now several first-rate ethnographies of "homeless" families and individuals living on city streets or in shelters.[3] Yet little attention has been paid to those who, like Alice, have ostensive "mental health" problems (to use the current but profoundly culture-specific idiom). This is partly because many scholars and advocates do not want others to get the wrong idea about people living on the streets. According to the best estimates, people known to be mentally ill comprised from one-quarter to one-third of those living on the streets and in shelters in the late 1980s and early 1990s.[4] But newspapers and politicians have sometimes amplified these numbers to depict the homeless as a witless, alcoholic lot and redirect attention from the economic and political factors that usually precipitate a lack of housing.[5] To counter this tendency, most sociologists and anthropologists have focused on those who cannot readily be portrayed as mentally ill. Much of the research on the homeless mentally ill has thus been left in the hands of psychiatrists and health services researchers, who usually rely on survey protocols. There has consequently been a "dearth of rich qualitative descriptions" on "how homeless mentally ill individuals live their lives and make meaning of them," as Paul Koegel observed in 1992.[6] Although a few more articles have since trickled into the scholarly journals, Koegel's finding that ethnographic approaches can provide a much-needed "different lens" through which to understand homelessness and mental illness still stands.[7] Such approaches can offer an antidote to "the language of pathology and images of the grotesque" on which, as Kim Hopper notes, official discourses on homelessness repeatedly draw.[8]

This kind of work can also help us to understand in more theoretical terms the linkages between culture, illness, marginality, and personhood. Medical anthropologists, in trying to discern such linkages and so move away from simplistic and reductive psychiatric categories of disease, have compellingly argued that the cross-cultural study of madness demands sustained ethnographic inquiry, particularly into the personal, "experiential" aspects of illness and healing.[9] These urgings parallel a more general call in anthropology for studies of experience, of consciousness, of bodiliness, and of sensory perception and knowledge.[10] Some contend that such studies are especially needed in settings of poverty and violence because they can help us to understand the pervasive impact of such settings on the people who live in them.[11] Common to these perspectives is the idea that we need to know more about what people from a range of different worlds go through in their everyday lives before we can develop integrative accounts of what those lives are about and thus try to avoid some of the assumptions that quietly but powerfully shape our understandings of human subjectivity. In her far-reaching essay "A Cyborg Manifesto," Donna Haraway argues that the only way to characterize the present state of political and technical domination in the world today is as "a massive intensification of insecurity and cultural impoverishment, with common failure of subsistence networks for the most vulnerable."[12] "But what people are experiencing is not transparently clear," she goes on to note, "and we lack sufficiently subtle connections for collectively building effective theories of experience. Present efforts—Marxist, psychoanalytic, feminist, anthropological—to clarify even 'our' experience are rudimentary."[13]

In considering the perceived hardships of people without permanent homes, I undertake a project similar to the ones noted above. This book offers an ethnographic portrait of the everyday lives and worlds of those who stayed, like Alice, in the shelter. It also tries to sketch what goes into the makings of human subjectivity on the margins of a late modern, post-industrial city at the close of the twentieth century.

Rethinking Experience

Explorations of "experience" are never straightforward, however, for once we begin to clarify its nature, we run into a host of problems. The intimate, experiential side of homelessness or any other abjection is just as mythic and just as cultural as the public, horrific side. There are also questions of how one goes about knowing what other people experience and the rhetorical uses to which expressions of experience are put. In turn, any attempt to build effective theories of experience is complicated by the fact that people's lives can entail very different ways of being. The category of experience is riddled with cultural assumptions, political tensions, pragmatic moves, rhetorical pitches, and subjective vicissitudes.

Rather than shy away from such riddles, however, I want to address them as directly as a zigzagging ethnography will permit. In so doing I want to sketch a way of thinking about social life that treats the category of experience not as a universal, natural, and supremely authentic entity—as many take it to be—but as a process built sharply out of cultural, historical, political, and pragmatic forces. Experience, often held to be the most fundamental aspect of being human, is here taken to be one form of life among many.

Behind this approach lie two fundamental concerns found in any study of "human experience." The first centers on the epistemic status of experience: How do we know what we know about experience, and what kind of knowledge does experience entail? The second relates to the ontic status of experience, or what experience, as an act, process, or entity, is assumed to be.

The first concern often boils down, in anthropology at least, to the idea that the native "experiences" to which ethnographers refer are supremely authentic ones—or at least more authentic and truthful than social relations, cultural discourses, or theoretical models. While references to the relation between experience and language, culture, or beliefs pepper many anthropological writings, few ethnographers address experience in more than abstract terms. When these writers try to hammer out the contours of experience, the wrinkles tend to take several characteristic forms. Some anthropologists draw on the concept of experience to provide the "missing term," as the historian E. P. Thompson wrote, through which "structure is transmuted into process, and the subject re-enters into history."[1] Some rely on it because it appears relatively free of the baggage that concepts like "self" or "mind" or "affect" carry.[2] Some anthropologists are interested in the cultural patterning of sensory experience, using experience as a correlative of the felt and the sensorial.[3] Others advocate phenomenological or "experience-near" approaches that try to cut through cultural discourses to touch upon "lived" experience.[4] Still others try to get at the moral aspects of everyday life, with experience involving an intersubjective medium of daily engagements.[5]

While these orientations call for diverse theories and findings, all stem from romantic sensibilities toward the incongruous and nearly unfathomable aspects of everyday life. They follow from Franz Boas's distinction between physical and historical-cosmographic methods, whereby "physicists" sought to "bring the confusion of forms and species into a system," and "cosmographers"—considering the phenomenon itself "without regard to its place in a system"—sought to "penetrate into its secrets until every feature is plain and clear."[6] Boas, Sapir, and Geertz have advocated the latter, ideographic approach, as have many American anthropologists. Yet, as the philosopher Charles Taylor notes, experientialist approaches also echo a "widespread aspiration" in post-romantic thought "to retrieve experience from the deadening, routinized, conventional forms of instrumental civilization."[7] Here, experience is held to be a truer aspect of life, rich enough to defy conceptual models. The sentiment accompanying this notion has passed from Schiller to Dilthey to contemporary anthropologists, who claim that theoretical and medical models fail to account for the intensely felt and personal dimensions of human life and suffering.[8]

For several scholars, lived experience is "the primary reality": "What comes first is experience."[9] Those who study "experiential truths" thus find they are investigating the most authentic, and most human, of anthropological categories.[10] In contrast, those anthropologists who do injustice to a society's plane of felt experience stand accused of "doing violence to the authenticity of the flow of lived experience."[11] Much of the impetus for "an anthropology of experience," as some call it, lies in the attempt to avoid such violence. Michael Jackson, for instance, does not want to "risk dissolving the lived *experience* of the subject into the anonymous field of discourses."[12] The emphasis is on felt realities rather than cultural categories, the near rather than the distant, and the sensate more than the semantic. The sensate implies immediacy, which in turn is said to carry authenticity.[13]

In the end, however, this logic is haunted by a problematic collapse of ontology and epistemology, of being and knowing, in which the supposed realities of experience are given the status of facts by the statements of anthropologists. The problem with taking experience as a uniquely authentic domain of life—as the first and last court of appeal—is that we risk losing the opportunity to question both the social production of that domain and the practices that define its use (after all, questioning cultural assumptions and social constructions is basic to anthropology). Connotations of primacy and authenticity lend legitimacy to the anthropologist's craft, but they can simultaneously limit inquiries to descriptions of the terrain of experience when what we need are critical reflections on how the terrain comes about.[14] Asking about experience can tell you about some things, such as how the everyday takes form, just as asking about labor relations or clan lineages can tell you about other things. None of these questions implies any supreme authenticity, merely fields of inquiry. I take the concerns, doings, and lifeworlds of shelter residents as one such field of inquiry.

Other anthropologists have raised similar issues, such that perspectives on the study of experience generally divide anthropologists into two camps. There are those who advocate an anthropology of experience that investigates, chiefly through phenomenological means, domains of life—pain, bodies, emotions—which one can only poorly apprehend through cultural analysis; and there are others who find that such an anthropology is both epistemologically unfounded, since one can never really know the felt immediacies of another person or society, and irrelevant to more important social and political concerns. Nevertheless, the word is of such value that even scholars critical of experiential approaches acknowledge that without it or something like it "cultural analyses seem to float several feet above their human ground," as Clifford Geertz puts it.[15] Experience, it seems, is a crucial element of contemporary academic thought in the United States. To try to write about humans without reference to experience is like trying to think the unthinkable.

This raises concerns about the ontic status of experience, for despite the apparent necessity of experience, as something that can and must be thought, its universality remains in question. We must ask if the act of experiencing is as essential or as commonplace as many take it to be. In listening to the debates noted above, for instance, one gets the sense that everyone knows what is meant by experience. But the word is rarely defined, and when it is defined, it typically involves a generic "we" (as in "We experience . . ."). That the category of experience goes undefined or is couched in universalist terms suggests that it is taken as a fundamental and unchanging constant in human life. The situation is similar to the one Heidegger faced in *Being and Time*. Experience, like Being, is seen as one of the most universal and emptiest of concepts. It requires no definition, "for everyone uses it constantly and already understands what he [sic] means by it," and it "has taken on a clarity and self-evidence that if anyone continues to ask about it he is charged with an error of method."[16]

In contrast to Heidegger, however, I want to argue that experience is not a primordial existential given but rather a historically and culturally constituted process predicated on certain ways of being in the world. Experience is the result of specific cultural articulations of selfhood (namely, a sense of self as possessing depth, interiority, unity, stability, and the capacity for transcendence) as well as certain social and technological conditions that foster and legitimate that sense of self.

The etymology of "experience" suggests how the concept has evolved in European thought. The modern English word "experiment" apparently best preserves the original meaning of "experience," although the latter also meant at first "putting to the test."[17] From this came an understanding of experience as "actually observed phenomena in order to gain knowledge of them," which in turn led to the more subjective "condition of having undergone or been affected by a particular event."[18] The modern subjectivist connotations of experience appear to be a recent innovation; the idea that to experience is to feel, suffer, or undergo is first recorded in 1588.[19] The implied interiority parallels the evolution of Western concepts of the self, particularly in terms of the "language of inwardness" that has increasingly come to characterize human agency in the West since Augustine.[20] Similar to the trajectory of the dominant form of selfhood in the West, which is widely believed to have been initially marked by exterior relationships to one's environment and later to have been moved toward a moral, reflexive agent, experience evolved from a verb denoting an external engagement with or "testing" of one's surroundings to a template marking a person's subjective awareness of that engagement.

Through time that awareness has grown increasingly introspective. In 1938 Lévy-Bruhl observed that:

Our current notion of experience bears the mark of certain mental habits that are peculiar to the civilizations of the West. Since classical antiquity it has been elaborated over the centuries by generations of philosophers, psychologists, logicians, and scientists. . . . The essential role of experience, as it has been described and analyzed by this tradition, from Plato and his predecessors down to Kant and his successors, is to inform the sentient and thinking subject of the properties of creatures and objects with which it places him in relation, to make him perceive movements, shocks, sounds, colors, forms, odors, etc., and to permit the human mind, which reflects on these data and on their conditions, to construct a representation of the world. The general notion of experience that has been thus developed is above all "cognitive."[21]

While twentieth-century musings have identified affective dimensions in experience, experience is now generally held to be a subjective, reflexive process that rests securely on a person's cognitive abilities to reflect on and make introspective sense of his or her engagement with the world. As Lévy-Bruhl, Hallowell, Lienhardt, and other anthropologists have pointed out, however, human functioning need not depend on such reflective assessments; rather, it can assume a range of non-introspective forms.[22] Experience involves only one, rather inward-looking arrangement of human action among many.

The stress on interiority ties into the affirmation of ordinary life that has earmarked humanistic thought and literature and relates to the Romantic sensibility that the most authentic truths lie in our selves.[23] A focus on the truths of personal revelations relates closely to modern religious concerns, particularly the Pietist emphasis on religious devotion, with personal experience, as "a state of mind or feeling,"[24] forming an integral part of the inner religious life. The inner states cultivated through such devotion reveal truths worth talking about. Raymond Williams notes, for instance, that nineteenth-century Methodists held "experience-meetings," or classes "for the recital of religious experiences."[25] Today as well, experience is rooted largely in individual agency. A person "has," "learns from," or "discloses" an experience. Privacy, individuality, and reflexive interiority are intrinsic to experience; no one else can experience my toothache, although someone might empathize with my suffering. Experience thus readily equates with a person's "inner life" or "consciousness" and is often considered synonymous with "subjectivity."[26]

The idea of interiority encourages some to try to understand the "very marrow" or "essence" of experience and leads others to suggest that "experience is sensual and affective to the core and exceeds objectification in symbolic forms."[27] The excessiveness of experience points to a second distinguishing feature: it possesses hermeneutical depth. The sense of depth, like that of interiority, ties into forms of meaning and selfhood common to the modern West. Erich Auerbach identifies the roots of some of these forms in the opening chapter of his magisterial *Mimesis,* wherein he details how the narrative form of the Greek Homeric poems differs from that of the Judaic biblical writings of the Old Testament.[28] Auerbach finds that Homer narrates the travels of Odysseus in such a way that all phenomena are represented as world-immanent. They are given objective, fully externalized form, fixed in a time and place, visible and palpable in all their parts, connected together in a perceptual foreground, without lacunae or "unplumbed depths," and with both people and things clearly depicted and brightly and uniformly illuminated. The biblical narratives, in contrast, convey only so much of the phenomena as is absolutely indispensable for the purpose of unfolding the story; all else is left as an obscure, transcendent background. Scripture conveys only the decisive points, leaving it to the imagination to generate connections. Here time and space, though mentioned, go undefined and call for interpretation, and the whole "remains mysterious and 'fraught with tension.'" Whereas the thoughts and feelings of the timeless characters in Homer (who age or change little in their lives) are completely represented, those of the biblical characters remain sketchy. In sum, the individual characters of the Old Testament are more complex than the Homeric personages; they possess various layers of consciousness, find themselves in problematic psychological situations, and develop through crises over time.

Auerbach keeps to the study of literary history, yet there are strong affinities with more recently discovered domains. Homer's representations of reality and personhood, for instance, recall recent discussions of forms of language and selfhood in non-Western societies, such as Samoa, and suggest how human beings need not depend on profound interiors or complex psychological dramas.[29] In turn, features of the biblical world of form—such as the opaque presence of unplumbed heights and depths, the multiplicity of meanings, the need for interpretation, and the idea of personal transformation and historical becoming—continue to resound, in attenuated form, in many Euro-American traditions (such as modernist novels, films, psychoanalytic thought, and hermeneutics, not to mention everyday life). Ideas of height and depth, of multilayered complexity, of a surplus of meanings calling for steady interpretation, and of an individual who develops through time lie at the heart of ideas of personal experience in the modern West.

The development of experiential depths has been a progressive one. According to Charles Taylor, while the writings of Augustine, Descartes, and Montaigne brought successively stronger declarations of human "inwardness," only with the expressivist yearnings of Wordsworth, Hölderlin, and others to discover and articulate our inner nature does this interiority come to possess significant, unfathomable depth—"a domain," that is, "which reaches farther than we can ever articulate, which still stretches our furthest point of clear expression."[30] In modernist times, the grounds of experience, rather than those of selfhood, have possessed the richest depths because experience is often seen as the foundation of human agency.[31] The import of experience is inexhaustible because experience, like a text or a work of art, carries a wealth of meanings that can never be conclusively interpreted.[32]

The hermeneutical depths of experience distinguish it from the subject matter of traditional cultural analysis. This kind of experience eludes social science analysis and resists easy symbolization. The idea of an abundant, semiotically rich plane of being entails the view that the only way to study experience fruitfully is to attend to the perimeters of expressions, stories, and social formations in which it is cloaked.[33] To say that "thick description" is the best method of analysis here is not to denigrate the available methods but simply to point out the kind of phenomena involved: experience is too complex, too subtle, and too private to be understood through anything but phenomenological ascertainments. Even then, "It's all a matter of scratching surfaces," as Clifford Geertz puts it.[34] Talk of surfaces, cores, and bone marrow suggests a shadow play of interiors and exteriors: we cannot penetrate the vessels of experience. The body is often held to be one such container, with the skin serving as an "envelope" within which, as William Faulkner writes, "the sum of experience" resides.[35]

Despite the immediacy, richness, and contingency that characterize lived experience, experience works on a principle of unity. John Dewey talks about the "inclusive integrity" of experience, while Michael Oakshott ponders its "concrete totality."[36] William James, Dilthey, Husserl, Merleau-Ponty, and others agree that the sum of experience is greater than its parts. Joyce's Leopold Bloom, Freud's Wolfman, and Proust's remembrances exhibit and exemplify the integrality of experience; memories, dreams, reflections, anticipations, and sensations combine into a whole in the sudden flash of an epiphany. The appeal to wholeness apparently relates, for many, to a desire to develop a concept that might safely encompass the many features of human agency, such as "thought," "feeling," "perception," "reflection," and "sensation."

Experience builds toward something more than a transient, episodic succession of events. The intransience of experience ties into the fact that it has a lasting and memorable effect on the person who undergoes it. "To undergo an experience with something," Heidegger writes, "— be it a thing, a person, or a god—means that this something befalls us, strikes us, comes over us, overwhelms and transforms us."[37] By undergoing an experience a person picks up something new: "Experience means *eundo assequi*, to obtain something along the way, to attain something by going on a way."[38] Experience transforms: it "does not leave him who has it unchanged," or so says Gadamer in his specification of a "genuine experience" (*erfahrung*).[39] To have an experience or to learn by experience suggests an education that can accrue in certain skills or knowledge, though this education hinges on a flux of subjective reflections that other kinds of learning (such as operant conditioning) do not. The Oxford English Dictionary notes that, since the sixteenth century, experience has involved "knowledge resulting from actual observation or from what one has undergone." Experience is thus the fodder for the kind of psychological developments or becomings that have characterized ideas of personhood in Europe since the Old Testament at least.

"To experience is to go along a way. The way leads through a landscape," writes Heidegger, drawing on the fact that *erfahrung* comes from the Old High German *infaran*, which means to travel, traverse, pass through, reach, or arrive at.[40] The landscape is organized along both spatial and temporal lines. Experience, by definition, collects itself through the rhythmic pacings of time. As David Carr, who draws from Husserl, puts it, "Our experience is directed towards, and itself assumes, temporally extended forms in which future, present, and past mutually determine one another as parts of a whole."[41]

Narrative typically helps to forge the sense of temporal integration. The idea that experience accumulates in time through stories builds on musings on the relations between forms of life and narrative orderings of time. From Aristotle to Heidegger to Ricoeur, the interpenetration of narrative and experience has grown stronger with the increased importance of literature in the lives of the educated. The present state of the art is that we can only grasp our lives through narrative, although one can and ought to question to what degree this apparently "inescapable" fact applies within as well as outside the modern West.[42]

Experience as a whole is subject to similar queries. In much the same way that the truth of sexuality grew out of an economy of discourses that took hold in seventeenth-century Europe,[43] so discourses of depth, interiority, and authenticity, sensibilities of holism and transcendence, and practices of reading, writing, and storytelling have helped to craft a mode of being known in the modern West as experience: that is, an inwardly reflexive, hermeneutically rich process that coheres through time by way of narrative.

Struggling Along

Given this complex genealogy of the idea of "experience," there are several ways in which we could proceed. We could try to ignore or deny its history and use the word in the most minimal and seemingly innocuous way possible—equating experience with simply being alive or sensately aware, for example. Or we could suggest that, because philosophers have gotten it wrong, we should try to wipe the slate clean and redefine experience in a less culture-laden, less bourgeois, or perhaps less masculine way. We could argue that the Western heritage presents only one, albeit variegated, strand of experience, with other traditions—Hindu, Muslim, Pintupi—advancing other versions.

None of these approaches appear to work, however. To me, any use of the word cannot but carry the traces of its heritage, and any attempts to dislodge the concept from its accumulated resonances would be like trying to extract a fly cleanly from flypaper.

We could, in turn, try to dispense with the category altogether and fall back on the idea of "consciousness" in describing the everyday. But this word is entangled in the same heritage and is perhaps even more thoroughly interwoven with the cognitivist strands that Lévy-Bruhl identified. Or it could be asserted that experience is a nonreality, a figment of the philosopher's fancy. But experience is very much a reality, or is in any case as real as other cultural phenomena: much evidence suggests that, at the least, many American families, therapists, and patients commonly live today in terms of experience as modernist philosophers, anthropologists, and others have articulated its manifold meanings.[1]

The best strategy might be not to try to redefine the category nor to dispense with it altogether, but rather to invest it with a specific meaning and set forth the conditions that must be present before experience can be ascribed to people. In turn, since experience as a form of life is only one possibility among many, it makes sense to infer that experience is found in distinct cultural-historical settings and that some people sometimes live in terms different from experience.

The latter appeared to be the case with many residents of the shelter. If we take experience to be simply a sensate awareness of life, or "to be alive when something happens" (which is the lowest possible common semantic denominator of "experience"), then everyone in the shelter experienced, for the worlds of all residents were marked by interiority and a sensate reflexivity. But, as noted above, experience entails much more, and the subjective and temporal contours of residents' lives often differed from those found in the unfolding of experience. By and large many residents did not live by way of a hermeneutically rich process that proceeded, cohered, and transformed through temporally integrative forms. Rather, they got along in life in terms of an acutely tactile mode of perception cued to episodic encounters. While there were many odd angles to the residents' lives, those lives often boiled down to a set of features that were perhaps best put into words by Alice Weldman, who would often say she was "struggling along" when asked how she was doing.

"How ya doing?" Louise Colbate, another resident, asked her one afternoon.

"Oh, struggling along," Alice said.

"Yeah?"

Alice walked away without responding.

Her response aptly described what life was like for her and many of the fifty others who slept on the basketball court. To "struggle along" was to proceed with great difficulty while trying at times to do away with or avoid the constraints and hazards strewn in one's path. The struggles implied strenuous efforts against opposition, hitting up against a world filled with noise, voices, bodies, pains, distractions, poverty, displacements, and bureaucratic powers. The process was double-edged, for while it involved the idea of carrying on with difficulty, it also spoke of the effort to avoid or do away with difficulties, hassles, or constraints— to the point, at times, of trying to block out everything in seeking a "degree-zero" way of being. Since one way to stop thinking about the cold or other distractions was to step out of the flow of time, the acme of this predilection was the pursuit of timelessness. To get away from the constant tensions and the fleeting distractions, some suspended the minutes or hours of a day. Too much calm could get to a person after a while, however, and many tried to find ways to keep busy without getting bored. An idle mind was an ill mind for some; pacing and other routines helped to lessen the worries that came with living in the shelter. Often the trick was to find a balance between sensory overflow (which could include "hearing voices") and walking around in a stupor. Many residents tended to work toward points of equilibrium, which often came down to a sense of stasis. The stasis, which made a good deal of sense, given how much was impermanent, unmanageable, and distractive in residents' lives, tended to grow more fundamental the longer a person stayed in the shelter.

While struggling along was the primary mode of existence for most shelter residents, more than a few also "experienced" at times, with patches of each modality filling their days. William Fordham, for instance, spent a lot of time away from the building during his seven month stay in the shelter. A tall, sandy-haired white man from New Orleans who settled in Boston for several months after spending time in other cities east of the Mississippi, William said that his family was in the egg business, producing ten thousand eggs a week. "My father has a lot of money," he said one day. "But I'll never see any of it. I visit my family from time to time, and they might give me fifty or a hundred dollars, but not much more. . . . The nurse called my brother last week, to see what she could find out about me. . . . I've seen over sixty psychiatrists. They've figured me out every which way." William dressed very well, often sporting dress shoes, slacks, and an Oxford shirt. "If I'm wearing a sharp suit," he said one night, "and have twenty dollars in my pocket, and can go to a restaurant like Wendy's, then I'm all set. I don't need a fancy job, and I don't need credit. . . . I tell you what. I'd rather have a Harvard degree in my hands than a million dollars, because that's respect right there." He was very concerned with proper appearance and behavior, in both himself and others, and spoke intensely at times about the state of the world. "The values of this country are falling apart," he told me one day. "It's an equal society now. The daughters of ditch-diggers are mixing with the daughters of doctors." He preferred smart clothing, pretty women, "proper," educated people, and long walks through Boston. "Tension builds if you stay in one place all day, whether you're mentally ill or not," he once said. Finding that going for walks helped to relieve tension, William would typically walk about five miles each day, drifting from the central Commons to the fashionable shopping area of Newbury Street to the artistically and educationally rich Fenway district and back again, and return around five o'clock to speak of his adventures.

"I kissed a woman on the lips today," he said one evening. "She was sitting on a bench, and she was crying, and so I kissed her. Now she wants to know where I live." The incident was more an adventure than an episode because it carried lasting meaning, future possibilities, and elements of suspense. "Episodes," Hans Gadamer writes in assessing Georg Simmel's equation of experience with adventurousness, "are a succession of details which have no inner coherence and for that very reason have no permanent significance. An adventure, however, interrupts the customary course of events, but is positively and significantly related to the context which it interrupts."[2] To use Heidegger's terms, the kiss befell William, struck him, overwhelmed and transformed him. He went along a way. The way led through a landscape. The journey through this landscape, with its landmarks, suspense, and education, is what many take as experience.

The idea of journeying is an important one for shelter residents, for movements through varied spaces inhabited and traversed by others appear to be integral to experience. To experience is to move through a landscape at once physical and metaphoric. In the shelter such movements were opposed to the repetitive ambulations of pacing, which ideally took a person through as smooth and unhindered a space as possible. Whereas many hovered close to the building, dealing with day-to-day contingencies, some ventured into the encumbered spaces of the city, an activity that often carried a sense of risk, anticipation, novelty, engagement, and storytelling. William's experiences, for example, emerged from a customary walk through Boston, the adventures that checked a traveler's gait, and a way of talking that gave form to those adventures.[3] His and others' daily excursions from and to the mental health center advanced the spatial and temporal makings of experience. Any walks undertaken readily broached the elements of opaque mobility, reflective wandering, and the narrative poetics that Michel de Certeau locates in what he calls "the long poem of walking."[4]

Others lived a similarly marginal existence in the shelter, which is to say that the political, social, temporal, linguistic, and sensorial features of shelter life did not engulf their lives. As I saw it, these people, principally those who were new to the streets and tended to look for and sometimes found jobs and apartments, lived largely within the folds of experience: they carried on in reference to constellations of inwardness, hermeneutical depth, renewal, cumulative transcendence, and narrative orderings of time. Nathan Ellison, for instance, was a young African American from Canada who ended up in the shelter after he lost his job out west, his car was stolen, and he got into trouble with the law. A month later he shared his thoughts on the people who lived in Boston. "The drudgery of their lives makes them lifeless," he said. "There's just a skeleton there, a frame. You see, there's a Cadillac, then a Porsche, and then at the end there's the Pinto. These people are the barest, the most simplest, you see what I mean? There's no life to them, no spirituality." I asked what caused the drudgery. "There's no transactions here," he said, "no business, no bidding for architectures. . . . In Boston, you have to be rich to be able to enjoy the city. You have to be a doctor, or a lawyer, or a basketball player." Nathan had a lot of fears and usually was a bit shaky. Nevertheless, he went out looking for an apartment and pushed his insurance claim on the car through the Boston courts. These activities led him to spend most days outside the building. He would generally return to the shelter around five o'clock to eat. About a month into his stay he started a Bible-reading group and began to mention the novel he wanted to write about "making it in the city today." His relatively short stay in the shelter, his desire to avoid Boston's privations, and his reflective focus on writing, spirituality, and urban transactions enabled him to lead a life different from those of most shelter residents, who struggled along more than they experienced.

Both "experience" and "struggling along" are patterned by longstanding cultural orientations, strengthened through a lifetime's interactions, such as a sense of selfhood as something unique, individual, and interior. They are therefore not mutually exclusive categories, in which the elements of one imply the absence or negation of corresponding elements in the other. Yet the two modalities do involve distinct phenomenal, aesthetic, and temporal features. The phenomenal plane of experience is a thoroughly reflexive one: to experience is to engage in a process of perception, action, and reflection couched in mindful introspection. Struggling along also entails a firm sense of interiority and reflexivity (which suggests the strong cultural dimensions of many, if not all, accultured peoples in the United States), but the reflections are not as intense as they are with experience. For shelter residents, the distracting sights and sounds of the building often prompted an acutely sensorial mode of awareness, which left little room or need for introspection or contemplation. Day in, day out, things happened much more on the retina, the eardrums, and the fingertips than in any detached haven of mind or body. Experience, then, implied a contained, integrative, hermeneutically rich, and occasionally transcendent adaptation of emotions, images, and lessons; struggling along entailed a diffuse and external rain of distractions that sometimes prompted more a retreat from the world than an incorporation or self-reflexive assimilation of its parts.

Experience entails an aesthetics of integration, coherence, renewal, and transcendent meaning—of tying things together through time. A good day for someone who is experiencing might be one in which there is a novel integration of personal undertakings, a tale to be told bordering on the adventuresome. The features of such a day build on the stuff of novelty, continuity, transformation, plots, and movement. A good day for someone who is struggling along, in contrast, might be a smooth one, where difficulties can be temporarily overcome, where a few bucks are earned, where the voices are not too bad, where tension is relieved through pacing, and where there are enough cigarettes to last the day. The ingredients of such a day draw from the forces of contingency, expediency, equilibrium, and stasis.

Pacing or sitting in the same spot for several hours each day has its consequences. The temporal order of experience, involving as it does a cumulative layering of events that build to a whole greater than its parts, proceeds along narrative lines of an Aristotelian bent, with clear-cut beginnings, middles, and endings as the ideal. The gist of experience is that it goes beyond the situation at hand, with past, present, and future mutually determining one another as parts of a whole. The temporal order of struggling along, in contrast, involves a succession of engagements, which can include a constant but purely episodic plodding of events. Alice's life, from an abusive upbringing to a nervous breakdown, and from a "happy," loner's life on the streets to the state's brutal confinement of that life, did tell a story of sorts. But her day-to-day existence in the shelter mainly involved events free of broader narrative frames.

The routines of shelter life could contribute to an episodic orientation toward time, with each incident taking precedence over any larger temporal matrix, as well as to the occasional need to stop the rush of events and find some point of equilibrium or stillness. In turn, economic constraints and the press of everyday worries usually directed residents' struggles toward temporally finite forms in which future, present, and past did not have much to do with one another.

George Orwell wrote of the annihilation of anticipation in *Down and Out in Paris and London.* "When you are approaching poverty," he noted,

you make one discovery which outweighs some of the others. You discover boredom and mean complications and the beginnings of hunger, but you also discover the great redeeming feature of poverty: the fact that it annihilates the future. Within certain limits, it is actually true that the less money you have, the less you worry. When you have a 100 francs in the world you are liable to the most craven panics. When you have only 3 francs you are quite indifferent; for 3 francs will feed you till tomorrow, and you cannot think farther than that.[5]

Lars Eighner, a writer who lived for three years on the streets of Austin and Los Angeles with his beloved dog Lisbeth, found that most of those days were filled with "empty hours" and "unrelenting ennui" wherein he could aspire to "nothing more than survival." "Every life," he writes, "has trivial occurrences, pointless episodes, and unresolved mysteries, but a homeless life has these and virtually nothing else."[6] Upon returning to the streets of Austin after hitchhiking to California and back again, he realized that the "reality of homelessness" entails the absence of narratives:

On our way to California I had my hopes. I was convinced at least once that we [he and Lisbeth], or one of us, would die before we got there. But either I would die or I would reach California, and what is more, the outcome would be clear within some few days. To progress was to get nearer California. Some days we progressed and some days we did not. Whether we would end in Los Angeles or in our graves, our direction gave meaning and measure to the days.
Such a structure is utterly lacking in a life on the streets.
Home is the natural destination of any homeless person. But nothing can be done in a day, in a week, in a year to get nearer that destination. No perceptible progress can be made. In the absence of progress, time is nearly meaningless. . . . A homeless life has no storyline.[7]

Homelessness and poverty have a way of throwing into relief aspects of life many take for granted, such as a narrative structure. They also throw into question the idea of experience, for life in the shelter often had no experience. As such, residents' lives were not especially excep- tional, since many in North America are undoubtedly subject to such struggles. Any differences between the lives of residents and those of others were more of intensity and duration than of kind. And while the disabling troubles associated with being "mentally ill" surely played a role in such struggles, it was largely a diffuse set of environmental forces, rather than any inherent will, heritage, or psychology, that led to such a situation.[8] Struggling along related to, among other things, a pauper's economy, a politics of displacement, a world of public spaces, and routines of fear, nervousness, and distractions.

A Critical Phenomenology

The presence in 1990s Boston of distinct ways of being, each with its own defining features, conditions, and constraints, suggests a need to rethink our approaches to the everyday. Instead of assuming that "experience," "emotions," or "narratives" are existential givens, ontologically prior to certain cultural realities, we need to question their origins and makings. As the great phenomenologists used to say, we need to place these concepts "in brackets" or "in abeyance."[1]

Ironically, this strategy calls for a reworking of how most phenomenologically oriented studies proceed. In the opening pages of *Speech and Phenomena*, Jacques Derrida shows that Edmund Husserl's phenomenology is shot through with a metaphysics of essence, presence, and authenticity, despite Husserl's assertion that his phenomenological method "excludes all 'metaphysical adventure.'"[2] In flirting with a similar metaphysics, anthropologists have come to equate phenomenological approaches with the study of "lived experience." The problem with this equation is that we can quickly gloss over the fact that, with a truly phenomenological approach, the idea and assumed nature of "experience" must be placed in brackets. Phenomenology after Hegel has been centered on the study of personal experience, individuated consciousness, and subjective perception. Since these notions are deeply rooted in Western cultural and philosophical traditions, however, a true study of phenomena would have to question even these categories from the start. As it is, many take the categories of experience and subjectivity to be universal constants, as if they were lasting transcendental categories the contents of which culture completes as rain fills a bucket. But a strong case can be made for the inverse: that the categories of experience, selfhood, personhood, and subjectivity are cultural and historical in nature; that what we take as "experience" or "agency" are born of a gamut of cultural, political, biological, linguistic, and environmental forces.

Of course, no method of inquiry can avoid metaphysics. Still there is value in studying people's lifeworlds from a phenomenological perspective, if only to parry the prevalent public images of homelessness with an account drawn from the homeless themselves. In so doing, however, we need to question received understandings of subjectivity, sensation, and the like. In my reckoning we need a critical phenomenology that can help us not only to describe what people feel, think, or experience but also to grasp how the *processes* of feeling or experiencing come about through multiple, interlocking interactions. Such an approach is phenomenological because it would entail a close, unassuming study of "phenomena," of "things themselves"—how, for instance, people tend to feel in a certain cultural situation. But the approach is also critical in that it tries to go beyond phenomenological description to understand why things are this way: to inquire, for instance, into what we mean by feeling, how it comes about, what it implies, and what broader cultural and political forces are involved. In addition, the phenomenology is a critical one because it tries to take into account the makings of its own perceptions.

The stress here is on the political because of the need to bridge phenomenological approaches and considerations of political economy. As it is, many politically attuned studies of social life neglect the finer questions of human agency and subjectivity, while many "experience-near" approaches are bereft of serious analyses of the political and economic forces that contribute to the apparent reality or nearness of experience. Anthropology is in dire need of theoretical frames that link the phenomenal and political. A few studies do make compelling links, but many concern themselves more with *what* people feel and know of pain, joy, or illness than with *how* they do so.[3] Studies of the latter are necessary, especially ones that convincingly link modalities of sensation, perception, and subjectivity to pervasive political arrangements and forms of economic production and consumption. Such work can offer insights into how political, economic, biological, and cultural forces intersect in constituting a person's or a group's lifeworld, as well as address the perennial critique that phenomenological approaches tend to neglect broader social and political dynamics in accounting for subjective realities.[4]

In 1977 Michel Foucault hit on the crucial idea while explaining to interviewers his "genealogical" approach to the constitution of human subjectivity:

. . . this historical contextualisation [in a genealogical study] needed to be something more than the simple relativisation of the phenomenological subject. I don't believe the problem can be solved by historicising the subject as posited by the phenomenologists, fabricating a subject that evolves through the course of history. One has to dispense with the constituent subject, to get rid of the subject itself, that's to say, to arrive at an analysis which can account for the constitution of the subject within a historical framework. And this is what I would

call genealogy, that is, a form of history which can account for the constitution of knowledges, discourses, domains of objects, etc., without having to make
reference to a subject which is either transcendental in relation to the field of
events or runs in its empty sameness throughout the course of history.[5]

Foucault could have been speaking of anthropologists, who sometimes
devise a transcendental subject that varies from culture to culture or
runs in its empty sameness throughout the course of humanity—even
though Gregory Bateson concluded years ago that any sense or presence of mind is immanent rather than transcendent in nature.[6]

In accord with Foucault's Nietzschean framework, I find it necessary
to try to account for the constitution of subjects within a specific cultural setting, such as the shelter. The impetus for this approach draws
on the orientations of Nietzsche, Heidegger, and Foucault with regard
to the historical and cultural conditions that lead to specific ways of
being. Nietzsche explored the web of political relations, historical patterns, and cultural values that make bodies, selves, and consciousness
possible. Heidegger sharpened these concerns into a phenomenological meditation on what he took to be the fundamental conditions of
Being. Foucault then situated Heidegger's meditations within a specific
history: namely, the political and cultural tides that launched the now
self-evident realities of deep, reflexive selves. Gilles Deleuze notes that
Foucault was trying, particularly in his later writings, to map out three
distinct but interdependent ontologies as they took form in the West:
power, knowledge, and subjectness.[7] Deleuze finds that these historically
contingent realities boil down to three fundamental problems, each
of which manifests itself differently in particular historical formations:
What can a person do, what powers can she claim, and what resistances
might she counter? What can she know or sense or articulate? What can
she be, or how can she produce herself as a subject?[8] In considering the
nature of everyday life in and around the shelter where Alice stayed, I
follow this tack in considering three interrelated sets of questions:

What can the residents of the shelter do? What are the dominant
relations of power in the shelter? How do these politics tie into local
techniques of psychiatric care? On what forms of political agency can
residents rely?

How do the residents know and communicate? How do they relate to
one another and to others who pass through their lives? How do they
use words? How do the pragmatic and rhetorical stances of residents,
shelter staff, and others tie into broader political concerns and modalities of care?

What are the residents' chief ways of being in the world? How do they
orient themselves in time and space? What are the sensate grounds of

life in the shelter? In what ways does the state try to change how residents feel, think, act, speak, and know, and what are the implications of these therapeutic efforts?

To begin to develop answers to these questions, we need to cast a wide analytic net and consider a range of forces and factors. After detailing the general lot of the homeless mentally ill in the United States, the history of the shelter, and the nature of my research there, I will turn to the architecture of the building where the shelter was located and the ways in which people used and made sense of the building's diffuse spaces and surfaces. This leads into a discussion of the layout of the shelter, its everyday routines and protocols, and what people made of their lives there and on "the street." Along with examining the political economies underpinning many of those lives, I discuss the maladies—"hearing voices," constant "nervousness"—from which people suffered and the ways in which Alice and others tried to "hold themselves together" through various actions and routines. As shelter residents frequently observed, one of the problems with hearing voices or being "crazy" was that it often made talking with others trying at best. After reflecting on such talk and the nature of social relations in the shelter more generally, I turn to concerns of the staff, who, in seeking to improve the lives of their guests, encouraged residents to speak, act, and think in ways quite different from their customary ones. Since the residents' and the staff's orientations to language implied different political stances and different kinds of agency, a consideration of the disparate linguistic, political, and epistemic orientations of residents and staff leads to reflections on the ways these orientations influenced how residents felt, knew, and acted in specific situations. The discussions thus build to an understanding of the multifaceted and pragmatically attuned modalities of sensing, knowing, remembering, and listening common to everyday life in the shelter. Through this inquiry, we can, I think, get a handle on the everyday. We can also get some sense of what it means to "struggle along" in the shelter. In so doing we may also obtain a more comprehensive, more fluid, and less categorical understanding of shelter lives than the idea of struggling along alone can afford.[9]

Questions of Shelter

Thinkers like Foucault, who emphasize the priority of cultural discourses in shaping our lives, tend to speak of incarnations of self or power as generic to an age. Yet while such approaches are useful in map-ping forms of mind and personhood specific to historical periods and sometimes show how these forms take shape in everyday life, they seldom consider how the stuff of personhood is built out of the events and doings of everyday life. They also tend to neglect the plurality of forces that occasion diverse ways of being at any moment within a society. To rectify this tendency we need to examine how patterns of sensation, forms of agency, or a sense of personhood come about in specific social interactions. Such a study requires not only a reading of broader cultural "discourses" in the Foucaultian sense of the word, but an ear toward mundane utterances, conversational exchanges, and day-to-day contingencies.

Contingencies were the rule in the Station Street Shelter where Alice stayed. Transitions and fluxes occurred frequently in 1991 and 1992, when I did my research. The interim, "acting" manager was soon to retire. Staff left for other jobs and new employees replaced them. Residents came and went, often without warning. People were unsure whether possible living arrangements would work out; economic options and resources varied over time; and there were rumors of the sale of the building to a local university, which would force relocation of the shelter and its residents. The early 1990s was also a time of economic hardship in the region, state budget crises, a Republican governorship, severe cuts in health services in Massachusetts, and a general push for "privatization," in which social services formerly run by the government were put into the hands of private, profit-driven businesses. Program cuts affected the shelter in two ways: residents lost case managers and treatment programs, and staff members worried about losing their jobs. In all, an air of impermanence and uncertainty permeated the shelter.[1]

The shelter was the product and its residents the recipients of two broad historical trends in the United States. The first entails the roots of, and political responses to, homelessness in the past century; the second, the nature of state-supported institutional care for those considered mentally ill. Although significant numbers of people have been homeless in the United States since at least the Civil War, this population and its visible presence on the streets, in shelters, or in makeshift homes has increased dramatically since the beginning of Ronald Reagan's presidency. The increasing number of homeless has largely been due to a tangle of macro-level structural forces, most notably: deindustrialization; urban decay and gentrification; the destruction of skid rows; a shortage of affordable housing in urban settings (especially in the residential hotels and flophouses traditionally used by men on the periphery of the labor market); the decline of jobs that keep many individuals and families above the poverty line; the dismantling of welfare programs that were intended to protect the poor; deinstitutionalization;

and a failure to provide housing for many of those deinstitutionalized.[2] While many countries throughout the world now have large homeless, displaced, and refugee populations, homelessness in the United States is primarily a question of economics, with many poor and marginal people finding themselves without jobs, without substantial resources to fall back on, and without permanent places to live. The problem is ultimately the failure of a modern nation-state and its market economy to provide adequate and sustainable housing for all of its citizens.

Throughout the 1980s and 1990s, shelters have been the most comprehensive and enduring response to the rise of homelessness, supplanting "skid row" as the most visible and common way station of marginal, disaffiliated, or underemployed men.[3] By the late 1980s shelters and soup kitchens in the United States serviced between 200,000 and 300,000 people a day.[4] By 1990, according to one survey, 5.3 percent of all adults said they had slept in a shelter or on the streets at some point in their adult lives.[5] In New York City alone, an intricate shelter system had by the mid-1980s radiated out into armories, old schools, abandoned hospital wards, and other facilities throughout the city, particularly in neighborhoods in advanced stages of urban decay; by the winter of 1987–88 the number of single men accommodated on an average night grew to more than 8,000, and some armories housed up to 600 men a night.[6] In Boston a similar but less centralized and less populated shelter industry sprung up in and around the city in the 1980s as a stopgap, symptomatic solution to the increase and increasingly visible presence of homeless men, women, and families in the city.[7]

Although the role of the relatively new phenomenon of "homeless shelters" in the day-to-day survival strategies and subsistence economies of the poor has yet to be adequately explored,[8] it is clear that shelters serve a variety of functions, including temporary and usually free lodging for those down on their luck, the warehousing of the poor and socially undesirable, and a refuge for the sick, the destitute, and the mentally ill. Similar in function to the "municipal lodging" of the nineteenth and early twentieth centuries, public shelter can be thought of as a kind of "hybrid institution" that, as Kim Hopper notes, has traditionally served two distinct functions, at times operating at cross-purposes to one another.[9] On the one hand, a public shelter must function as a place of respite or temporary aid for the unemployed during times of economic depression. On the other, it must routinely be available "as an option of last resort for the penniless without friends or family, for the physically disabled, for those so crippled by alcoholism or mental illness as to make any but the most menial and intermittent work impossible."[10] While the first function assumes that unemployed or underemployed people will return to the labor force whenever possible, the second is custodial in essence, serving to house or repair a damaged, disagreeable population. In the past two decades, shelters in many major cities have thus emerged as a mix between a degraded type of public housing and a new form of institutionalization that often sustains rather than alleviates a state of impoverishment and dependency among its patrons.[11]

The institutional function of public shelters relates in part to the so-called deinstitutionalization that began in earnest in the early 1960s, when many long-term residents of psychiatric hospitals and asylums were released and assigned to community-based treatment centers with the idea that such facilities would provide more humane and less expensive care for the chronically mentally ill. As is well known, the plans did not go as well as their architects envisioned they would. To begin with, the number of people released into the community was more than existing services could manage. In turn, many proposed community treatment programs went unrealized and patients often left hospitals without any provisions for care, employment, or housing. In addition, many states proved reluctant to allocate funds for community-based services, community mental health centers delayed or resisted providing services to the chronically mentally ill, and many communities preferred not to have the mentally ill live in their neighborhoods. Finally, those formerly interned in asylums frequently met with social, psychological, and financial difficulties in living on their own or in group homes.[12] In time, thousands of people with severe and persistent mental health problems, · unable to obtain or maintain a place to live, ended up staying on the streets or in shelters, with little or no income, with few resources to fall back on, and rejecting or rejected by existing mental health services. It appears that fewer than a quarter of the homeless in the late 1980s had actually spent time in state mental hospitals. Yet, as Christopher Jencks notes, many more who would once have been sent to a mental hospital were now sent to the psychiatric service of a general hospital or were treated as out-patients. In other words, well over a third of today's homeless (and undoubtedly the majority of those who bedded down in the Station Street shelter) would have been locked up in the 1940s.[13] Deinstitutionalization thus led to a significant increase in the numbers of mentally ill people living in shelters or on the streets or migrating between hospitals, halfway houses, and shelters. While psychiatric hospitals still house many Americans on either a temporary or a long-term basis, shelters have willy-nilly succeeded state psychiatric hospitals in lodging large numbers of those considered mentally ill, though often without the resources to provide the kind of care common to psychiatric hospitals.

Deinstitutionalization is by no means the main reason that up to a third of the homeless today are those deemed mentally ill, however. The problem of homelessness has been likened to a game of musical chairs, in which the chairs represent affordable apartments and the players the poor seeking permanent shelter in those apartments.[14] In the past two decades a range of economic, political, and other structural forces have not only reduced the number of chairs. They have added players to the game. Most social scientists and policy experts, intent on underscoring the economic and political factors involved, would profess that, outside the evils of poverty and racism, it is an equal opportunity game. Yet it is important to note that people considered mentally ill have a harder time than most obtaining or holding onto an apartment. In the past two decades a scarcity of low-income housing, coupled with neighborhood resistance to the development of new housing for mentally ill individuals, has increased the competition for low-cost housing; poor people with mental health problems have regularly lost out when competing with others for increasingly scarce housing resources.[15] In addition, many of those who "hear voices," hallucinate, are extremely fearful, or have great difficulties in relating with others have come to live apart from their families; they are thus denied the kind of shelter that others can rely on in times of difficulty. Many find it difficult, if not impossible, to take the necessary steps to find an apartment. Those who do try to locate a place to live often find that landlords refuse to rent to them. Some cannot come up with the money to pay the up-front costs of acquiring an apartment, and others are evicted when they fall behind on rent. Some stay in psychiatric hospitals from time to time and thereby risk losing their apartments. Still others lose their apartments because they act in socially inappropriate ways or simply lack the skills to make it on their own. While many find lodging in group homes or shared residences, many also come to find themselves on the streets or in shelters, where most of them have a hard time. Research conducted in American cities in the 1980s found that, in comparison to homeless people who were not deemed mentally ill, homeless people who were diagnosed as mentally ill remained without housing for longer periods of time, had more barriers to employment, were in poorer physical health, had less contact with family and friends, and had more frequent contact with the criminal justice system.[16]

This was much the situation in Massachusetts, despite its comprehensive and relatively attentive state-run mental health care system: one 1992 study estimated that 2,500 to 3,000 homeless mentally ill individuals were living in Massachusetts, with 1,500 to 2,000 in the metropolitan Boston area alone.[17] Before the early 1980s there was little organized government policy toward the homeless in Massachusetts. During the so-called economic boom years of the mid-1980s, however, the state government, pressured by advocates for the homeless, developed a series of initiatives designed to respond to the increasing number of homeless individuals and families in the state. Along with gearing efforts toward prevention, constructing permanent housing, and providing emergency and supportive services, the Dukakis administration focused on expanding and improving the psychiatric services and housing options available to the mentally ill.[18] One important result of this focus was the construction and funding of three shelters in Boston designed specifically for the mentally ill. By the early 1980s it had become clear to the area's homeless advocates, social workers, psychiatric case managers, and shelter staff and managers that there were a number of mentally ill people living on the streets or in shelters, with little access to clinical care, often preyed on, and perceived to be a potential danger to themselves or others. Since the existing "emergency" shelters lacked the means to provide sufficient care, the Massachusetts Department of Mental Health (or DMH), which oversaw the provision of mental health services in the Commonwealth, concluded that the state should provide temporary housing for the homeless mentally ill in the form of specialized, service-oriented shelters with comprehensive clinical care and social support programs.[19] DMH therefore set up the Station Street shelter in early 1981 in an old school in Roxbury, a lower-class suburb at the southern edge of Boston. Soon after it was opened it was moved from Station Street its present location in downtown Boston. The original name stuck, however.

DMH established two other shelters, both in remote areas. One was located in the leaky, windowless basement of a condemned building on the grounds of a hospital in southwestern Boston; the other, which provided special programs for substance abusers, was set up in a defunct sanatorium next to a detox center on an island in Boston harbor. Although the shelters had their own supervisory staffs trained in mental health services, they were managed from above. Each offered forty to fifty permanent bed assignments and lockers, on-site psychiatric nurses and other staff trained in mental health services, and referrals to day and prevocational programs at community mental health centers.[20] They existed both to attend to the special health needs of the mentally ill and to keep this population away from the perceived dangers of the "generic" shelters (so called because they tried to provide accommodations for anyone who asked, not just the mentally ill or substance abusers). As Stan, the acting manager of the Station Street shelter, recalled, however, the city of Boston also established the shelters in order to "get them [the homeless mentally ill] off the Commons." They therefore served as state-run but impoverished gated communities.

The desire of many state and city officials to remove apparently homeless and crazy people from the Boston Commons in the early 1980s, when the homeless became a pressing "problem" in the downtown area of Boston, attests to the ever-dwindling public sphere in American society. Public domains, once accessible to most, have been policed in such a way that the kinds of activities and peoples permitted in them have been increasingly narrowed to fit mainstream norms. The desire also attests to the often violent, apartheidlike divides in the country, in which the segregation of various minorities and peoples has coincided with the spread of mono-ethnic neighborhoods, gated communities, new technologies of policing and population control, and increasingly authoritarian methods of regulating the poor.[21] Artifacts of the state's investment in the spatial control of marginal populations, many shelters function as de facto poorhouses in which poor people and other undesirables are kept apart from the American mainstream.[22] It is thus fitting that two of the DMH shelters were set up on waste spaces on the outskirts of the city, out of sight and beyond the reach of most social and economic commerce. In function they bore some resemble to the *Narrenschiff* or "ship of fools" of fifteenth-century Europe, in which the mad were rounded up and confined to ships that sailed from town to town along the Rhineland rivers.[23] Yet here internment, not embarkation, was the most crucial symbolic rite. "Shelters are always subterranean," said a man who lived for a while in one of them. Although located on the ground level of the mental health center, the Station Street shelter had a similarly desolate, bunkerlike air to it. Yet since it stood in the middle of a bustling downtown area, a few blocks west of City Hall and a couple of streets over from the Boston Garden, many preferred it to other shelters.

The shelter was set up in a gymnasium on the ground floor of a large community mental health center. The center itself formed one-third of an even larger State Service Center; the other two sections were devoted to agencies of Education and Welfare, and Employment Security and Health. Conceived in the late 1950s, when large urban renovation projects were all the rage, the State Service Center was a product of the large-scale plans devised by state and national governments in the 1950s and 1960s to build and operate comprehensive, state-run facilities attending to the needs of its citizens. These concerns had their genealogies, of course. According to Foucault, "government" exploded as a general problematic in sixteenth-century Europe, in part because of ever-increasing populations and ever-expanding economies on the continent at that time.[24] The result was that caring for national populations soon became the ultimate end of government: "In contrast to sovereignty, government has as its purpose not the act of government itself, but the welfare of the population, the improvement of its condition, the increase of its wealth, longevity, health, etc."[25] In 1960s Boston, urban planners tried to answer their era's questions about governing (how to govern, how to rule, how to improve the welfare of a population) by building a massive, centralized, and rationalized government center that housed in one megastructure agencies devoted to the needs of the population.

The state's provision for mental health in this structure is significant because madness became a clear "matter of state" in the United States only in the latter decades of the nineteenth century, when publicly supported, state-run asylums succeeded community-run county almshouses as the main facilities for the care and housing of the mentally ill.[26] In concurrence with the "invention" of the asylum in nineteenth-century North America and the ever-increasing centralization and rationalization of state control over welfare, social services, and education in the twentieth century, state-run asylums and psychopathic hospitals became the dominant forms of care and housing for the mentally ill (especially for those who could not afford private care) until the 1950s and 1960s. Then a series of initiatives helped to launch community mental health programs throughout the country focusing on outpatient facilities, preventive strategies, and psychiatric care for more than just the severely ill.[27] The community mental health center in which the Station Street shelter was lodged was one of the first and largest of such programs. But, from the start, most of its services were based on traditional medical methods, and it soon became a symbol for the unwillingness of the psychiatric establishment to implement more innovative practices encouraged by many advocates of the community mental health movement.[28] From its inception the mental health center and its patrons were under the jurisdiction of the state government, the Department of Mental Health, and affiliated psychiatrists.

In the early 1990s the center consisted of a Byzantine complex of offices, bureaucracies, and referral services that managed, supported, and documented various mental health services. Each of the main programs, which focused on different populations as defined by their distinct needs, could be understood as being integral to a particular era of services. The center as a whole thus comprised an implicit timeline of social philosophies and psychiatric technologies, and thus distinct considerations of people, space, time, power, and well-being. A locked, in-patient psychiatric hospital on the top floor (by all accounts a forbidding, oppressive place, usually unnamed by the people who spent time within it) was reminiscent of the asylums and psychopathic hospitals that dominated in mid-century. "Step by Step," a popular fourth-floor social club for the mentally ill, which Alice and other shelter residents attended during the work week, professed the humanitarian, community-centered approaches first launched in the 1960s and 1970s. Below that was a "homeless outreach team," whose employees anticipated a new wave of streetside, triage-like services in providing case management services for mentally ill residents in area shelters and went out to the streets at night to search for potential patrons.[29]

The shelter itself, a novel hybrid of the almshouses and asylums of an earlier era, attended to the ever-increasing numbers of itinerants that became publicly visible in the early 1980s. In addition to providing room, board, and psychiatric services, the shelter professed some of the features of psychiatric hospitals and other "total institutions" that Erving Goffman outlined in his classic study *Asylums,* including: a single rational plan of action promoted by a unified supervisory staff; the regimented regulation of daily activities, usually carried out in the immediate company of others; and a wide range of "secondary adjustments" and "underlife" activities, such as "knowing the ropes" or setting up informal economies.[30] But the lack of a fixed barrier between the world of the institution and the world at large, as well as the relative absence of "a deep initial break with past roles," made the shelter a not-so-total institution.[31] It therefore carried the vestiges of an earlier culture of incarceration and psychiatric care, though it set them in the more deinstitutionalized present, itself founded on a network of institutions that were less entrenched in a particular locale than concerned with activities and procedures.[32]

In constant contact with other service providers, the shelter's staff received referrals from the homeless outreach team, sent violent or suicidal residents to the psychiatric hospital or other psychiatric institutions, and encouraged their "guests" to attend the social club or other day-treatment programs. Kathleen Hirsch, a journalist, summed up the idea behind all this in *Songs from the Alley,* her 1989 account of homeless women in Boston:

[Station Street] remained part of an unfinished dream, the centerpiece of a comprehensive case management program for the homeless mentally ill that had never developed. The program's designers had envisioned psychiatric referrals from the other shelters to [Station Street], one-on-one case work, rehabilitation centers, and ultimately, permanent residences for the deinstitutionalized mentally ill. None of this had materialized.[33]

Hirsch's judgment was unduly harsh. Although the shelter and its sister services did not function as comprehensively as the designers might have envisioned, the staff did manage to get people off the streets and out of other shelters. They were also effective in helping residents develop ties with psychiatrists, case managers, and "rehabilitation centers," as well as get onto the Social Security entitlement system and find more permanent places to live.

The shelter's mandate, to provide temporary housing for people known to be mentally ill, set the criteria for admittance: to gain a bed in one of the shelters, a person needed to be both homeless and mentally ill. To be "homeless" was to lack any permanent residence in an apartment or house. To be "mentally ill" was to carry a psychiatric diagnosis such as "schizophrenia," "bipolar disorder," or the like. A person usually received such a diagnosis through previous engagements with the mental health establishment.[34] A "guest" arrived from a local hospital, another shelter, or the streets, often through contact with one of the city's "homeless outreach" teams. Entry into a shelter was sometimes a gradual process, with homeless outreach workers, shelter personnel, and potential guests meeting to decide on a course of action. When people were admitted into the shelter, they usually arrived with looks of mild apprehension and large plastic bags filled with possessions. Members of the staff then showed them where to bed down, explained how the shelter operated, and met with them to discuss concrete plans to find more permanent places to live.

Until such a place was found, a person could remain in the shelter as long as he or she abided by the shelter's rules. A person who needed to stay temporarily in a psychiatric hospital could do so without fear of losing his or her place in the shelter. Some residents stayed in the shelter for a few weeks. Others lived there for several years and are therefore best thought of as "sheltered" rather than "homeless." In 1992 a few were in their seventh or eighth year, to the consternation of staff, who worried that these "permanent fixtures" (as the manager once referred to a shelter veteran) might never acquire more "permanent" accommodations. People typically left when they found another place to live, hit the street, looked for a better life outside Boston, returned to a psychiatric hospital, or were kicked out due to infractions of the shelter's rules.

There were usually about thirty men and twenty women in the shelter, with a turnover of three to four people per month (in 1991, forty people left the shelter and forty others took their places). While there were constant shifts in the composition of the population, those staying in the shelter were predominantly white (about a third were African American, Asian American, or Latino), from the Boston area, and from lower-class or lower middle-class families. A sample survey of the shelter residents—conducted in the second half of 1990, shortly before I began research—found that 49 percent were in their twenties or thirties, 71 percent were white (compared to only 40 percent in three generic shelters surveyed), 30 percent had less than high school education, and 97 percent had been homeless for one year or more.[35] While issues of race, gender, and ethnicity daily played themselves out, and some white residents were blatantly racist, these were not the most important social constructs at work: a pervasive "drama of difference" took place in which those living in the shelter, identified as "guests," tended to orient themselves in terms of values derived largely from living on the streets, in shelters, or in psychiatric hospitals, while those working in the shelter, identified as "staff," advanced the dominant values of American middle-class capitalist culture.[36] While residents actively participated in this drama, they also tried at times to establish a sense of alikeness and equality among themselves and staff members.

A few staff members said that their guests considered the Station Street shelter the "Rolls Royce of shelters." Although I did not hear residents profess the same enthusiasm, many did find it to be one of the better shelters in the Boston area (the survey noted above found that 87 percent of those interviewed considered themselves "satisfied with the shelter"; 79 percent said it was better than other shelters).[37] People were satisfied in part because, situated as it was in downtown Boston, it was better located than the other two DMH shelters, and in part because it was much safer than any of the city's generic shelters. The Pine Street shelter, one of the largest and best known of such shelters and used by many residents, was notorious for its crowded rooms and dangers. "You wouldn't want to stay there," cautioned Martin, a young white man who had "seen" several shelters in Boston before coming to stay in the Station Street shelter. "It's terrible. There's some undesirable characters there. The bottom floor is the worst. There's lots of drunks sleeping there, throwing up all night." "I don't like Pine Street," added Simone, another resident. "People lie down in the lobby. You can't even pass a finger through the crowd there." "This is the best shelter by far," Martin said. Simone nodded her head in agreement.

Safer and less crowded than the generic shelters, the Station Street shelter also allowed its guests to maintain the same bed and locker area for the duration of their stay. In generic shelters like Pine Street, one had to line up at a certain time in the afternoon and then go to a newly assigned bed, cot, or mat each evening. "You don't have to sit outside in the rain and the cold, like you have to at Pine Street," explained one man. "It's kind of boring living in the shelter. But at least here, I'm out of the rain," said Greg, who lived for a while in an abandoned building. "People feel safe in the shelter," Bill, a staff member, told me. "A lot of people feel that things are not going to get out of control here. Once they're here, they don't want to move out, because it's threatening. The strategy then becomes, 'How can I stay here?' "

The strategy of the staff, in turn, was to maintain the temporary nature of the accommodations and to make it clear, at meetings and in conversations, that the shelter was "not a home."[38] This meant that while staff members gave priority to one of two main functions of public shelters—namely, serving as an option of last resort for the mentally ill—they maintained that it could be only a temporary refuge. "As I've said before, it's not as if this is our own home," Stan, the acting manager, declared in a group meeting when several of his guests were complaining that they could not choose the movie videos that they were most interested in watching. The movies in question were bloody horror films, which the staff thought might frighten some residents. "It's a transitional shelter," Stan continued, "for people *on their way* to their own homes. Once you get there, you can watch what you want. . . . When living alone, you can do what you want. But people here are living in a community. You have to respect the man or woman next to you." When Stan finished speaking a woman stood up, said "I don't have to listen to this," and left the meeting area. As the staff saw it, in living in a transitional group setting, people gave up specific liberties that came with living in a "home."

Many residents relied on a similar image of home when asked if they thought the shelter was one. They invariably answered "no" to this question. Some said the shelter was "not a real home" because it did not have the "feel" of one. While some held that it lacked the creature comforts and utilities of a home, most said it lacked the privacy and freedoms associated with one's own place. For Nina, home meant "the freedom to do what you want, like have friends over and cook food." Another woman said that "home is a place to wash one's clothes, cook, and eat," stressing that personally carrying out what one needed to do in order to live was integral to having a home. Many emphasized the importance of freedom of action. "Home is where you can sleep all day," Tommy said. When others spoke of getting their own apartments, they often mused on the possibilities of sleeping, eating, and smoking when and where they wanted to.

These liberties were curtailed in the shelter. Residents could not always do as they pleased, largely because the staff upheld a regimented schedule of activities. Anyone staying in the shelter was expected to shower every other day, leave the shelter from 9:30 in the morning to 3:30 in the afternoon, perform a rotating set of chores, dine at five, take any prescribed psychiatric medications in the evening, and return to the shelter by nine at night, unless a "night pass" had been requested and granted. If a person broke any of the shelter's rules, he or she could be punished. Discipline included banishing a person "outside" the shelter for an hour or two (typically for acting up, swearing, or talking too loud for too long) or sending him or her "out for the night" for more troublesome acts, such as threatening or insulting another person. While the latter punishment was "the final form of discipline"—to quote the manager—because staff could only bar people from the shelter if they stole or took drugs, there was also the threat, if one "decompensated" too radically, of being restrained and taken by police to a psychiatric hospital for confinement, evaluation, and psychiatric care, which often involved heavy doses of neuroleptics.

The staff held that the rules were there "to provide structure to your lives," as a nurse told several residents one evening. Residents found that the numerous restrictions, as well as the way they were asserted, were unpleasant and infantilizing. Fred said that the shelter was "not a home" because there were "too many rules and regulations." "I didn't like it there much. You have to put up with so much shit," said another man soon after leaving the shelter for an apartment.

"It's a question of choices," one staff member put it to a group of residents gathered for a meeting one evening. "Take Freddy, for instance. He has choices. If he wants to stay here instead of in-patient [the locked psychiatric ward on the fifth floor], then when he's feeling nervous and anxious, he can either come up to us and ask for more medication, or he can try to throw a door through a window." Fred nodded his head and smiled in childlike, accommodating agreement. Residents resented these kinds of lessons. "They treat you like children here, not like a person," Julie told me. "Some people are not fit to live in a place like this," Kevin said. "They don't adapt so well. You have to be here at five at night and need a pass if you want to stay out past nine." Nevertheless, there was some truth to the management's stance on the "question of choices," however infantilizing that stance could be. People put up with the rules and regulations and the perceived lack of privacy and freedom in the shelter because they had few other feasible options. Sleeping on the streets, staying in a generic shelter, crashing at a friend's or relative's place, or bedding down in a psychiatric hospital were not attractive options to most. And while many would have preferred to live in an apartment, these were usually hard to come by or keep.

Five Coefficients

The need for housing, and questions as to which kind of accommodations best suited "the chronically and persistently mentally ill," led to the research project with which my fieldwork was formally linked. The project, itself part of a nationwide comparative study, tried to assess the effects of two housing models on the welfare and well-being of the "consumers" participating in the study. To begin this project, "housing officers" and case managers recruited prospective subjects from the three DMH shelters. Once a person agreed to participate in the study, he or she was randomly assigned and relocated to either an "independent

living situation" or an "evolving consumer household." The former category denoted studio apartments located in public housing facilities in
Boston; the latter, five shared, staffed residences expected to transform
themselves over time from arrangements resembling traditional group
homes to cooperative living situations managed by the residents themselves. In which of the two housing situations did people fare better? The
researchers tried to answer this question by measuring the participants'
clinical status, physical health, length of domicile, and other outcomes.[1]

My job was to develop an ethnographic understanding of the social
worlds from which participants came in order to help the research team
gain insight into the participants' concerns, lifestyles, sensibilities, motivations, and previous living arrangements.[2] In an attempt to learn about
one such world, I began to spend time in the Station Street shelter in
early March of 1991 and continued to frequent it for several days and
evenings each week until August of 1992. My arrival came on the heels
of a social policy research team that conducted surveys in the fall of
1990 of several shelters in the Boston area, including the Station Street
shelter. The response to that team was not particularly auspicious for my
own work. Team members had asked residents a series of questions —
such as "Have you thought of killing yourself in the past week?" — that
apparently troubled residents and annoyed the staff. Taking the staff's
account of these events to be an expression of concern that yet another
nosy researcher was in their midst, I tried to assure them that I would
simply hang out in the shelter, talk to people in a low-key way, and observe their daily doings. They understandably remained wary, but since
there was no choice but to let me work there, they hoped I would be no
more intrusive than "a fly on the wall," as one authority put it. With the
exception of Lisa, a young staff member who introduced me to many of
the residents and shared her thoughts on particular events and general
shelter life, my relations with the staff remained cordial but distanced,
with neither party revealing much to the other. My research interested
the shelter manager in part because, as he intimated one day, he wanted
to learn if there was any way he could make shelter life less "comfortable" and so indirectly encourage his guests to seek more permanent
housing elsewhere. I revealed little of what I was learning — and worry
today as to the uses to which this book might be put.

Much of what I learned came from my sidelong participation in and
observation of the daily life of the shelter and its surroundings. To preserve confidentiality, I was not allowed to read either the residents' case
records or the log notes kept by the staff, nor did I attend any of the
staff's private meetings, except for a few that pertained to the research
project itself. Since structured or unstructured interviews would have
unnerved everyone, and I did not want to use a tape recorder while

among residents, I spent much of my time hanging about, listening to and entering into conversations, and then finding a place to write down the gist of these exchanges. One disadvantage of this method was that, without access to written records or private discussions, I have been unable to develop a sufficiently systematic understanding of the staff's world of practice or the larger systems of care that residents patronized.[3] My perspective is therefore slanted more to the points of view of the residents than to those of the staff, and much of what I know is gleaned from everyday conversations. Another drawback was that my notes on these conversations, which typically contained quasi-verbatim accounts, lacked the precision that tape or audio recordings could have provided.[4] However, as many anthropologists have found, especially those who have worked among homeless populations, the advantages of unassuming participation in daily activities, during which one can develop lasting, informal ties with people, often outweigh the benefits of information obtained through surveys and more intrusive methods.[5]

From the start, residents identified me as being part of the research project and would sometimes ask if I could "get them housing" when they first spotted me in or around the shelter. I would explain that I had no say in the matter, that I was only working in the shelter in order to figure out what it was like to live there. People would then usually say something to the effect of, "Oh, well, it's not a bad place to live, as far as shelters go"—or that the shelter was "lousy," "pretty good," or "a good-for-nothing dungeon." Our exchanges took off from there.

These and other conversations were both the cornerstone of my research method and part and parcel of everyday life in the shelter. In his *Western Apache Language and Culture*, Keith Basso notes that "the resources of a language, together with the varieties of action facilitated by their use, acquire meaning and force from the sociocultural contexts in which they are embedded, and therefore, as every linguist knows, the discourse of any speech community will exhibit a fundamental character—a genius, a spirit, an underlying personality—which is very much its own."[6] The genius of the residents' speech communities tied into the give and take of conversation. The shelter was very much a conversation-based reality, perhaps more so than other social worlds. Daily life constantly involved people approaching, speaking with, and then walking away from others. Almost all of the exchanges of information, monies, goods, and resources took place through face-to-face conversations that residents had with other residents, the staff, or other patrons or employees of the health care system. Talk was so frequent that Carla Bataille worried she was "giving her personality" away, and this "depressed" her. "All's you can do is overhear people's conversations, so I might as well join this one," she once said to two of her neighbors. The reciprocal give and take of economic exchanges assumed the tempo and plotting not of a story but of a conversation, with the participants playing out call-and-response sequences through time. Other phrasings were phatic in nature, working to keep the lines of communication and exchange open. While a few residents disliked the repetitive pitch of the exchanges, most acknowledged that they valued "having a conversation" since it provided them with companionship and an opportunity to exchange, share, and reciprocate.[7]

Conversations were of such commonplace significance that in this book they function, like the shelter's air of impermanence and uncertainty, as a coefficient or constant factor. The data and the rhythms of these pages are founded on the contrapuntal, give-and-take sequences of people talking with one another in occasional, unassuming, usually candid, and often humorous conversations. Many of the sentences voiced below, which imply a language of "she said," "I asked," and "he answered," should be heard in this key.

I often did the asking and residents the answering: "Why do you ask so many questions?" Eva asked me one day. I told her I was just interested in what she thought. "Well, can't we just sit quiet-like for a while?" she replied. While a few residents wanted nothing to do with me and thus were left alone, others rightly took my curiosity for a sincere interest in their lives and were generally glad to talk to me. At times they found our conversations refreshing for their absence of therapeutic motives and directives, and came to see me as distinct from staff. But while the political underpinnings of my stance were probably more opaque than the staff's, the stance was political nonetheless. Residents and I became "objects of desire" for each other.[8] While I was trying to develop a systematic, book-bound understanding of life in the shelter through a close reading of conversations and a fly's-eye view of actions and interactions, my informants were concerned with their own politics and often drew on my attentiveness to voice their concerns about the shelter, the staff, or their lives in general.[9]

The pitch of these concerns ties into another coefficient in this book: that of rhetoric, whose basic function I take to be "the use of words by human agents to form attitudes or to induce actions in other human agents."[10] Since residents had little direct political might of their own, one of the more effective ways for them to get things done or to get others to act in certain ways was to try to persuade, convince, cajole, complain, or express feelings of pain or distress. Both residents and staff sought to do things with words. Words also did things on their own, regardless of the intentions of their utterers.[11] Both the rhetorical stances, in which people attempted to persuade or get others to act in certain ways, and the pragmatic consequences, in which the words themselves promoted certain meanings and realities, relied at times on a language of referentiality (as when a person said they were anxious or afraid). But often the referentiality was quietly persuasive in spirit. The quotations that follow should therefore be read not as direct and unambiguous references to the real but as subtle efforts in larger political games.

In fact, the coefficient of rhetoric implies a coefficient of power. Each action, interaction, and conversation should be understood as being set within the relations of power common to the shelter and its stream of doings and practices. Most often staff members possessed the ability to do what they sought out to do, whereas the residents needed to resort to a range of tactical actions to get things done. Their respective uses of language—which, as detailed below, commonly implied a physics of movement, coercion, enticement, and persuasion—tied into their political stances and the different powers they wielded.

One of the dominant manifestations of power in and around the shelter was the act of obscuring. Staff members obscured the lives of residents by displacing them to less visible spaces and residents sometimes cloaked their lives and concerns in obscurity in an effort to avoid the staff's bureaucratic gaze and powers. These practices took place in a building known for its maddeningly opaque architecture, and in an institutional setting where nothing was certain, where many facts were confidential, and where people came and went suddenly, often without informing others. All this made for ways of knowing predicated on opacity, surface knowledge, contingencies, and diverse planes of meaning—as well as for a book that toils with these ways of knowing. Behind this everyday murkiness, however, lay a powerful bureaucratic order comprised of the jural, economic, and medicinal offices of the state.

Despite the drama of difference played out been staff and residents, the lives of various residents were as different from one another as they were from the lives of the staff. People came from diverse backgrounds and upbringings, faced unique problems, and professed individual wants and sensibilities. They therefore cannot be depicted as a single-minded collectivity.[12] Yet the difference that really stood out in the shelter was something more than the heterogeneity found in the average social science treatise: the residents' oddities made them "different" from most Americans. They often acted, thought, and spoke in ways that were, by most accounts, just plain weird. "Everything I thought was weird. I used to change it round to look different," one man, diagnosed as schizophrenic, told two clinicians of his first rush of madness.[13] The residents likewise thought differently at times. One day Joanne, the designated "housing officer" of the research project, held a meeting with several residents in an effort to drum up interest. Debra Joyce, who had arrived at the shelter a month before, said she would very much like to settle in an apartment but wanted to live where there were no church steeples. "I can't stand it," she said with great conviction. "They should knock down some of them on every block. You can't even run from them." In the odd silence that followed Joanne tried to accommodate Debra's views by saying, "Well, as my mother used to say, 'There's no pot so crooked that it ain't gonna fit.'"

Although Joanne's response had the merit of not casting Debra's crookedness in pathological terms (and carried the implicit message that she, too, could find a place to live, especially if she participated in the housing project), her mother had it wrong, because the residents fit in poorly, if at all. To a considerable degree their eccentricities accounted for many of the circumstances of their lives. Their ways of talking or acting often perplexed or frightened others; known to be "crazy" or "mentally ill," they were stigmatized for their oddness and came to live on the margins of everyday social life. As a matter of fact, a single-minded attribution of differentness would probably be the best way to characterize the residents' lives if it were not for the intense pain and isolation that they suffered. To investigate whether such differences or "pathologies" are biological, psychogenetic, social, or political in nature would require a different study altogether; their origins cannot be debated here. We do need to take note of the differentness, however, and in a way that does not attempt to make weird thoughts look appropriate. Along with the coefficients of conversation, rhetoric, power, and obscurity, a constant measure of differentness runs though this book, much as—as Bronislaw Malinowski found—a "coefficient of weirdness" peppered the magical chants of the Trobriand Islanders.[14]

"A Crazy Place to Put Crazy People"

The building in which the shelter was lodged was known for its eccentric irregularities.

The mental health center, of which the shelter was a part, was located in the Massachusetts State Service Center, three blocks west of City Hall, at the upper, easterly crest of the area formerly known as the West End. The West End was populated by immigrant families until the late 1950s, when the Boston Redevelopment Authority declared it a slum area and slated it for destruction and redevelopment. By January 1962 the winding streets and 2,700 households were replaced by medical complexes, luxury apartment buildings, and a billboard that boasted to commuters leaving the city "You'd be home now if you lived here."[1] These renovations coincided with the building in the 1960s of an expansive Government Center in the area just to the east of the West End. Along with the State Service Center, the complex included a new City Hall, a State Building, a County Courthouse, and assorted office buildings and parking garages. Finding, as one architectural writer puts it, that "it had become just too difficult to try to run a city, a state, and coordinate with the federal government from offices scattered widely all over town," and hoping to "boost what was then Boston's only growth industry, government," Mayor John Collins and his administrators promoted and authorized the construction of the Government Center soon after he took office in 1960.[2] Construction of the various buildings went on for several years after that.

The call for redevelopment projects in the 1950s and the later critique of these projects in the 1960s grew out of the embattled aesthetics of urban planning of the twentieth century. In the wake of the First World War, a group of visionary "International Stylists," led by Walter Gropius, Ludwig Mies van der Rohe, and Le Corbusier, felt the need, as Mies van der Rohe put it, to "create order out of the desperate confusion of our times."[3] Pursuing the renewed modernist dream of a "clean slate" in both art and urban living, they sought to make cities places of Hellenic order, where houses would be "machines for living," isolated skyscrapers would dominate open parks, footpaths would be elevated above ground, and automobiles would replace pedestrians on the streets, which should be straight and radiant rather than curved and obscure.

By the 1950s the aesthetic of purity and technical order—which for many came down to "slum-clearance, the provision of sun, light, air and green space"[4]—had snowballed into a series of redevelopment projects along the eastern seaboard. Highways and skyscrapers were replacing the so-called "disorder" of urban enclaves, poor families were losing their homes, and the streets of New York, Boston, and other cities were turned into "empty landscapes of psychosis."[5] "You'd be crazy about it in summer," a Boston planner told Jean Jacobs, an important critic of urban renovation projects, about the colorful, mazy North End. "But of course we have to rebuild it eventually," he added. "We've got to get those people off the streets."[6] Such sentiments and their implications for urban planning led Jacobs and others to condemn "the dishonest mask of pretended order" brought on by Le Corbusierian ideals. "A city cannot be a work of art," Jacobs concluded, and she and others sought to restore the active street life for which many pined.[7]

The 1962 planning board for the proposed State Service Center was apparently concerned with both the need for an expansive government center and the desire for a "street-scale" architecture that would complement the existing roadways. The first plan for the Center—which was

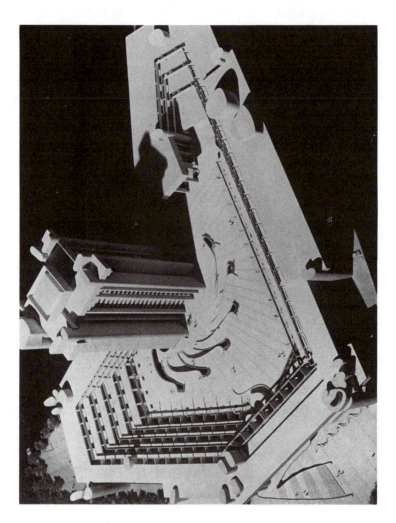

Figure 1. 1964 model of the State Service Building. The mental health center is in the lower left; the tower and section in the upper left were never built. Reprinted by permission from *The Architecture of Paul Rudolph*, ed.G. Schwab (New York: Praeger, 1970), p. 18. Photo Paul Rudolph.

to house three agencies: Employment Security; Health, Education and Welfare; and Mental Health—called for three buildings, to be designed and built by separate architectural firms. The Mental Health building was slated to be designed by a Boston architectural firm, with Paul Rudolph, a Yale "Brutalist" architect, as consultant. Although the firms together came up with a comprehensive scheme for the whole complex, which would resemble an Italian town of small buildings, no one was completely satisfied. Then one day Rudolph walked into a meeting of the architects with what he called "a stake with a tail": a tower circled by a set of low buildings enclosing a plaza (see Figure 1). The other architects, charmed by Rudolph's ideas, named him design coordinator of the project, in which the firms would collaborate to produce three buildings merged into one monolithic whole.[8]

Rudolph's solution drew on several different architectural traditions. Rather than construct several separate buildings, as was originally planned, he successfully argued that the three buildings should be united within a single "megastructure," such that "they form a specific space for pedestrians only." On the one hand, Rudolph desired in the post-functionalist tradition of Le Corbusier to create a "monumental" architecture, built of massive concrete blocks and pillars, which could serve as a "focal point" for the city and "could undoubtedly indulge in certain excesses"; the excesses echoed the later "inside-out" architecture of Le Corbusier, which permitted curves and whimsical shapes to frame right angles and straight lines.[9] On the other hand, instead of regarding the street "as an enemy" by constructing freestanding buildings, Rudolph sought to "add to the city" by creating a piazza-like space in which pedestrians and workers could rest and walk without feeling intimidated by the monumental scale. His solution was to provide a "double-scale" encompassing both street-scale and monumental-scale spaces. To achieve this Rudolph planned a multistory tower that "would announce itself from a great distance, acting as a pivoting point for the whole complex," and so "allow the scale of the complex to hold its own with tall adjacent buildings." Three adjoining buildings were to circle the tower, creating an "interior bowl of space" that would effect "a plaza evocative in shape, size, and feeling of the Piazza del Campo in Siena and the Piazza San Marco in Venice."[10]

To balance the tension created by the tower, Rudolph designed the three linked buildings so that a more "intimate" scale would be felt on both the "street" and the "courtyard" sides of the buildings. He sought to create this more human scale—to complement the excessive, monumental scale of the tower—by "stepping back" the walls on the courtyard side and by placing "fixed elements such as stairs, elevators and toilet cores at the 'knuckles,' or turning points of the streets."[11] He also designed the height of the buildings in such a way that people standing close to them on the street side could see only the area around them and not feel intimidated by the tower and the structure as a whole.[12]

To further relate the buildings to the streets and so "humanify" the complex, Rudolph "articulated" the lower exterior spaces of the buildings' concrete walls with an array of irregular and intricate formations, from spiral staircases and curved benches to receding, cavelike interiors. The experiment contributed to Rudolph's "long and continuing search for ways to modify space for results of feeling, mood, mind, and symbol."[13] In line with Frank Lloyd Wright's desire to create houses that assimilated natural forms and offered a "cave-like sense of intimacy,"[14] Rudolph introduced a "topographical architecture—hills, valleys, streams, cliffs, precipices, caves, grottoes, and so forth." And in accord with Wright's call for "continuity" in buildings, Rudolph highlighted the "movement of space" in both exteriors and interiors, particularly through "connections" between one volume of space and another.

In all, while Rudolph worked to uphold the structural principles of the International Style (exposed structures, "raw" concrete), he also sought in his handling of interior spaces to "activate the imagination" and "satisfy people's psychological needs" with a range of perceptual and tactile effects.[15] He accented "unused or waste space" as well as used space because the former "nourishes the subconscious."[16] He proposed that the "rooms" of the building's exterior should "have varying character: solemn, awesome, refined, quiet, hectic, dynamic, goodtime—depending on use."[17] Surfaces of the walls, inside and out, were designed in the New Brutalist tradition, of a rough concrete "corduroy" texture in which "light was fractured in a thousand ways and the sense of depth was increased" (see Figure 2).[18] In turn, the fusion of monumental and primitivist sentiments would ideally lead to a mythic, superhuman structure, a "rough poetry" in the Brutalist vein.[19] In hindsight, Rudolph's blueprints, with their hybrid design, playful eclecticism of themes, and excessive monumentality, sounded a death knell for modernism and the inevitability of a postmodern aesthetic (Robert Venturi launched his postmodern manifesto, *Complexity and Contradiction in Architecture*, in 1966).

Rudolph, who once told *Time* magazine that he wanted his buildings to end as "beautiful ruins," never saw the Center completed as he had envisioned it.[20] "The reality never matches the imagined" he rued a decade later, when he was still writing of his plans in their pristine form.[21] The makings of the *brut* corduroy exteriors were so expensive—the building reportedly cost $84 a square foot to build[22]—that only two of the three buildings were completed and workers never began construction on the "pivoting" tower. The center officially opened in 1971, with

Figure 2. Rudolph's "corduroy" surface.

rusting, unconnected iron bars jutting out of the building's unfinished, jagged edge of concrete on the eastern side, and a few staircases ending in mid-air. In 1991 office workers parked their automobiles in the sandy lot, or "gaping wound,"[23] where the tower was to be (see Figure 3). Thirty feet above the makeshift parking lot stood the wind-swept, usually vacant plaza, which abruptly ended with a curving chain-link fence on the eastern side. "If it had been completed," says one of Rudolph's apprentices, "it would have been one of the great urban-design achieve-

Figure 3. The "gaping wound" of the plaza: the unbuilt tower.

ments of the twentieth century. . . . But as an incomplete project, it is less than the sum of its parts by a long shot. It just does not work."[24]

In the 1980s and 1990s the building, which hosted, inside and out, a maze of winding staircases, cavelike recesses, and a harsh "corduroy" concrete surface, tended to affect people strongly. "It's a dysfunctional space," "It doesn't welcome out to the community," "It's a grey mass, uninviting, scary" claimed people who worked within and around the area.[25] Architects called the building an "unfinished symphony" or "primitive monstrosity," psychiatrists told of getting lost for hours in the building's "hallucinatory" inner chambers, and visitors described feelings of "discombobulation" when in the building's midst. "Madhouse," a 1987 *Boston* magazine article on the building and its patrons, held that it was "one of the strangest buildings in the world"—calling it "a brutal citadel of despair" that held "seven circles of madness"—and likened it to the animal "madness" of one of its residents: "[The building] is, like the world inside Tony's head, riddled with serpentine corridors, dark alcoves, and elaborate staircases—one of which ends in thin air."[26]

The equation of psychiatric and architectural madnesses was commonplace. "It's a crazy place to put crazy people," one psychiatric intern told me, apparently in reference to the air of danger and insecurity the architecture was thought to bring. Many were concerned and some out-raged that the building housed people with mental health problems. Others disliked the particular ways in which it activated the imagina-tion. "The building has lots of open spaces, and is perfect for some people at times," said Lisa, who worked as a staff member in the shelter. "But for others, it's hard on illusions. It's cold to the touch, like a cave. It seems like the structure isn't really fit for the people." "The building is dangerous," Bill, another staff member, told me. "Especially with the corrugated walls. On the plaza level, they had to put up a fence and seal off the area. People used to jump off a certain part of the building and break their knees. There's a lot of crazy designs, stairways that go nowhere. And it was never completed."

The themes of madness, danger, inhumanity, pointlessness, and in-completeness common to many perceptions of the building were closely tied to the building's architectural features. Although Rudolph never made the association between the form and function of the mental health center in print, one can easily conclude that he designed it in such a way that it might embody what he and others took to be some of the core features of madness: errancy, aimlessness, deviance, unpredict-ability, and irrationality. These features contrasted sharply with the "ar-chitecture of reason and functionalism"[27] found in the other two wings of the building, which had more monolithic structures, direct lines, and practical, usable spaces.

At the same time, the building's incompleteness added to its dis-concerting presence. In a 1977 essay that refers at length to the "not yet completed" State Service Center, Rudolph offered the following thoughts: "The balancing of thrusting and counterthrusting spaces, often rushing through the blue, outward and upward, leads to the most dynamic of all interior spaces. However, if this thrusting of spaces is not brought into equilibrium, it causes most people to immediately feel a sense of disorientation and unease. They are actively repelled by the space, because it is felt too much. This agitated and turbulent handling of space is unique to Twentieth Century architecture."[28]

Rudolph, I take it, thought that the tower would have contributed to the desired balance: while the street-scale buildings would create a space of crowded intimacy, brimming with cliffs, streams, caves, and grottoes, this topography of the unconscious would be balanced by the multi-story tower. The tower would give perspective to the turbulence below, and pedestrians walking along the perimeter of the building would not feel lost because they could get the tower back in sight by stepping away from the fluidity of the outer exterior.

It is clear that without the tower the building never achieved its in-tended balance. To draw from Rudolph's vocabulary, the "thrusting"

Figure 4. The "sandcastle" stairwell: northwest exterior.

spaces of the exteriors had yet to be brought into equilibrium by a "counter-thrusting" space. As it stood in 1991, the megastructure created a sense of excessive and restless movement because the "movement of space" that Rudolph had sought was accentuated by its incompleteness. "I always thought of it as melting," Sam, a local college student, said of the building, which he often used to walk by. "That's the key image for me. It's sort of eerie, like those staircases. They seem to spill out. It used to remind me of when we were at the beach, we would build sandcastles, and we would squeeze some watery sand and some mud would drip down. The stairs seem like that. They look soft, stepped on" (see Figure 4). When I mentioned Rudolph's philosophy of space ("The movement of space has a velocity, for space flows much in the manner of water from one volume to another"),[29] Sam replied, "Yeah, that's a good way to put it, better than to say that it's melting. The stairs are like waterfalls. They're flowing. The stairs are smaller on top, then they get larger, like a waterfall, as if it's been eroding."

The continuity of the State Service Center reminded me, in turn, of some of Wright's achievements—such as "Falling Water," as the Kaufmann house is known—although it lacked their grace and intimacy. The building was constantly flowing, melting, erring. It could not be pinned down. An illusion of order haunted it, particularly along its southern front, which consisted of linear concrete slabs and columns arranged in a monumental, civic manner. Yet toward its northern rear, downhill and away from City Hall (and, significantly, the sun), the order began to break down, and the floating staircases of Rudolph's "subconscious" architecture took over.

Many shelter residents offered their thoughts on the building. Richard Groton, for instance, speculated that the building's erosive movement would be controlled if a tower were to overlook it. A straggly, bespectacled, reputedly ill-behaved white man in his early thirties, Richard came to the shelter in April 1990 and was still there in the summer of 1992. He told me that in 1978 his mother had kicked him out of their home in a working-class neighborhood in East Boston, telling him, "Well, now you'll need to do something." Since then he had been staying in shelters. When I met him in the spring of 1991, he said he planned to stay in the shelter another three years or so: "I'm trying to get out of the red-light district now. But I'm also looking after my best interests," he said in a customary mix of metaphors and introspection, noting that he most wanted a job, a girlfriend, some money in his pocket, and, in due time, a place of his own. Although he admitted to being "very social" and so might get lonely living on his own, he said he would be sure to go out and form "social interactions." His history of employment was one of failures: he said he was fired at Burger King because he "couldn't keep up." When asked, he said he felt happy when he had a few bucks in his pocket and sad when people took advantage of him.

A sensory misfit of sorts, Richard liked to touch things and interacted with the world largely through tactile means. "You ever see some statues?" he once asked. "Yeah, they're cool. You can touch 'em and all that." He also liked to touch people in an attempt to be "affectionate," as he put it, and was constantly trying to interact with others. "Some people tell me to fuck off, others don't say anything, others don't seem to mind," he said in reference to the responses his approaches incurred. His habits, which bothered some residents, especially annoyed the staff, who preferred that people look but not touch. As might be expected, he often got into mild trouble for "inappropriate touching," getting people riled up, or having angry outbursts. The staff would then "discipline" him by making him sit down on a couch close to the staff desk, stay out of the shelter for an hour, or spend the night elsewhere. "He's just a crazy, mixed-up kid," his friend Stuart explained one day when Richard reported that he had drunk vodka the night before with some "bums."

Despite a juvenile demeanor, Richard was intelligent, perceptive, and articulate. When talking about himself, he would become thoughtful and was often insightful about why his and other lives were the way they were. He also had a knack for colorful metaphors that sometimes confused his listeners but just as often got at the heart of what he was talking about. I allowed him to guide me through the cultural, semi-otic, and architectural recesses of the mental health center, and listened attentively to his critique of the towerless building.

"A tower," he said as we stood atop the outer plaza, "would suck in space and all the traffic, but without a tower, the place is useless. . . . If there was a tower, it would keep all the jerks from running down the streets." Hasty drivers, that is, would be slowed by an unwavering announcement from afar. Yet without the tower, and a "gaping wound" in its stead, the spaces of the building ran on.

For Richard the building was a "dead space" because "it's right across from the Charles River and there are trains swinging by all the time and the bus is running twenty-four hours. It's like a consumption of people's, I don't know, a consumption of their well-being, I guess." The hectic flow translated into a space that was useless and distracting—and a population that was restless and aimless. "There are stairs goin' to nowhere someplace," Richard said. "I've seen people in here, poppin' pills, switchin' channels on the TV at night."[30]

If anything, the half-finished quality of the Center added to the confusion fostered by Rudolph's imagination. I found that those who had yet to learn their way through the labyrinth often got lost because they could not pin the building down. They also got lost because they could not find any unlocked entrances. In 1964 *Progressive Architecture* explained the building's rationale: "Entrances to the buildings will be unmistakable in this scheme. The towers of the tall building will act as 'pivoting elements' to lead to the plaza and the other buildings."[31] Without the tower, people lost their perspective. Visitors unfamiliar with the building tended not to approach it from the plaza side, where most of the open doors were (particularly at night and on weekends), because they assumed the plaza was an interior space. People therefore looked to the exterior for the entrances. But these entrances remained locked at night and throughout the weekend. One evening, soon after I began frequenting the shelter, a taxi driver with sweat on his brow rushed up to me as I was leaving the building. "Excuse me," he asked excitedly. "Do you know how to get *inside* this thing?! I've been driving around for half an hour and I haven't found any way in!"

The Sea of Tranquility

Anyone who did locate the sliding glass doors at the shaded northwest corner of the Mental Health building, which were open only during business hours, first had to pass through a circular expanse about a hundred yards wide and seventy-five yards deep that was bordered by the building on one side and two streets on the other. With its perimeter defined by a concrete ridge, the area suggested a quiet, shallow, waterless pool. "I always thought of it as a sea of tranquility," said Stuart Coopan of this courtyard-like space (see Figure 5). Stuart was a young and usually talkative white man who lived in the shelter for about eighteen months until he found an apartment he shared with friends. While in the shelter he spent much of his time either hanging around the lobby, where he talked to himself or to people he knew, or visiting certain areas of Boston. "It's actually more like a chasm," he went on. "You can see an indentation, you know, where it drops down from the street, and that area always seemed peaceful to me. It's a slow-motion space. You could walk with your shoes untied and see the people walking about. You don't have to exert yourself. The space sort of carries you along."

Others, including myself, also found this carefree, "shallow and still" area (as Rudolph christened it) to be shored by the busyness of the streets and the "hustling, bustling" backside of the building. Many residents and other frequenters of the mental health center liked to sit on the benches lining the area and talk with friends, sit quietly, or look out onto the passing traffic. "It's open here, you can see the sky," said Helen Kessler one summer day as we sat on the benches facing the streets. Helen was an amiable, multi-talented Korean American in her late forties who had moved from Kansas to Boston in the early 1980s and had lived in the shelter for over three years. During her stay she played chess, worked for a few dollars a day in the lunch kitchen at the social club upstairs, wrote poetry in the evening, "babysat" another woman who "kept saying she lost her mind," and dreamed "dog dreams" or "dreams that don't mean anything." Although Helen had been a cook and indeed had often worked several jobs at once, she had trouble finding a job that she would like. English was Helen's second language, and while she spoke it very well, she had difficulty moving her jaw with ease; this was apparently due to TMJ, or temporomandibular joint pain dysfunction syndrome. According to Helen, the malady had begun a decade ago when her former husband had poured acid into her mouth while she was asleep. The husband was also psychologically abusive, and so she had left him. She had two children from that marriage who lived on the west coast: a daughter in college and a son who worked in busi-

Figure 5. The "sea of tranquility."

ness. She proudly showed me photographs of both children, who sent her money on occasion.

Several years ago Helen wrote her "life story" and, without making a photocopy of it, sent it to CBS News in the hope of having it published. She later inquired about the manuscript by letter and phone but could not reach anyone in New York who knew of it. She therefore needed to write the autobiography again, and planned on doing so once she moved into her own apartment.

One day I asked how long she had been in the shelter. "Too long," she said. "It's like I'm part of the building now." In the spring of 1991 she received word that she would be getting an apartment of her own. She was glad to learn this but was also worried that she would not have enough money to pay for rent, food, clothing, medicine, and cigarettes. To cover these essential expenses, she wanted to find a job waitressing—being a cook took too much time. Since she tired quickly she would need to work in the afternoon and then return again in the evening.

Helen was pleased to learn that she was going to get her own place. "I've had enough of group homes," she told me. "You have to understand that people are sick here. They have problems. There's nobody here that I would want to live with. Even Peter. He's sick in his own way. Moody. Doesn't talk to us. I couldn't live with someone who's moody. I'm sick too, but not so bad. I'm getting better." Around the time that she was to move into the apartment, she grew nervous. "I'm not ready to move out yet. Nervous breakdown. I need to calm my nerves," she said one day as we sat on the benches lining the sea of tranquility.

Helen moved from the shelter to a studio apartment ninety minutes away by bus, and for several months I rarely saw her. Although she spent a lot of time in her apartment in order to write her life story and cook, she eventually started to come to the Center every day because her apartment was "too small." "I can't breathe when I'm at home," she said. "I think I'm going crazy. I turn on the fan and open the windows, but it doesn't help. I feel black inside, in my lungs and my nose. I know it's illogical, but I still can't breathe. I really need to find a bigger place."

Before and after she moved into her own place, Helen spent many late afternoons sitting or lying on one of benches, and many early evenings in the lobby next to the shelter. She found the building, and especially the sea of tranquility, to be "open" enough for her to spend her time sleeping, talking, or panhandling: "I like buildings that can fit a thousand people, like this one. I don't know what they did—so many squares and circles. It's beautiful! Perfect. Just right." She did say once, however, that she got "scared" when she visited the upper floors of the building. "I have bad dreams when I go upstairs. I think it's gonna collapse."

"I sleep here," she said of the benches that bordered the sea. "Sometimes I come here, lie down, and watch the cars and people until I fall asleep. I always wake up feeling good."

"Why is that?" I asked.

"I don't know. It's calm, sort of sweet."

For Helen and others, certain spaces directly affected how they walked, spoke, thought, and felt. Richard found that the building's dead spaces consumed people's "well-being" while its directionless stairs coincided with the pill-popping, channel-switching actions of its residents. Stuart found that the sea of tranquility carried him along in a slow-motion, shoes-untied gait. The openness of this same space made Helen "feel good," whereas going upstairs scared her and gave her "bad dreams," and her studio apartment choked her breathing. She felt that it was illogical, crazy even, that the size of an apartment could influence one's physiology. But the above considerations suggest that she was right: spaces could have moods and physiologies as much as people did. The features of buildings and apartments had a contagious effect on the people who lived in those spaces, especially when they spent a lot of time in the same place and came to feel as if they were "part" of a building.

"Too Much"

Once people stepped into the sea of tranquility, the building confronted them with a clear choice: they could ascend the stairway into the open area above, which led to the upper plaza, or they could descend into the darkness of the ground floor, which in a few steps led to the shelter. The spiral staircases twisted up toward the plaza's expanse, which seemed even more open and lacking beside the ghost tower. "It's got no feeling. It's a dead space. There's no use to it," said Richard. "And it's dangerous. You could fall off the front."

The plaza's unbounded openness worried many, including Fred Wiessner, a childlike but physically imposing white man in his mid thirties who often migrated from the shelter to the locked psychiatric ward on the top floor because of the violence he committed on himself and threatened on others. "It's kinda scary," Fred said of the top floors of the building. "When you look down, it seems like nothing's below you." For more than a few the open air of the plaza, which seemed to fall away without boundaries (see Figure 6), hinted at a violent instability. "Can I push you off the edge?" Richard joked when I suggested a walk around the plaza. His decision not to accompany me was indicative of the general sense of the area. "I never go up there," Stuart said, in reference to the staircase leading up to the plaza. "It's a bit too high for me. . . . I never look up there. I'm always looking toward the door—to see who's in there."

Stuart was referring to the ground floor entrance, which led into the lobby next to the shelter. In contrast to the "sea" or the plaza, this area was defined not by an atmosphere of lack or terrifying freedom but by a space that could be felt too much. The stairs obscured the entrance, blocking much of the light that could have fallen on it and heightening the sense that one was descending into a cave or underworld (see Figure 4). "It reminds me of death," Richard said of the area. "'Cause I'm inside it. 'Cause people come to stay inside and take pills and don't know whether it helps or not." Others, mostly nonresidents, spoke of being overwhelmed or frightened by the building's spaces. "I went down those stairs, the spiral ones," an ethnographer said of her first visit to the shelter, when she entered the building through the plaza side and walked down the interior curved stairwell to the lobby. "I thought I was climbing down into a cave. I didn't think I'd be able to get out."

This sense of losing one's way, of being engulfed or of feeling too much, is similar, it seems to me, to the feelings evoked by "the sublime," as it is variously defined by the British political philosopher Edmund Burke in the eighteenth century and his contemporary, German philosopher Immanuel Kant. For Burke, whereas the beautiful consists of all those sensations that give us pleasure, the sublime involves those natural phenomena—sea storms, darkness, forces vast and unmanageable—that fill us with an "idea of pain and danger, without being actually in such circumstances."[1] Kant, in turn, suggests in his *Critique of Judgement* that the sublime derives less from the natural world than from "the cast of mind" that shapes how we cognitively approach that world. With the dynamical sublime we are faced with a force so powerful that we would fear for our lives if that force were actually able to threaten us (e.g., watching a lightening storm from a safe enclosure). With the mathematical sublime we encounter some vast or formless object "that overwhelms our capacity to comprehend it *as a totality* in terms of sense-perception or imagination."[2] For Kant, one example of the mathematical sublime is the finding that, if one stands "very near" the Egyptian pyramids, "the eye requires some time to complete the apprehension of the tiers from the bottom up to the apex; and then the first tiers are always partly forgotten before the Imagination has taken in the last, and so the comprehension of them is never complete."[3] Kant adds, "The same thing may sufficiently explain the bewilderment or, as it were, perplexity which, it is said, seizes the spectator on his first entrance into St. Peter's at Rome. For there is here a feeling of the inadequacy of his Imagination for presenting the Ideas of a whole, wherein the Imagina-

Figure 6. View east from the plaza.

tion reaches its maximum, and, in striving to surpass it, sinks back into itself, by which, however, a kind of emotional satisfaction is produced."[4] Here and elsewhere Kant suggests that the pleasure we achieve from the mathematical sublime derives from the reminder that we have "a faculty of the mind surpassing every standard of Sense"—namely, Reason. The feeling of the sublime contains a painful awareness of the power of Reason to go beyond our sensory impressions. When we are faced with a vast object, such as an infinite number, we are checked by its sheer and overwhelming force; we feel a sense of boundlessness, of "violence to the imagination." Our imagination tries to assess the object in its entirety, but fails; the failure makes us pleasantly aware of the ability of Reason to accomplish what the imagination cannot.

While Kant's celebration of the saving graces of Reason might now seem outmoded, there is still something compelling in his grasp of a sublime moment. Kant found that the sublime derived from a sense of "formlessness, an absence of form." A comparable feeling of "formlessness" characterized the responses of many to the intimate spaces of the State Service Center, for people often had difficulty comprehending the building as a whole. As noted above, Rudolph designed the building with a "double-scale" in mind: the tower would balance the forces of the encircling exterior structure. Without the tower, however, there was only an illusion of scale. One could step away from the building and view it from afar, but the linked buildings lacked the central "announcement" that a tower could have provided, and one faced a range of ruins. In contrast to the linear John Hancock Tower in central Boston, for example, whose entirety could be grasped in a single glance and so was not overpowering, the Center could project a feeling of boundlessness. Though people had a sense of the building as a whole, of a "megastructure," most could not conceive of it through perceptual means.

When standing beside the Center, people, sheltered or not, held onto the desire that the building conclude in a bounded form. Yet because the upper levels were "stepped back" and so could not be seen from the ground level, it was only possible to "read" the building, as Rudolph put, "as a single floor." "You can only see one floor from here. That's all," Stuart said as we stood in his sea of tranquility. Richard expressed a similar frustration one day when he said that sitting on the sandcastle stairwell made him feel "restless" because "there's too much to look at." For him, the northwest exterior was a "nocturnal space," because "people can't see it." "It's a bit too large," he said, "and you can't really see it well. . . . Maybe if they took a bench or two away, you could see it better. But as it is, people don't want to visit. It's a dead space—or a puzzle that's never been finished." As with Kant's structures, an opacity arising from perceptual overload frustrated the viewer.

The first floor of the building, which loomed over pedestrians like an inverted pyramid, could enhance the frustration and restlessness Richard spoke of, in part because it was impossible to see more of the building than that which was directly in front of a person. "I hope it doesn't fall on us," was the typical response of shelter residents when discussing the exteriors of the building; the nervous quips correlated with their feeling of being overwhelmed. The spaces of the building, inside and out, conveyed a sense of excess, of something added. With Burke's sublime, "the mind is hurried out of itself, by a crowd of great and confused images; which affect because they are crowded and confused."[5] A similar crowdedness characterized the State Service Center. Because there was too much to look at, it imposed a violence on the imagination. People could relate only to parts of the building rather than to its entirety. "It's weird," said Sam, the college student, when I asked his impression of the building as a whole, "but now that I'm talking to you, I can only recall bits and pieces. The more I talk about it, the less I can picture the whole building. I can only think of the little staircases."

To be able to think only of little staircases recalls a contemporary semiotic reading of the Kantian sublime. Thomas Weiskel finds that a sense of the sublime can occur when there is either too little or too much meaning in a discursive moment.[6] With the latter, or "poet's sublime," a word or image "contains" so much that there is nothing we cannot "read into" it.[7] With the former, or "reader's sublime," which compares to Kant's mathematical sublime, there is an excess of signifiers that we fail to comprehend because we cannot match them with a signified. When the fission between signifier and signified occurs in the reader's sublime, "the feeling is one of *on and on*, of being lost. The signifiers cannot be grasped or understood; they overwhelm the possibility of meaning in a massive underestimation that melts all oppositions or distinctions into a perceptual stream; or there is a sensory overload."[8] Simply put, there is a lack of tangible meaning; an object or force hints at a meaning, but that meaning always seems beyond our reach. At this moment the imaginative faculties are checked or suspended, and the mind collapses in its inability to assign meaning. In fact, Neil Hertz points out that, while Burke and others write of being temporarily "baffled" or "checked" by a sublime moment, later thinkers, such as Kant and Wordsworth, speak of a more profound "blockage" of the mind's movement.[9]

In order to "right the balance" between signifier and signified and so recover a stable meaning, Weiskel suggests, the perceptual field must be slowed.[10] One way to halt the flow and thereby release the mind from its failure to imagine or conceptualize is to substitute "strong images" for what one cannot adequately think.[11] With the Center, an inability to "picture the whole building" led Sam and others to grab onto bits of imagery. "It's a free-floating Rorschach test," said another student of the building. To pin the building down, Sam drew on a "key image"— that the building was melting like the sandcastles he had built at the beach. While Sam resorted to metonym, taking a part—the little stair-cases—for the whole, each person found his own trope. "I just hope the building doesn't fall on us," Ian, a shelter resident, said one day as we sat beneath an overhanging exterior wall, then quickly added, "Some guy was hit by a car today. Up by the Commons. His hair and blood were still on the windshield."

"What made you think of that?" I asked.

"I don't know. I don't know. My mind could of done that, though."

That people made sense of the building in overly rhetorical or imag-istic frames rather than on its own, concrete terms related to the fact that the building remained open and unstable. When a space was felt too much, a person tried to control it with his or her own net of repre-sentations. A point of blockage sparked a whirl of substituted meanings: the building became "an unfinished symphony," a "brutal citadel of de-spair,"[12] or, in my own musings, Kafka's Castle, Borges's labyrinths, and an image of the sublime itself. In effect, the building absorbed mean-ings and feelings. As Richard put it, "I think the building is made of people's dreams, and conversations, and minds—and architecture. Yeah. The building has people's emotions in it. When people breathe onto it, when they look at it, or touch it, then what they're feeling goes into it, like that."

Beautiful Ruins

For Kant, the "emotional satisfaction" produced by the sublime derives from the realization of the powers of Reason. For Burke, the pain and terror brought by the sublime achieve a catharsis; they "clear the parts, whether fine, or gross, of a dangerous and troublesome incumbrance."[1] Yet it strikes me that any satisfaction achieved with a more modern sub-lime relates to the pleasure felt when standing in the midst of ruin. Meaning can tumble like a house of cards, the loss of a solid perceptual footing can undermine one's identity, a building can fall apart. While one can witness or facilitate the collapse in a variety of ways, the thought of the collapse can alone effect a vicarious delight. Freud's Thanatos comes to mind, although the drive toward destruction seems more cul-tural than instinctual.

In the modern West, devastation is most often made beautiful in heroic historical movements, when great monuments seize the imagination. The pairing of heroics and devastation ceases to be ironic when one realizes that these movements often arise from the ashes of pre-existent disorder, such that dreams of immortality signal an imminent demise. Rudolph, for instance, pursued an aesthetics of destruction when he wished for his megastructures, built on the fallen "slums" of the West End, to end as beautiful ruins. While the phrasing echoes Le Corbusier's dictum that "Architecture is that which makes for magnificent ruins," the sentiment recalls the "ruins principle" of the Third Reich: Hitler and Spier designed their monuments so that they would decay majestically, like the remnants of Athens.

Rudolph's wish was quickly fulfilled, for people often take the unfinished State Service Center to be a place of ruin. "What was to be a grand central plaza," rails the "Madhouse" article, "is now a desolate tundra of crumbling concrete, sloping eerily toward a rusting chain-link fence that rims a concrete precipice. Sumac and weeds have taken over the concrete planters. . . . Rubble marks the spot where a majestic 25-story tower was supposed to rise."[2]

According to Richard, the building's uses eroded as quickly as its structure. "They shouldn't have a shelter here," he said. "The building doesn't have any use anymore. It should be torn down. It was getting too old-fashioned, and the concrete and stuff don't have any meaning any more. The spaces in this building were probably better used in the sixties, when everybody was doing acid and coke and stuff. But now I don't think they use it so well. . . . The times have changed, but the building hasn't."

David offered another opinion. "I think it would have been nicer if it was finished," he said. "I wonder what it would be like if it was."

"But you know," I said, forcing the issue, "some people say they like the building as it is."

"Yeah, I can see that," he said. "I sort of like it too, in a way. You know when they say, 'You're so ugly, you're beautiful'? The building's like that. It's so ugly, it's beautiful."

It might be that a ruin can be beautiful only if it accords with a sensibility that values collapse and decay in their own right.[3] George Simmel found that we value the ruin because it is a place where "The past with its destinies and transformations has been gathered into this instant of an aesthetically perceptible present."[4] Yet when a building emerges and declines within the same artistic era, it acquires special meaning. Architects have begun to build ruins intentionally, so that their dwellings are, from the start, simulacra of ruined form, with the present intensified and fulfilled for the future. The narrative pacing is of such intensity that the present is already seen as past, and that past lingers in the pale of

ruin. "Ruins helped ground our shaken identity in a rapidly transform-
ing world," writes David Harvey in glossing Simmel's essay.[5] Lately, ruins
have become our identity at times, with some identities shaken more
than others.

Framing the Homeless

Basic to the sublime disorders of the post-industrial age, then, is a common sentiment: whether it be the occasional thrill of semantic collapse
or a yearning for structural decay, there is a delight in the fall. The architects of Boston's homeless—politicians, journalists, consumers, psychiatrists, ethnographers, and the dislocated themselves—are tempted by a
similar aesthetics of decay when invoking or depicting these people. As
I understand it, confrontations with Boston's itinerant often evoke sentiments similar to those conjured by Rudolph's ruin. This is not to say
that the cultural history of the homeless is identical to that of the sublime. But the ways in which many people respond to and present what
they take to be the sublime can, I believe, help to explain how many
commonly respond to and present what they take to be the homeless.

The homeless can be felt too much. Those living on the streets and
in shelters are disturbing because they threaten assumed paradigms of
meaning. Their presence can effect an excess of meaning for which the
American imagination has yet to account. To escape a sense of blockage,
those confronted by the homeless resort to irony, mythic themes, and a
rough poetry to give meaning to their encounters. These strong images
achieve a poetics of homelessness that deploys the perceived qualities
of animality, death, and darkness within an aesthetic of ruins.

We can take as a model of this semiotic rupture the opening words of
the article on "compassion fatigue" cited earlier.[1] The "peaceful civility"
of the breakfast scene is "rudely—and horribly—interrupted" by the
presence of a man "bleeding heavily from the nose." An animality rich
beyond words shatters the beauty of the setting: "His shrieks filled the
cafe, and a thick mixture of blood, mucus, and tears dripped down his
face." The man wails and screams incomprehensibly. There is too much
here to make sense of.

While the author notes that the "storm" passes when friends calm the
man, I find the account serves witness to a secondary resolution. The
author re-creates the scene for his readers, but it is through the act of re-
creation, of re-presentation, that his mind seems able to right itself. The
rhetoric of the article, with its tropes and images, removes us from the

point of blockage threatened by the intractability of the man's presence. By poeticizing an unsettling moment, the moment ceases to disturb. The author puts a lid on formlessness by giving it a tangible form. To talk about the homeless (or any other presence that lacks stable form) can quickly lead to a poetics that situates the talk within an architecture—a rhythm or structure that gives form and meaning to the formless.

At times an author's words embrace an aesthetic. In the article on "Compassion Fatigue," the threatening presence of a bleeding man is paired with "peaceful civility." By situating the perceived qualities of the homeless within an aesthetic structure—wherein pain clashes with beauty, and ironies abound—the threat becomes a fiction, a piece of art. The aestheticization of the homeless, evident in this and other tales, stems in part from some of the more problematic aspects of artistic representation. Jacques Derrida tears at these aspects when he shows that the Kantian aesthetic involves a paradoxical relation to the matter of the *parergon*, the frame or border of a work of art which is both distinct from, and necessary to, that work or *ergon*.[2] While the *parergon* is excluded conceptually from a painting, it nonetheless serves to enhance, determine, and size up a painting to such an extent that the *parergon* fulfills a lack inherent in the work. The work needs what it excludes. In contrast to essentialist views of art, which posit distinct borders between the beautiful and the mundane, Kant's own analysis of art and the sublime seeds the idea that such borders are unstable.

Derrida's reading of the Kantian sublime wreaks further havoc with notions of both bounded and unbounded art. Kant found that the sublime marks the limitations of the aesthetic, precisely because the sublime seems to lack or exceed the *parerga* characteristic of the beautiful.[3] Derrida sums up Kant's views by drawing on the colossal, which Kant took to be the prime example of the sublime: "If art takes form by limiting, indeed by framing, there can be a *parergon* of the beautiful, the *parergon* of a column or the *parergon* as column. But there cannot be, it seems, any *parergon* of the sublime. The colossal excludes the *parergon*. First of all because it is not a work, an *ergon*, and then because the infinite is presented in it and the infinite cannot be bordered."[4]

Derrida shows that this truth is too neat, for how can one present the infinite if it cannot be presented? In other words, any presentation of the sublime must entail some sort of frame, determination, or "cise." The sublime is defined less by its absence of frame or measure, as Kant suggests, than by its constant passage over, and transgression of, borders. As a result, one needs, when talking about the sublime, to hang a frame around it. In trying to convey a sense of "too much," one must settle for an "almost-too-much." And since the use of frames implies the ornamental, presentations of the sublime tends to clothe coarse and threatening qualities within an aesthetic. Kant is clear on this: "The sublime is not an object of taste. It is rather, the feeling of being stirred that has the sublime for its object. But when an artist exhibits the sublime to us, by describing it or clothing it (in ornaments, *parerga*), it can and should be beautiful, since otherwise it is wild, coarse and repulsive, and so contrary to taste."[5] As J. M. Bernstein notes in quoting Derrida, the aesthetic is a consequence of the fearful qualities of the originary sublime: " 'There is an excess here, a surplus, a superabundance which opens an abyss (*Abgrund*). The imagination is afraid of losing itself in this abyss, and we step back.' The stepping back is the aestheticizing of the threat, making it no threat, only a representation, a fiction."[6]

Derrida's take on the Kantian sublime does not necessarily hold true for all sublime encounters, for there is no inherent reason that the modern sublime, found in nature or in cities, needs limits or borders. But his reading does help make sense of literary and artistic portraits of the modern sublime, which try to present the unpresentable. It also helps to explain presentations of the homeless, which often grapple in a similar fashion with the unsettling. With the *Boston Phoenix* article, the threatening presence of the bleeding man is framed by the beautiful. A drama unfolds. There is a "balance or reconcilement of discordant qualities," as Coleridge says. The aesthetic—a familiar one in Western literature—can be a cliché and is perhaps best modeled by Auden's lines:

And the crack in the tea cup opens
A lane to the land of the dead.[7]

Similar to Auden's image, the peaceful civility of music and coffee cups is ruptured by the potent constellation of a "homeless" man: blood, mucus, and tears. Yet while Auden's words open onto a further darkness, the cafe rupture is a re-created one; the dramatic framing of the threat sutures the wound. Tensions linger, but they are artful ones. We still glimpse the horrific, but it is tamed through the balancing of blood and carnations. The tones of irony or tragedy are evident in other tales as well: a wilding sneaks into a library, a morgue is set up in a museum, and a homeless man is gunned down in front of the White House. The homeless have been framed.

Due to a complex play of media productions, urban sensibilities, and built form, then, the homeless are the recipients of a mythology. The mythology, with its air of animality, death, and the underworld, stands on two acts of the imagination. There is an immediate confrontation with the homeless, which can involve a glimpse of the unsettling, and there is a retreat into strong images that cast the homeless as beautiful ruins. The reason for the anxiety and the nature of the poetics hinge on cultural sensibilities: a late modernist orientation toward light, form, and space indirectly structures both the State Service Center and imageries of homelessness. In Boston and other American cities, buildings, like streets or bodies, can become open or closed, dark or light. They can be felt too much or not enough. We encounter wild, Dionysian places and ordered, Apollonian ones. There are tortured, serpentine streets and straight, reasonable roadways; flowing, errant spaces and steady, tranquil ones. While the distinct features of urban spaces can seem endless, most build on the sensibilities of late modern discourses and the debate over architectural and imaginative forms. In modern times there has been a recurrent need for clean, well-lighted places as well as a fascination with the waste spaces of urban life.[8] Perspectives on the Center reflect the need for light, the strain of the formless, and the sentiments that certain "dead" or "nocturnal" spaces can evoke.

A poetics of darkness similarly infects current perspectives on the homeless, for the homeless are often said to inhabit the ghostly netherworlds of cities. The modern need to "create order out of the desperate confusion of our times" soon converts into a will to "get them [the homeless] off the Commons." All that does not shine in the light—the unmanageable, the formless, the obscure—is sided with death and the wild, and the homeless are kept from public places. There is a mythology of homelessness that situates the homeless in a deathly underground. Yet there is also an active production of homelessness, for the myths instruct us how to treat people, construct shelters, and write sentences.

Sensory (Dis)Orientations

Since people's feelings could become part of the State Service Center when they touched, looked at, or breathed onto it, the building felt different and meant different things for different people, at different times, and from different vantage points. The building could not be read like a book, with a single meaning: its uses and meanings tied into one's position in space and one's place in society. While many of the residents of the building, more familiar with its nuances than most, found the unusual architecture to be dangerous and "distracting," they also knew the structure as a place of safety and protection, a sanctuary where they could stay and avoid the openness of Boston's streets. People without homes used its vacant corners as their "offices" or as places to rest, be with others, sell drugs, have sex, or sleep off a drunk. The building was a "castle" to some. It was "solid" and "wouldn't leak."

"It makes me feel distinguished," said Simone Jacobs, with a majestic wave of her hand. Apparently a childhood refugee from Nazi Europe, Simone, who worked for a long time as a secretary, often spoke in a large, raspy voice of numerous persecutions and ailments. "I love this building," she went on. "The building is strong, clean! It helps me to be healthy. It makes me feel like God!" I asked her why that was. "The columns! The windows!" she said with another sweep of her hand, "It's very spacious, and it's very crowded here. So it helps. It fascinates me. You know, they did all the walls by hand?"

Other residents appreciated the building for similar reasons. "It's a terrific building. I like the architecture. It's interesting," Henry Williamson told me. "I think it's tremendous," said a woman new to the shelter, as we sat and talked one day. "Me too," said the woman seated next to her. "It's nice, sort of strange. The walls are odd. There's so many turns and squiggles," Peter Vaughn said.

Some were not so taken with the building, however. One man told me that "it's intimidating. It feels like a dungeon," while another resident said, "It reminds me of a medieval castle." One day, while talking with Richard and his companion Ian in the lobby, I asked Ian what came to mind when he thought of the building. He thought for a second, then said "Fuck! That's it: Fuck!" I then asked Richard what words came to mind when he thought of the building. "Solid, drafty, condemned," he said.

Richard summed up how residents commonly valued the building for its unanticipated uses. Some appreciated its "solid" nature, in part because the arrangement of concrete slabs, columns, and walls led many to find solidity, permanence, and safety in the structure. "It's solid, concrete. It won't leak," Walter Rech told me. "It's kinda nice," Nina Anderson said. "It's a stone building. I like that it's stone, because it won't burn. It's fire proof."[1] Others appreciated the building's expansiveness. "I like living here a lot," said Helen of the shelter and the building at large. "It's like living in a mansion. There's a lot of different places to go."[2]

Many of the spaces—tucked into "caves," set beneath staircases, or stretched out along long, narrow, dead-end corridors—were hidden from the immediate gaze of others, so that people could sit or lie unnoticed by others. Some, however, got lost at times in the labyrinthine structure. "I think the building is interesting," April Berreman said, "but you can get lost pretty easily. There's five different levels here." "It's a unique building, but it could be dangerous," Henry told me one day. "The stairs can be dangerous. You don't see where the steps drop. I fell one day. I missed the last two steps. It's confusing, with its winding stairwells. I used to come in here to pick up my meds, and I would get lost. I couldn't find the room and then I couldn't find the way out, even though it was just one flight up."

The building's architectural features often occasioned a sensory disorientation among its users. The "inside-out" style, combined with the same surfaces within and without, clouded distinctions that one might ordinarily draw between interiors and exteriors. The movement of space in the building and the connections of one volume of space to another made it difficult in spots to know precisely which floor one was on, where one actually was in the building, or whether one was descending or ascending. The corduroy surfaces fractured sound as well as light. The intensity of light in certain corners and hallways, the lack of light in some caves and chambers, and a correlated inability to gauge the time of day contributed to its confusions. "It's so dark," said a poet friend of mine who once attended AA meetings in the building, which she condemned as "an insane mud castle built by someone who wanted to die." "There's really no light from any windows," she added. "And there's no hands on any of the clocks. Didn't you ever notice that? There's no hands on any of the clocks in the building at all! You can never tell what time it is!" Although there were working clocks in the building, certain areas could readily give the sense that there were none to be found. Then again, the absence of a clock would disorient or unnerve a person only if he or she counted on there being one. Most residents did not seem to mind.

In all, the building's features sometimes made it difficult to maintain one's orientation in space or time. Certain spaces within or close to the building did help to clarify where one was, but this made any passage through more obscure domains all the more disconcerting, for people then moved back and forth between states of clarity and opacity as quickly as they stepped from one volume of space to another. Like the clocks with no hands, the building's structure teased people's expectations. "Maybe people are encouraged to use their imagination that way," Stuart said of the building's odd arrangements, "but I think it's too complicated for a mental health building. I think it could cause people to become confused or disoriented, maybe." [3]

Although patrons of the mental health center—particularly those who were new to the building—did get confused and disoriented at times, the spatial and sensory complications sometimes worked to their advantage. Residents and other inhabitants of the mental health center made use of its secretive, labyrinthine form, which offered obscure nooks and crannies. They could take cover in the sublime, inhabit the building's perceptual cul-de-sacs, and go unnoticed. In *Formations of Violence* Allen Feldman details how the holding cells and interrogation rooms run by the police and the British army in Northern Ireland—

made of pure white spaces, without relief or variation, and bereft of clocks, daylight, sounds, and language—evoke a sensory and temporal disorientation among paramilitaries imprisoned for interrogation.[4] As he notes, the unvarying white spaces of the prison cells and interrogation rooms advance an "exhaustive exposure in which nothing can be hidden or disguised, in which there are no recesses or depths, only the self reduced to a figure against a ground—a diagram."[5] The mental health center advanced a comparable sensorium, but one distinct in several ways, for its distractions, blind spots, and sublime features permitted the possibility of retreat, hiding, or obscurity. Both edifices disoriented, but the center's discombobulations often served the interests of the residents and other frequenters of the building. Feldman's account, which adds to a range of studies that underscore how state regimes or aggressive agents try to terrorize a populace by invoking a sense of disorientation, concludes that the security, resistance, and self-integrity of prisoners in Northern Ireland lay in the restoration of time and agency.[6] The denizens of the Center, in contrast, found a measure of security and control in the disorientation itself; they would probably agree with guerilla fighters, chess players, and Brer Rabbit that opacity or ambiguity is sometimes the best defense against the strongholds of the powerful. Yet while residents took advantage of the building's briar-like confusions, there were important limits to such defenses. Unlike guerrilla fighters or IRA prisoners, any political resistance among residents was atomistic and reactive, with their actions and their quests for opacity ultimately fueling their dependency on the Center. Individuals tried simply to stay within the building and did not work toward more organized and collective political actions that might lead to their release from the shelter. The political orders that ruled the Center went unchallenged. In the end, one had to ask who was tricking whom.

The residents' sole advantage lay in the fact that they knew the building better than most and so were more familiar with its perceptual oddities. Kevin put it this way: "It's a building you have to get used to. It's like going to a mall downtown. It seems very shiny at first." Much as an unfamiliar shopping complex can be optically bewildering until one makes the necessary sensory adjustments, the Center required a habitual reorganization of the senses. Constant use of the building's spaces and knowledge of its irregularities could lead to new perceptual habits.

The variable presence or absence of such habits helps to explain why those who spent less time in the building—mental health workers, case managers, psychiatrists, support staff, and the participants of various meetings—were less comfortable within it. The way employees walked, bore themselves, and used their bodies differed from that of residents. Georges Dumézil notes that many early Indo-Europeans understood that a well-organized society consisted of four categories of peoples: celestial "saints," "sages," and "priests"; atmospheric "kings," "warriors," and "bureaucrats"; terrestrial "craftsmen" and "laborers"; and subterranean "barbarians" and "savages."[7] The social blueprints of the Center involved a similar hierarchy, with celestial politicians, atmospheric bureaucrats and psychiatrists, terrestrial nurses and staff members, and the presumably subterranean "homeless mentally ill" occupying different levels of the building and its outlying areas. Uses of bodies tied into different cosmic statuses and social roles. Most of the politicians, bureaucrats, and staff members walked quickly through the building's corridors and rooms toward their destinations: an office, a meeting room, or exit. Remaining erect and upright, they did not sit or lie in any of the "unused" or "waste" spaces, nor did they rest against the walls. Many walked through the common areas with eyes straight ahead so that there was as little engagement as possible with people whom they did not know. In line with the predominance of vision in modern American and Western European cultures, they tended to assess and make sense of the building and its inhabitants through optical, non-earthy means.[8] For most, any tactile contact with or earthy knowledge of the building was unwelcome, primarily because they took the surfaces of the building to be dirty, the walls to be dangerous, and olfactory sensations to be unpleasant. Employees usually wanted their bodies to be upright, bounded, autonomous, free of contact with their surroundings, and purposeful in their actions and movements.

Residents, true to their subterranean status, commonly made use of bodies that were in close, porous, and interdependent contact with their surroundings and their associates. Using and knowing the building through various kinesthetic as well as optical means, they inhabited a range of unused spaces (often to avoid the direct gaze of others) and sometimes used the walls for support. And although they usually considered certain places, such as the bathrooms, unfit for human habitation, most of the floors, staircases, benches, and corners were well-suited for temporary, idling occupancy. This variable kinesthetic orientation held true for human interactions, for there was more bodily contact between patrons than between employees (or between patrons and employees). To rely on Richard's words again, whereas employees and visitors tended simply to "look at" the building and its patrons, residents and other long-term frequenters also "touched" and "breathed onto" it and them. They therefore used and knew the building and most of its occupants through different, more marginal, and more visceral ways of sensing.

The Walls

The walls, both inside and out, remained forbidding, however. Phenomenologies of space, like Gaston Bachelard's *The Poetics of Space,* usually attend to the mood, symbolism, or geometry of certain areas, such as a home, a corner, or an avenue.[1] But the makings of the State Service Center suggested that the very surfaces and tactility of built spaces played a strong role in the doings and imaginings of its users.

The architects, "brutalist" by trade, designed the walls so that light would be "fractured in a thousand ways" and the sense of "depth" would be increased. To achieve this effect, most of the vertical surfaces of the building (which Richard took to be "rough and spiny, like a jellyfish") were made of a rough "corduroy" concrete inlaid with small stones, broken pieces of rock, and different-colored glasslike fragments; the concrete was then chipped away at with hammers to roughen its surfaces (see Figure 2). Each wall contained a series of ridges, with each ridge, spaced about an inch and a half from its neighbors, jutting out to form a narrow edge about an inch from the back surface of the concrete. This narrow edge was set, like the rest of the concrete, with dull or sharp stones and mineral fragments. In the shelter, mice were known to scurry up and down the ruts between ridges in the winter months.

Inside the building, the fractured depth envisioned by Rudolph, which related to the striated, multitextured surface, often translated into a sense of oddness, darkness, and potential danger. Although some residents liked the surfaces' whimsical air, most disliked the walls, finding both the texture and the sharpness ominous. "I don't like this building," Eric Oberg told me. "The guy—whoever built this—must have been on drugs. Whoever thought of making the inside of a building like the outside?! And that kind of wall is a lawsuit right there. You could fall against it, or be pushed into it."

One of the greatest fears that people had when living in the shelter was of being thrown against the seemingly razor-sharp walls. "The building can be dangerous," Richard once said. "If you were fighting with someone, they could push you flat against it." Others often said much the same, although I never saw anyone actually throw someone against a wall. One man who stayed in the shelter for a few weeks hinted he might do so, however.

"How's it going?" I asked him one day as he was leaning against a wall.

"I wish it was," he said.

"Uh-huh?"

"A man's head could be split in two against this wall. Alls it would take is one push, and he'd be dead."

"I see what you mean," I said, unsure if he had me in mind.

"And then maybe I could take my radio off of him."

"So someone has your radio?"

"Yeah. I just bought it brand new. As a matter of fact, I had it out on the nightstand this afternoon, so I could listen to it tonight."

He then walked away.

A person's head was generally seen as most vulnerable to the potential violence of the walls, a violence that could be realized by either the acts of others or harm inflicted upon oneself. "That's—I don't know why they would make walls like that in a mental institution," Martin Aaron said in exasperation one day, when I asked him what he thought of the walls. "People are known to knock their heads against the wall in hospitals, and that could split your head right open." Martin's concern reminded me of Sylvia Covert's thought that "Maybe there are some soft heads that like, are helped by, the [building's] hard surfaces." In this architectural imaginary, the building was taken to be solid, hard, and sharp, whereas heads—particularly those sported by residents—were soft, vague, and vulnerable.

Due in part to the sharpness of the walls, people also spoke about the way in which the surfaces inhibited any tactile or bodily contact. "You can't even rest against the wall," my poet friend said in disgust. "It's impossible to do. You have to remain upright." Her concern, which tied into her inability to maintain a solid perceptual footing in the building, was a common one among visitors and mental health care workers, particularly in the locked psychiatric ward. This area, unlike the shelter proper (which consisted of standing partitions arranged in a gym), was lined primarily with corduroy surfaces. The ward's architecture was held to have an offensive, even inhuman air to it, partly because of the potential violence of the walls and partly because people had to refrain from any tactile contact with its surfaces.

While many nonresidents maintained a chasm between the building's structure and any bodily contact with it, residents of the shelter and the psychiatric ward often did, in fact, lean against the walls when standing or sitting on the floors, which again attests to the different perceptual and bodily orientations of residents and nonresidents. Residents nonetheless rested gingerly against the ridges, with no great comfort. Richard once told me that "nobody can paint or clean the walls, so nobody can touch them." Given that the walls were one of the few objects that Richard was unable or unwilling to touch, the statement hinted at their dirty, impersonal, and untouchable nature.

Roots to Earth

Despite their dangers, the walls protected those within them. Many found refuge in the building from the streets, the police, and the potential violence of everyday life. It sometimes seemed as if each person heeded a distinct geography of fear and safety. Wendy Dyer, for instance, told me one day that she only felt comfortable "in this building and around it." She was particularly frightened of East Boston, where her ex-boyfriend lived. When I asked Julie Mason what she took to be safe places to stay, she named the shelter, the building, and Virginia: "People don't die in Virginia. Here [in Boston], they do." Julie Mason found the streets and subways to be especially unsafe. Rose Crecco told me, in turn, that she preferred to stay inside the building rather than outside. "It's nice to come inside," she said. "Why is that?" I asked. "I don't know. It can be so open outside. There's too much air, maybe, and if you have no place to go . . . [then waiting outside gets tiresome]." She said she felt "safer, more secure" inside, "because it is nice and closed inside."

The fears of more than a few women related to the abuse they suffered in life. Rose said she was raped when she was a young woman, Helen's former husband had tormented her, Wendy feared assaults by her former boyfriend, and Alice said she was psychologically abused by her parents. When Alice told me this, I asked if she thought others in the shelter had suffered abuse. "I look around sometimes," she said, "and think a lot of people were sexually abused."[1] Some women wanted to have nothing to do with men, and most were wary of the affections and bodily proximities of men.

For these and other reasons, many women and men stayed close to the building. Bill, a staff member, told me that people usually did not leave the building on weekends. "They feel really safe in the building," he said, "and are threatened by venturing outside. Few individuals venture out." With a few exceptions, such as Helen, who enjoyed the openness of the streets, I found this to be true as well.

Some nonresidents also found the Center to be a sort of haven from the streets—to the occasional consternation of mental health bureaucrats. Thelonious, a charismatic African American in his mid-thirties, often spent time at the social club on the fourth floor, where he wrote poetry, played cards, and participated in various group activities. Most nights he slept on one of the concrete benches that bordered the sea of tranquility beside the rear of the building.[2] One afternoon I sat with him on a bench and asked why he came to the Center. "Sometimes," he said, "it's just too distracting outside. That's why I come here, to get away from that. But sometimes people here are just as bothersome. Some of them act much younger than me, and so I feel I can't go anywhere."

"You just have to take it as it comes," he said of living on the streets. He did not like to bed down in a shelter because "being comfortable is sometimes more important than safety." In a shelter, he said, "you get rules, regulations, and a social worker always watching over you." Sleeping outside, in contrast, brought "peace of mind, if not peace around the ears." That is, it could be noisy as well as extremely cold—he once slept on a bench in winter when it was thirty degrees below zero. But at least one skirted the unnerving rules and steady gaze of shelter staff. Thelonious found that the Center was "one of the safest places in the city." "You don't have two hundred cutthroats walking by all the time. And the security guards sit over there," he said, nodding to a spot across the street. "Besides, it could be unsafe either inside or outside somewhere. You don't know what could happen." He said at first the police used to bother him when he was sleeping outside, but they no longer did. "There's a lot of poor people around this building," he said. "They need to stay here."

Like Thelonious, others spent much of their time in or around the Center even though they weren't staying in the shelter or the psychiatric ward. Many of them regularly attended the social club during the week and were "poor people" who, as Thelonious noted, "needed" the Center for a variety of informal reasons. On Veteran's Day, which fell on a wintery Monday in November, Mitch put it more generally. Even though the social club and most other programs were closed (the shelter remained open throughout the day), many of the regular clientele, who mainly lived alone or in shared apartments, still came to the building. "They have nowhere else to go," he said. "They have homes, but they're used to coming here, so they come every day. Where else can you go? Everything costs money. And with libraries closed, what can you do? You can't go anywhere. It sucks. Everything costs money."

Poverty limited where a person could stay or go. The down-and-out were excluded from a range of other public institutions in Boston, either because they did not have the price of admission or because shop owners or the police displaced them if they loitered for any length of time. Many frequented the Center less for its official functions—mental health care and social rehabilitation—than for the possibility of a free and relatively safe, "solid" place to stay and a way to be around others without spending more than a few dollars on food, cigarettes, or coffee. The decision makers at City Hall and the shopowners in the downtown area probably did not mind this informal arrangement, since it kept "crazy" people out of sight and "off the Commons."

Shelter residents and others often sought out particular sites in which they found comfort. The spots usually varied according to the time of day and a person's mood. Nancy Ange, for instance, told me that a "comfortable spot" for her was on the fourth floor of the building, "in a hallway with pictures." Simone, in turn, would often stretch out during the afternoon on a patch of grass at the far, northern end of the building, with her back to the shelter ("It's peaceful, quiet. I like to get away from all this *mess*," she explained one day with a disgusted sweep of her arm). At night she often ended up underneath a stairwell. "This is my favorite spot," said Roy Lerner, a man who lived for over two years in the shelter, when I approached him one day as he sat resting against the back of the elevator cavity, facing the shelter. "I try to find a favorite spot and sit there every day, like roots to earth."

A lot was involved in such encampments. Many promised a modicum of privacy—which, for residents, meant going unseen and unheard by others. They also entailed a sense of the familiar and possibly the comforts of a home. However makeshift or illusive these nests might be, the residents valued them, given the unsettled nature of their lives. Some, like Roy, found a measure of consistency, solidity, and stasis in the routine of sitting in the same place every day.[3] Others sought refuge in quiet places. Irving Jackson, a middle-aged African American who lived in the shelter for seven years, found that he sometimes needed to get away from the constant interactions and distractions found around the shelter. A thoughtful and kind-spoken man who spent much of his time on his own but in close proximity to others, Irving often spoke contemplatively on a certain theme, usually to no one in particular. At times his words stretched into a lengthy monologue that centered on biblical themes, such as Moses, the Resurrection, hope, and the Judgment Day. "I don't want to tell a sad story," he began one day. During the monologues he often said "hello" to people as they walked by, but he somehow conveyed the sense of wanting to be alone; sometimes he wore sunglasses that made him look unapproachable. He liked to sit in what he and others called "the plaza," a cavernous, usually quiet room on the third floor that was often occupied by sleeping or resting folks when not used for more official purposes, like Alcoholics Anonymous meetings. "I've been up here since 9:30," he told me late one afternoon. "I got here at 9:30 and slept until 12. Then I had lunch. I come up here. Too much noise, conversations downstairs. Same old conversations. Cigarettes, coffee. Coffee, cigarettes. I've been living here a long time and I'm getting tired of it."

"Do the [Capitol] Police bother you when you're sleeping here?"

"Na. Not really," he said. "I guess they figure that we're tired of TV, cigarettes, conversations. There's too many violent movies downstairs [in the shelter]. So they let us stay up here. . . . Sometimes they have meet-

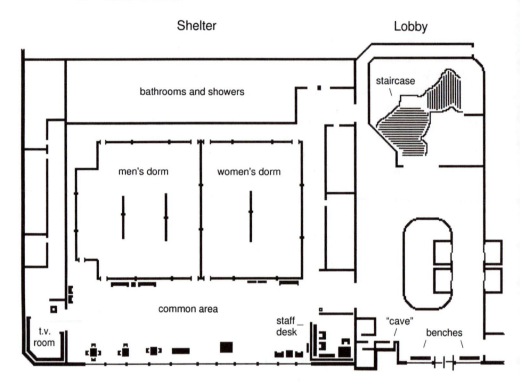

Figure 7. Map of the shelter and lobby.

ings up here, AA meetings." He then said "Hello, Stanley" to a man dozing on a bench.

Many hung out in "the lobby," which was next to the shelter (see Figure 7). To get to the shelter, a person needed to pass through the lobby after coming in sliding doors that stood to the right of the shelter's entrance, walking down a spiral staircase that descended from the next level of the building, or stepping off one of four elevators that stopped on each of the five floors of the building. In the lobby was a set of bathrooms between the shelter and the sliding doors, and a cafeteria on the far side of the sliding doors, opposite the entrance to the shelter. Two elevator shafts stood to the left of the cafeteria, along the wall. Another two, which directly faced their counterparts, stood in the middle of the lobby and were encased in the *brut,* corduroy concrete walls. Set on the back shoulder of this central column, on the shelter side of the lobby, was a pay phone, which in turn faced a soda-vending machine and a snack-vending machine that stood flush against the outer wall of the shelter. Most of the conversations that took place in the lobby happened by two benches that were set to each side of the sliding doors.

A marketplace of sorts for the building's citizens, the lobby was a place of commerce and converse. People bummed cigarettes, traded and borrowed possessions, hammered out loan and repayment schedules, and discussed a variety of other arrangements. It was a good place for people who wanted to talk or be with others but a poor one for people who wanted to be alone.

While the shelter was the staff's domain, the lobby belonged provisionally to the residents. Both groups understood that the lobby was not a part of the shelter and that the rules of the shelter could not necessarily be enforced in the lobby. Staff members would intervene when there was trouble and would often walk through or stand in the lobby, but they did not exercise the same authority that they did in the shelter. "I still get a sense that I'm not supposed to be there," Lisa said one day after she went to talk with people in the lobby. Asked why she thought this, she said, "I think it's because I'm the one who has to move people on during the day, when they're not supposed to be there."[4]

Residents often preferred to hang out "outside" — that is, in the lobby rather than in the shelter — even though there were only a couple of uncomfortable benches to sit on. When I asked Amy why she liked to stay in the lobby rather than the shelter, she said with a giggle, "You can kiss each other!" The general consensus was that people could act more freely in the lobby than they could in the shelter. The lobby functioned like one of the "free places" that Goffman found in psychiatric asylums, in which "ordinary levels of surveillance and restriction were markedly reduced" and where "the inmate could openly engage in a range of tabooed activities with some degree of security."[5] It also worked as an anti-structure to the shelter's structure. Mikhail Bakhtin notes that the marketplace in Rabelais's time carried a language, uttered by itinerant hawkers, gypsies, medical quacks, and obscure déclassés, of freedom, frankness, curses, and carnivalesque flair and laughter.[6] The marketplace of the lobby had a similar reputation and thus helped to shape the actions and habits of people who hung out there.

Several crannies offered a bit of privacy. Between the sliding doors leading out of the building and the entrance to the shelter was an alcove with an opening about four feet wide that expanded into a small room about eight feet long and five feet wide. While the room served ostensibly as an open janitor's closet and held a locked electric circuitry board (atop which one man stored bottles of tea), it also smacked of one of the "unused" or "waste" spaces Paul Rudolph took pleasure in designing. "It's really like a cave. Everyone uses it at different times," Lisa explained one day. Shelter residents or nonresidents who needed a place to sleep or rest used it the most. Anthony, a man who, on leaving the shelter, stayed in several places in Boston, told me that there were three places to sleep in the building, besides the shelter itself: "in the plaza, under the stairs [in the lobby], and inside that wall." That the room for some stood "inside" a wall gave it an air of intimacy, and it was known as one of the places where people could have sex or sleep. One rainy March afternoon two men slept in the room for several hours, resting their heads on each other's shoulders and clutching bottles in their hands—"dead to the world," or so said a police officer when he tried to wake them at eight, when he needed to lock the lobby doors. The officer finally succeeded in waking the two men, who then drowsily walked out of the building.

At the far end of the lobby, opposite the sliding doors and past another set of glass partitions and doors, was a spiral staircase, made of polished concrete slabs and *brut* corduroy sides, that curled up majestically toward the first floor and arrived directly to the right of the desk of the Capitol Police, a city-run security force that patrolled the State Service Center and other state-owned buildings in the city. People often sat or stood at the base of the stairs in order to drink coffee, smoke a cigarette, or be alone for a few minutes. In the evening hours, once the foot traffic had died down, people would sit on the stairs, usually about halfway between the ground floor and the first floor, so they could not be seen or heard by anyone in the lobby or the Capitol Police above.

Because the staircase arched up toward the next level, there was an expanse of "waste" space beneath its frame that offered some protection from the gaze of others. One of Anthony Scola's three sleeping places, this was where Carla Bataille slept for several months when she was "homeless." Several others had bedded down there as well. Still more liked to lie there in the afternoon or evening.

"I wanted to go where it was quiet," Rose said with a sheepish laugh one day when I came upon her seated against the curved wall to the right of the stairwell. As noted above, Rose usually preferred to stay "inside" rather than "go out" into the excessive openness of the city. Most evenings she could be found close to the stairwell, by the lobby benches, or at the end of a long corridor that stretched around the back of the stairwell enclosure and ended at a door that led to the cafeteria kitchen. Rose, more than others, would sit by herself at the end of the corridor, a few feet from the kitchen door, with cigarettes, soda, or coffee at hand. On occasion I would exchange a few words with her.

"So, is this your spot?" I asked one summer evening.

"Yeah," she said with a laugh. "It's nice here. Quiet and cool. Nobody bothers me." Sometimes people did bother her, however. One evening she was visibly upset because a man had followed her "back there" and kept talking to her.

Others were likewise bothered or bothered others in turn. Often the clashes related to different and sometimes incompatible uses they wished to make of the building. Throughout the day, but especially in the morning and early evening, people who worked in the mental health center passed through the lobby in leaving or in going to their places of employment. While case managers and counselors would often say "hello" to the residents they knew, other employees, unfamiliar with the lobby's inhabitants, would often enter through the sliding doors with eyes straight ahead, push the button to summon an elevator, and wait uncomfortably until the elevator doors opened.

Contact between residents and employees was occasionally antagonistic. During my first day at the shelter I watched a woman enter the lobby, walk up to the elevator doors, press the button to summon the elevator, and look down at Richard, who was lying against the wall between the two elevator doors, with his frame and legs on floor and his head atop a boombox that blasted a rock song through scratchy speakers. "Turn that off!" the woman yelled. "You're not allowed to play that in here!" Richard leisurely moved his hand down and turned off the radio. After the elevator doors closed behind the woman, he turned the music back on and lay down with his head against the base of the wall.

Since the lobby meant different things to different people at different times—serving alternatively and often incompatibly as a commuting lane to and from the building's offices, a thriving market, an informal social club, an extension of the shelter proper, a site of deviance and transgression, a place to hide, rest, or be alone, a refuge from the streets, and a cave to sleep off a drunk—people wrestled over its meanings and functions. As Stan, the shelter's acting manager, put it, the lobby was a "microcosm of modern society" because it embodied the tensions and contradictions of public space in a democratic nation-state.[7] Was the lobby a public space? Should everyone have equal access to it? Did anyone have the right to live in or consistently inhabit such a space? What if the presence of some made others feel uncomfortable? Should the space be limited to those who engaged in "proper" (or at least more officious) economic, governmental, and social activities? Should shelter residents and other itinerants resign themselves to living on the margins, or should they actively assert their presumed right to frequent public spaces and so remain visible to others? These were some of the questions that the staff and, perhaps more importantly, the administrators of the mental health center debated.

Shelter residents and other frequenters of the Center heeded and at times tested the ever-changing answers to those questions. During my time in the shelter, people were allowed to hang out in the lobby during the late afternoon, evening, and overnight, but were prohibited from "loitering" there during the ostensive workday, when they were expected to be present at jobs or treatment programs. During the day staff members, responsible for their "guests" and often pressured to keep them from the lobby, would ask them to "move on" to where they were supposed to be. At other times a set of agreed-upon, unspoken rules of comportment held sway—as when the woman said that Richard was not "allowed" to play a radio, which implied that he and others *were* permitted to do other things. In effect, the inhabitants were permitted to stay in the lobby during nonbusiness hours as long as they didn't make trouble. The patrons of the social club, the patients of the psychiatric ward who could take leave from the ward, and other confederates of the larger society of mental health consumers could also linger in the lobby. But those considered outsiders—such as the two men asleep in the cave—were customarily asked or forced to leave the building because, I gathered, they were thought not to belong there.

On the Basketball Court

Entering the shelter from the lobby, people passed through a set of industrial blue doors bearing the words

ALL PURPOSE ROOM
NO SMOKING

and walked into the confines of a gym complete with shower rooms and a basketball court that provided the grounds for the men's and women's "dormitories." In crossing the border between lobby and shelter, people entered (or left) a specific domain of social and political relations.

Upon stepping into the shelter, people first encountered "the staff desk," immediately to the left of the entrance (see Figure 7). The term "staff desk" was metonymic, for it referred to an area, enclosed within a four-foot-high bureaulike partition, that included a couple of chairs, a small desk with a phone, assorted supplies and storage areas, and a working clock set high enough that it could be viewed from afar. Residents and staff alike understood that the desk area was off-limits to residents. "You're not supposed to be back here, Julie," the staff nurse said one day when Julie Mason reached for a paper cup behind the counter of the staff desk. "It's a big no-no." "I know," Julie said. "I just needed this." The counter, about three feet across, was not only a barrier separating the desk area from the common area of the shelter and the activities of the staff from those of the residents. It also served as a storage area for the staff's various supplies, records, and pharmaceuticals; a flat surface on which the staff dispensed medications and read and wrote documents; and a space of interaction between staff and guests, with the guests most often receiving the staff's verbal and medical dispensations. Despite being in a corner of the room, the staff desk was central to the life of the shelter. Its location enabled the staff to keep a constant eye on those entering and leaving the shelter and to talk to people as they walked by: "I have your meds," and "You're on the shower list" were commonly heard directives.

Usually attached to the support columns that stood close to the staff desk were fliers announcing meeting times and other events, such as holiday celebrations and departure parties for people leaving the shelter. On the standing partition which served as a wall separating the women's dorm from the common area of the shelter there was a map of the United States, a "Free Meal Guide" to Boston's soup kitchens, and a list, in neat block letters, of the shelter's rules:

SHELTER RULES:

Guest responsibilities:
1. Leave the shelter on time. 9:30 am
2. Store all personal belongings in your locker
3. Keep bed area neat and clean
4. Shower every other day
5. Wash and dry clothes weekly
6. Clean-up after eating and smoking
7. Smoke only in designated areas
8. Participate in shelter chores
9. Respect the privacy of other guests
10. Return to the shelter by 9 pm, unless you have a pass until midnight

There is to be no:
1. Violent behavior
2. Threatening of staff or guests
3. Abusive language
4. Possession of weapons or harmful implements
5. Damaging of shelter property, or staff or client property
6. Stealing
7. Use of alcohol, or illegal substances
8. Smoking in dorms, or non-smoking areas[1]
9. Food or drinking in the dorms
10. Loitering on the ground floor between 9:30 am and 3:30 pm

Most of the fliers faced the entrance, at eye level, so that when people walked into the shelter they eyed an expanse of written information. Writing, also evident in the announcements and broadsheets, was enacted by the staff's customary reading, documenting, and displaying written objects. This space of writing was the only area of the shelter that bore printed words; it was thus all the more pronounced.

The "dorms" were built of standing plywood partitions, about ten feet tall, which enclosed two areas in the center of the basketball court, beneath the metal-framed backboards that remained folded up against the ceiling. The men's dorm was closest to the staff desk. Each of the enclosures contained twenty or more beds set up in barracks style. A tall, freestanding locker in which a resident could store belongings accompanied each bed, which stood about five feet from its neighbors and was readily visible from other locations within the same dormitory. Curtains hanging from rods above the entrances served as makeshift doors and blinds while providing easy passage to and from the dorms. Male residents could enter and occupy only the men's dorm, and female residents the women's dorm. Although female staff members entered the women's dorm at liberty without announcing themselves, they would typically shout "Staff entering the men's dorm!" when entering the men's dorm. Male staff members would do much the same when entering the women's sleeping area.

The absence of walls between the beds and the ease with which residents and staff could pass through the dorm areas made the shelter a pseudo-private space with a mix of public and private features. While serving as a kind of gated community for the down-and-out, removed from the polity of public space and the horrors of generic shelters, it nevertheless did not approach the intimacies and feel of private space or time as understood by most Americans. It entailed a semi-public communal bedroom, managed and monitored by employees of the state, whose distinctively modern sociospatial arrangements were perhaps first anticipated in an extreme form by Kafka in the opening pages of *The Trial*, wherein several warders intent on arresting K. enter his bedroom, intercept his breakfast, inspect his nightshirt, pick out clothes for him to wear, and arrange for three office clerks to accompany him to the bank where he works.[2]

Just to the right of the shelter entrance, opposite the staff desk, was a corridor formed by the gym wall on the right and the outer side of the women's dorm on the left. The corridor led to the showers and toilets in the back of the shelter, and, on the right, to a second passageway connecting the shelter and the lobby. This door remained unlocked only when the shelter was officially "open"—during weekday mornings, afternoons, and evenings, and all day on weekends and holidays.

Close to this rear passageway was a room, usually locked, that contained a bounty of foods and assorted supplies. The room was known as "the token store" because it was where residents could redeem the tokens they had earned for performing various chores (such as watering plants or cleaning tables) and duties (such as showering every other day). Each of these acts merited a certain number of paper tickets which in turn could be used to pay for items at the store: three tokens for a candy bar, seven for a bar of soap. The store, which was open for about twenty minutes every evening around seven o'clock, was usually run by a staff-appointed resident.

When entering the shelter and passing the staff desk on the left, people could walk in a relatively straight line from the entrance to the far end of the gym. In so doing they stepped through a common area that was bordered on the right side by the standing partitions of the women's and men's dorms, and on the left side by expansive, connecting windows that looked out onto the northernmost grounds of the Center, themselves bordered by a chain-link fence. The windows, which by design could not be opened, admitted a fair amount of sunlight during the day. A few plants had been placed toward the desk side of the common area, with several more suspended from the ceiling, close to the windows. The common area also contained a set of cushioned chairs and couches, as well as several tables and wood stands, that provided the shelter's main public seating areas.

A small bookcase stood against the partition marking off the women's dorm. The location of the bookcase—between the staff desk and the entrance to the women's dorm, but closer to the latter—designated it as something within the outer orbit of the staff's space of writing but chiefly for the use of the residents; it was thus a link between the two domains. In fact, as people walked away from the staff desk into the common area, pictorial images—from prints of Renoir and Van Gogh's *Starry Night* to the television screen—replaced worded signs. When the smoking ban went into effect in the shelter, a simple, primary-process prohibition—NO SMOKING—became the only lasting piece of writing in the common room. When I noted to Lisa, a staff member, this slide from writing to image and hence, as I saw it, from culture to the wild, she replied, "Yeah, and it's true that the more primitive people hang out in the back room, watching TV."

The "back room" was a separate area at the far end of the common area, away from and opposite the entrance to the shelter. A set of doors could close this room off from the common area. The first part of the back room contained a curved set of cushioned seats set against a curving corduroy wall. Anyone seated there faced a metal stand, with a color television set, placed flush against the far wall next to the doors.

Although the area, often occupied by residents who wanted to watch television, was also known as "the television room," it was not in fact an enclosed room: to the left of the television set was a corridor that wound back toward several locked offices which were used by the staff for meetings, to store records, and to do paperwork and conduct other activities in private.

The fact that the "television room" was seen as a room of its own rather than an unshored cavity of space suggests how the nature of space in the shelter was different from that in the lobby. Residents and staff alike understood the shelter not as a vague expanse but as a finite assortment of distinct and functional sites: the staff desk, the men's and women's dorms, the token store, the television room. Each bed and locker in the dorm areas were seen, in turn, as a person's "individual space." The shelter was still multifunctional; the original appellation of "all-purpose room" still fit. Yet in contrast to the lobby and many other areas in the building, where space was forever diffuse, polysemic, and multifunctional, the shelter's spaces were clearly demarcated and more singular in their function and meaning. There were spaces for writing, observing, bathing, medicating, sleeping, and eating. Each area carried a specific theme, function, and set of social and political relations, with each bed area serving one person's needs just as a piece of private real estate might. Some aspects of this spatial design appeared to promote the kind of "therapeutic environment" found or intended in many psychiatric hospitals and asylums, in which an air of consistency, unambiguity, harmonious proportions, simplicity of function, and clarity of purpose is sought after.[3] Other aspects reflected the staff's interest in creating an ambiance of personal rationality and industry: at some point in the transformation of a basketball court into a machine for living, the shelter became a rationalized, routinized domain of order and functional utility not unlike the distribution of space in many modern factories or offices.

The functionalist, unambiguous orientations to space engineered by the staff were sometimes at odds with the more associative, participatory spatial orientations of residents, such as Helen or Richard, whose bodies and minds could be profoundly affected by the qualities imbued in a certain place. When Richard told me that the lobby reminded him of death because he was inside it and because "people come to stay inside and take pills and don't know whether it helps or not," I asked him if any other parts of Boston reminded him of death. "Yeah," he said. "East Boston."

"Why's that?"

"Because airplanes are always falling down there. Because people are always not finishing projects they started. Because they're trying to do things they don't know how to do. They mess things up."

"But why does all that make you think of death?"

"Because death becomes part of you."

For Richard and others, such constellations of meaning had a way of affecting the residents of those places, as if the symbiotic relation between a place and the people who inhabited it was a direct and contagious one. While many Americans would probably find such a principle to be a bit irrational if not downright crazy, it would make a great deal of sense to other peoples in the world, such as the Tamil of India and Sri Lanka, who commonly understand that the bodily substances and psychological dispositions of humans are forever mixed with and influenced by the substance, qualities, and "flavor" of the soils where they make their homes.[4] But since in this life at least Richard lived in Massachusetts, not in Tamil Nadu, and in a homeless shelter to boot, he and other residents had to mind the state's more functionalist, disenchanted, and dominant orientations to space and learn how to negotiate the spacings of the shelter as well as the zones "off-limits" to them as they settled into daily routines.

Smoking and Eating and Talking

The nature of these routines suggested that the construction of time in the shelter was akin to the makings of space, such that a distinct "chronotope" or time-space configuration (to use Bakhtin's word) governed life on the basketball court.[1] The chronotope, promoted by the staff in myriad ways, involved a span of finite, clearly defined, habitual, and reasonable activities.

On weekdays residents had to leave the shelter by 9:30 in the morning, unless they were physically unwell. If they wanted to eat the free breakfast served in the cafeteria they had to rise by 8 o'clock or so. From 9:30 to 3:30 they were expected to attend the jobs or treatment programs in which they were enrolled. Those not so occupied roamed the streets or found places to sleep or hang out in the Center's unused rooms and corridors. By three o'clock, a half dozen or more residents were usually waiting in the lobby in anticipation of the shelter's reopening. Most looked tired and did not talk much. Often someone would open the shelter doors and peer at the clock above the staff desk to check the time; the act signaled to the staff that there were people waiting. The staff's rebuffs signaled back that they were in charge.

Around 3:30 a staff member would open the shelter doors and announce, "The shelter is now open." Those waiting would then gather their possessions and walk into the shelter, where a range of activities took place throughout the remainder of the afternoon. Most people would lie down on their beds for an hour or so in order to rest or be alone before doing something else. Some would seize the opportunity to wash their clothes. A few would shower and shave, or wait in line to take a shower; after showering they would walk over to the staff desk and ask to be taken off the "shower list." Some would perform the chores for which they were responsible or complete tasks in order to earn extra tokens. Some would return to the lobby, where they would sit on the benches, pace, smoke cigarettes, or talk. Others would journey to a convenience store and return with food or coffee, which they consumed either in the lobby or in the common area of the shelter. Still others would sit in the common area, either by themselves or together. Some would listen in outward silence to walkman radios. A few would sit in the back room and watch television for a while.

Around 4:45 people would begin to line up in front of the cafeteria to wait for its doors to open. Many would be quite hungry by this time (some often went without lunch). Shelter residents were usually joined by the "in-patients" from the psychiatric ward, who were escorted by several staff members. At 5 the cafeteria workers would open the doors and people would stream in, line up in order to be served the free dinner meal, and then carry their trays to tables, where they would sit down and eat. By 5:30, when it was usually shut down, the cafeteria would be empty save for a few stragglers. The lobby, however, would be occupied by a wealth of people mingling about. By this time most residents would have returned, and would be engaged in activities similar to those of the afternoon. Sometimes people would play cards with one another or work on puzzles. Occasionally the staff would rent a video and show the movie in the front of the common room, by the staff desk.

From 4 to 7, when her shift usually ended, the staff psychiatric nurse would dispense medications to those who took them. She would usually announce that the medications were "ready." People would then line up to take them with juice served in small paper cups. The nurse would try to summon those who did not line up from the lobby, the common area, or the dorms.

At 7 the token store would open for twenty minutes or so, announcing with a shout, "The token store is now open!" Those interested in buying something would amble over to the store, present their tokens, and then return with their purchases to tables in the common room.

At 7:55 people usually gathered in the television room to watch the lottery drawing on television. Debra Joyce was a particularly reliable patron of this event; "Here comes the numbers lady," one woman said as she approached one day. "Oh damn. Nobody here will get a number," Barbara Harpham said one night when her numbers did not come up.

During the evening, when the place would quiet down somewhat, staff did not need to attend as much to the guests. Residents would settle down to various activities or states of being, sitting or pacing or smoking in the lobby, sitting at the tables in the common room, watching television, or lying down in their beds. Many would go to bed by 9, in part because the medications they took made them feel drowsy.

All residents were instructed to return to the shelter by 9, unless they had previously asked for, and been granted, a "night pass." As a rule, if they stayed out past 9 without such a pass, they would not be permitted back into the shelter that night.

Staff members continued to monitor the shelter and cover the staff desk throughout the night until a new shift of workers took over in the morning. Throughout the night, more than a handful of people would be up and about. Some would watch television, some would sit at the common tables, some would talk from time to time with staff, and some would sit or pace in the lobby. Most often these were people who could not sleep well at night because they felt "restless" or "nervous," and who spent much of the day sleeping in the Center's unused rooms. Due to the constant nighttime activity, many residents complained that it was difficult to sleep well in the shelter, although most agreed that the sleeping conditions were better than at the Pine Street shelter or on the street.

On weekends and holidays the shelter remained "open" throughout the day, which meant that the residents did not have to vacate it from 9:30 to 3:30. Many took this as an opportunity to sleep through the day, and the shelter was usually quieter than on "workdays." Others engaged in much the same activities that took place during most late afternoons and early evenings. Some lingered in the lobby. Few ventured outside the building for any length of time. One reason for this was that the sliding glass doors in the lobby remained locked on weekends and holidays, making it more difficult for people to pass in and out of the shelter. (To leave the building on these days, one had to walk up to the third floor, pass by the police desk, and then walk around the building's interior fold.) Another was that many were afraid to spend a great deal of time out in the city and preferred the safety and relative comfort of the shelter. A lack of spending money also limited peoples' options and movements. As in other shelters, weekends passed slowly for most.[2]

The routines were regimented for several reasons. The exigencies of communal living and the shift-oriented schedules of the staff's labors led to a focus on standard times. This shipboard sense of routine tasks and activities owed much of its character to the kind of temporal orientations common to factories, military regiments, hospitals, almshouses, and total institutions in modern industrial societies, in which designated stretches of time (like a "workday" or "workweek") are calibrated to the minute, hour, or day in order to promote disciplined, synchronized, and productive actions or labor.[3] Staff members promoted these routines in part because they wanted their guests to learn how to act and think in better accord with the rhythms of time inherent in work settings and mainstream American capitalist culture. They therefore woke residents in the morning, assigned specific chores, maintained the "shower list," and kept them honest about their duties, plans, and appointments in part to establish an ethics of responsibility, self-discipline, reliability, and personal integrity. They also tried to get residents to lead more active lives. The use of tokens, undoubtedly inspired by behavior-modification psychologies, encouraged personal industry because it rewarded the residents for undertaking and completing certain tasks. The tasks themselves centered on discrete, temporally finite activities performed by individuals, most of which—showering, doing laundry, watering the plants—could be completed in a few minutes. The staff also hoped that having fixed times for activities and protocols—which often ran on the hour or half-hour, day after day, and usually in accord with specific locales suited to these occurrences—would encourage a scheduled, "planned" orientation toward time and a general sense of "structure" in residents' lives.

At the same time, the lack of variation in these routines—whereby nothing much happened out of the ordinary, and if something did happen, it was usually an unanticipated, unwelcome event—accorded with the staff's desire to create an air of regularity, consistency, and dependability. This orchestration of regularity and order echoed concerns that dated to at least the pre-Civil War era, when the superintendents of asylums for the insane sought to comfort, reform, and possibly cure their patients by instilling a sense of precision, order, punctuality, and steady labor.[4] Some residents were assured and put at ease by the unsuspenseful regularity of events. "They train you to be crazy upstairs," Carla said of the psychiatric hospital on the fourth floor of the building. "They crack a whip up there. They don't do that here [in the shelter]. They're calm here. When I first moved in here, I didn't adjust well. I was defensive and I flipped out. But now I'm getting settled in. They have you do things gradually here, which I think is a good thing to do." The shelter's staff worked to secure a sense of stability, calm, and gradual but steady development—all of which contrasted with the breakneck suddenness of being crazy, flipping out, or cracking whips.

In all, a system of values was embedded in the uses of and calibrations of time. One consequence of the dominant reckoning of time was a strengthening of the hierarchy of power, for the staff prescribed the activities and tempo of shelter life and the residents had little choice but to follow suit if they wanted to remain in the shelter. Other consequences included routines, a focus on distinct activities conducted by individuals, and boredom.

"Wasn't Sunday so boring?" Carla Bataille asked another resident one Monday afternoon.

"No," her companion said.

"Well, it was boring to me. It's boring day after day."

The set schedule led many to base their lives on the routines. Soon after Mitch moved into the shelter, he told me that he had started to drink coffee because of the need to keep a "routine" in the shelter. Eva, in turn, had a set way of doing things in the morning. "I get up at five," she explained one day, "and take a shower. At six I have a coffee and a cigarette. At seven I eat breakfast. Then I rest for half an hour. At nine I go up to Step by Step." In listening to people talk in and around the shelter, I noted that others also mentioned the timing of specific actions or events: "At six-thirty I went to the store"; "I left the shelter at nine o'clock." Residents' awareness of time made sense, given how much of shelter life was calibrated in hourly and half-hourly periods. While it is true that much of North America has kept an eye on the hour hand for some time now, what made these recollections distinct from other methods of telling time was that it was the primary way in which people chronicled their lives: references to specific days of the week, dates in the month, or months or seasons of the year were much less frequent. Weeks and months did have a rhythmic quality to them: one day followed the next, weekends followed the workweek, and disability checks arrived around the first of the month. From what I understood, however, for many residents much of the present week or month had a hollow feel to it; specific dates and the calendric flow of time did not mean as much as they might for others. Louise once said that she was mad at her case manager because she had not spoken with her "for six weeks, six months, six years—something like that." One day I realized in talking with Richard that he knew neither the day nor the date. When asked about this, he laughed and walked over to the calendar by the staff desk to figure things out. "It's Tuesday, the 14th," he said a moment later.

For many the routines dulled over time. "I was doing good at first," Julie said of her stay in the shelter, "but then I got settled in. Everybody's so used to doing nothing here. There's nothing to get you going." Evonne said that there was "no structure" in the shelter; she would forget how "boring" it actually was. "You must be going crazy here, hanging around so much," Kevin told me soon after I began research in the shelter. Asked why that might be, he said, "Because there's nothing to do!"

"I like living here," said Barbara, an elderly woman who used a magnifying glass to read the TV guide. "But it's getting kind of boring. The same thing every day. Monday, Tuesday, Wednesday, Thursday, Friday, and the weekends are the same old monotony. I get nervous doing the same thing." Martin said he "walked around too much" because he had nothing to do with his time. Estelle, a steadfast companion of Barbara's in the television room, said she had been there "too long": "It gets the same all the time. No change. A year here and a year at the other place is way too much. Too much for me at least. . . . I get robbed nearly every day." I once asked Peter Vaughn what he thought about the possibility of growing old in the shelter. "Well," he said, "the days and nights are long here. It [growing old] would seem twice as long." For most residents the passage of time in the shelter was slow, monotonous, uneventful, unhurried, and predictable.

Getting "settled in" was therefore double-edged. The process helped some adapt to a sane and quiet existence. As Julie noted, however, it could also make "doing nothing" the general state of things. The worrisome idea that, the longer a person stayed in the shelter, the more he or she "settled in" and grew accustomed to "doing nothing" was a common one. In talking about this unwanted slide into a habitual steady state, wherein even getting "robbed" had its dreadful routines, residents distinguished between action and passivity, between doing something and doing nothing. These distinctions often came down to a more fundamental one between motion and stasis. In the extreme a person could end up not doing anything besides existing in an acutely stationary state of being or thinking. I once asked Richard what it was like to live in the shelter. "It sucks," he said. "Why is that?" I asked. "'Cause I get into a rut, and you just think about what you're doing, the jobs you don't have." "How do you get out of a rut?" I asked. "Talk with your friends," he said. As his friends he named a handful of people, including several staff members.

For Richard, who was concerned about missing out on what he thought a young man should be doing with his life (living on his own, establishing a career, courting a girlfriend), getting into a rut entailed a sense of "just" thinking about what he was doing—and so, in effect, what he was *not* doing—and the jobs he did not have. Living in the shelter meant getting into a rut much of the time or suffering the "shelter blues" when he felt depressed or worthless. The rut itself smacked of a wanting inactivity. Richard got out of the rut by doing something: namely, by talking with friends—or by "touching people," "mixing things up," or "acting crazy." Through such contacts, exchanges, or disturbances, the spell of negative stasis was broken and Richard was active once again.[5]

A similar focus on "doing something" was evident in how others described their days. When I asked Rose one evening what she had done that day, she said: "Oh, you know, the usual boring stuff: smoking and eating and talking." When I asked where she had been, she said: "In and out, in and out, and I paced a bit today." I later asked Roy how he spent his days. "I go up to the social club," he said, "smoke cigarettes, drink coffee, listen to music, talk with people, you know." For Roy, Rose, and others, for whom a phrase like "you know" implied activities taken for granted, basic human actions such as eating, talking, and walking became full-blown activities in their own right. This made sense given the regimented routines of shelter life, in which daily life often centered on these actions. Everyone could of course leave the Center at will and engage in potentially more active doings if they desired. But this was a big "if." Rose, for example, hugged the shore of space and time in hovering along the building's western perimeter during the day and in sitting at the end of the long corridor at night.

Others lived similar routines. The way people spent their time, as well as how they spoke of spending their time, related to their needs to be doing something, to their desires to maintain a sense of calm in their lives, and to the task-oriented routines imposed by the state. Routines and desires fed into each other. The temporality of the shelter was akin to that in the total institutions studied by Erving Goffman, every one of which, he found, "can be seen as a kind of dead sea in which little islands of vivid, encapturing activity can appear."[6] Goffman held that "such activity can help the individual withstand the psychological stress usually engendered by assaults upon the self."[7] While there was a bit of truth to this assessment as far as the shelter went, my sense is that residents created archipelagos of activity in response both to the hollow, static feel of the shelter's routines and to the worries that came with consistently more active engagements in life. Many did the usual boring stuff—smoking and eating and talking—because it enabled them to be "doing something" in ways that did not jeopardize the air of calm and safety implied in the building's routines. They actively created a sense of active, passing time, both in the moment of doing something and retroactively, in reflecting on how they spent their days. If I could coin a new verb, it would be "to ing," with a gerund form of "inging." Residents did a lot of inging for the sake of doing something. While their actions were tuned to a culturally and institutionally informed set of temporal orientations, they also made, through their actions, the time they were in at any moment.[8]

We cannot speak of a strong narrative line here, for while people told stories and events tumbled along, the episodes seldom built to a narrative wholly dependent on a poetics of coherence, continuity, and climax—as narrative has usually been defined. The shelter fixed time as an episodic, steady-state order.[9] The routines of the clock, the realities of power, the influence of pharmaceuticals, the constant exchanges, and the relative lack of privacy and structure created a sensitivity to singular moments, exchanges, and desires. There were eddies when the mundane occurred and whirlpools when someone was restrained or hospitalized but much of the day, week, and month consisted of a vast sea of routine. Because of this event-dependent organization of time, people recalled specific actions and events—everyone talked about the time Walter punched a nurse—but had little reason to notice the potential links between events or the motivations for actions. The poetics of memory were more like those found in Beckett than in Proust; recollections depended more on momentary occupations than on deftly woven remembrances of times past.

Barbara and Walter were sitting on the benches in the lobby outside the shelter. She asked him to go the store to buy her some cigarettes and a soda. He returned to the lobby, handed her a can of Pepsi, a pack of cigarettes, and some coins, and sat down on the far bench with a soda of his own.

"Where's the rest of my change?" Barbara asked.

"What's a few pennies?" Walter replied.

"A few pennies are a few pennies, that's what they are, especially when they're mine."

The two sat and drank their sodas. Despite the exchange, there was no catharsis to the dispute. They both appeared to be angry, but everything seemed to diffuse quickly. The conversation involved less a narrative frame (as I would have anticipated) than a poetics of exchange, confrontation, finite acts, and momentary occupations.

When the occupations changed, the memories sometimes evaporated. "You have a child?!" Carla asked a woman seated next to her on a lobby bench. "Yeah? Excuse me, I forgot. I've been moving back and forth between hospitals, moving back and forth between the hospital and this place, and I forgot." Like Evonne, who found that the lack of structure in the shelter led her to forget how boring it was, Carla realized that constant displacements led her to forget something she once knew, as if a person needed a solid footing to remember. People regularly remembered a great deal. When they did forget something, however, their inability to recall an event clearly or why it occurred could relate to several factors: constant movements from one place to another; the cognitive and affective differences of those considered mentally ill; the wear and tear of pharmaceuticals; the focus on single actions and encounters; and a training distinct from the more mainstream arts of memory. I once asked Ian where he slept the night before he returned to the shelter after a stay in a psychiatric hospital.

"I forgot," he said.

"How could you forget?" I asked. "You just came back yesterday!"

"I can't use my memory all the time," he said. "You see, I never learned how to use my memory like most people do. I have to think about something at least three times before I can remember it."

Displacement and Obscurity

Carla's migration from the shelter to the hospital and back again was political in nature. Though many residents sought to root themselves in particular locales, they were uprooted in turn.

In the winter of 1992, the shelter staff held an "open" and "mandatory" meeting with the residents of the shelter soon after an elaborate and sensitive smoke-detector system was installed. A few minutes into the meeting, one resident questioned the appropriateness of a new rule, proposed by the shelter manager, that would banish a person from the shelter for a night if he or she was caught smoking.

"I don't think it's fair to throw people out for the night," the woman said.

"It's the final form of discipline that I have," the manager said in response. "Because I can't bar people from the shelter. If you have a better way . . ."

"Don't you put people out for an hour?" the woman asked, referring to a common practice of banning people from the shelter for an hour when they acted inappropriately.[1]

"But the fire stuff [smoking cigarettes] is more serious. Any institution has some rules, and if you break them you have some consequences. Some people need help. And if you don't accept it, we have to use the back-up services, and some people are sent to the hospital. It does happen."

The group then went on to consider other topics.

Several things were taken as self-evident in this exchange: discipline was necessary; discipline helped some people to act appropriately; and while the degree of discipline depended on the seriousness of the infraction, it typically took the form of dislocation (at issue was whether eviction for a night or for an hour was most appropriate, although some were sent to a hospital when necessary). To care for someone, the logic read in the extreme, was to displace them. The focus on displacement fit with many other actions in and around the building in which the shelter was located. Staff members would "move" shelter residents on if they loitered in the lobby during business hours, and police woke people and often told them to leave if they were found sleeping in the upstairs "plaza." "Moving people on," an act in and of itself, often had a therapeutic air, for it kept people active and mobile.

That the movements often involved disciplinary actions, which themselves tied into a comprehensive system of mental health care, is noteworthy in part because the nature of the discipline was at odds with that integral to one of the more important models of power and discipline to come our way in the past fifty years: namely, Michel Foucault's considerations of "disciplinary" power in the industrial age, in which discipline involved confinement, surveillance, and detailed organizations of human action. Two common disciplinary acts in the shelter—displacing people, and obscuring the lives of those displaced—made its realities of power distinct from those in strictly panoptic arrangements.

For Foucault, the arts of discipline were best exemplified by Jeremy Bentham's plan for the Panopticon. Although Bentham devised the Panopticon at the end of the eighteenth century in an effort to find ways to control and monitor prison populations, he quickly saw the utility of his invention for other practices, such as the care of the sick or the education of the young. Within his "all-seeing" structure, people were to be confined in such a way that their actions could be observed by an unseen guard seated in a centralized tower. According to Foucault, such architecture created a space of "exact legibility."[2] The panopticon offered a "house of certainty" that left "no zone of shade."[3] An art of distributions specified that each individual had his own place, and each place its individual.[4] A system of light governed the flow of power, such that individuals were constantly visible and knowable and power was continuous and homogeneous. The details of time and writing in the panopticon implied "an uninterrupted, constant coercion"; discipline worked through themes of detail, certitude, presence, and immediacy.

Although the panopticon was never built in its ideal, original form, Foucault contends that the "model" of power inherent in this system of visibility "spread" throughout the industrial age to pattern the technologies of prisons, medical practices, and educational reforms, all of which were—and to some extent still are—predicated on the production of tangible knowledge and "docile" bodies suited for capitalist production. This disciplinary mechanism created "individuals" whose histories, pains, and anatomies were classified in the service of technologies of production and reformation. With the arts of medicine and psychiatry, bodies were personalized (as individual "cases"), made visible, and potentially transformed. With disciplinary power, time was partitioned into discrete, operational segments in tune with the demands of capitalist production. Writing worked to organize, record, and connect these moments into an integrative chronicle of detail. Hierarchies assured the "capillary" functioning of power in the disciplinary age; power pulsed through a society like blood through a body. An anonymous network of power relations, coursing from top to bottom and bottom to top, "held" the whole together in a web of interdependent forces that met the needs of capitalist production. Disciplinary power tended to be productive; it enabled, molded, and transformed. Discipline arranged a positive economy through specific arrangements of time, space, and selfhood that effected an interdependent, self-producing chain of positive effects. Foucault sums up these thoughts in sketching out the general disciplinary functions of the panopticon: "This enclosed, segmented space, observed at every point, in which the individuals are inserted in a fixed place, in which the slightest movements are supervised, in which all events are recorded, in which an uninterrupted work of writing links the center and periphery, in which power is exercised without division, according to a continuous hierarchical figure, in which each individual is constantly located, examined and distributed among the living beings, the sick and the dead—all this constitutes a compact model of the disciplinary mechanism."[5]

Despite substantial differences in the organization of power in eighteenth- and nineteenth-century France and twentieth-century Boston, differences that would make any direct historical comparison limited at best, elements of panoptic forms of power were evident in the architectural and institutional layout of the State Service Center. The Capitol Police, aided by video cameras that monitored certain passageways, kept watch over the entrances and exits from the building, while the psych ward, a descendent of the asylums of mid-century, was an enclosed, segmented space that inserted individuals into fixed places and supervised and regulated their movements. The shelter, with its centralized, state-supported authority, panoptic "staff desk," and techniques of observation, note taking, medicating, and therapeutic advice, was no stranger to these themes either. Staff members dispensed pharmaceuticals, noted in logbooks the actions, moods, and whereabouts of their "guests," implemented a set of rules, and could inspect at will possessions, bed areas, and lockers. Although guests could leave the not-so-total institution of the shelter whenever they wanted and had a degree of freedom unavailable in a psychiatric hospital, methods of observation, instruction, and normalization were in effect. As Thelonious, the man who slept on the benches outside the building, put it, in a shelter you got "rules, regulations, and a social worker always watching over you."

The "rules" often boiled down to a handful of practices and relationships. In his study of Foucault's thought, Gilles Deleuze notes that "a relation between forces is a function of the type 'to incite, to provoke, to combine.'"[6] Each relation between forces, in other words, involves a customary action that effects something in the world. "In the case of disciplinary societies," Deleuze adds, "we should say: to allocate, to classify, to compose, to normalize."[7] In the shelter, disciplinary functions of this sort existed alongside such functions as to observe, to organize, to medicate, to shelter, to inform, to interpret. While each function had its own genealogy, they were all enacted with little reflection on their logic or histories, as if they were a handful of rites whose origins and purposes were lost with previous generations of mental health workers. But they were powerful nonetheless and ingrained themselves in the thoughts and actions of staff and residents alike. To gaze steadily at another, for instance, could imply a certain relation of power. "You can't watch me while I'm writing," Thelonious told me after he asked to borrow my notepad to sketch out a poem and I joined him on a bench where he planned to write down some thoughts on "Attitude Adjustment." "What am I going to do? I'll have to sit and watch you owe me twenty [dollars]," one resident said to another, who had failed to pay back some money he had borrowed. "I'm not the only one who watches you," Catherine said to Wendy one day, apparently in reference to a celestial observer. "So what," Wendy replied.

Yet while panoptic forms of power were alive and well in and around the Center, they coexisted with other forms. Much as Bentham's panopticon was for Foucault the "architectural figure" of the disciplinary age, so the Center—a testament to the Icarus-like grounding of modern artistic and political visions—is for us symbolic of the nature of power in 1990s Boston.[8] While the architectural plans for the Boston State Service Center contained the ideals of centralized government control and a concerted distribution of space that centered on a panoptic tower, many contemporary users have taken advantage of the tower's absence, a decentralized "ruin," and the errant caves and corridors of Rudolph's waste spaces.

I once showed a photograph of the original model of the Center to Thelonious and asked for his thoughts on the building as it now stood. "It's a good thing they didn't make it like that," he said, in reference to the original plans. "If there was more color, more fortitude, then there would be less freedom. If they had the towers, you could be watched every moment. They could have cameras in the hallways. Nobody wants that."

For Thelonious, a stronger, more monumental building would have been more restrictive. Finding, with Foucault, that diagrams of power soon spread to other domains, he concluded that the construction of a centralized tower would have created a panoptic scene in which people in and around the building could be watched through cameras at every moment. Without any towers, however, cameras could not hold sway. The building's biography and its contemporary uses apparently set up a situation in which techniques of light and observation could not fully succeed, as if the building was originally primed for a panoptic structure but the reality never came to match the imagined one.

Thelonious's observations point to some of the differences between the Center and Bentham's "all-seeing" structure. Compared to the Panopticon, the Center was a house of uncertainty. It was opaque and weighty. A system of light and knowledge organized its key coordinates (particularly within the psychiatric hospital and the shelter) and could penetrate into its farthest reaches, but the architecture also permitted zones of shade or opacity where shelter residents and other frequenters of the building could remain alone and go unnoticed. These various rooms, caves, and dead-end corridors became important only when they were valued; abandoned "nonplaces" lingered in obscurity until government forces revalued them as "places," such as when a vacant room turned into an office, and the squatters moved on.[9]

The migrations entailed a tempered freedom of movement and volition. Foucault found that the panoptic mechanism "reverses the principle of the dungeon; or rather of its three functions—to enclose, to deprive of light and to hide—it preserves only the first and eliminates the other two."[10] The Center continued to enclose—although the enclosures were less steadfast than they were in the age of asylums—but it also gave life to acts of hiding and obscurity. Darkness, which a panopticon would rule out, once again protected, although the darkness was double-edged. Shelter residents could hide in the building's nooks and crannies, seek obscurity, and remain "estranged from society," as Alice did. To do so, however, they had to opt out of organized or collective forms of political action, stay clear of zones of comfort, police safety, therapeutic care, and high finance, and root themselves in spots that lacked full-time value and significance to others.

The logic of these spatial evaluations related to the economics of power in Massachusetts in the early 1990s. Given a limited wealth of capital and the state government's vision of concerted and thrifty government resources and services, the state had the means to invest resources only in certain times and places, which meant that not every place or time could be fully maintained and monitored. The state government thus constantly faced the question of how to best use and maintain the rooms and corridors of the State Service Center, with the most effective responses to this question tied to thriftiness of energy and finances expended for particular activities. The Capitol Police, for example, maintained a centralized spot at the main entrance to the building and kept most of the other entrances locked at all times, but they spent less time monitoring the numerous rooms and corridors of the building, especially ones that had little active value. These same rooms and hallways were sparsely decorated and minimally heated. The state, lacking enough resources to monitor time and space completely, came to value some hours and locales more than others. The scope of this evaluation was an ever-shifting one.

With this schema of value, humanitarianism, the hallmark of modernism and the industrial age, was a dying craft. The sentiment to care for and possibly transform people (still quite strong among shelter staff and social workers) stood in the shadow of the government's concerns for risk and capital. "The building takes priority over the people," one staff member said of the actions of the Capitol Police. "The police," he said, "are here for the property, and all the grounds of the government center, not for the people." The police neither cared for nor especially monitored the shelter residents, although they did get a chuckle out of their presence at times. There was more thought put into the control of spaces and property than of people. When the police did interact with the residents, the welfare of the building and its institutions was most at stake. Care was largely custodial.

The priority of place over people helps to explain the proclivity to dislocate. "The police, they often tell people to get up, or they leave them alone. Often they will tell them they can sleep until eight [p.m.] or so, then they must leave," said one shelter resident of the dynamics of the upstairs plaza. While the deadlines noted by this man were most likely established because public meetings were held at those times, the man was understandably more interested in knowing when there were no meetings in the room—when, in other words, the room lacked value to others. His movements and those of his sheltermates were reactive in that they relied on spaces and times unwanted by others. They could inhabit vacant rooms at off-hours, and the police would "leave them alone" at these times, but when the rooms were needed, they had to move on.

While power often entailed the ability to make people leave or remain in a single location (an ability that residents generally lacked), the staff and police opted for displacement because they had few other options. Since it cost so much to lock people up, it was easier to displace them. In fact, the fiscal crisis of the late 1980s and early 1990s led the state to suspend several of the acts of confinement and normalization that many modern forms of discipline have entailed. As an officer said one rainy afternoon when asked by the shelter staff to evict the two men who were sleeping off a drunk beneath a stairwell in the lobby of the shelter, "If we arrest those guys, nobody will take them. There's no place for them. There's no longer any detox center." The officer woke the men and told them to leave the building.

Like-minded displacements occurred in the shelter. Foucault notes that "one of the primary objects of discipline is to fix; [discipline] is anti-nomadic."[11] In the shelter displacement was one of the primary functions of power; punishment was hyper-nomadic. As noted above, discipline customarily included throwing a person "outside" the shelter for an hour or sending him or her "out for the night" for more egregious acts. While the latter punishment was the "final form of discipline" because staff could not bar people from the shelter unless they stole or took drugs, there was also the threat, if one "decompensated" too radically, of being restrained and escorted by police to a psychiatric hospital for evaluation. So, while the displacements sometimes involved movement from one system of visibility to another (from the shelter to a hospital, for instance) or from darkness into light (from the streets to the shelter), they more commonly involved movements from a zone of light to one of darkness. An imminent threat was to be kicked out onto the streets, a domain of muteness from which many were trying to escape. Unlike the supreme effect of the panopticon, which was to render visible, the imperative was to obscure. Lives, bodies, and actions were threatened with oblivion.

The play between value and valuelessness and meaning and meaninglessness, ever-present in the Center, also took form in the techniques of observation common to the shelter. The arts of writing as defined by Foucault were quite important in the shelter, but they registered acts more in terms of significance than of detail. The staff, rooted in a space of writing, kept daily notes on the activities of their "guests" (in part, to maintain continuity of care between different shifts of workers and to develop long-term understandings of a person's behaviors and potential "progress"). But only significant actions and transgressions were inscribed. Import took prominence over certitude and repletion. Not everything was worth writing about, and many events remained below the threshold of observation and description. The same sensibility held for visual observation: lockers, possessions, bodies, and psyches were inspected only when something seemed to be wrong in criminal or pathologic terms.

The poetics of significance here—of *something important happening*—folded back onto perceptions of time, such that time tended either to coalesce, like gravitational fields, into intensities of meaning and activity, or to become dispersed in expanses of tedium. Rather than tend toward ideal points of maximum speed and efficiency,[12] time worked along a continuum of clarity and opacity, which, like the features of local space, related to a schema of value and valuelessness. There were set times in the shelter—up at 8, out by 9, lunch at 12, back at 3:30, dinner at 5—but once people stepped outside the circle of shelter time, clocks held little value in how they went about their days or nights. Instead of proceeding by the minute or the hour, shelter residents tended to work in response to the schedules of others, inhabiting spaces at times when others did not want them. In general, residents and other patrons of the Center most often operated along the trash end of the spectrum of time, where time was diffuse, unmarketable, and so lacking in partitioned detail.[13]

Local sensibilities thus centered less on ideas of transparency and omniscience than on strategic and slightly nomadic appropriations of, and control over, distinct times, places, and activities. Any differences between Bentham's Panopticon and the State Service Center were largely ones of shading, of minutely different distributions of force, than of kind: whereas the Panopticon detailed an art of visibility and productivity, the Center made some use of these themes but simultaneously effected an art of obscurity and displacement. Both of these arts, which carved out realities and rendered self-evident certain ways of doing and knowing, tied into larger economies of meaning and value. If, as Foucault argues, power in disciplinary societies was characterized by its diffuse, capillary, and uniform nature, then power in and around the Center was characterized by its intensive, coagulative, and uneven qualities; it centered on specific sites of value instead of working, without division, according to a homogeneous, continuous hierarchy. Different formulas of power prevailed at different times and in different domains of life. Zones of discipline and surveillance, which worked to domesticate and normalize actions, were in effect, but other, more obscure zones were also involved.

A Physics of Homelessness

In Mike Leigh's 1993 film *Naked,* Johnny, a splenetic youth down on his luck and without a place to sleep in London, seeks shelter one night in front of the glass doors of a well-lit commercial building. Despite the poor lighting outside the security guard inside the building notices Johnny sitting on the stoop. The guard, who later says his job is to "guard space," gets up from his desk, walks over to the doors, unlocks them, takes a step outside, and asks without malevolence, "Got nowhere to go then?"

"I've got an infinite number of fuckin' places to go," Johnny fires back. "The problem is where you stay. You with me there?"

Johnny's comment conveys the plight of the two men who sought refuge in the lobby "cave," as well as of those we have more generally come to call "the homeless," who, by definition, have many places to go but seldom can find a place to stay. The manifest physics of these movements—of going, not staying—itself relates to political relations that determine who can stay, who can go, and where one can be at any one time. If the dominant philosophies of the West are tied to a metaphysics of presence, dwelling, and stasis, as many have implied and some have argued, then the homeless suggest an alternate history of absence, dislocation, and movement. A distinct sensibility of power coincides with this history. A number of explanations have been proposed to account for the rising numbers of people who have found themselves living on the streets, sleeping in cars, or bedding down in shelters in the United States in the last twenty years. A decrease in the availability of low-income housing and single-room occupancies in urban settings, a lack of steady employment for unskilled workers, the release of long-term mental health patients from psychiatric institutions, and a scarcity of community support programs to assist those people once they hit the streets have been identified as the main culprits.[1] Although each of these explanations has its advocates, and the numbers suggest that they all have more than a bit of truth to them, they have generally been treated as distinct causal pathways without any underlying political forces or cultural sensibilities tying them together.

A basic, multiform physics apparently does drive such dislocations, however. If the State Service Building tells us anything, it is that a system of displacement and obscurity, rather than one of confinement and visibility, dominates the politics of homelessness in contemporary Boston and elsewhere. Power no longer needs to be capillary or essentially productive; it is more efficient to focus on the valued sites in society. Indeed, several sociologists contend that in Europe and the United States governments have withdrawn rather than invested resources, capital, and services from the *banlieu* and "inner cities," to a point where state-controlled systems of education, welfare, and police discipline are relatively nonexistent.[2] The present art is one of strategic appropriation rather than one of exhaustive visibility. Just as in the telling scene in *Naked*, in which there are zones of light (which the security guard protects and prohibits others from inhabiting) and zones of darkness (in which Johnny tries to find shelter), urban settings today include distinct times and places, some of which are valued more than others. The most valued sites are policed in such a way that the poor and others are forcefully kept away. We maintain and control the resources, the knowledge, the means of production and of visibility, the actions imply; you can have what is left—the refuse, the excess, the waste spaces, the night—until we find another use for them.

The homeless inhabit zones of darkness for much the same reasons that the shelter residents found refuge in the caves and corridors of the Center: they have few other options. Again, the darkness is double-edged. Bentham held that power should be invisible and unverifiable, creating an aura of uncertainty for the prisoner, who, as Foucault puts it, "is seen, but he does not see; he is the object of information, never a subject in communication."[3] To an extent the homeless are now the invisible, the unverifiable. This is only because they do not count for much. The irony is that activists for the homeless want them to be seen and counted. The 1990 U.S. census received heavy criticism from activists, who believed that the numbers of homeless in the United States were grossly underreported. Services were ultimately at stake. To be counted, in other words, was to exist, to be registered as a person, even if this came down to being simply the object of information. To linger in silence or obscurity, which many "homeless" people were forced to do in order to survive, was to lack value or significance to others.

"It must be some kind of experiment or something, to see how long people survive without food, without shelter, without security," said a woman who lived around Manhattan's Grand Central Station, when asked, in 1980, what she thought about being homeless.[4] Despite government policies to the contrary, there is no grand experiment at work. There is a method to the madness, however. The decreasing availability of jobs, the increasing shortage of low-income housing, and the release of long-term patients from psychiatric hospitals all relate to changing evaluations of human welfare and activity. The age of discipline, taking "humanity as its measure," celebrated the positive benefits of human activity and encouraged the detailed organization of human thought and agency.[5] The present age, taking government budgets as its measure, upholds the vestiges of this tradition, but the humanitarianism associated with it is dying; human welfare sometimes does not count for much in its own right. As the space-guarding Capitol Police would be quick to admit, there is often more thought put into the care of economies, assets, and services than into the care of people. The difference in emphasis ties into larger economic conditions: the demands of production have changed since the industrial revolution and Ford's assembly lines, and now not all people are needed as productive forces. It is no longer necessary or important to work the entire population of a society into a positive economy of bodily discipline. One indirect consequence of this is that there is little economic or moral value in maintaining a large stock of low-income housing in urban settings, in providing continuous employment for all members of a population, or in "rehabilitating" people in psychiatric hospitals. That being so, ever-increasing numbers of people are finding themselves on the street or in shelters.

Hearing Voices

"The doctors have no name for my illness," said Julie Mason, a usually pensive African American woman in her early thirties who lived in the shelter for a year before moving into an apartment provided by the housing project. "I hear voices, telling me to hurt myself. But I don't talk back. It's not so bad. Others are a lot worse."

She told me this in March of 1992, soon after I began research in the shelter, on one of the many occasions that we sat at a table to talk. She spoke slowly and hesitantly, as if searching for words with arduous care. "My family is what you would call dysfunctional," she said. When I asked how a family came to be dysfunctional, she looked at me as if I was a naive child and said, "Practice!" In outlining her theory of practice she explained that her family had "no morals whatsoever." Her mother lived in Boston, her father lived in Virginia, her stepfather lived in Chicago, her two brothers were doing drugs, her sister stole away a former boyfriend. "It's not a close family," she said. She very much wanted a place of her own where she could live with her two daughters, who had been adopted by her sister and were now living in Virginia, and she hoped that a new living arrangement might make that possible. She spent much of her time by herself, sitting quietly with others or visiting her boyfriend, a young man who used to live in the shelter but had since found an apartment in South Boston.

Julie said she was trying to block out the voices. Medication helped. "I also hallucinate," she said. "Once I saw a man in the dorm, just standing there. I went over to try to find him, but he wasn't there. . . . Once I was living in a house and I saw a man dressed in black and a woman dressed in white. They told me to 'Go away. Leave this house now.' My daughter thought I was crazy. I couldn't sleep for four nights." I asked if she was angry or sad about being ill. "No," she said. "I just hope the illness doesn't get worse. I can live with it if it stays like this."

Soon after Julie moved from the shelter into an apartment, she received a visit from Lisa, the staff member responsible for the housing needs of residents. "She's not well," Lisa said when I asked about the visit. "She's a mess. Her sweat glands were swollen, as if after taking drugs and her body wanted to purge the drugs. [But] She claims to have stopped taking drugs. She's glassy-eyed, and has become very inarticulate. I couldn't get a response from her. I don't know what's wrong with her."

A week later Lisa and I went to see Julie, who was living to the south of Boston, in a building inhabited mostly by elderly people. Her studio apartment was small but well-kept. Except for the glimmer from a television set at the foot of the bed, there was not much light because Julie kept the blinds shut throughout the day. Julie said she had stayed "inside" for the past five days, not going out at all, and watching television, because she felt "safe" inside. She also told us that, several days before, when she was really "out of it," an electrical outlet spoke to her and caught fire several times. Lisa thought Julie was much better, saying that she appeared "less tired, more together, with it."

Like Julie, many residents faced a slew of maladies, afflictions, and troubles that waxed and waned. People suffered differently. Some felt "depressed" or "tired," while some were "manic" at times with "grandiose thoughts." Some were known by the staff to have "fixed delusional systems." Some found that they were unable to think clearly and could not think and speak as well as others did. Some said that they "hallucinated," seeing or hearing things that were not there on second glance. While some were "paranoid," more said they felt "anxious," "nervous," or "restless." Some simply found that there was "too much pressure" from living. Some "lost it," "fell apart," went "crazy," or "flipped out once in a while." Nathan said he was on "the borderline": "Things could go easily wrong." Others referred loosely to psychiatric diagnoses. Peter, for instance, said he was a "bipolar," but he mostly described himself as feeling "lousy."

Many heard voices distinct from those common to everyday social interactions. "I hear voices," Larry noted in one of the men's health group meetings. "Young women telling me that they're easy to sleep with. That scares me, it scares me." Wendy said that she got headaches when the voices were bad, which usually happened, she explained, when people like her boyfriend yelled at her, telling her she was no good. She tried to get rid of the voices by yelling and telling people how she felt. "But I can't do that here," she said. "You can't yell into the phone here [to tell someone, like her boyfriend, how she felt]." The voices provoked laughter or torment. On any given day there would be a few people in the lobby or shelter who were laughing to themselves, looking pensive, or talking less to themselves than to the voices they heard. Those who heard such voices distinguished them, as Julie did, from the stream of thoughts they knew as their inner voice as well as from the ordinary utterances of people around them. As with visual hallucinations, however, people sometimes heard words spoken but were unsure whether someone had actually said them.

While people usually referred to their own ailments in terms of their subjective, psychological aspects (feeling lousy, hearing voices), they tended to speak of the problems of others in terms of their behavioral, social aspects (throwing things around for no apparent reason, talking in incomprehensible sentences). There were, in turn, perceived degrees of sickness in the shelter, with some residents known to be worse off than others. The continuum ranged from Richard, who did not hear voices but who acted "inappropriately," to Sylvia, whose fears kept her from stepping far from the building, to Nancy, who was known for shuffling up to people and telling them that she had lost her mind. Many felt that they were not as sick as others. "Some people have more psychiatric problems than I do," Peter said. "You have to understand that people are sick here," Helen said, in explaining why she did not want to share an apartment with anyone from the shelter. "They have problems. I'm sick too, but not so bad. I'm getting better." In turn, those staying in the shelter understood that they were generally more "together" and less "crazy" than those interned in the in-patient psychiatric ward on the fourth floor of the building, which was known as a place where "they locked you up" for acting in violent or severely deviant ways: "He doesn't even belong here. He should be on the fourth floor!" Rose once said of a man who was "bothering" her in the lobby.

Psychiatrists had the final say as to what someone was suffering from and, by implication, who belonged where. As residents saw it, psychiatrists tried to "name" their ailments and "figure out" what was wrong with them. In so doing, doctors tended to cast residents as "characters," as Amelie Rorty uses the word.

The qualities of characters are the predictable and reliable manifestations of their dispositions: and it is by these dispositions that they are identified. . . . Characters are, by nature, defined and delineated. If they change, it is because it is in their character to do so under specific circumstances. . . . The psychology of character rests in physiology. . . . The physical constitutions of misers or people with choleric or sanguine temperaments will set the ways in which they develop habits under various sorts of social conditions; within limits, it is their character that determines their responses to social and environmental conditions, rather than these conditions determining their character. . . . To know what sort of character a person is, is to know what sort of life is best suited to bring out his potentialities and functions. . . . "To be a character" is to maintain a few qualities, nourish them to excess until they dominate and dictate all others.[1]

Although psychiatrists got to know some residents as individuals, they knew most of their "clients"—who they usually saw for fifteen minutes or so every week or two—as predictable, fixed, and definable characters. In efforts to determine how their patients would act in the present and future, how they would respond to social and environmental conditions (such as being homeless), and what sort of life best suited them, the psychiatrists tried to identify what character a person was: manic-depressive, paranoid schizophrenic, substance abuser. They usually did so by drawing upon their clinical expertise and by consulting the great encyclopedia of modern negative character traits, the American Psychiatric Association's *Diagnostic and Statistical Manual of Mental Disorders,* or DSM.[2] The residents' crucial character traits were often physiologic at base, or could at least be altered through psychopharmacological means. By knowing a person's character and thus his or her physiologic makeup, one could alter that makeup to effect changes in his or her personality.

Psychiatrists were generally more successful in identifying those who could be taken as "characters"—those, that is, whose distinct psychological qualities (mania, dysphoria, undue fear, moodiness, constant drinking, etc.) dominated and dictated all other personal qualities. But they had names for no more than a few "illnesses" and did not know what was wrong with some. While many residents were keenly aware of the limits of the psychiatric system—and, like Anthony, tried to "use" the system as such—they also hoped for a clean diagnosis and a name for what ailed them because, they thought, a diagnosis could lead to proper treatment. This desire for a proper diagnosis might have related to a perhaps universal need among troubled peoples to divine a "causal agent" in their pain.[3] Despite constant trips to psychiatrists, however, the ailments rarely fit neatly into the categories to be found in the pages of the DSM. Some residents nevertheless took their ailments as concrete, singular, and durable "mental illnesses" rather than as diffuse sets of problems, perhaps because this helped them to attend to the cognitive messiness or to avoid responsibility for their problems, or because doctors encouraged them to see their problems in that way. "You see how quickly I get angry?" Wendy asked me one day. "Sometimes I yell out at the top of my voice, or throw things. You can tell I have a mental illness, can't you?" You could tell what her character was, that is.

Some denied such identities and characterizations. "I'm not crazy, just defensive," Carla said. "I was mentally abused, but I am not mentally ill," Alice said. "I'm not a nut, just a man born under circumstances out of his control," explained Richard. Most were uncomfortable with the labels but still admitted in complex ways to having problems. Mitch Anderson, for one, had concerns about being considered mentally ill and "fitting" into the shelter crowd. A self-professed "independent" white man in his mid-forties, he spoke of an earlier life when he was a trucker and went on drinking binges: "Now it's time to stay sober." "I'm a bi-polar manic," he told me once. "Do you know what that means? My mind gets really high."

Before coming to the shelter, Mitch "squatted" for three years by the Cambridge River, in an abandoned building in which he set up a tent and kept a small stove, his various possessions, and a slew of cats, the last of which kept him company and the place free of mice and rats. He also set up a skeleton by the entrance to the building to keep the kids out, although in general the building was safe thanks to police officers who napped in their cruisers on a neighboring street. The building burnt down, however, when the "young punks" who hung out there started a fire. With no place to stay, he got a bed in the shelter, though he still walked over to the building every other day to feed his cats.

Of his stay in the shelter Mitch once said with a knowing look, "It's been noteworthy," then added, "I'm not complaining." "Can you see that I'm enjoying this?" he asked me one chilly November night while resting his feet on a heater. "I wouldn't want to live with some of these people, though. They're like cats: if you get to close to them, they'll scratch!" At that time he planned to stay in the shelter at least through the winter in order to save some money and get a place of his own. He took pride in the fact that he had learned how to "squat" and said he knew of different places to sleep in the city, such as in abandoned buildings or under stairwells leading down to subways. "These city people," he said, in reference to his sheltermates, "they don't know how to take care of themselves. If they get kicked out for a night they won't know what to do."

In the spring of 1992 Mitch moved into a group home through the housing project. After that I saw him once a week or so, when he dropped in at a day program in the mental health center. I found that he was less comfortable around me then, as if he no longer wanted to be considered part of the shelter crowd. Even before the move he saw himself as unlike most of the shelter residents, whom he took to have serious problems.

Like Mitch, many of those staying in the shelter distinguished between those who were "normal" and those who had problems; they did not welcome the awkward identity that came with being considered mentally ill. Most acknowledged that they were "sick" or had specific problems—such as hearing voices, excessive nervousness, or feelings of paranoia—but did not like the idea of being considered "crazy," "schizophrenic," or "psychotic." The difference lay in the nature of the characterizations: diffuse problems were seen as distinct from but combated by oneself, whereas the fixed identity of being "crazy" was held to be integral to a person's existence. Henry, for instance, said that psychiatrists had described him in his records both as having a psychosis and as being psychotic. "I have a psychosis," he said, "because I see things that aren't really there. But psychotic to me means that you're violent, always lashing out at people. I'm not that way. . . . It kinda hurt me to be called a psychotic." The implications were moral: to be psychotic was to be something less than fully human, without control over one's actions, and set apart from the social and ethical realities of others. It came down to a difference between "having" an illness or "being" one.[4] Most found that they fit into the former category. But since many of their problems involved the disruption of faculties that most urban Americans would probably take as basic to human functioning, such as thinking, perceiving, feeling, and speaking, the problems were unnerving. In the long run people's stances, which rested on pervasive cultural understandings of illness and health (including the idea that madness was, in fact, an "illness"), implied that the "self" or the "I" with which they identified was somehow separate from the ailments that plagued them, as if they were saddled with something "other." Most acknowledged the phenomenological aspects of what ailed them (such as hearing voices or stoppages of thought) but were ambivalent toward, suspicious of, frightened by, and sometimes downright hostile toward the singular, all-defining characterizations made by psychiatrists, case managers, and shelter staff. The latter parties valued the psychiatric classifications because they were useful in determining the most effective plans for treatment. But most residents disliked the labels, even though many still wanted to name what was wrong with them.

One reason that people worried over and sought to avoid labels is that they were stigmatizing. Many of those who bedded down in the shelter would have agreed with Erving Goffman that a stigmatized individual is "reduced in our minds from the whole and usual person to a tainted, discounted one."[5] Julie, for instance, said she did not want a "Special Persons" pass for the Boston public transportation system (also known as a "crazy card") because that would make her "different, not normal" and "in need of special consideration." Nina, a bright, cheerful young African American woman, summed up how many felt. When asked how she liked living in the shelter she said, "Well, I have to be honest. It's not the best, because there's a stigma that comes with living here, because people think that you've got something wrong with you."

At the same time, residents themselves heeded the idea that the shelter was a place for people who were different, and they often held that their sheltermates had something wrong with them. Some tried to avoid the impurities of affliction. "I like to go in there late at night," Ian said of a shelter he used to frequent, "and take a shower and get into bed. I like it because I don't have to see people who are crazy or sick or diseased." Many said they wanted to leave the shelter because "crazy" people were living there. Some, like Mitch, sought to be "normal," if only for a spell. "I want to have normal things, live a normal life, with normal friends," Helen said. Sam Kinch was known to take "vacations" from the shelter for several days at a time. He would ride the subway up to Copley Square, where he would spend several evenings in the bars. Bartenders would call a taxi when he became drunk and dispatch him to a hotel or back to the shelter. "He knows people are crazy inside [the shelter], and he says he wants to get away from that," Lisa said. To be normal required movement to another place and involvement in a different social world: one could only be normal by being around normal people. This meant that being normal in the shelter, where "sick" or "crazy" people were the mean, was nearly impossible. Sylvia, for example, said that she sometimes went for walks around North Station, a busy metro area close to the building, and mingled with the pedestrians there without directly engaging with them. "It feels good to be around people—it's exciting there—and to feel almost normal," she said, then added: "One day I was walking around and saw a woman staring down at the ground, and I thought, 'Oh my god, do I look like that?'" But the vacations were inevitably temporary. She and others settled for feeling "almost normal" because they could not escape their troubles or their sheltermates for long.

Those staying in the shelter understood well that it served as a way station for people known to be abnormal. Their quests for a measure of normality implied the existence of a set of norms and common standards, potential deviations from those norms, and a broader community of mutual evaluators who minded the norms and ruled on the deviations. As such, the residents' concerns were integral to a specific historical and cultural configuration in which society-wide ideas of norms, normality, and abnormality were central to how people construed social judgments, legal institutions, issues of health and illness, and notions of morality and inequality.[6] This helps to explain why, for many, it was not simply a question of feeling lousy, of "hearing voices," or of being tainted by or bothered by others, but one of being characterized as abnormal. Similarly, some were not necessarily in search of health, wealth, or spiritual redemption. Rather, they simply wanted to be normal. To be normal or almost normal was to pass as "anyone" and go unnoticed in a crowd. To be thought of as "crazy" was to deviate from the norm, to not measure up, to be singled out, and, if without substantial resources of one's own, to have to bed down with others who weren't normal. While most fluctuated between feeling normal or abnormal as they went about their daily routines, the unwelcome and irresolvable reality of the latter in their lives troubled more than a few.

Holding It Together

Like Julie and Eva, who had to give up custody of their children, many residents were neither overly angered nor saddened by their troubles. Instead they dealt with their problems day by day. Although few thought that complete health was possible, all hoped their ailments would be alleviated or at least would not worsen. Roy Lerner, for instance, spoke of his current state of being as if commenting on the weather; a florist by trade, he considered himself an "observant" person who understood flowers and people. He often noted the presence and severity of "voices" in his report. "Good. I feel good. My spirits are up today," he once said when I asked how he was doing. "Sometimes I'm up, sometimes I'm down. It's God's will. We can't do anything about it." For several months Roy had a painful rash on his legs and had trouble walking. He soaked his legs each night to alleviate the swelling. "My legs have been bad for a while lately," he said. "I don't know why." Medicines didn't do anything for him. "Some days I feel like my old self," he said. "Other days I hear voices all the time. I can't stand it. They're just there. But all days, I feel spirited, full of cheer." A month later Roy said that he no longer heard voices and that he was no longer seeing the psychiatrist. "No more voices," he reported.

The vagaries of Roy's ailments paralleled those faced by other residents. Sometimes people were "up" and felt like their old selves, sometimes they were "down" and couldn't stand it. The voices and bad legs came and went. They seemed to be "just there," without human volition or evident causation, and would not go away permanently. Each malady, "mental" or "physical" in character, was temporally and phenomenologically distinct. They involved both the incidental — once Julie saw a man — and the durable. Residents understood that they had little control over their ailments, perhaps in part because they were mostly seen as distinct from the self. Yet people usually managed to feel "spirited," if not as cheerful as Roy, and continued on with their lives, even when the ailments harped.

In trying to mend their lives, people often aimed for a provisional state of health by "staying calm" or grabbing onto a sense of coherence, stasis, or painlessness. Richard told me that people got out of hand when they got "unglued." When you are glued together, he said, "you know what you're doing, and you can tell other people what to do, how to get a job, how to get out of the shelter." When you are not glued together, "the body feels sort of tired, you feel nervous, and you get anxiety fits, and you don't know what to do with your life, and you stop looking out for your personal hygiene." Thinking that his syntax of "and . . . and . . . and" nicely conveyed the patchiness of the sequence, I asked him what led a person to become unglued. "I don't know," he said quietly. "Low self-esteem, maybe. Not knowing what to do with your life, and then you walk around the streets looking for work." When unglued people were together, he explained, it got all screwed up because they got on each others' nerves.

Becoming unglued was reminiscent of the dreaded "decompensation" that the staff identified when confronted with the breakdown of a resident's baseline psychological functioning. Both the residents' existential, corporeally attuned imagery and the staff's psychological, therapeutic idiom hinged on a sense of dismemberment and reassembly, with the act of staying glued implying an effort to maintain (but never to integrate fully) the faculties of one's life. That the elements of a life were tenuously held together also meant that they could be dispersed or come unglued. The staff at times helped or forced residents to tie things together; the choice of verb here depended on how one looked at it. "He said he didn't think he could hold it together," Henry said of Ian a day after he was taken to a hospital, "so they called the police. When he saw them he started to fight them and say he didn't want to go, but they had him on the ground and handcuffed him. They tied him to the cot all the way." One can read into these acts a forceful attempt to physically and symbolically bind a person who couldn't hold it together on his own. Henry, in turn, saw the psych ward as the place where "they put you back together." A few migrated from institution to institution in an enforced search for the most appropriate care.

Residents worried about holding things together for several reasons. They feared losing control of their actions. They also feared being restrained and sent to a hospital. The two concerns were interrelated and involved parallel movements in space. The theme of "control" was a common one in conversations, particularly those held with the staff. Carla said that she would "flip out" on occasion and would not know what happened. Richard spoke of "losing it." Julie said that she often got angry: "Sometimes it goes so quickly. There's nothing you can do about it." Events of this sort typically involved a uncontrollable dispersal from the self: one would "flip out" or "lose it" or it would "go so quickly." Words, objects, or fists could be released uncontrollably or unknowingly. Wendy, for instance, said that she would yell at the top of her voice or throw things when she got angry. Staff members were quick to respond to anyone who said she could not govern herself any longer, because such statements often foretold the possibility of violence. Thus the staff tied Ian down and sent him to a hospital when he said he didn't think he could "hold it together." A lack of control and integrity often signaled two kinds of displacements: an immediate, uncontrollable movement of words and fists away from the body; and a secondary, enforced movement from the shelter in an effort to recover a sense of control and integration. While people associated illness with movement and transience, they often measured well-being in the ability to stay in one place: "He was backsliding, and then he backslided some more. He got violent and he had to leave the place," Stuart said of a former roommate of his.

Partly for these reasons, people tried to establish a sense of calm, quiet, balance, coherence, and rootedness in their lives. These concerns, which went beyond the presumed craziness of hearing voices, seeing things, or thinking irrationally, involved an implicit aesthetics of the everyday, in which well-being was marked by themes of integration, control, calm, and presence of mind, and feeling sick or lousy was marked by fragmentation (wherein people were "a mess," "fell apart," or could not "hold it together"), lack of control (people could "lose it" or "flip out"), nervousness (feeling "anxious" or "restless"), and absence of mind (feeling "out of it," dull-witted, or inarticulate).[1] The cultural reach of these sensibilities was evident in how users of the Center made sense of the structure, for people regularly drew on similar images of fragmentation, dispersal, incompleteness, absence, and unrestraint in accounting for the building's architectural and perceptual disorders. Outside of the perceived dangers of the walls, the strong affinity between the kinds of problems that shelter residents had to contend with and the kinds of problems invested in the building was one of the main reasons that many thought it was a crazy place to put crazy people: the errant, confusing architecture could add to or reinforce a person's fears of dispersal and unconstraint.

Since a sense of integration and control was hard to hold onto, attaining it was usually less a question of improving one's lot in life than of maintaining one's present status. "My doctor thinks I would be fine if I only found a job and worked," said Martin Aaron, a likeable twenty-two-year-old white man and self-professed "punk" with sandy blond hair who had moved to Boston from northern California a year before and came to the shelter after living on the streets and staying in shelters in Cambridge. "But I can't even hold it together long enough to make myself a peanut butter and jelly sandwich. I tried it once in the hospital, but I couldn't do it."

Martin liked to wear jeans, black boots, and a black leather jacket with the emblem of Megadeth inscribed on the back. He also liked a thrash band called "Stormtroopers of Death" and owned a black cassette case filled with "metallic" music tapes. Martin was just the name he went by; he said he got very angry when people used his real name. One day I asked him about his family and whether he had any contact with them. "I don't want to talk about that," he said after a pause.

Martin said that drugs and alcohol were the cause of his illness. He drank all the time before coming to the shelter, he said, and when he suffered a respiratory arrest, he had been taken to the hospital. Eventually he went to a psychiatric hospital and then to a shelter. "I think that I might have been trying to commit suicide, unconsciously. . . . I would have been dead now, for sure, if I didn't stop drinking."

Martin heard voices, "bad voices," and heard and saw things that were not there. He became most "anxious" in the late afternoon and during twilight, but didn't know why that was. He was also paranoid at night. "It's not a personal angle," he told me one afternoon, "but I can't stop from thinking that there might be a nuclear holocaust or an earthquake —but not a hurricane, because you know that's coming. I know this isn't rational, but I can't stop thinking about it. And I find myself turning the radio on every ten minutes to see if there's any news." This all started in the past year, he explained. After a bad acid trip he began to get paranoid and hear voices. Since then he became paranoid whenever he got high. "Right at this moment," he said late one afternoon, "I have this impending sense of doom—that something terrible is going to happen in a few minutes, like this ceiling could fall in on us." One day, after he said something about being a "bipolar," I asked if anyone had figured out what was wrong with him. "No," he said. "They don't have a clue."

"Do you think your problems will go away some day?" I asked.

"No, I don't," he said.

When I first met Martin in September of 1991, he had boils on his thigh and a toothache. "I don't think anybody would want to be me right now. There's just too much going wrong. But they tell me it's Maya testing me." A practicing Hindu at the time, he read the Bhagavad Gita and attended a Hindu temple in Boston. "Sometimes I get into really evil moods," he said. When I asked if he meant he got depressed, he said, "No. I'm almost always depressed. Being evil is different than that." He said the evil came from getting really angry and wanting to put a "hex" on someone, which was a skill he learned when he dabbled in black magic some years back. But lately he had been trying to put his energies into more spiritual things and was thinking of joining the Catholic Church. "I don't know how some people can have no religious beliefs at all," he said.

Though Martin had thought of going back on "dope" or heroin to calm him down and help with his ailments, "that would mean I'd have to wear my jacket all the time." He therefore relied on the drugs prescribed by his psychiatrist as well as any Valium he could get on the side. The Haldol he took helped him to sleep. "After taking it, I'm out like a light. If I didn't take it, I would be up paranoid all night." He took another medication for a while that made him irritated and constipated and dried out his mouth, but it kept him from getting depressed. "If I'm off my meds I have a real tough time," he said. On another occasion he said he had been "sleeping all the time lately." I asked if this could relate to his medications. "Maybe. I've been taking a tranquilizer lately." One night, with the staff's help, several residents rented *The Return of the Living Dead* at a local video store. Martin said that he and Henry would have to watch the movie just after dinner because they would have already taken their medications and would get sleepy soon after.

"Life is pretty crummy, don't you think?" he asked me one day. "I expect to spend the rest of my life holed up in some hotel room, drawing pictures, smoking cigarettes, listening to music, watching TV. That's about it." The worst thing was feeling that he was not contributing to the world—he wished he could be doing that. He thought about moving back to Los Angeles or going to San Francisco: "I've heard that they'll forward your SSI checks if you give them an address."

Martin left the shelter after five months, for an apartment he found through a friend. "It's good to get out of the shelter," he said a few weeks after his move. "I didn't like it there much. You have to put up with so much shit." Yet he continued to frequent the social club in the building. "I like it here," he explained. "I can just come in and watch TV and listen to my tapes." He then spent much of his time hanging around his apartment, listening to music, and drinking beer. "Mostly I've been getting drunk every day," he said. A few weeks later he said that the drinking got to be pretty bad and a friend suggested that he smoke dope instead, which he had been doing. That, combined with his medication ("It's like Valium"), got him "pretty numb."

Others lived similar lives. The problems had no clear origins and no foreseeable ending. Like Martin, most expected to live with an illness, in poverty, without a steady job, in hotels and apartments, among friends, apart from one's family and children, passing the hours, trying to hold it together. Time itself was affected; the expected permanence of the illness shaped people's orientations to everyday activities as well as the projected and actual course of their lives.

Yet while the quality and tempo of one's life tied into the assumed chronicity of the illness, the chronicity was very much a cultural production. In contrast to some societies, in which a bout of madness is often a temporary, unstigmatizing state that can often be remedied through ritual means, mental illness in the United States and elsewhere can be a lifelong identity, integral to a sense of selfhood.[2] As Sue Estroff puts it, chronicity is that painful process by which is worked "a transformation of a prior, enduring, known, and valued self into a less known and knowable, relatively recent, devalued, and dysfunctional self."[3]

Many factors apparently contribute to such chronicity, including culturally mediated relations between illness and selfhood, societal understandings of the reputedly durable, biological nature of many mental illnesses, social and environmental factors that increase the severity of the course of an illness like schizophrenia, and a hungry mental health care system that requires a steady clientele of sick people.[4] As for the relations between self and illness, the ways people like Martin and Peter were identified and came to identify themselves played an important role, for DSM character traits like "paranoid schizophrenic" or "bipolar" could contribute to "a fusion of identity with diagnosis"[5] and so work to create the sense of a lasting, unchangeable, and sometimes quite knowable character: namely, that of someone forever crazy, ill, abnormal, or disabled. In general, the roots of any lifelong debility might lie less in an individual's brain or mind than in culturally systemic ways of meaning and knowing: those cast by others or themselves as being in essence "psychotic," "schizophrenic," or durably "sick" can become the direct casualties of what Roland Barthes once called the "disease of thinking in essences."[6]

Taking Meds

Martin tried to numb himself from worries and nervousness through licit and illicit drugs. Others medicated themselves as well, but usually with pharmaceuticals regulated by the state and prescribed by a psychiatrist. Some were on a fixed and steady plan of antidepressant, antianxiety, or antipsychotic medications; by definition, these antidotes countered some malady or symptom more than they fostered a new state of mind. Others repeatedly returned to "their" psychiatrists so that they could adjust the kind and amount of medications prescribed. The adjustments had a hit-or-miss quality to them; different antidotes and dosages were tried until something worked.

The psychiatric nurses on duty administered the medications in the morning and early evening. In the evening a nurse arranged the pills in small paper cups set out on a tray, announced it was "medication time," and called out a litany of names. A handful of residents would then line up to take the pills with cups of juice or water. The dispensations were ritualistic in flavor, with patrons queuing up for the evening Eucharist. The nurse would also try to catch people as they passed by the staff desk and tell them that she had their "meds."

Although residents could refuse their medications at any time, they needed to tell a nurse of their decision so that she could log it in her notes. While many medicated themselves quite willingly, some resisted and thereby risked a trip to a hospital if they "decompensated" substantially. A few staunchly resented the impositions, especially those who, like Alice, had little faith in the psychiatric system. But in the end most of them were, like Alice, forced to take meds. For better or worse the state altered people's moods, thoughts, and actions by recalibrating their physiologies. Bodies were political domains over which individuals and institutions wrestled for control.

The use of meds enabled the state to monitor people in ways distinct from an earlier era of psychiatric care. As many have noted, one of the main contributing factors in the "deinstitutionalization" of the late 1950s and 1960s was the development and use of new and more effective psychotropic drugs, such as Thorazine, that helped to quell the behavioral disorders associated with schizophrenia, manic-depressive psychosis, and other severe ailments.[1] With these innovations, which enabled patients to be discharged from asylums and hospitals, came a shift away from the kinds of "disciplinary" power arrangements that involved confinement and constant visibility toward "societies of control" that involved modulations of people in an open terrain.[2] The advance of psychiatric medications has not only contributed to these new power arrangements, however; it has been integral to them. The use of such medications helps to explain the decreasing utility of panoptic models of enclosure and surveillance. By the early 1990s, states no longer found it necessary to confine a marginal, "crazy," or potentially dangerous person like Alice in a closed space for months or years on end. Her life could be administered in such a way that she could move about freely much of the time, and could seek out obscurity on occasion, but also had to "check in" at designated times and take medication. These arrangements enabled the staff to evaluate residents systematically. They also helped the state to modulate people's lives in time (in setting up specific times for medication) and space (in limiting how far one could range between medications), thus adding to the shelter's role as a site of circumscription. If a person started to "act out" or "decompensate," her dosages could be recalibrated. If someone refused to medicate, as Alice did at times, she risked losing her place in the shelter and chanced being sent to a psychiatric hospital, where she would be "locked up" and forced to take meds. With this medicalization of surveillance, the meds governed a person's actions through the sheer force of their chemistry.

Psychotropic drugs were clearly present in the sensory range of everyday life. They helped residents get rid of the "voices" and, for some, reduced levels of anxiety. In making a body shake or stiffen, however, they also induced it to speed up or slow down. Many got "hopped up" or felt "hyper" on meds. "I think it's this medicine that's making me anxious," Stuart said. "I really do. Whenever I take this medicine, I get anxious. I get the shakes and I feel hyper." Henry's medications made him feel "excited": "I can't sit down for five seconds," he said. "I can't concentrate." "You might have noticed that I'm shuffling around a bit," Roy said one day as we stood by the railings along the entrance to the lobby. He was shifting from foot to foot from the akathesia caused by

Haldol, a neuroleptic pharmaceutical. "It's the Haldol shakes. It's okay. I'm less nervous today." "I'm sorry about going on about New Orleans," William Harding said one evening after raving on about life in his home town. "But I get kinda hopped up after taking my meds. For about two minutes, you get hopped up after the meds, you see, and then it's all right about thirty minutes after. Then everything's okay." When William walked away, Mitch came over and said with a wry smile: "We get to hear about New Orleans all the time, seven days a week." His comment underscored the ways in which medications not only altered people's minds or bodies, but colored their relations and communications with others.

The presumed actions of medications touched on the kind of aesthetic sensibilities that patterned the recognized forms of illness and frailty in the shelter: at their best, the pharmaceuticals worked to integrate, reconnect, rebalance, clarify, steady, and calm a person's innards or faculties. "I just took my medication—to smooth out the joints," Joey told me one afternoon. Eva took antidepressants to make things "fit together again." "When I'm depressed," she explained, "the chemicals stop connecting with one another. The medications make the chemicals connect, like fingers tied together. That's what my doctors say." Henry, in turn, said that his head was "a mess" until a medication helped him to regain his "equilibrium."[3]

The art of medicating was a delicate and ambiguous one, however. Ralph told me that there was no "gray line" with his medications: not enough and he heard voices, too much and he walked around stiffly in a stupor. Others mentioned similar side effects. "That's because of their medications. They make you walk real stiff," April said when I told her that the "in-patients" who descended to the cafeteria each night from the psychiatric ward reminded me of zombies because of the slow, shuffling rigidity of their movements. Others displayed the repetitive, rocking motions common to psychiatric wards. For many, medication was one way to get desensitized. They made Richard go into his "own little world." At their worst, the meds excited, stiffened, immobilized, dulled, clouded, and debilitated.

"I don't think I should have to take meds. They could be destroying my brain," Ian said of his pharmaceuticals, which were supposed to stop his "Grandiose Thoughts."

"I think meds are wonderful," Larry said in a meeting of the men's health group. "They make me feel good."

Most residents, acutely aware of both the advantages and disadvantages of taking medications, combined Ian's and Larry's stances. They held attitudes similar to those expressed by the patrons of a mental health program in Madison, Wisconsin, that Sue Estroff studied in the 1970s: some were quite positive toward medications, some were ambivalent, some were neutral, and some were negative.[4] Attitudes changed as the severity of the ailments and side effects varied. Some hated the side effects but were grateful because the medications quieted the voices and helped them to think clearly. Some disliked the medications because they contributed negatively to their social identity: the need for medication, as well as its outward effects, signaled that a person was mentally ill.[5] Some were frustrated by the idea that they would probably have to be medicated the rest of their lives. For many, medications involved, like the possibility of "naming" their illnesses, a vague hope more than any solid expectation, with the future unknowable and redemptions slated for some but not others. "I'm hoping the medications will make me feel better," Peter said once. "They haven't done anything yet. I'm just waiting, hoping, that they'll do something."

For all the biological bases of the medications, everything about them—from their political uses to their identity-making capacity to the sensations effected when they coursed through one's veins—had a cultural tint to it. To be sure, the ways in which people suffered, the ways in which they and others tried to remedy ailments or "hold it together," and how they thought of illness, well-being, and abnormality in general were patterned by culturally pervasive, institutionally mediated, and occasionally contested orientations to self, other, bodiliness, and time.

The Street

"Compared to the streets," Tommy said of the shelter, "it's a pretty good place."

Indeed, to understand why people slept in the shelter for months or even years, given its monotonous constraints and routines, we need to know something about "the street." References to the street or streets did not imply specific, nameable roadways or neighborhoods but instead involved a general sociogeographic domain that intimated a specific way of life and certain frames of mind.

With the notable exceptions of Mitch and Alice, most residents disliked life on the streets. They spoke of the street as if it was a single location with a singularly forced sensorium of fear, cold weather, isolation, and transience.

Roy, like others, said the street was a "pretty tough place." He used to panhandle in front of Dunkin' Donuts and kept mostly to himself for "safety reasons." Ralph said he had lived on the streets "from time to time" and had even eaten out of trash cans when he was desperate: "I ain't proud of some of the things I did," he said.

Tommy and Greg said they slept in subways when on the streets. The former spoke of eating at McDonalds and Burger King; the latter, of people stealing money from his pockets.

Logan was sleeping in a warehouse by the Cambridge River before he came to the shelter. "I had all my utensils there—a shelf, a bed—but it was getting cold." When the warehouse burned down he slept in one of the trains in the train yard behind North Station. "You try not to think about the cold too much," he said, "even if your thoughts wander. Then you go to sleep, wake up, and get the hell out of there."

"Because you're afraid?" I asked.

"No. Because it's cold!"

Women in particular spoke of the fear and isolation of the streets. Sylvia, who lived there and in different shelters before coming to the Station Street shelter, said that the streets were "terrible." She spent many nights just walking around, unable to sleep, "so frightened, terrified, afraid of being accosted." "The street makes you feel lonely, afraid. It makes you feel like crying," said Evonne, who recalled "wandering" around the streets and occasionally sleeping outside until she discovered the shelters. She then lived for six years at Pine Street. For Rose, life on the streets was "pretty lousy." Women more than men had to contend with the threat of rape and physical assault. They also had to deal with private matters such as menstruation in an inhospitable, semipublic arena.

These and other recollections echo those of researchers and street dwellers who have commonly found that life on the streets of American cities often boils down to discomfort, tedium, precarious sleeping arrangements, makeshift subsistence strategies, and random acts of kindness, indifference, abuse, and violence.[1] Street living can involve police-enforced displacements from storefronts, parks, and other public areas. It can also entail a surreal social existence wherein people sleep, eat, and bath on the spatial and temporal fringes of the public sphere. Social relationships often consist of a combination of affiliation and isolation, in which "quick and easy conviviality and an ethos supporting the sharing of modest resources are counterbalanced by chronic distrust of peers and fragility and impermanence of social bonds."[2]

People known to be mentally ill are notable exceptions to this kind of sociability, however. They have consistently been found to be the most isolated of street dwellers, perhaps in large part because of their suspicion of others, the voices they overhear, their preoccupation with private troubles, and their difficulties in communicating or getting along with others.[3] Researchers have also found that the chronically mentally ill, sometimes popularly known as "space cases," are frequent victims of street predators; they are more likely than other homeless people to be assaulted or robbed.[4] Since talking to others can be dangerous, keeping to oneself has its benefits. Any isolation is not necessarily self-willed, however. Many city dwellers do not want to associate with people talking to themselves or in apparent disarray, and so employ what Irvine Welsh, the author of *Trainspotting*, calls "that special talent people have: pretending nutters are invisible."[5] Many of those thought to be crazy are thus assigned against their will the role of the untouchable or its North American equivalent, the unspeakable: someone, that is, to whom you should not talk or respond.

Many shelter residents thus have spent much of their time on the streets alone. They told me that they just did not talk to anyone there. Peter, who felt "alone" on the streets, said that they were "hard to take." He slept under bridges and "hid" for a week in a hole that he camouflaged with leaves and cardboard. "There's no one to talk to. It's scary," he noted. Others found shelter under bridges, in subways, in abandoned warehouses, or in empty trains, where they could sleep or hide from others.

Julie, who lived on the streets for a couple weeks before arriving at the shelter, said that the isolation could snuff out a person's will to talk to and be with others. "People in the street don't talk to anybody," she said. She wore a Red Sox T-shirt, twisted a piece of paper, and paused after each sentence. "A part of you dies on the street. Your spirit dies. You lose the wanting to live inside; also, the wanting to talk with someone. That part dies too. . . . Once you're outside, you can't come back inside. You can never be the same, or talk or live inside [again]. . . . On the street, you can get robbed, beat up, knifed. It's dangerous. I would have lived on the street, but I never found a place that seemed safe. . . . The street is tough. Homeless people are dying out on the streets. You lose everything but a sense of survival."

The social and linguistic isolation pressed on street dwellers helps to explain why some lost the desire to talk with others (it might also help to explain why the media often portray the homeless as solitary, mute, and incomprehensible creatures). Since dwelling on the street could mean months of living on the margins of language, communication, and sociability, some found it difficult to return to living "inside." A person's very nature changed, particularly one's capacity for communicating with others. The longer people lived on the streets, the less they lived as social beings.[6]

Some aspects of this muteness became clear to me around 5:30 one evening when an unkempt man in ragged clothes walked into the lobby, stood by the entrance to the cafeteria, and peered in at the people eating dinner. Dan, the staff member in charge of the dinner watch that night, observed the man as he stepped toward the shelter, then said: "Don't go in there." The man turned around and walked toward the cafeteria. "If you want to come into the building," Dan said, "you have to go outside and walk around to the main entrance." He guided the man out the sliding doors and shut and locked the doors behind him. The man, having never spoken, stood outside and peered in through the glass for a minute, then walked away.

The man's silence reminded me of something Richard once said when I asked if he knew any of the women who lived on the downtown streets. "Oh, the bag ladies, they just look at you and think about you," he said. As suggested by the essays of many journalists, visual rather than verbal discourse dominated encounters on the street. It was also evident, from the incident with the mute man, that once you stepped outside, you could not come back in; you lost the desire and ability to talk to others. Dan's actions were perhaps typical of the kinds of deeds that made this so. The man was excluded for his unsightly appearance, his unwillingness to play by the rules, and, perhaps, for his queer silence; his exclusion no doubt added to his isolation, silence, and passivity. Strict divisions were thus maintained between the building and the streets, between "inside" and "outside," between belonging and unbelonging, and between communication and silence.

The language that people used conveyed quietly but powerfully their recollections of being completely alone when on the street. A constant focus on first- and second-person singular pronouns—on a distinct "I" or "you"—pointed to the way in which a person could remain detached from the realities of others and suggested that life on the street was dramatically subjective, personal, and singular. When people did mention encounters with others, it was usually with an anonymous, impersonal "someone."

Certain turns of language were also indicative of the street's uncharitable force. Peter confirmed that the streets were "tough" and "hard to take." "If you're on the street," he said, "you get beat up, disrespected, cheated, and robbed. . . . Street people are very uncouth. The mentality is, 'Nobody gives a damn about me, so I don't give a damn about nobody.' " Such accounts cast personal agency as something passive and reactive; linguistically and politically, a person was more patient than agent, with "the street" assuming a direct agency at times. The street *made* you feel lonely and afraid, or made you feel like crying. People on the streets didn't do things so much as have things happen to them. A person passively accepted or responded to the forces of the street more than he or she actively engaged with or challenged them. If you were on the street you got up robbed or "disrespected." There was not much choice in the matter. The commentaries were also highly prescriptive, in the sense that they described what the street would be like if you happened to find yourself there: "If you're on the street, you get beat up." They were also cautionary, for they involved both a warning and a moral: "Nobody should have to be on the streets," Carla said after telling me of her days there.

The force of other agents helps to explain the demeanor of several young men—such as Greg, Tommy, and to some extent Roy—who came to stay in the shelter after living in isolation on the streets or in abandoned buildings for several months. In contrast to the veteran patrons of the psychiatric system, each of these men struck me as quiet, wary, and strangely inactive, as if they only spoke or acted in response to someone else's words or actions. "It's as if they aren't all there," I noted to myself during my research; what seemed to be missing, and what I was taking for granted when talking to others, was the capacity for direct and voluntary action. Psychiatrists would probably attribute this inactivity to the "avolition" or "inability to initiate and persist in goal-directed activities" that is thought to go hand-in-hand with schizophrenia.[7] But given that the doctors tend to root almost everything within the ailment itself, and given that not all diagnosed "schizophrenics" in the shelter professed the same demeanor, it appears that a certain environment was at work. The demeanor of Greg, Tommy, and Roy led me to surmise that the sense of passive, trepid inactivity fostered by the streets led to a general but attentive agentlessness among some.[8]

As most residents saw it, people were negated and reduced by prolonged exposure to the street. Along with losing the desire to live inside and to talk with someone, people also lost their self-respect at times. "He looks like hell. He must be staying on the street," one man said of an acquaintance he ran into outside the building. Along with a disheveled appearance—a visible clue that someone was staying on the street—the end result was typically the stripping of sociality, a raw state of anxiety, and the redundancies of walking, hiding, eating, and bumming for change or cigarettes. You maintained the few words, possessions, acquaintances, and memories that you could, moving around "like a ping-pong ball," as one man described his plight.

In effect, the streets could come close to effecting a civil death, in which people ceased to be fully social human beings. If we follow dictionary definitions and take "personhood" to mean the state of being a socially recognized and engaged human being, acknowledged by law as the subject of rights and duties, with a distinct character or "personae," and the bearer of faculties of communication, reason, and moral judgment, then it is evident that for many residents the streets diminished a sense of personhood. As Grace Harris notes, in societies throughout the world personhood can be "bestowed or removed, confirmed or disconfirmed, declared or denied."[9] The personhood of those staying on the streets of Boston could often be disconfirmed and denied. There was surely a sense of selfhood—of a reflexive, embodied "I"—but that self was sometimes stripped of the social, moral, and linguistic connotations inherent in American ideas of personhood.

One strand of this depersonalization involved the way in which others looked upon street dwellers. In his essay on the Balinese cockfight, Clifford Geertz writes of how, when he and his wife first began fieldwork in Bali, the Balinese treated them as if they were "not there." "For them, and to a degree to ourselves, we were nonpersons, specters, invisible men. . . . people seemed to look right through us with a gaze focused several yards behind us on some more actual stone or tree. Almost nobody greeted us; but nobody scowled or said anything unpleasant to us either, which would have been almost as satisfactory."[10] The homeless faced a similar kind of inattention in American cities. In trying to skirt any engagement, people often disregard panhandlers or street dwellers, treating them as shadowy untouchables to be overlooked. The inattention, which often comes close to a lasting, ritualized excommunication, can add to a dweller's sense of being a ghostly nonperson, absent and silent in the world of others. This dynamic must be disturbing and dissonant for those who face it: while one readily takes oneself to be a fully ordained person, that assumption can be checked or canceled by the actions or inactions of others, leading to a situation in which an individual can become, paradoxically, "a person of no existence."[11]

The characteristic features of the street tied into how residents remembered time spent there. In speaking of what happened to them or how they ended up there in the first place, many spoke in impressionistic hues, as if recalling a vague dream whose sensorial or psychological features took prominence over any detailed plot or integrative schema. Often absent from their recollections was a sense of purpose, or any reason for their actions or the actions of others. Louise, for instance, spoke of being on the streets once: "I didn't know where I was going," she said. Peter, in turn, said that a person hit him once: "I don't know why he did that," he said. And when asked how he came to live first around and then within the State Service Center, Roger, a man blinded by cataracts who for seven years slept "where he could" on the streets, said: "I don't know. I can't answer that." Although Roger might have wanted to keep a painful history private, my guess is that he could not understand his homelessness according to a single causal timeline. This possibility should make us question what we take to be a personal history. In general, those who had spent time on the streets did not and perhaps could not respond with any precision to the "who, what, where, when, and why" questions that guide most mainstream historical accounts in the modern West. What they remembered most was fear, isolation, cold, constant worries, reductions, feelings of despondency and hopelessness, and assaults on their dignity.[12] The mood of times past was more significant than any plot.

To my ear, memories were often dreamy and drifting. Greg Bagnel told me that he lived for a while in an abandoned building until someone from a psychiatric hospital visited him and then later returned with the police. "I can't remember," he said, when asked whether he left on his own. "One night I was scared of something," Peter said of his nights on the street. "I pulled an alarm because I was scared, and the fire engines came. I told them I was scared and alone and I thought that if I pulled this alarm, they would be able to make me feel good. They threw me in jail for that." Although this memory—anchored in fear, the prospect of comfort, and further abuse—was distinct, with a minor plot of its own, it was set apart from any other occurrences, storylines, or larger temporal context.

The moody, non-linear bent of many memories apparently tied into the orientations to time and cognitive processes (some would say "disorders") found among many known to be schizophrenic. Louis Sass notes, for instance, that many diagnosed schizophrenics speak in self-reports of "the immobility of time, of the loss of past and future, or of the difficulty of arranging remembered events in the correct order."[13] As one man diagnosed with schizophrenia told his psychiatrist, "I feel as if I've lost the continuity linking the events in my past. Instead of a series of events linked by continuity, my past just seems like disconnected fragments. I feel like I'm in the infinite present."[14] While shelter residents usually did not lose touch with the past, several, especially those who were known to suffer from schizophrenia, did tend to recall their pasts by way of dreamy, disconnected fragments. People often remembered dates, names, and specific acts and interactions as if they were reciting a court docket: "On December 5, 1987, I broke into a real estate office," Ian said one day. But personal motives were often not so significant or memorable: "I don't know why I did this," he added. "Maybe cause I wanted money, I can't remember." And then, as if an afterthought: "See, that's why I wonder about these drugs."

Yet other, less psychogenic factors also figured in how residents remembered time spent on the street. The reductive, nonreflective, pain-avoiding aspects of street life suggested a certain sensorial environment. Many of the great chroniclers of fin-de-siècle Europe, from Baudelaire to Benjamin, found that city life was, in contrast to the pastoral scenes of country living and earlier epochs, built out of a discordant rush of distracting stimuli and unnerving discontinuities. Georg Simmel, for instance, observed in 1911 that the "sensory foundations of mental life" in the metropolis were based on "the rapid telescoping of changing images, pronounced differences within what is grasped at a single glance, and the unexpectedness of violent stimuli."[15] Robert Musil, in turn, wrote in *The Man Without Qualities* that all big cities were "made of up of irregularity, change, forward spurts, failures to keep step, collisions of objects and interests, punctuated by unfathomable silences; made up of pathways and untrodden ways, of one great rhythmic beat as well as the chronic discord and mutual displacement of all its contending rhythms."[16] For many who stayed in the shelter and ventured out into the city from time to time, the streets of Boston offered a similarly discombobulating cacophony of sounds and images. In general, however, recollections of a lengthy stint on the street did not invoke themes of distraction or discordant stimuli. For many the sensorium of the street involved a corporeal existence in which a person's senses and ability to make sense soon became dulled in response to excessive and brutal demands on those senses.[17]

At times, the feelings or assaults that people recalled were highly corporeal ones, centering on specific bodily pains and violations. Richard once said, "When you're homeless, you end up with just your body because you don't own anything else." If this is true, and it appears that it often is, then this degree-zero corporeality might have contributed to the kind of memories people took as their own. Or perhaps people remembered bodily states and eventualities so well because life on the streets was profoundly corporeal from the start. In any event, bodies sometimes became the most prominent instruments of engagement, awareness, and retrospection.

These and other memories were precise and vivid, yet in such a way that talk of the street involved less a narrative history of events than an impressionistic bundle of sensations and events. As noted above, the temporality of poverty, idleness, and dislocation probably had something to do with the absence of integrative narratives. Lars Eighner has concluded that "a homeless life has no storyline," and indeed, few storylines were to be found in the residents' recollections of the street.[18] Each phenomenon, sensation, feeling, event, or interaction was distinct from and unrelated to other such occurrences: a person hit Peter *once*. Events and sensations tended to be isolated conceptually and temporally from other events and sensations. And yet similar *kinds* of occurrences clustered together, such that it became a rule that when you were on the street, you got beat up, cheated, "disrespected." Any distinct recollections of being beaten fused into a generic, incidental fact.

All this made the physics of time and space on the street distinct from those found in the shelter.[19] The dominant chronotope of the street was one of drifting unmoored, with few clearly demarcated events or places. People measured time and moved through space according to usually intractable constellations of power, bodies, concerns, and eventualities. They did not so much do as have things done to them. In the shelter, people were more the agents of their lives. They acted and moved about in predictable, clearly defined expanses of time and space, with the "whys" and "wherefores" of such actions more readily at hand. There, others did things *for* people more often than they did things *to* them. Understandings and recollections of everyday life entailed distinct doings—even if only smoking and talking and eating—more than they did durable impressions, feelings, or eventualities. While bodiliness still mattered immensely, the force of feeling was different. In the shelter, feeling arose more from temporally discrete acts than from diffuse, durable states: "feeling" was closer to the spirit of a verb than a noun. Most of the doings still went on without a strong narrative frame, however, for the shelter fixed time as an episodic, steady-state order. In both street and shelter, then, the features of time and memory were closely wedded to the stuff of language, space, and agency.

Secondness to Firstness

In the long run, the uncouth, isolating, reductive, and bodily aspects of the street patterned how veterans knew of, spoke of, and remembered that terrain. They also led many to seek out a refuge like the shelter. The street's distractions, contingencies, and potential violence amplified fears and anxieties. People oriented themselves on the sensory range between "nervousness" and "staying calm," with many bedding down in the shelter in hopes of finding more of the latter. "I'm okay. I feel safe as long as I'm in the building," Joey said when asked how he was doing one day. Greg said that the place as a whole was good for "detuning," which I understood to be the process of dampening the shrill pitch of everyday life: "There's not much pressure here," he said. Sylvia, "desperate to find an answer to the rambling" of her mind, was looking for a place "to recover from the shock of the elements outside." She said she would stay in the shelter until it was safe for her to move out.

We can better understand the nature of residents' concerns, as well as their orientations to time, space, and action, by drawing on the turn-of-the-century phenomenological writings of the American philosopher Charles Peirce. Building on a mathematical logic of possible forms of action and interaction, Peirce contends that there are three "primal ontological categories"—firstness, secondness, and thirdness—that are neither inventions of his nor mere classificatory devices; they spawn the world and its structures of interaction and intelligibility. "The first," he writes, "is that whose being is simply itself, not referring to anything nor lying behind anything. The second is that which is what it is by force of something to which it is second. The third is that which is what it is owing to things between which it mediates and which it brings into relation to each other."[1] Each of these categories—so intangible that they are less like conceptions than "tones or tints upon conceptions"—are rarely found in their pure form but are involved in any phenomenon, either singularly, in combination, or in what Peirce calls "degenerate" forms.[2]

The first category, "firstness," is hardest to describe because it signifies a quality in itself, in its original state, before it is thought of, differentiated, verbalized, or defined in contrast to something else. Peirce therefore usually portrays the idea of firstness through imagined scenarios.

Imagine, if you please, a consciousness in which there is no comparison, no relation, no recognized multiplicity (since parts would be other than the whole), no change, no imagination of any modification of what is positively there, no reflection—nothing but a simple positive character. Such a consciousness might be just an odor, say a smell of attar; or it might be one infinite dead ache; it might be the hearing of a piercing eternal whistle. In short, any simple and positive quality of feeling would be something which our description fits that it is such as it is quite regardless of anything else.[3]

"Firstness" is Peirce's name for a monadic quality that abides in itself, undifferentiated, and prior to any recognition or analysis of that quality. It is therefore predominant in feeling, as distinct from objective will, perception, or thought. And since firstness involves nothing more than a "positive qualitative possibility," involving potential rather than actual "existence," its attributes are freshness, presentness, immediacy, newness, originality, freedom, spontaneity; it has no unity and no parts.[4]

Whereas the category of firstness refers to the phenomenon of a singular quality, secondness refers to any interaction involving two elements, or the force of a "second" on a first. Peirce uses the examples of feeling resistance when pushing against a door and of being poked on the back of the head with a ladder while walking along a sidewalk; both events carry the "brute fact" of the other, of the "not," over and against the ego, and so demonstrate the existence of both the self and the other. Secondness is the category of effort, of dyadic tension and opposition, of brute and factual contrast, of seconds striking against the senses. It entails the element of "struggle," which Peirce defines as "mutual action between two things regardless of any sort of third or medium, and in particular regardless of any law of action."[5] Whereas the category of firstness is "so tender that you cannot touch it without spoiling it," that of secondness is "eminently hard and tangible."[6] While firstness can be found in an eternal piercing whistle, secondness can be found in a whistle that breaks in on our consciousness; the event creates a shock that splits our consciousness into a before and after. Secondness thus involves an undeniable shock that makes its presence known. It is the category of "existence"—"that mode of being which lies in opposition to another"—for only in the dyadic polarity of struggle and resistance does existence become manifest or indeed possible.[7] And yet such existence "is an affair of blind force," without intelligibility, habit, or generality.

Habit and lawlike generalities are involved in the category of thirdness, however. They define it, in fact, for a third mediates between and brings into relation a first and a second. As Robert Corrington notes in explaining Peirce's concepts, "Thirdness, as a category, refers to the power of mediation that brings the earlier dyadic structure into a higher form of relationality, a relationality that is intelligible and that manifests lawlike regularity."[8] While thirdness cannot exist apart from firstness and secondness, for it exists in its role of mediation alone,[9] it always transcends that which it mediates. As Isabel Stearns puts it, "It goes beyond actual instances, without which it would have no existence, to signify still other conceivable instances to which it may refer in the future."[10] Thirdness implies a combination of habit, purpose, and reasonableness; it involves a "directive tendency" that guides and influences habitual and lawlike (but flexible) modes of behavior.[11]

In accord with these qualities, there is a strong normative, moral dimension to thirdness that is absent in either firstness or secondness. Whereas firstness is the realm of mere potentiality, and secondness the realm of brute, morally unappraisable action and reaction irrespective of any law, thirdness is the realm of "conduct." Indeed, Peirce often argues that thirdness is moral per se. Partly for this reason, he values thirdness over secondness and firstness. At times he considers thirdness as the "thread of life," or as a "gentle," "healing force" that repairs through mediation the breaks created by secondness. As Corrington notes, Peirce holds that thirdness "is the most important for the life of the self and the evolving universe" because it integrates, synthesizes, moderates, anticipates, regulates, guides, and begets "sympathy."[12] To his credit, however, Peirce makes room for distinct forms of consciousness and acknowledges the important role that secondness plays in "the rough and tumble of life"—something which Hegel's philosophy, for one, does not.[13]

As Peirce himself makes clear, the categories of firstness, secondness, and thirdness are rarely if ever found in their pure form. Each moment and each life involves a mix of the three categories. Yet it appears that different lifestyles and perhaps even different societies involve differently patterned combinations, which relate to some extent to political forces. Peirce holds that secondness "is forced upon us daily; it is the main lesson of life."[14] In the United States, it is forced on some more than others. Some are able to buffer themselves from disruptions and sharp pokes to the head, or they hire others to manage their share of seconds for them. Others have secondness thrust upon them.

The politics of secondness are often geographic in form. For many Americans, certain real estate is valued for the absence of secondness that it promises; for many shelter residents, the force and significance of secondness was perhaps no more apparent than when living on the street. There was a strong degree of secondness evident in how many residents spoke of the street. "Secondness," Corrington writes, "comes to us in a series of surprises. It is as if the self is constantly overtaken by seconds that enter from the fringes of awareness to impose their directionalities on consciousness."[15] According to Peirce, the kind of consciousness that falls under the category of secondness is one of "altersense": "The self and the not-self are separated in this sort of consciousness. The sense of reaction or struggle between self and another is just what this consciousness consists in."[16] Much the same could be said of life on the street, which was often "an affair of blind force," to use Peirce's words, with most situations involving dyadic encounters between a first and a second (which helps to explain why residents' recollections of the street so often involved the pronouns "I" and "you"). Street dwellers got cheated, accosted, and robbed by vague, impersonal "seconds." The weather, cold and inhospitable, could shock the senses. These conditions contributed to a temporality of individual "facts" and "events." The "if-then" logic of these facts ("If you're on the street, then . . .") smacked of the active-reactive physics of secondness. The common absence of purpose and reason in actions—as when Louise didn't know where she was going or when Peter didn't know why someone hit him—suggests that the dyadic relations were often bereft of intelligibility, reason, and meaning. As Elliot Liebow puts it in his ethnography of homeless women, "There is a coarseness, a rudeness, even a brutishness to life in shelters and on the street."[17]

The streets sometimes bore such a pure quality of secondness that it could exhibit the untainted, positive qualitative possibilities inherent in the category of firstness. While such a claim might seem contradictory at first, Peirce accounts for it in detailing how there can be a firstness of firstness, a firstness of secondness, and a firstness of thirdness.[18] One can strive, that is, to get at the purest possible conceptions of the qualities imbued in the three categories. As he notes, "A firstness is exemplified in every quality of a total feeling. It is perfectly simple and without parts; and everything has its quality. Thus the tragedy of King Lear has its first-ness, its flavor *sui generis*."[19] The streets also had their firstness; they had a flavor distinct from that of any other domain. And the fact that the streets had such a quality of firstness to them sheds light on how people recalled and spoke of that terrain, which was often described, signifi-cantly, as a single force or entity: "the street." As noted above, people portrayed the street in vague terms, in which distinct events and facts — the hallmarks of secondness — fused into single, sensorially rich images. For many the images had the air of the preverbal, undifferentiated "feel-ings" or "qualities" that characterize firstness. Peirce held that firstness could involve the consciousness of "one infinite dead ache." The streets could foster such a consciousness.

There was a quality of thirdness to the streets as well. Apparent in people's accounts were general principles, schemas, and prescriptions that patterned and directed their actions. The very orderliness of the secondness created a kind of thirdness of secondness. The order of con-duct was largely one of fear, isolation, polarity, and reactions that con-stantly forced awareness of threats, difference, and otherness. Just as Peter said of life on the street, that "Nobody gives a damn about me, so I don't give a damn about nobody," so the conduct of the streets was generally conditioned by persistent secondness and a dyadic, unsympa-thetic, "me-against-the world" morality.

Since people did not need to worry as much about being harmed or worn down in the State Service Center, seconds in and around the shel-ter were neither as numerous nor as severe as they were on the streets. This was one of the main reasons that people sought refuge in what was appropriately called a "shelter." A good place for "detuning" and for "smooth days," the shelter helped people to recover from the shock of the elements outside.

Nevertheless, residents found that they still had to contend with too much otherness, too many interruptions, too many brute facts, and too many "nots." Many of the seconds in the shelter involved distracting sights and sounds that entered from the fringes of awareness. "It's hard to get a decent sleep here. Someone is always singing a song," Helen once said. Some of the secondness resulted from the commands and instructions asserted by staff, which entailed an "absolute constraint" on residents "to think otherwise."[20] Some of it, in turn, involved the pains people felt, the "voices" they heard, or the distractions they suf-fered. In general, schizophrenia has often been known to involve states of mind that attend in exceptional and wearisome ways to any and all perceptions, sensations, and environmental cues, with little ability to screen out distractions or unnecessary stimuli: "Too much movement," one diagnosed schizophrenic complained of a visit from his mother.[21] People staying in the shelter had to contend with similarly discombobulating movements and noises. Their ailments increased the intensity of seconds in their lives, and everyday fears and distractions heightened their distress. People spoke of being "emotionally tired" and unable to deal with "distractions" when they arrived in the building. "We're sensitive," Carla explained to Larry one day. "We can't deal with things. Every little thing bothers us, and we can't take shit. That's why we're here. We're not like the people outside [who lived apparently normal lives]." By living "inside" she and others could remain one step removed. On another occasion Carla told me that she needed to be "familiar" with an area before she was comfortable. She didn't want to be in a place where she always had to be "on the look-out." "It's the adjustment that's the problem," she said. "It's okay when you're well. But when you're sick, it's hard to start off fresh each day." Considerable effort was required at times to act, think, move about, and get on in life.

Alice's idea of "struggling along" touched on such efforts, for the act implied strenuous, motivated efforts against opposition—hitting up against something. That "something" usually entailed a world of noise, voices, pains, distractions, poverty, displacements, and bureaucratic powers—a world, in short, of secondness. The struggles suggested a fundamental engagement between a first and a second, between a consciousness and a world at odds with that consciousness. Yet while this engagement could sometimes seem like an affair of blind force, without intelligibility or habit, people crafted routines founded on their interactions with a multitude of seconds. Alice struggled *along* as if moving upstream, with her exertions assuming an expectable, continuous air through time and space. Struggling along could therefore involve a kind of "inging" on a par with the routines of smoking, eating, or talking.

In general, residents set up routines in order to mediate the distractions, skirt any impinging fears or afflictions, and so mold the secondness into a kind of thirdness. Mitch's effort to maintain a "routine" in the shelter, Roy's attempt to sit in the same place each day, Carla's need to be "familiar" with an area, and her and others' desires to get "settled in" all involved, I believe, efforts to instill a thirdlike sense of habit, regularity, and order. "It's all right, it's better than nothing," Joey said when I complemented him on a new coat that he bought at a discount market. "I'm trying to hang in there, you know. Hanging in is good. I'm all right as long as I'm busy. My father says an idle mind is an ill mind." Hanging in—good enough for many—helped people to attend to everyday life. People stayed busy by talking, pacing, smoking cigarettes, and carrying out chores and errands. They engaged in these activities not only to get things done or to pass the time but to instill a sense of calm, stability, and safety. The staff thought that the "routines" were "self-defeating" because they negated opportunities for active engagements in life. But they promised many residents the best chance for a relatively sane existence outside of hospitals. As in the street, however, the mediations, rules, habits, and sensibilities were founded on the principles of secondness: the main interactive frame and moral economy of the residents' worlds was dyadic and reciprocative, as if most social, economic, and linguistic transactions involved dialogues between a first and a second.

Along with establishing habitual routines, residents sought refuge from seconds in various ways. As noted above, Thelonious, the poet who slept on the concrete benches outside the Center, found the discomforts of the street better than the hassles of shelter life. Unfortunately he sometimes found that it was just too "distracting" outside and so came to the building "to get away from all that." The people there were just as "bothersome," however, so he could rarely stay in any one place for long. "Hypersensory residualness wants to be within equatorial lines" went the last line of one of his poems. Given the hypersensory climate of the Center, in which sights and sounds lingered like unshakable residue, he and others tried, often unsuccessfully, to maintain some balance between comfort and distraction. Some tried to find their own private seas of tranquility. Irving liked to go up to the plaza to "get away" from the tiresome noises and conversations of the shelter and lobby. Rose sought out the end of the corridor in the lobby because it was "quiet" and "private" there. Others would similarly find spots to be alone or would wear headphones to block out noise or the voices they heard.

A few tried to escape secondness by searching out firstness. In sketching the nature of firstness, Peirce holds that he can "imagine a consciousness whose whole life, alike when wide awake and when drowsy or dreaming, should consist in nothing at all but a violet color or a stink of rotten cabbage."[22] Some residents also imagined and sought out such a consciousness. They apparently wanted to achieve a state of monadic being or a pure quality of feeling that might permit refuge from the rude consciousness of seconds in and around the shelter—much as Alice felt that she would be okay if she could "block out all the rest" by reading the Bible for sixteen hours each day. Richard, who easily got caught up in the doings of others, said he "used to pick up a newspaper, you know, and hold onto a word, and that would calm me down," and Ralph worked on puzzles because they helped to "calm" him. Each of these efforts involved the focused contemplation of a single element, quality, task, or domain of meaning. "Contemplate anything by itself— anything whatever that can be so contemplated," Peirce writes in arguing that consciousness is made up of qualities of feeling. "Attend to the whole and drop the parts out of attention altogether. One can approximate nearly enough to the accomplishment of that to see that the result of the perfect accomplishment would be that one would have in his consciousness at the moment nothing but a quality of feeling. This quality of feeling would in itself, as so contemplated, have no parts. . . . It would be a pure *priman*." [23] Peirce paints such a picture to demonstrate that "there is nothing else in immediate consciousness. To be conscious is nothing else than to feel." [24] But the example also suggests that one could envision and desire such a primal quality of feeling.

Some residents apparently did just that. On occasion they tried to invoke a trancelike state by reading the Bible, holding onto a word, sleeping, finding a private spot in which to dwell. More rarely, and depending on cash flow, they tried to find a smooth plane of joy or numbness through dope, crack, pharmaceuticals, or alcohol. These and other efforts to find firstness were probably not very effective, however. The idea or possibility of firstness was perhaps more significant than the success or failure of efforts undertaken to reach such a state.

In trying to replace secondness with firstness, some people tried to step outside the flow of time. For Peirce, the temporality of secondness —much like the temporality of "the street"—is one of individual events and brute facts, of abrupt accidents and coincidences, and of punctuating interruptions. Firstness, in contrast, involves a pure, undifferentiated state of qualitative possibility, and is therefore bereft of time altogether. "Secondness," Peirce holds, "is the predominant character of what *has been* done. The immediate present, could we seize it, would have no character but its firstness." [25] As Corrington puts it, "There is a sense in which firstness is not in time. The pure feeling, which is passive and open to a sense of quality, does not occupy a stretch of time. Firstness is the generative source *of* time rather than a product of time and its flow." [26]

Those who sought out firstness apparently had in mind a similar sense of timelessness. Holding onto a single word or reading the Bible for hours on end was an effective way to stop the flow of time, which, at least on the ground floor of the Center, was commonly punctuated by the interruptions and eventualities characteristic of secondness. "The building," Richard once said, "keeps you out of your own little world. It's kind of distracting."

"What do you do when the building distracts you?" I asked.

"Play dead."

To play dead was to stop existing—or, in Peirce's terms, to stop living in secondness. For many residents the immediate present promised through firstness involved a sense of stasis and quiescence. Since one way to stop thinking about the cold or other distractions was to step out of the flow of seconds or block out sixteen hours at a stretch, the acme of this predilection was the pursuit of timelessness. In contrast to Peirce, then, who found that the fundamental attributes of firstness were freshness, immediacy, potential, and spontaneity, residents valued firstness more for its qualities of atemporality, calmness, and undifferentiated monadicism. They desired firstness because it was unlike the bothersome hardness of secondness. These desires and the efforts they begat were probably not unique to the shelter's residents. While the idea of firstness might not necessarily be relevant, desirable, or even thinkable to many peoples outside of Europe or North America, it does seem to recur in the hankerings of many Americans and Europeans to sleep, to lose oneself in a book, to live in neighborhoods of sameness, to invest in crack cocaine or heroin, to "veg out" in front of a TV set, to "get away from it all," or to find some still point in time and space—as when Hamm of Beckett's *Endgame* fancies that, if he can hold his peace and sit quiet, "it will be all over with sound and motion, all over and done with." [27] Perhaps what made the residents' lives distinct was that, even though the idea of "shelter" promised a refuge from secondness, conditions were such that firstness was extremely hard to come by. Getting a taste of it required strenuous effort.

The danger for those who built their lives around secondness and firstness was that they could lose the knack for feeling alive—or for feeling anything at all. Since shelter life, despite its many distractions, could be too mundane, it was sometimes difficult to keep active or maintain a sense of autonomy. "I'm dissolving into the building up there," Joey said of his forced stay in the locked psychiatric ward on the fifth floor. He then added, "When I was homeless [staying in the shelter], well, geez, I could get out, smoke a cigarette in the lobby, take a shower. But upstairs, we're locked in." His comment recalls Helen's statement that she had lived in the shelter for so long that it was like she was "part of the building now." Both perspectives suggest that people could meld into their surroundings or become engulfed by a larger field of firstness if they stayed in one place for days or weeks on end.

Others referred to similar affinities between setting and constitution. "Sometimes I go to my bed area," Eva said, "and it seems so kinda gloomy, dark. It looks moldy, though it isn't really moldy, you know?" Evonne found that the shelter was "like death row," and said she sometimes saw the same faces in different shelters. "How does that make you feel?" I asked. "I don't feel anything," she said.

The idea of not feeling recurred. "I lost my mind," Nancy said in introducing herself one day. "What does that feel like?" I asked in the course of the conversation. "I don't feel. I don't feel. I feel numb," she replied, invoking what the German psychopathologist Karl Jaspers called the "feeling of not having any feeling." [28]

One day Martin showed me a poem he wrote called "Sheol," which is the word for the Hebrew netherworld. The poem told of the Los Angeles street scene, where "people are hanging out, with no thoughts, no feelings."

"I don't know what I was thinking about then," said Henry of a razor he put to his wrist a few years back. "I guess I did it because I was really depressed. When I cut myself, I felt alive, more alive than I felt before. Anyway, I wasn't depressed any more after that."

The sensory range involved a continuum between "feeling nervous" and "staying calm," movement and stasis, timeliness and timelessness. Nervousness implied an act of feeling; calmness implied a static state or a moment of quiescence or unfeeling. The former belonged to the passage of time; the latter, ideally, was bereft of it. Given this antipodal lot, it made sense to try to get out of an insensible funk by making oneself "feel more alive"—as when Henry cut himself, or when Richard touched his neighbors to rid them and himself of the shelter blues. Then again, many found that there was too much feeling in their lives, and few appreciated Richard's contact. Residents wavered between wanting to feel more, or less, of the world.

Pacing My Mind

Another way that people dealt with things was to pace. Some did not pace at all. I never saw Fred, Helen, or Peter pace, and Irving seemed somehow too regal to want to work his body so. Richard sometimes paced when others did; he shadowed Brian at times, as if the contagion of movement was another way for him to get in touch with people. Men paced more than women, although it was unclear why this was so. Perhaps the difference lay in the culture, in the medications that men took, or in how those medications affected them. More likely it was because women in the shelter found that they risked more in moving about.

People paced in different ways and for different reasons. Some found it helped them to think or concentrate, others found it to be calming, and yet others used it as a means to burn off restless energy or to find some sense of equilibrium. Rose, who said she liked to pace because it "relaxed" her, would do so in the afternoon, outside, close to the western edge of the building, by one of the main roads. Usually looking pensive and worried, she would walk, with head down, in a straight line to a concrete column, then turn about and glance toward the street. She would then walk, with head down, to a second column, turn, look out, and walk back to the first. She said that she often waited there for her brother-in-law, who would drive up in a car and talk to her for a while and hand her some money through an open window. Her movements had the air of a much-needed but ultimately ineffective rite that might help to put the world in order and ease her worries.

Hector, in turn, would frequent the same two territories each evening. Before six o'clock, he paced outside the building, around the hand railings that led out from the sliding doors. After they locked the doors at six he paced in the lobby.

Others paced in the lobby, whose doughnut-shaped core, with the enclosed elevator shaft in the middle, made it ideal for repetitive circumambulations. "Yeah, I've paced the lobby," Henry told me. "How would you define pacing?" I asked. "It's when you walk around, when you need to think," he said. "Do you pace when you feel nervous or restless?" "No. When I want to think." He explained that some places were better for this purpose than others. The lobby was a good place, he said, "because it has a clear space, and you can circle the elevators." The shelter, in contrast, was not so good: "There's too many pillars—and too many people."

Brian also paced the lobby, usually in the late afternoon or evening (after taking medication), and often with soda bottle in hand, sidestepping anyone in his way without breaking his stride. His hands and eyes were often active as he added to the converse of the moment: "The token store is now closing! Last chance for alcohol. I used to be crazy, but now I'm not," he said in turning a corner one evening.

Brian's peripatetic gait was the exception. Most were more like Kevin Halpern, a white man in his mid-thirties who stayed in the shelter for a year before moving to a group home set up by the housing project. Kevin was a quiet and thoughtful person who sometimes paced during the day; he spent many evenings in the common area of the shelter, where he would write poetry or read (one night he was reading a book on education "by some guy named Dewey"). One day I asked him what advice he would have to a newcomer to the shelter. "Live one day at a time, don't get ahead of yourself, and don't get too worried," he said. "Worries" for him were the main problem in the shelter; they threw off the equilibrium, the balance. "If you have to get copies for something, or records at the hospital, it can get compressed in here, because of the close quarters and tight spaces." He got to feeling "tight inside," "constricted." On top of this his medications made him feel "excited": "I can't sit down for five seconds. I can't concentrate."

For Kevin, "pacing up and down" was the way to change his "luck." It also helped to use up energy, "so much energy from the meds." He showed me one of his poems, which consisted of four lines jotted in a notebook:

Pacing the floor
pacing my mind
walking the floor
walking my thoughts

As the poem implied, pacing involved repetitive rhythms and the graphing of spatial and mental movements. For Kevin and others, pacing involved actions at once physical and mental, a way of moving through space that, through the details of moving and thinking, helped to carve out a distinct kind of space and time. It came down to a particular "technique of the body," as Marcel Mauss might say: a learned, habitual, effective form of bodiliness that involved a physio-psycho-sociological assemblage of series of actions.[1] The technique was effective in that there was usually a point to the pacing, which, depending on the person or the day, could be either to relax, to address the Haldol shakes, or to zone out for a while. The specifics of the technique—continuous, repetitive, solitary ambulations in a circumscribed space—helped people to attain these goals. Pacing helped Kevin to burn off excess energy and to relieve his worries as well as his sense of constriction and confinement. In trying to "walk" and so unwind tight thoughts Kevin, like others, took voyages *in situ*, moving about the lobby in a way that skirted encounters with others, so that he could in fact "pace" his mind.

Indeed, people did not pace *to* any place, as they did when moving or traveling. They simply paced, which is why "pacing" was an activity readily couched in the form of a gerund. It was therefore not like going for a walk, for the former was intensive and the latter, extensive. The difference related to the distinction between movement and speed. "Movement is extensive; speed is intensive," the philosophers Gilles Deleuze and Félix Guattari tell us: "Movement designates the relative character of a body considered as 'one,' and which goes from point to point; *speed, on the contrary, constitutes the absolute character of a body whose irreducible parts (atoms) occupy or fill a smooth space in the manner of a vortex*, with the possibility of springing up at any point."[2] The residents' pacings involved speed more than movement: they did not move extensively from place to place as in a journey, but rather stepped intensively. That people actually moved through space and often through areas occupied by others was usually not one of the criteria of pacing but rather an unfortunate hindrance to it. Most of those who paced did not care to move in space, in large part because journeys through space brought tensions and problems. They simply wanted to move, and through as smooth and unpopulated a space as possible. Sometimes approximating a thirdness of firstness, in which stretches of aloneness or stillness were fashioned into ritualized, steady-state routines, pacing was a way of moving without frequently brushing up against others and without stepping into any significant flow of time. For many it entailed a useful compromise between having too much restless energy and wanting to think or be alone. Pacing therefore did not foster the "long poems of walking" that Michel de Certeau identified in his musings on big city life, and which William Fordham cultivated when he hiked through Boston each day.[3] Nor did it have much to do with ideas of journeying, suspense, transformation, or hermeneutical depths. Given this, it would be difficult to contemplate an "experience" of pacing, since ideas of pacing and experiencing were usually antithetical to one another.

The Give and Take

Wages are low on the margins of society. Many of those who came to the shelter from the streets, psychiatric wards, or other shelters brought little money with them. While a few managed to save one or two thousand dollars in a bank, most existed on a bare subsistence level, living from month to month, bartering goods, and borrowing and loaning money in a local economy founded on principles of exchange and reciprocity.

The majority of Americans known to be mentally ill live economically meager lives. Most are poor, with average annual incomes from $3,000 to $7,000, and unemployment rates as high as 85 percent.[1] Their impoverishment helps to explain why so many are homeless. According to several major public policy studies, a majority of the 1.7 to 2.4 million Americans considered "long-term mentally ill" live in inadequate housing or are homeless.[2] Many find it difficult to hold down full-time jobs or find part-time work that is not overwhelming, since most unskilled part-time jobs in urban centers are in the service sector and often require constant contact with a demanding, impatient public. Many employers, in turn, do not want to hire people known to have mental disabilities, in part because they fear that the unpredictable moods and behavior associated with mental illness (often indicated through poor hygiene and shabby clothes) will be bad for business.[3] Since the early 1980s, state governments have increased efforts to develop vocational rehabilitation programs and sheltered workshops for the seriously mentally ill. But these programs typically do not pay well. The vast majority of those considered mentally ill do not have "real" jobs, and many do not earn enough to live on.[4] These factors often lead to vicious circles in which people's ailments hinder their ability to work at the same time that a lack of income exacerbates difficulties and pressures faced in daily life. As Sue Estroff and her colleagues note, "Having a severe, persistent mental illness very often means a life harshened by the presence of financial and material deficits as well as clinical impairment and social dysfunction."[5]

Shelter residents encountered all these problems. The 1992 survey found that only 7 percent of them considered themselves employed, while 32 percent were looking for work (compared to 22 and 42 percent of those staying in three generic shelters).[6] Many residents would have liked to have jobs, but only ones that suited them well. Helen Kessler, for instance, wanted to find work waitressing and often looked through the want ads in local newspapers, but since she tired quickly she knew she could not work a long shift. Others spoke, as Richard did, of being fired from jobs because they "couldn't keep up." Still others felt they were not ready for full-time employment, principally because their ailments or medications kept them from working in a productive and steady manner. Louise told me that although she would like to get a job, she would need "a smooth day" at first, just ringing up the numbers on a cash register, before she could do it for real. She couldn't "react" to people when she had a job, she said; "I can't hold that in my mind. I can't sit still." Nancy said she could not think well and could not remember things: "I couldn't keep a job because I can't take care of myself." Nerves, fatigue, social conflicts, and fears of messing up often got in the way. Nevertheless, some worked odd jobs around the North End or participated in state- or city-run work programs that paid a token salary around or below the minimum wage. In general, residents' understandings that they couldn't work well or keep jobs contributed to the sense that they were dysfunctional and disvalued. These understandings had powerful consequences, especially in a capitalist society in which an individual's ability to work and "contribute to the world" is so highly regarded.

The main income of most people in the shelter came from state or federal benefits; the 1992 survey found that 86 percent of the residents received benefits of some kind—almost always Supplemental Security Income (SSI) and Social Security Disability Insurance (SSDI)—compared to 52 percent of those staying in three generic shelters.[7] Until the 1960s and 1970s, when many people were deinstitutionalized, state governments that operated large institutions for the mentally ill provided for their charges' basic subsistence needs: food, shelter, clothing, and health care.[8] In recent years, although SSI nor SSDI were never meant to replace income for disabled persons, both have become the de facto major or sole source of support for many persons deemed mentally ill. Beneficiaries remain well below the poverty line, however, with insufficient funds for securing and maintaining permanent housing.[9]

Of those shelter residents who received state or federal benefits, the income, usually from $400 to $450 a month, often did not last the month. But those who saved money could have their benefits cut if they accumulated more than $2,000 in a bank. Some, particularly those who were living on the streets and were not part of any health care system, did not receive any benefits at all when they arrived at the shelter. Like thousands of others with mental health problems, they had no personal financial resources to speak of.[10] They usually remained almost penniless until they established some form of government assistance, usually with the staff's help. This required rounds of documentation that usually took weeks or months to complete.

Many of those who collected welfare, SSI, or SSDI checks on the first of the month spent much of their money within a week's time. Often there were loans to pay or things to buy. Some went on pleasure binges as soon as they had cash on hand, buying food, clothes, drugs, or alcohol until they were broke. Those who received weekly allowances faced similar constraints. Julie Mason would often be broke by the middle of the month. Once she told me that she was flat broke and had already borrowed some money. "How are you going to manage the next two weeks?" I asked. "Just be broke," she said with a matter-of-fact shrug of her shoulders. Fortunately it was possible to remain broke in the shelter for weeks on end. Room and board (two meals a day) were free, which left cigarettes as the only pressing need. And one could bum for these if necessary.[11]

People supplemented their incomes through "shadow work," which usually involved participation in the "makeshift economies" of Boston's poor, and various other means.[12] Some panhandled on the streets, some received cash from relatives, and a few scavenged for cans in the trash and recycling bins around the Center. Some traded or sold items that they found or no longer needed or wanted. Some played the lottery, although they lost more money than they won; a few, like Brian, thought that lottery tickets were "a waste of time." Others worked odd jobs or learned to labor in sheltered workshops.[13]

Residents regularly borrowed money from one another. The going rate of interest for a loan was 100 percent: if Helen loaned Mitch five dollars today, he needed to pay her ten by the following week. Many loans for two or three dollars were paid without interest, however. Those who were broke often continued to borrow until they received money of their own, but then needed to repay their loans and were soon broke again. From time to time, lenders, who had to watch how much money they had "out" to others, approached borrowers to find out when they would get paid. "When you gonna pay me?" Anthony said to Larry one day. Larry rested his chin on his hand for a moment, then said, "Next Monday." "Okay, okay," Anthony said, and the two parted ways.

"Do you have the dollar you owe me?" Wendy asked Susanne when she sat next to her on the lobby bench. When Susanne ignored her, Wendy cautioned: "This will be the last time, then." "I can give you sixty cents," Susanne said. "I had a lot of big bills to pay."

"What am I going to do?" one man said to another in the lobby one evening. "I'll have to sit and watch you owe me twenty."

To sit and watch another person could be a strong statement in the shelter, where forms of political authority often involved standing still with a steady gaze. That was the most one could do, however. Since one could neither force nor bully another into paying back a loan, those trying to collect on loans constantly had to ask when they would get their money. People usually repaid their loans—often dollar by dollar— although a few had a reputation for defaulting. "Irving gets no credit. He owes me too much," Anthony Scola told me one week, when he was "overextended."

Anthony, an agreeable, gregarious white man in his early fifties, made a living out of loans. A month after he left the shelter for a room in a group home run by the housing project, I asked him if he still came to the building a lot. "This is my office!" he said. "This is where I write letters, where I read the want ads, where I make my phone calls!" An entrepreneur, he lent money out to others at high interest rates (in a typical week, he lent out $80 and expected $160 in return), drummed up various jobs, bet on the dog races, slept on the cheap, and looked for the best deals on items for sale. "Do you think I could use a new pair of pants?" he asked me one day. "I think I'll go to Pine Street, where they give you free clothes." One week he tried to get Nancy to work for him selling flowers. He planned on paying her ten dollars a day, and making eighty for himself. "I'll sell the flowers for one dollar each, and they'll cost me twelve cents apiece," he said with a mischievous smile.

"She's a mental patient, of course," he said of Nancy. "She can't do nothing else. She says she wants to kill herself. I'm not like that. I just use the system."

"How do you use the system?" I asked.

"The psychiatrist wants something from me," he said, "and I get something out of him. We're both doing it."

Anthony lived in the group home until March of 1992. "The people working there kept after me," he explained. "I had to get out." He said he was looking for "free living jobs" in Alabama or New Mexico: "They'll put you to work in a resort, and sometimes they'll give you a place to stay." He said he also wanted to go down to New York City to the "School of Panhandling" so that he could learn how to ask for a dollar. When I asked him how profitable panhandling was, he said, "One guy once put a twenty dollar bill in my shoe. Another one put a bill in my hand. Usually I only get dollar bills, though. Some people give me seventeen cents in change, you know. That's all they got, naturally."

In April of that year he said he found a job in the Catskills for the summer and another in West Palm Beach for the winter: "I'll get four-forty an hour, naturally, plus food and housing." At this time he was living in a three-bedroom apartment in Brookline. "It's unoccupied now," he said. "I know the caretaker. He lets me stay there and I help him out. But I have to maintain a quiet presence. They don't like bums in Brookline. They kick you out! They want to keep the prices up, so they keep the bums out!" Other nights he slept in the basement of a building where he got a key from a locksmith for forty dollars. "I only stay during the night," he said when asked if anyone bothered him. He also stayed (usually for a price) in the apartments of other patrons of the mental health care system. "I have a lot of friends," he once said. I took it that many of these friends were people to whom he loaned cash or traded.

In June Anthony was back at the Center, unshaven and wearing a gray overcoat atop a baby-blue suit. I asked where he had been for the last two months. "Here and there," he said. He told me that he planned to go to Europe, but now that the two Germanies were united, it didn't work out. "I'll stay out for awhile," he said. Around this time one man said that Anthony must be "staying on the street" because he "looked like hell." Lisa used comparable terms in describing him one day: "He always looks ragged, dirty. He wears a dirty coat, with long pants down to the soles of his shoes."

While Anthony made an art out of drumming up cash, finding temporary jobs, sleeping on the cheap, and "using the system," others tended to the dull compulsion of economic activity (to use Karl Marx's words) through like-minded if less systematic means. Insufficient funds led many to forage for money, food, cigarettes, coffee, and economic niches. People usually ranged the Center or the downtown area but sometimes traveled afar in search of jobs or places to live: stapled on the board facing the entrance to the shelter was a map of the United States, with routes penciled in from Boston to Baton Rouge and from Boston to Albuquerque to San Diego to Tijuana. While most women tried to stay in a single place, many men moved "here and there" and so stayed nowhere in particular. "I'm just here for the winter," Roy said, when I met him in October of 1991. "The problem with apartments in the winter is that the landlord can kick you out. And if you try to camp out, the police come along. That's how people are." The sensible thing to do was to find, as Roy did, a place where they could not readily kick you out, or to maintain, like Anthony, as quiet a presence as possible in basements and vacant flats. But even with street smarts, the economics implied movement, marginality, and impermanence. Anthony knew this well—"She's not smart enough. You gotta know what you're doing!" he said of a woman who wanted to leave the shelter—and he managed his finances accordingly.

The economies of shelter life also implied constant exchanges. Along with negotiations over loans, many verbal exchanges between residents involved people asking others for cigarettes. "Can you give me a cigarette?" Stuart asked Joey one night. "See a doctor," Joey replied. As Joey's quip implied, the lack of cigarettes often presented more pressing problems than a shortage of money because many residents were physiologically dependent on nicotine. One could "just be broke" for weeks on end, but it was hard to go more than a few hours without a dose of nicotine: "I'm nervous. I need a smoke," Eva said decidedly to herself one day. When people lacked the money to buy cigarettes, they made use of a host of ritual dialogues.

One afternoon Susanne walked over to Helen, who was sitting on a bench in the lobby, and asked her for a couple of cigarettes. Helen did not respond. Susanne then asked for a few dollars. When Helen still did not respond, Susanne added: "Maybe my check will come in a day or two." Helen took out three cigarettes and gave them to Susanne, who walked away apparently content with the transaction. This sort of ask-and-you-might-receive dialogue happened repeatedly. On another occasion Alice approached Helen in the lobby. "Can I trouble you for a cigarette, Helen?" she asked. Helen made no movement whatsoever. "Helen, may I have a cigarette?" Alice asked. Helen silently drew a cigarette out of her pack and gave it to Alice.

Alice preferred not to buy packs of her own because she feared she would then smoke constantly. She therefore needed to ask others when she felt the urge to smoke. "Jesus. You just asked me!" Walter once said to her when she asked him for a cigarette. One week she took advantage of the fact that a new man had just arrived in the shelter and, not knowing well how things worked, was giving out cigarettes left and right. Most newcomers would stop giving out cigarettes soon after they got settled in and picked up the local mores. Several weeks after moving into the shelter, Martin told me that he decided to give out only one cigarette a day. He was doing this, he said, "so people get the message. I can't be giving out cigarettes all the time." Some compromised by selling a pair of cigarettes for twenty-five cents.

The exchanges went on. One day Irving Jackson was talking, partly to me, partly to himself: "Moses was a wise man . . ."

Nancy walked up and interrupted: "Irving, can I have a cigarette?"

"I don't want to hear that, Nancy," Irving said. "We're doing the same old song and dance."

Much of everyday life repeated the same old song and dance: the bumming, selling, and sharing of cigarettes, food, and items such as walkman radios. Most of the exchanges occurred in the marketplace of the lobby (which is one reason why Irving often sought refuge upstairs). A barter economy existed in which people traded what they had (and others wanted) for something that they wanted (and others had). Tokens could be exchanged for cigarettes, radios for friendship, and sex, at times, for money. "If you have the money," Martin said, "you can get anything you want on the street." During his stay in the shelter he bought Valium on the street for a dollar a pill and was trying to get a constant supply set up in the building. Drugs, cash, food, friendship, and bodies flowed in and out of the building in a vast exchange network.

Language was integral to the exchanges. It served as a medium for the negotiation of trades and as a marketable item in itself. Much as Judith Irvine has noted for the political economy of language in general, talk and sociability did not come cheap in the shelter.[14] Words, bearing a "commodity candidacy" of sorts, could acquire a limited exchange value, as when a few kind words set someone up for a free cigarette or a cigarette was offered in exchange for conversation.[15] One day Nhor, a Vietnamese man who lived in the shelter for a year, struck up a conversation with another resident and then asked for a dime. While Nhor, who did not have a good understanding of American culture or the culture of the shelter, made the connection between language and money overly apparent, others similarly found that words, sociability, and other linguistic performances could be exchanged for other goods, such as a cigarette or two. "Can't you talk to me, even after I gave you a cigarette?" Amy said to Wendy one afternoon as Wendy was getting up to leave the table where they had both been sitting. Amy used to live in the shelter but had since found a place of her own; she still liked to come and hang out in the shelter, but could only do so, the staff warned, if she was "visiting" one of the residents. She was therefore dismayed that her provisional host was not going to stay with her and so not follow through on the exchange of words for a cigarette.

The promise of a cigarette worked better for Amy on other occasions. One day Greg walked over and sat down at a table with her. "Amy," he asked, "do you have an extra cigarette?"

"Only if you sit with me."

"Okay."

Amy slid out a cigarette, gave it to Greg, then said: "You better remember me when I need a cigarette."

"I will."

They smoked in silence.

On another occasion Tommy walked around the shelter for a while, went into the lobby, then returned and walked over to Amy, who was sitting at a table in the common area, hoping to attend a meeting of the women's health group to be held in the next hour.

"Amy, do you have a cigarette?" he asked.

Amy gave him a few, then asked if he would go to the store for her. He nodded his head. "Buy me some candy balls, and a pack of cigarettes, and buy a pack for yourself," she said in giving him a ten-dollar bill.

Tommy left, returned ten minutes later but with the wrong brand of cigarettes, went back to the store, and finally returned with Amy's cigarettes and candy.

"Can I have some candy?" he asked while by her side.

"Why don't you sit here, Tommy," Amy said in handing him a few of the candy balls. "Don't you want to sit with me?"

"Okay," Tommy said.

He sat down, and, while eating some candy, nodded his head "yes" or "no" to Amy's questions.

"Why don't you shave?" she asked.

"I usually don't got no tokens to buy razors with," he said.

"You're nervous, Tommy," she said. She clasped his hands in hers and shook them lightly.

They sat without speaking for a minute, until Amy said, "Give me a kiss, Tommy."

Tommy leaned over and kissed her on the lips. Amy smiled.

Later Amy gave Tommy a dollar to go buy a soda from the vending machine in the lobby. Tommy did so and returned with a can of Pepsi, which they shared.

"Here's some money," Amy said. "Go buy yourself a pack of cigarettes."

"But you just bought me one."

"That's okay. You're good to me. You go to the store for me."

After finishing the soda and pocketing a few more candies Tommy got up and walked out of the shelter.

Among residents and their associates, social ties and economic exchanges were fundamental to one another. But neither was prior to or reducible to the other. The line between conversation and commerce was not clearly drawn. There was an economic edge to many social interactions and a strand of sociability in many economic exchanges. The dyadic, call-and-response sequence of many events in the shelter, itself rooted in qualities of secondness, had a great deal to do with these interactions and exchanges. Economic and social interactions alike implicitly involved an idea of "converse" that carried both linguistic and economic connotations: to converse was to live or keep company with, to deal with, to have acquaintance with, and to talk with another. "Talking" to others could, in fact, entail ongoing socioeconomic contracts. "Bruce, can you talk to me today?" Larry asked Bruce one day in the hope of getting a loan repaid.

"Yeah," Bruce said. "Can I give you twelve [dollars]?"

"That's great. That will make the week easier."

A few days later, while huddled together in the lobby, Larry advised Bruce not to be stern in lending out money. He told him one had to "work in international waters," "give some room in between," and think about "the give and take." The advice captured well the ethics of a place where money could be tight but where debts and bad deals were not soon forgotten.

Several features characterized the give and take. Economic interactions between residents largely involved barter, with the residents trading their wares—including words and companionship—at the going rate. The interactions were negotiated, in that transactions bore certain conditions: Amy would give Greg a cigarette *only if* he sat with her; she was dismayed that Wendy left her *even after* she gave her a cigarette. The interactions were dialogical in that they tended to involve social engagement between two people. And they were immediate and incidental in that they usually pertained to the situation at hand rather than any long-standing agreements. But since people usually wanted to continue to exchange with others in the future, and those who had reputations for miserliness or unreliability had a tough time doing so, an ethics of trade applied in which people were motivated to act fairly.[16] For traders, it was important to be trustworthy. For borrowers, it was important to pay back one's loans. Leniency had its merits when lending. In general, it was a good idea, as Bruce advised, to work in international waters when negotiating the terms of barter and usury, and give some room to negotiate. People also shared or gave away food, drink, or cigarettes on occasion. They apparently did so in order to make amends for the times when they bummed for cigarettes or to cultivate good will among their associates. People, knowing quite well what it was like to go without, also gave food, cigarettes, or spare change to those who were broke.[17] The spirit of barter and gift giving in the shelter carried over to social interactions in general, for these tended to be contractual, dialogical, incidental, and driven by sentiments of doing right by others. In tandem with the religious and cultural values that people professed, moral sensibilities among residents related to the practicalities and vulnerabilities that came with borrowing or lending money, having or going without food, and conversing face-to-face with one's neighbors day after day. These sensibilities, then, involved consciousnesses that were open to woundings and hunger and mindful of the regard of others. A different set of circumstances would have entailed a different kind of ethics.

As a matter of fact, the residents' ethics and understandings, and thus their local economy of SSI checks, loans, barter, and Maussian gifts, often clashed with those of the staff. "It's foreign to them to think about money," one staff member told me in accounting for how residents would often spend all their money soon after receiving checks at the beginning of a month, borrow money at extremely high rates of interest, skip out on paying jobs, or "blow" their money on cigarettes, fast food, or other seemingly insubstantial items. Despite the staff's sincere concerns, however, it would be better to say that it was foreign for residents to think about money in the same way that staff members did. In a 1989 volume *Money and the Morality of Exchange,* Maurice Bloch and Jonathan Parry contend that—the assumptions of many anthropological studies to the contrary—the meanings attributed to money are not inherent in any single idea of "money" but are rather incorporated in distinct cultural practices.[18] The point held true for the shelter, which housed at least two economic sensibilities, two distinct "regimes of value," and two divergent understandings of, and temporal orientations to, money.[19]

Residents focused more often than not on the day at hand. As they saw it, the advantages of having ten dollars today more than offset the disadvantages of owing twenty next week *if* that ten could be put to good use. The motivations for residents to spend their money quickly related to the provisions of shelter life. Since those staying in the shelter did not need to worry about room and board, money could be spent on other needs, such as cigarettes or lottery tickets. And a person could "just be broke" when his or her cash ran out—although, when the next check arrived, it was hard to resist buying the things that one previously went without. With no refrigerators on hand, residents could not store perishable goods and so had to buy food at convenience stores or fast food chains when they wanted something besides cafeteria meals. These costs quickly added up. Many residents also tended to "spend down" in using their money to provide for immediate wants and needs. Rather than calculating the total amount they had to spend and then spreading that amount evenly, if thinly, over a specified period of time—which is what their case managers would have liked them to do—those who "spent down" used as much of their money as it took to make desired purchases at any given moment, without worrying about the cost or whether they would run out of cash. As one woman who moved from the shelter to a shared residence put it, "My motto is, if you got it, you gotta spend it!"[20]

The obligatory tone of the woman's motto, in which one had to spend whatever money one had, related to some extent to street life, where cash was likely to be lost, stolen, or borrowed. Money spent quickly was beyond the gaze and reach of others. Not to be discounted, either, was the influence of SSI, which forced people to spend by jeopardizing the benefits (income, health insurance, medications) of those who accumulated more than a stipulated amount of cash. Perhaps most important, however, was poverty, which could encourage people to seize the moment. Assuming that they would never be in a position to afford a comfortable standard of living, residents sometimes invested in moments of pseudoprosperity, splurging on pizzas, boom boxes, or narcotic highs.[21]

Whereas many residents tended to focus on their present needs and wants in accord with the give and take of their lives, the staff encouraged them to embrace a long-term teleological sequence in which the future ideally held more value than the present. In line with the main tenets of a capitalist state, they advanced a regime of value that focused on individual labor and earnings, monetary savings, mathematical calculation of holdings and expenditures, and rational investments in products and activities that might pay off in the future.[22] In effect, given the perceived "foreignness" of money for residents, the staff tried to naturalize their guests to what they took to be the proper meaning and value of money. They stressed that it was important to work for one's money, to plan ahead, to budget one's finances, to avoid spending one's money all at once or wasting money on insubstantial items, and to avoid falling into debt. When necessary they tried to impose a "payee" system on a few spendthrifts, whereby a case manager would budget a person's monthly finances and dole out a weekly or daily allowance. The staff also implemented the "token" economy, a system they found was generally effective both in getting people to do things and in getting them to act responsibly and appreciate the rewards of work. This economy was imbued with the "capitalist realism" that Michael Schudson finds in American commercial advertisement, for it succinctly represented the virtues of a capitalist lifestyle.[23] Given that scholars and policy makers were then professing that residents and others should be considered "consumers" of the mental health care system, it could well be argued that the Department of Mental Health was trying to make good capitalists out of its charges.

Residents followed the staff's advice at times and managed their finances in the ways staff wanted them to. But they usually invested more in the moral economy of exchange and reciprocity, in which money or tokens were two types of commodities among many to be bartered and exchanged. The token economy, for instance, consisted of an odd mix of meanings and values. While the staff hoped that the message imbued in the economy would carry over to the residents' lives in general—much as a pigeon in a Skinner Box will learn to press the bar, even though it does not always receive pellets — the perceived link between effort and reward could go to the other extreme, for residents often wanted tokens for *any* chorelike duties asked of them. ("Do you want a token for doing that?" one of the staff nurses asked me in a cheerfully sarcastic voice one afternoon as I replaced the bottle on the water cooler.) Many of the exchanges of labor for tokens thus reflected the work ethic and rational calculations of capitalism, but also the lobby's reciprocities, loans, paybacks, and ongoing conversations. "Bill, I took a shower," Larry said as he passed by the staff desk one evening. "Now you owe me eight tokens. Eight tokens. I'll get them when I get back."

Stand Away

"I think a lot about him leaving. He bummed a lot of cigarettes from me, you know," Larry said to Lisa and me as we sat a table in the shelter. He was referring to his pal Bruce, who two days before had moved into a halfway house provided by the housing project.

"Oh, yeah. You also seemed to get a lot in return," Lisa replied.

"Yeah. We treated each other right. I don't know. He kind of let it go the last week. I lent him some money the last week, ten dollars one day and some cigarettes the next, but I guess he thought I was setting him up."

"Maybe, you know," Lisa said, "he was trying to get some distance from this place, and break away from here."

"Yeah. Maybe so."

As with Bruce and Larry, whose interactions together mainly involved exchanges of cigarettes, money, and lottery tickets as well as negotiations on those exchanges, many ties between residents rested on an ethos of exchange, reciprocity, and short-term trust in which people tried to treat each other "right." Sometimes they involved a solid bond: Barbara and Estelle shared a lot of things, including food, cigarettes, and *TV Guide*, and Bruce and Walter were continuously making exchanges when they lived in the shelter ("Bruce and Walter are like that," Larry once said, tying two of his fingers together). Other exchanges were more incidental but involved a similar spirit of sociability. Helen, meanwhile, went out of her way to "help" other people, like Carla, who she said was "sick in the head. She talks funny. She says the opposite of what you say: if you're on one side, she's on the other. She puts cigarettes into cups, even if there's an ashtray nearby. She didn't want to go into the cafete-

ria with only one door open. . . . I need to watch over her. I pat her
back when she gets upset, and she calms down. The staff can't take care
of her, they have too much to do as it is. She needs someone to watch
over her. I'm the only one. When I feel that someone needs help, I help
them until they get better."

Helen's caring attentiveness was more the exception than the rule.
Despite the few friendships, the focus on conversation, and general concerns, especially among women, for the well-being of others, many had
a tough time talking at length with their neighbors. They tended not
to sustain solid relationships; indeed, focusing on their own concerns
and welfare often led them to ignore those around them. "To tell you
the truth, I haven't been paying much attention to people in here,"
Martin said in early January, when asked how the people in the shelter were handling the winter holidays. Evonne's ills made her keep away
from "social areas." "I have no friends," she said, "just people I recognize. . . . I have my own routine." Sylvia Covert, a white woman in her
late thirties who had lived in the shelter since 1985, also spent a lot
of time alone. Cursed with an electrified, somatic version of the evil
eye, she felt that she gave people painful charges whenever she touched
or looked at them. Everyday interactions consequently troubled her. "I
can't form deep friendships with people," she said. "I can't confide emotional problems with them. I can't look at them."

When Sylvia first heard of the housing project she was happy to learn
that she might get a place to live. "Oh my God," she once said, "if I
ever got a place to stay after all these years. . . ." From the start she was
adamant about wanting to live alone. "It's not because of wanting to be
haughty in my independence," she explained, "but because I need to. I
can't look at people. Besides, I'm used to being alone." As it turned out,
she was assigned to "independent living," which meant she would have
her own apartment. But when she visited the building and found that
she "hurt" people when she looked at them, she said she could not live
there in good conscience, fearing she would harm children and elderly
people living there. The staff thought she was afraid to move out because she had established a routine in the shelter that she found safe
for herself and others. She continued to stay in the shelter.

While Sylvia and Evonne built their lives around routines that kept
them from social areas, the sociability of others depended on how well
they felt at a particular time. Their sociability was often geographic in
form. The location that Rose chose in the evening indicated how well
and how sociable she felt. At times she would sit on one of the benches
in the lobby and talk amiably with those around her. At others she
would sit pensively in a corner with her head down, hostile to intruders.

"Don't talk to me! I don't want to talk," she scowled one evening as I approached. "I'm sorry for talking to you that way last week," she said with a smile the following week, "I didn't want to talk to anybody. I was in a bad mood."

People tried to stay clear of others' moodiness. As Mitch put it, some would scratch if you got to close. While some lashed out only occasionally, others were known for their gruffness. Many found Ralph hard to talk to during his stay in the shelter; he had a knack for contradicting everyone. "I wasn't sure if I wanted to be friends with him," Peter said after Ralph quit the shelter, "because he was always kind of gruff. I don't think he liked people that much. He was always keeping to himself, doing puzzles or whatnot."

Sam Kinch, the man who periodically vacated the shelter for the bars at Copley Square, had a similar reputation for being unapproachable. A thin, wiry white man in his fifties who had lived all his life in Boston, Sam stayed in the shelter for four years until his physical health became so poor that he required hospital care. He could often be found sitting at a table in the middle of the common area, facing the staff desk, so that he could watch the staff's proceedings from afar. "Well, fuck you," he said one day in the direction of the staff at a time when they were talking and laughing while puttering about the staff desk. He was normally in possession of several cups of coffee and often spoke to himself while fidgeting with empty creamer cups and plastic spoons and knives. Because he spoke in a quiet, raspy voice his words could be difficult to understand and his wit easy to underestimate.

Sam had numerous medical problems: he was missing one lung, had lost sight in one eye, and was an alcoholic. "Actually, the drinking is a form of self-medication," a staff member told me. "I have a hard time staying alive, a hard time breathing," he told me one day. "Not feeling well today," he said on another. "I hurt myself before. I fell down and lost consciousness. I have to take care of myself, not talk too much. I have to keep my mind sharp, in case I lose consciousness again." He said this in part, I believe, to justify why he couldn't talk with me too much. We therefore sat together without talking. "I'm in a bad mood, okay?" he said on another day, and I backed off. "I have a good day so long as nobody bothers me," he once said. "I need to behave myself," he said on yet another day, toward the end of his time in the shelter. One staff member thought the notion of Sam's behaving himself might have related to the fact that he thought he was getting to be an old man and could die soon.

Others were wary of Sam. "The guy never eats," Mitch said. "Just coffee and sugar. We might be watching him commit suicide right now. . . . He's always got a [plastic] knife in his hands. He'll yell at you if you get too close: 'Son of a bitch!'" "That guy," said Martin on another occasion, "is the only one here who bothers me. He yells at you if you ever get too close."

Despite residents' efforts to give each other space, disputes were common. People, unglued or not, got on each others' nerves. Few held lasting grudges, however, and conflicts were largely incidental and soon forgotten. "You're burning my coat"—"Fuck you" went one exchange. Another went as follows: Sam and Fred were arguing in the dorm area, with voices raised. Sam then left the dorm area and sat close to the staff, by the window, but alone, so he would not be bothered.

Sam's movement away from the site of the argument was a method commonly used to avoid or end a conflict. The staff tried to prevent escalations of conflicts by encouraging people to "walk away": "When a person bothers you, just walk way," Peggy, the staff nurse, advised Fred. One day, about twenty minutes into the dinner hour, Louise, who had lived in the shelter for several months, rushed out of the cafeteria and said in a loud, angry voice, "I'm not going to put up with that kind of shit!" Lisa, who was sitting on a bench, asked her what was going on. Louise complained that Dan, Lisa's coworker, had yelled at her for doing something that she did not actually do. "I was just sitting there, minding my own business," Louise said in an unsettled voice. "Perhaps you need to take some space," Lisa said. "Yeah, right," Louise huffed and walked away.

The interaction between Louise and Lisa conformed to a common script that frequently involved tension, the presence of staff, and an unresolved separation. When residents got mad or upset about something, they would often "take some space," go for a walk, or be told to take a "time out." When I asked one man what people did when they got angry, he said, "You have to avoid the person, not talk to them. If you're verbally abusive, you have to take a time out for an hour and try to settle the dispute with a staff person present."[1] In contrast to the stasis that could come before or after a conflict (Louise, for instance, was "just sitting there" before the trouble began), anger was nomadic. The logic here, as with the lack of personal control and integrity associated with being mentally ill, related to the local contours of space, power, and restraint: if you were angry or verbally abusive, you had to leave; if you did not leave, you would be forced to leave. Staying calm, in contrast, enabled one to stay put. At work was a subtle metaphysic of language that linked anger and verbal abuse with movement and isolation, and restraint, consensus, and communication with stasis. Anger and verbal abuse typically entailed a movement away from something—from the shelter, from the lobby, from the building. Communicative acts typically entailed a stationary act—sitting down to talk about what was going on, being stopped at the desk, or having a staff member present to settle things. All interactions had a spatial cast to them.

For the most part, the themes of separation and distance held for all social relations in the shelter. "It's the rule of the shelter to stand away, when asking for cigarettes or anything else," Anthony said. "They tell us to keep our own space, to just have friendships," Larry told me. But the risk of conflict, the rule to stand away, and the tendency of people to keep to themselves led to a general consensus among residents that the shelter was "not a place to make friends," as Julie put it. "I've been trying to make friends for a while now, and I haven't made any more. It's kinda hard around here [in Boston]," said Martin, who told me he had four friends: his ex-roommate, his girlfriend, and his two stuffed animals. Roy Lerner said he did not talk to people in the shelter much, although he did some mornings. "I keep to myself," he said. "I have no friends here. A few acquaintances. It's not possible to have friends." "You cannot have real friends here. People are sick in the head," Helen said. "If you ask me," Barbara said, "there's just fair weather friends here. There's no real friends here, only acquaintances." For Barbara, who complained of lending money but never seeing it again, friends were those you knew for a long time and learned to trust in a mutual way, whereas acquaintances were those "you know from day to day and mainly give and take money." "Everyone here has problems," Julie once said. "Each goes their own individual way. So I have no real friends here. I have a lot of acquaintances. It's a prerequisite."

The "prerequisite" of having numerous acquaintances served two needs: to keep one's distance from others, for reasons of well-being; and to maintain contact with others, for reasons of economic exchange. Such concerns support the anthropological truism that social orders emerge out of the environmental needs of a people. In fact, the transfer of money, food, and cigarettes involved innovations in sociability that reflected the constant focus on one's socioeconomic welfare and, at times, the distanced mode of communicating. The styles of relating that emerged were as much economic as social. "You can't have a real good friend these days," Irving said one day as we sat in the plaza. "What is a good friend to you?" I asked. "Someone who's there when you have whiskey, cigarettes, you know."

While some lamented the lack of "real friends" in the shelter, others found comfort in the detached but constant companionship that characterized shelter life.[2] "I like it here," said Helen. "It's good here because I don't feel lonely. There's always people to talk to here. In an apartment by myself I was going crazy, losing my mind." Helen said she liked to be around people but tried not to get too involved in their lives because they could cause her to have a "nervous breakdown." A few preferred to live in the shelter precisely because it did not offer lasting bonds. "I think the shelter is the ideal situation for me," Alice said when I first met her. "Unlike a halfway house, there are enough people around that I don't feel the need to maintain deep ties with others. Yet there are also enough people around that I don't get too lonely." Later, when the housing project led to a steady turnover in the shelter, I asked her if all the new faces affected her life. She shook her head no, then said: "It's like a big bus station to me, with people passing through. But that's usually okay with me. I can talk to some people, but I don't get too close." The ideal for Alice, Helen, and others was neither intimacy nor isolation. The difficulty was finding the right balance, especially given how much of life was beyond their control.

Often the sociability to be found in the building took distinct and frail forms. Warren Nations, for instance, was a white man in his early thirties who lived in a single-room-occupancy apartment on the outskirts of Boston. I often saw him riding the subway to and from the downtown area, sitting alone and talking to himself in an outwardly belligerent voice. Many evenings he could be found in the Center, either in an empty room upstairs, where he worked on his "testimonies" and law suits against the state, or at the base of the stairs that curled up from the lobby. Usually he would stand and face the lobby; sometimes he would play an imaginary guitar in tune with the music from a Sony walkman. "I come here to see Brian, and to socialize," he said one evening, when I asked why he came to the building. "He does his thing, and I do mine." Warren's thing was to stand on the lower end of the stairwell, while talking under his breath and looking through the glass window toward the lobby proper, where Brian was doing his thing, which was to pace quickly around the elevator shaft. His distance from the lobby, and the glass doors and windows separating him from it, enabled him to observe the activities there without directly participating in them.

Warren, like others, liked to be around and "socialize" with people but also preferred to keep to himself much of the time. I believe he found it difficult to hold a conversation with someone for long but still wanted to maintain distanced contact. His desire to be alone in the company of others recalls Ellen Corin's finding that "schizophrenics" in Montreal who demonstrated a style of "positive withdrawal" in relating to others—maintaining "distanced" and often highly routinized social relations with acquaintances and family members—were rehospitalized less often than patients who sought more intensive contact with family members but who were simultaneously excluded from family life.[3] Apparently, a tendency to "disinvest" from close relations with others, pursue contact "at a distance," and remain relatively "detached" from the social world at large helped many to stay within the community. Perhaps Julie had similar arrangements in mind when she said it was a "prerequisite" to have only acquaintances in the shelter, for many of those who lived in the shelter proper preferred, like Warren, to keep to themselves or seek the company of others in communal silence: Rose sat alone at the end of the corridor, Julie and Peter played a game of cards with little conversation, and Wendy sat and smoked a cigarette next to Sam because she knew he would not try to talk to her. Some preferred to sit in on the edge of conversations. One day Brian sat down at a table adjacent to the one where I was sitting and talking with several people. He got up fifteen seconds later and walked out of the shelter. Bruce, in turn, could often be found with coffee in hand in a corner of the shelter. He would say "Hi, Bob," "Hi, Helen" to people who walked by, but seldom engaged in any lasting conversations. In fact, one reason that many frequented the building was that there they could keep to themselves in the company of others. The Center served as a kind of "safe harbor," which, like chain restaurants, shopping malls, single-room-occupancy hotels, and some airports, provided a social setting with both low demands and the possibility of distanced participation in a social world.[4] While some agencies of the state might have found that this was a self-defeating escape, it was, for those who sought out such marginal stances, a fragile but effective way to maintain a measure of sanity in everyday life.

In the long run, the ubiquity of acquaintances that one knew "from day to day" made anonymity more the rule than the exception. Except for a few close ties and love interests, lives remained separate. "It seems that people don't want you to get to know them," Peter said. "People sit in groups, groups of their own. I see them. They're strangers to one another." "Nobody knows anyone!" Lisa said one day in disbelief, when a couple of residents seemed not to care that Tommy and Greg were leaving the shelter to move into a group house. "Isn't that so weird? And they're happy with that."

Other departures followed suit. A few weeks after the first few residents left the shelter for houses provided by the project, I asked Richard if he knew how they were doing in their new homes. "No," he said. I then asked if he had thought of visiting them.

"No," he said, then added: "I didn't really become friends with them, you know. But I'm gonna miss Peter's pizza. . . . People don't miss people here too much when they leave."

"Why is that?" I asked.

"Because they forget."

"But they miss Irving, don't they?"

"Some, because he was always going to the store for people." People missed the socioeconomic benefits of being acquainted with him, that is. Relations ceased when the commerce and the grounds for the relations did.[5]

The rapidity with which many people left the shelter (when quitting it, in finding another place to live, or in being sent to a hospital) and the reluctance of staff to talk about the private affairs and whereabouts of their "guests" added to the anonymity. The way the residents saw it, people suddenly appeared or disappeared. After a long weekend I asked Richard what was "new." "Different faces, different places," he said nonchalantly. I soon learned that Jeff was no longer living in the shelter, and asked Mitch if he knew where he was. "I don't know, he just disappeared," he said, then added: "See, that's the thing. People just disappear one day. You sort of miss them and sort of don't miss them. And when you ask where somebody is, it brings it home all at once." Likewise, when Ian went into a hospital, nobody knew where he went nor did they give much thought to where he might be. Often the changes in faces were evident, however. "One night," Evonne recalled, "I came in and saw the heavy-set woman sleeping in Estelle's bed, and she was there the next night too. I wondered who she was."

Although people often came to know others—and quite well, at times —through verbal, auditory, and tactile modalities, first contact was commonly visual. People encountered "different faces," as Richard put it, or noticed different bodily forms, as Evonne found. Indeed, familiarity was first and foremost founded on a physical, visual presence or absence: a person either appeared or disappeared. This kind of surface knowledge was compounded by many things, including the staff's code of privacy, the rule to stand away, the prerequisite of having acquaintances, the general uncertainties and contingencies of everyday life, and the anonymity of the shelter itself, which lacked any public sign identifying the gym as a place of residence. There were also, as the manager noted in a discussion of shelter policies, "layers of decision makers that would boggle the mind." Knowledge in the shelter was customarily transient, unstable, and partial; often one couldn't pin down what was going on. While shelter residents took advantage of the Center's opacities, sublime features, and perceptual obscurities, they also had to live with the limits on knowledge and certitude that came with bedding down there.

The confusion of identities could apply to one's surroundings as well. "I always seem to wake up and not know where I am, every morning," Barbara said. For Evonne, Barbara, and others, it was principally at night, when the features of space and time lost their edge, that identities and locations were in question. Sometimes the uncanny sight of fifty transient people sleeping on a basketball court in the basement of a massive state building hit home. "Are you going to miss this place?" I asked Helen toward the end of her last week in the shelter.

"No," she said, then added, as if to justify her sentiments: "You don't know what it's like to live here. It's funny living here. When you wake up in the middle of the night and think about the big building you're sleeping in and you turn and see all the people sleeping next to you, it's like that."

"Like what?" I asked.

"Psssssshh," she said.

"You mean like it's strange, weird?"

"Yes."

Ragtime

"One guy gets me coffee in the morning, and I give him a dollar," Joey told me once. "So it's worth it for me. But the guy is kinda hard to talk to sometimes."

One reason that people found it difficult to converse with others was that talk often involved different planes of meaning that built on diverse principles of association.

Some phrasings relied on an exuberant, associative semantics of concrete metaphors and metonymns. "You're gorgeous," a woman said to me, "you have a house and two kids and a dog in Brookline." "I've been to Ohio for so long," Fred said when he returned to the shelter from the psychiatric ward. "When I go to sleep," Louise said once, "it feels like someone is sticking pins into my eyes, and I go down, down, down."

Some people engaged in conversations with themselves in a stream of allusions and digressions, as if Joyce's Leopold Bloom were to muse aloud as he roamed Dublin. "Moses was the greatest fighter. He never lost a battle. . . . The Bible should be read in a quiet atmosphere," Irving said to no one in particular one day, but with all the intonations of a gentle conversation. "That reminds me of a guy I know," Stuart said to himself while sitting in the lobby. He then proceeded to discuss the ins and outs of his friendship with him.

Some would laugh privately at something the "voices" said or tell the voices they heard, "Shut up!" or "Stop it!"

Some found exceptional meanings in events and actions where others did not: the patter of rain was a warning that people were trying to hurt you. Staff and psychiatrists, working from a different frame of reference, saw these "paranoid" interpretations of reality as "delusional."

Some people related to language in a concrete, literal fashion. When Lisa and I visited Julie Mason in her new apartment after she moved from the shelter, I found the room confining and the space private, and so asked Julie if she wanted "to go out for a coffee." I meant the question in the broadest sense of going someplace to sit and talk. When she said no I thought she understood the general import of the question. When I asked her the same question a few minutes later, she again said "no." It then dawned on me that she might be hearing me in a way different than I intended, so I asked, "Would you like to go for a soda?" "Okay," she said.

Julie's understanding of this and other exchanges recalls the clinical finding that people with schizophrenia often respond more to the denotative than to the connotative meanings of words; they take a word or phrase as representative only of the specific objects that they are considering at the moment ("coffee") rather than as representative of a group or class (going somewhere to talk).[1] As one author puts it, "schizophrenic listeners are more likely to be biased by the 'strong' or 'preferred' meaning of a word than the meaning of a word in its sentence or discourse context."[2] For Julie, a coffee was a coffee, although we need not deem her way of hearing things pathological.

In any event, the semantic confusion Julie and I encountered points to the gist of the matter. Since each of the associative principles that gave life to different phrasings drew on distinct but linguistically sound ways to express meanings, problems in the pragmatics of communication arose when a metaphoric statement was taken literally or when a personal soliloquy was offered or taken as a social conversation. Each plane of meaning had its own logic, although the logics were often more associative than deductive—parts were taken as wholes, one image took the place of another, words were what they concretely stood for, or a web of signs pointed to a greater design of meaning. As with the differences between the system of "resemblances" and the system of "representations," which for Foucault distinguished the "epistemes" of Renaissance and Classical thought, planes of meaning in and around the shelter, each entirely sensible on its own once its premises were accepted, were not commensurate.[3] The ways that references were drawn, signs interpreted, or meanings effected did not match up with one another.

Unlike Foucault's history, however, the different semantic orders were voiced at the same time. This inevitably resulted in confusing moments. Indeed, many of the spats between residents related to the incommensurability of different semantic orders. While the staff held that the conflicts often occurred when people "lost control" or were stressed out, I found that they were just as often the result of diverse planes of meaning. The phonology, grammar, and syntax were as sound as that used by any American, but conflicts arose when references were drawn inappropriately, signs were interpreted in ways different than they were intended, or conversations took different paths.

Take Richard Groton, for instance, whose need to "touch" people and things in order to stay calm had linguistic correlates in what he and others saw as an extreme impressionability. "Don't be doing that," Brian told a man who was trying to get Richard to sell his radio for ten dollars. "He's not like you or me. He's highly suggestive. If you give him an idea, he listens to it right away." "Yeah!" Richard said with an eager smile. The immediacy of Richard's "listening" was evident in how he copied the actions and views of others and readily did what others told him to do.

With this grammar of impressions, whereby Richard touched things and was touched by others, people's thoughts and feelings influenced matter—and matter had a hold on people. Something of this metaphysic was evident in his understanding that the lobby and East Boston made him think of death because "death becomes part of you." For Richard, there was often an immediate correspondence between different domains or entities, such as the symbolic space of the lobby and the person who frequented that space. In a bit of contagious magic, death became part of a person, and a person's moods stained the stuff of buildings and cities. In general, his way of speaking was characterized by an intimate relation between mind and matter, as if his use of language was governed less by a division between these two domains than by their constant coupling. The couplings related directly to the large number of metaphors, similes, and other poetic tropes in his speech. Richard was constantly spinning a web of significances that linked words and feelings and matter through a contiguity of qualities whose most essential features were often colored by the defining aspects of his life: a sense of failure, despondency, and marginality. His use of language evinced a thicket of metonymns that linked parts to wholes in an immediate, existential fashion. The couplings also involved metaphors and similes that linked two, often radically dissimilar, semantic domains. For Richard, being homeless was "like being a crack in a concrete wall. . . . 'Cause you don't hold everything together, and people start to look at you as if you're poor or something." "If you were behaving, they would give you strawberries," he told a neighbor. While Boston was "like a forest" because people would give you a cup of coffee, the shelter, he said, was "a dime-store floozy house." And when I asked him where everyone was on a sunny May afternoon, he said, "People are out trying to pick up the pieces of their shattered lives, I think." He also said once that he was "trying to get out of the red-light district," and on another occasion that "reading and the weather are related." Although I have yet to grasp why this was so—or why Boston was like a forest—I did find that it was the direct and tangible coupling of various domains, through either metonymic or metaphoric relations, that characterized much of his speech.

By definition, a metaphor is "a figure of speech in which a word or phrase literally denoting one kind of object or domain is used in place of another to suggest a likeness or analogy between them."[4] The less obvious or cliched the comparison, the more striking the image usually is. But there are dangers in being too opaque. In his *Poetics* Aristotle observed that "It is a great thing, indeed, to make a proper use of the poetical forms, as also of compounds and strange words. But the greatest thing by far is to be a master of metaphor. It is this one thing that cannot be learnt from others; and it is also a sign of genius, since a good metaphor [literally, to metaphorize well] implies an intuitive perception of the similarity in dissimilars."[5] Richard "metaphorized" all too well. His couplings were often too dissimilar for their own good; his evocations of death and strawberries tripped people up in their imaginative leaps. As Aristotle might hear it, his metaphors were "drawn from too far afield," his diction too "unfamiliar," his poetry "either a riddle or gibberish," such that his expressions often failed "to carry the hearer with them."[6] "Don't worry about him," Estelle whispered to me one day as Richard spoke; "He's just mixing things up, to get you confused."

Confuse he did, but unintentionally so, often fusing one domain of meaning with another. He baffled one man when he referred to the staff desk as a "car," and he tripped up Larry when he complained that the staff "was always telling us to take pills and trying to give us shots" (that is, tell them what to do), to which Larry responded, "But I don't get you. They want you to take a shot?!" Misunderstandings thus took flight when metaphors were taken literally, as Richard himself sometimes observed. "I like Ian. He's cool," he said one day after Ian walked by. "That's great. Does he like you?" I asked. "I don't know," Richard said, then drew on a metaphor to explain why people disliked the use of tropes: "Nobody likes nobody around here," he said, "because they want everything to be in black and white instead of color."

Peter Vaughn, who lived in the shelter for several years, was one of those who preferred things in black and white. A tall, heavyset, aging white man with sad eyes and a Santa Claus beard, he spoke softly, pausing between sentences. When talking, he would look me in the eye once in a while, then look down again. "I'm not much of a conversationalist," he said, after someone tried to reach him by the pay phone in the lobby and he sent word that he was not to be found. "What can you talk about every day? That you had two sodas at the social club?" He said he had no friends in the shelter but would like a few. "It gets boring when you don't have any friends. It's nice to share stuff with friends, talk a bit."

Sometimes Peter felt sick: "I feel lousy. I hear voices. And I feel anxious a lot." He said he had an "anxiety disorder" and so was always "feeling nervous," although the nervousness often translated into displeasure with life in the shelter. "Sometimes," he said, "I feel like I'm taking up space that I shouldn't be taking up." All the same, he was afraid of what would happen if he got better. "I'm afraid," he said, "that someday people are going to say that it's time to leave, that they'll say, 'You're not crazy so you can't live here.' . . . I got barred from three shelters already. I'm not ready to move out. I need to do things." Yet he said he would like to have a place of his own one day.

Around this time Peter was thinking about the possibility of moving into one of the housing situations provided by the housing project. Finding that he didn't know how to do things like buy clothes, use an automated teller machine, or get around on the subway, he worried about what it would be like to live on his own. He also worried both that everything was moving so fast and that he was unable to do anything in preparation for moving out, even though his counselor wanted him to do so. When he heard that he would be living with other people, he stopped worrying about being isolated and feeling lonely but began to fret about the nature of social ties in the house. "People here don't seem to care much," he said. "They punch holes in the walls or shout all the way down a hallway. Who's to say it won't be like that in the house?"

Peter spoke often of the words and actions he did not understand. He occasionally walked out of meetings between staff and residents, which were often semantically and pragmatically wild affairs. "Sometimes I walk out, because they don't seem to make sense sometimes, and I don't understand what they're saying." Combined with a lack of understanding, some of the actions hurt him immensely. "One day," he once said, "a person who works here asked, 'Why do you look unhappy?' I was just sitting there. That made me unhappy. I don't know why some people would want to make someone unhappy." Peter was a literalist of the emotions. A presumption of unhappiness made him unhappy.

Peter found that he had as many difficulties with language as he did getting things done in the city. One problem was a "blocking" of thought and speech common to people with schizophrenia.[7] "I have a lot of trouble talking," he said. "I can think the words, but I can't say what I'm thinking. I don't know how other people can do it." He said he was bothered by the staff, who tried to get him up in the morning. He usually did not feel well in the morning and had a tough time getting up but was unable to explain his difficulties adequately to the staff. "For some reason," he explained, "I have a hard time expressing things that other people do easily."

Peter said that there were a lot of things that he could not "figure out," like "why there are so many violent people in the world." He seemed bewildered by life as well as tired and despairing of such bewilderment. The confusions of the shelter compounded his concerns. "The problem with living here," he said, "is that people are fickle. They don't make sense. They're talking ragtime all the time."

"What's ragtime?" I asked.

"Oh, It's talk about the sky falling down or cows on the roof. It doesn't make any sense. How can you listen to that?" He went on: "It's awkward. People seem rational when they first sit down with you, but then, the next thing you know, they're bouncing off the walls. One second people are nice—but only when they want something. The next, they're shouting names at you. They turn on you in a second. . . . The other night Richard was walking around with a blanket over his head. I don't know what he was doing. And there's some guy here who's talking about God all the time."

Like a few other residents, Peter had to deal each day with slownesses of body, speech, and action. He found it hard to get up in the morning, he found it difficult to say what he was thinking, and he needed to take his move from the shelter one step at a time. In turn, a lot of things were bereft of secure meaning for him. His desire for clarity, order, and understanding was confounded by the actions of other shelter residents, who, he found, sometimes acted without apparent reason or predictability. Peter put a moral twist on these actions, for he disapproved of and was apparently hurt by their sudden and nonsensical air. Others found him "moody" but calm and sober. "Peter is the only one who makes sense to me here," Richard once told me in Peter's presence. "He doesn't talk ragtime."

To "talk ragtime," as I came to understand it, was to speak by way of the "loose," dreamlike associations between different sequences of speech, tangential asides, obscure references, neologisms, intense and stilted verbalizations, and other peculiar and often noisy phrasings common to—and often thought to be indicative of—schizophrenic speech.[8] While I only heard Peter and Richard use the term, their choice of words was on the money, since dictionaries note that, along with referring to a jazzy music characterized by a syncopated melodic line, "ragtime," like "ragtag," "ragged," "ragtail," and "raggle-taggle," connotes disorderly, patchwork, and disreputable themes or actions. To rag, meanwhile, is variably to play, sing, or dance in ragtime, to wrangle, to be noisy and riotous, to engage in rough play, or to tease, torment, or annoy in a rough manner. Such offbeat talk, quite common in the shelter, was syntactically and phonetically correct. But since it usually made ready sense only to the speaker, despite his or her intentions to the contrary, someone like Peter could not easily "listen" to it. In fact, one person known to talk in ragtime would normally be unable to make out the ragtimes of another.

Whereas Peter had trouble coming up with words and tended to situate meanings in a literal, black-and-white frame of reference, Ian Greene, a white man in his late twenties who stayed in the shelter for several months, was often faced with a mania of possibilities. One day he told me he wanted to construct a giant boxlike structure around the universe and have people live inside it.

"I don't think I'd like that," I said. "I like to have a lot of sunshine around."

"Not me. Not me," he said quickly. "I'd put the sun out."

Ian, who said his medications were supposed to stop his "grandiose thoughts," had twenty-seven ideas that he hoped to market if he could only get the market rights for each one, although he had to find out if a person could copyright an idea and would take his case to the World Court if it came down to that. He tended to present as many linguistic possibilities as creative ideas. When I asked him how he found the building, he said, "I don't know. When you say, 'How do people find this building,' that could mean so many different things. How do you know that's it, that it stands for the whole thing? It could be something else entirely, you know? I mean, sometimes I think something in my head and the language comes out otherwise. It's different, you know. Maybe other people do it different, but that's how my mind works." On other occasions Ian spoke of his "mind" in similar terms, as if it was constantly racing ahead while he tagged along, figuring out the semiotic clues it left behind.

Others got "hopped up" at times and talked in linguistic circles as much as they paced in spatial ones—as when William Fordham "went on" about New Orleans after taking his medications. For the most part, these racings of the mind resulted in a profusion of talk, in which people spoke intensely about this or that to drive their points home. Often any hearers of such talk—symptomatic for clinicians of "pressure of speech"—could only listen and try to follow along, as Mitch noted when he said that they got to hear about New Orleans "all the time."

Sometimes the abundance of possibilities could make a person freeze up, as when Brian excitedly said that he could not talk when I asked him if he was going to be leaving the shelter. In contrast to Peter, then, who faced a lack of meaning in the world and had a tough time finding words to match his thoughts, others found there was too much meaning. As Ian put it, one phrase could mean "so many different things"; it could connote so many ideas or possibilities. Peter and Julie often zeroed in on what things denoted, whereas Ian and Richard spoke of what things connoted. Peter's orientation was hypo-semiotic while Ian's was hyper-semiotic. These orientations to meaning reflected general ways of being in the world: to use Susanna Kaysen's terms, while some slogged through a world of "viscosity," in which thoughts and perceptions moved slowly and bodies felt sluggish, the lives of others were characterized by "velocity," in which perceptions and thoughts on those perceptions raced quickly through their minds. Some moved along a continuum of these states in accord with their moods, their nerves, or their medications.[9]

A complement to the manic hyper-semiotics of linguistic production was a hyper-semiotics of interpretation. A common practice was to read a great deal of meaning into things that other people would not find unduly significant. Julie, for instance, sometimes felt that people were planning to kill her on the street. "When a group of people are together, laughing," she said, "I think that they're talking about killing me. Once there were two men in the subway and so I thought they wanted to kill me. Me and my daughter got away from them, so that the door was between us." Martin, in turn, was "paranoid" day and night. He heard voices that commented less on his own life than on the general state of the world. He knew that his fears were irrational, but he could not stop thinking about them and so turned his radio on every ten minutes to see if there was any news of a terrible disaster. At times, it seemed that there was an exceptional, connotative meaning to the events people could cue into. All one needed to do was to look for the right signs. But since the signs often had a hermetic cast to them, and were especially suited for private interpretations, others were often unable to follow the implications of meaning. "I care not to associate myself with pee pee," one woman said in disgust as she left the room where Martin and I had been talking. Though I was unsure what she was talking about, I did eventually understand that she did not like to be around men and so probably considered us to be as tainted as urine. Others drew on similarly private systems of meaning, which usually left others bewildered. During a meeting of the men's "health group," in which a nurse was showing residents how to use condoms, Brian walked up to the doorway, stuck his head inside, and said, "I just want to say that I don't approve of prostitution or pornography in the Combat Zone."[10] He left, and the nurse and I looked at each other in bemused perplexity.

A fair amount of literature, devoted to what one book calls "the language of psychosis," tries to come to grips with the odd and heterogeneous speech patterns associated with schizophrenia.[11] The analyses either attend to the discourse of those considered schizophrenic as if they stood alone in the world, like characters in a Beckett novel, waiting to utter monologues to be assessed by clinicians and researchers, or examine how such discourse is understood (or not) by psychiatrists and therapists. Little is said, however, about what takes places when the "patients" return to their everyday social worlds, which are usually populated by family members or other patrons of a mental health care system. Keith Kernan and Sharon Sabsay recently noted that mentally handicapped individuals "continue to be studied solely as clinical entities, not as persons immersed in the stream of social life."[12] Much the same holds true for those considered mentally ill.

One evening Eva had something to say about the shelter's rocky stream of social life. Nathan was telling Helen and me about a "nonfiction novel" he aimed to write "about making it in the city today, not yesterday, you know what I mean?" Eva walked by, held out a cross at him for several seconds, then flicked her head as if snapping out of a reverie. "I thought you was a demon," she said. "I thought you was a demon! We don't understand one another. We don't *understand* one another!" Then she said, more to me than to Nathan, "We live in the same place, but we don't *know* one another. And that's how most arguments get started around here!" The rest of us looked on in confirming silence.

Words of course could mean different things for different people. The intention of the sender of a message might not converge with the interpretation of the receiver of that message. Indeed, often there was no mutual conversation, centered on a single, shared topic, but rather a hub of words that branched off into distinct corridors of meaning. These diverse lines of thought could swing around to other frames of reference from time to time. A pack of words would find a home in someone else's speech, but the meaning often picked up a different shading, and the talk would never settle into a single frame. At times, the two-ply conversations went on without much of a hitch. "You see, we need a good government," Ian said to Roy. "But Ian," Roy responded, "it would be righteous, right?" Both appeared satisfied with the import of the conversation, although the implications were different for each man: a civic discourse and a moral-religious discourse crossed paths, commented on one another in a momentary confluence of meaning, then continued on their merry ways.

Often, however, people got upset with certain statements. As I walked into the lobby one day, Rose was standing by the elevator, facing toward the benches, and shaking her fist at a man who was hanging around the lobby. "You're my brother, he's my brother, everyone's in my family, in a way," he was saying. "I ought to hit you right in the face!" Rose yelled, apparently peeved at the man's pitch for metaphoric brotherhood.

Confusions arose when the metaphoric was heard literally. "You're an angel," Wendy said to Nancy one afternoon as they sat in the lobby.

"I'm not an angel," Nancy said.

"You do *look* like an angel."

"No. I'm not."

They also arose when the literal was taken metaphorically. "Where's your cane?" Hector asked the usually cane-wielding Estelle as she hobbled through the lobby. "You shut your mouth!" she snapped back, then turned to me and said "He's talking very dirty!" Whereas Hector took the cane for what it literally denoted—an aid for walking—Estelle heard him use the word in a sexually suggestive way.

In turn, a steadfast commitment to a particular turn of language could create a standoff of meaning. "All good things come to an end," Estelle said to me while sitting on a bench in the lobby. "I heard all good things come to those who wait," said Larry, who was lying on the floor with hands supporting his head. "No sir! No sir! That's what my father used to say!" Estelle cried.

And the soliloquies, so common in the shelter, sometimes sparked tension, especially when another person found an interpersonal design in them. "Are you talking to me?" Fred asked Sam, who was talking to himself while seated at a table across from Fred. "No, I'm talking to myself. Jesus Christ!" Sam said. "Well, you're looking at me. Turn your head when you're talking!" Fred shot back. Since the intonations of a soliloquy could easily be mistaken for those found in a social conversation, Sam needed to make it clear—by not looking at Fred—that he was only talking to himself.

"Who?—What's Your Name?"

Although the shelter was very much founded in a conversation-based reality, the social life there was such that people enjoyed contact and quick exchanges with others but tended not to sit down and participate in extensive conversations. To "sit with" someone was to engage in a long and stationary conversation, usually while seated at a table in the common room or television room. More incidental socioeconomic exchanges typically took place on foot, which enabled one to "stand away," if necessary, when asking for things. Some preferred not to sit with others: "I don't sit with anyone," Peter said; "I don't like to sit," said another man. In general, talk was brief.

One reason people found it difficult to have a conversation with others is that one's companion could end up talking to herself. As Julie said, "Would you want to have a conversation with someone who is talking to themselves, who is caught up in their own conversation?" To be "caught up" in one's own conversation—or to respond to one's voices, which it often came down to—was to fail to acknowledge cultural conventions requiring that a person direct his or her speech to anyone attending to that speech.

"Do you want to sit here?" Susanne asked Greg one day as he passed by a table in the shelter where she was sitting, smoking a cigarette. Greg sat down without saying anything. Susanne began to talk to him, but the conversation soon ended in an allusive monologue on her part. Greg got up and left. Susanne watched him walk away, looked around the shelter, looked down, and stopped talking. Once Irving started a soliloquy while sitting on a bench next to Debra, a fortyish woman who had recently moved into the shelter. "There's a rich man," Irving said, "and there's a poor man. A rich man has a false pretense. . . . A secret of a Greek cannot be known." Debra nodded her head at first but later appeared to be uncomfortable with Irving's continuous monologue. She stood up and walked away after finishing her cigarette.

As Erving Goffman notes, people constantly engage in and acknowledge acts of being together or "with" one or more social beings, as when two or more people stand off to the side of a party and talk.[1] The residents did so as well, but sometimes an interpersonal "with" would suddenly switch into a situation in which a person was only with himself. Greg apparently took Susanne's question as an invitation to form a "with" with her. But when she fell back into a monologue in which he could not readily participate, he got up and left. Debra did much the same when she first (mis)took Irving's commentary as one to which she was expected to respond—which was an easy thing to do, given how "conversational" his words were in rhythm and tenor—then found that he was simply talking to himself. While Debra was uncomfortable with the situation, perhaps because it was a relatively new one to her, veterans of the shelter simply got used to it, although they did bemoan the state of things. "People here, talking to themselves, it's hard to have three conversations at the same time," Irving once told me. The idea of three conversations at once is noteworthy because it suggests that in many verbal exchanges between two people in the shelter there was a conversation between the two but also a side conversation that each person held on his own.

Another reason for the brevity of conversations was that residents often found it difficult to follow them through. One had to deal with the perceived moodiness of others, the occurrence of diverse planes of meaning, the tendency of some to talk to themselves, and the unaccounted for violation of commonly accepted maxims of cooperative conversation (such as "be relevant," "avoid obscurity of expression," "avoid ambiguity," "be brief," and "be orderly").[2] All this made the "mutual tuning-in relationship" that Alfred Schutz deemed essential to communication difficult to sustain at times.[3] People tuned out as much as they tuned in. In general, the risks of confusions, disputes, standoffs, and mis- or re-interpretations led some to keep conversations to a minimum. When Joey told me that he felt safe as long as he was in the building, he continued to talk to me at length although I was unable to follow all of his prolix allusions and references. He might have noticed my confusion because he suddenly shifted gears and said, "I get into trouble talking to people. I can get them mad somehow. So I figure I shouldn't talk to people." "But you get along with me," I said. "Yeah, I do, I do. I figure I should keep with people my own size, you know. My own size."

People relied on a range of makeshift efforts in conversing with people. While some kept to their own political size or preferred to talk with those who worked within the same plane of meaning, some tried to find something in common to talk about: "See," Debra said to Larry one afternoon soon after she moved into the shelter. "We have something to talk about. We both play the numbers. We see each other on the same street, doing the same thing, looking for numbers." Others kept to themselves. Julie, for instance, seemed to enjoy being around others and having quick exchanges with them but did not care much for extensive conversations. "Yes, we've talked from time to time," she said when I asked if she knew a certain person. Her response implied the idea that, beyond recognizing someone visually, to really know someone was to talk with that person more than once.

For the most part, people like Julie, Wendy, and Fred talked from time to time, but seldom got into extensive conversations with each other. Something of the nature of communication was evident when people sat down in the cafeteria to eat dinner: people tended to sit apart from one another; those who sat at the same table usually kept silent or occasionally exchanged a few words. There were also times when people did not want to talk at all. A common way to refrain from interacting with others was to go off by oneself, seeking refuge in the plaza or in one of the building's nooks or crannies. Others blocked off the constant patter—and at times diminished the strength of "the voices" they heard— by listening to walkman radios for hours on end.

Some sought the company of others in communal silence. "Can we just sit here quiet-like for a while?" asked Eva after I tried to strike up a conversation. She had joined me at a table one evening when she was feeling "kind of nervous tired." Greg, who was usually very quiet ("I sit on the couch, by myself. That's okay," he told me when I asked how he spent his time), was apparently also searching for quietude one afternoon when he stepped into the television room and looked around as if to see whether any garrulous or unnerving neighbors were there.

Finding that only Tommy, a taciturn presence like himself, and I were there, he sat down on one of the cushioned seats. "Do you want a cigarette?" Tommy asked. "Yeah, thanks," Greg said. Both sat and smoked and watched television without further exchanges.

Greg's wariness and taciturnity were apparently related to the nervousness he sometimes felt when conversing with others. A few weeks before he was to move into a house provided by the housing project, I asked him how the rent would be taken care of. Ralph, who was passing by at the moment, overheard my question and shouted over, "It's a *big* mistake to share rent with others!" On hearing this Greg appeared to grow nervous. He lit a cigarette, kept his head down, and knotted his fingers in Ralph's direction.

The staff, in attending to nervousness of this sort, tried to create specific, ritualized frames of interaction with a few residents who were acutely anxious around others. Once a week a staff member would play a few rounds of Trivial Pursuit with Colin, an elderly man who spent most of his time alone and was, I was told, extremely paranoid. While asking each other trivia questions from the stack of cards that came with the game, they would discuss issues in Colin's life, such as doctors he had seen, medications he had taken, and how his week was going. From what I gathered, the meetings constituted one of the most substantial face-to-face interactions Colin had each week.

Residents likewise interacted with each other in ways that engaged a measure of mutuality, affection, and intimacy. One day Hector went up to Wendy, who was seated on a bench in the lobby, and silently held her hand for a half a minute. He let go, walked outside the building, and laughed. She stayed where she was and began to smoke a cigarette.

A few days later Fred sat down in the lobby next to Wendy and patted her on the back. "Hi, Wendy," he said.

"Hi Fred. How ya doing?"

"I love you," Fred said endearingly.

"I love you, too," Wendy said with a laugh, but appeared a bit uncertain about the closeness. She got up and left.

Sometimes, however, it wasn't worth the effort to try to converse with someone. One afternoon Simone walked out of the women's dorm, saw me, said "Hello," and sat down across from me at the table. I asked how things were going for her. "Not so good. As good as they can be in this place," she said.

Nancy appeared and sat down with us at the table. She looked at Simone, and said, "Who?—What's your name?"

Simone opened her mouth as if to speak, paused, then said, "Never mind."

"Oh."

After a few seconds of silence Nancy turned to me and said, "I lost my mind. Do you think you could get it back for me?"

"No," I said, disappointed that I could not talk more with Simone. "I don't think I could do that."

Simone watched me, perhaps to see how I would respond to the interruption, then got up and left. Nancy continued to look at me.

Most of the literature on language suggests that people living in the same community or society inhabit the same linguistic and semiotic reality. While this may be true in many situations, it was not the case in the shelter. Life there involved distinct semiotic systems, different planes and intensities of meaning, distinct lines and possibilities of interpretation, different speeds, and thus, to an extent, different realities, ways of being, and orientations to time and space. People spoke different languages, some as metaphoric as Shakespeare's Sonnets, some as literalist as a *Nouveau Roman*, some as speedy as Kleist's stories, some as semantically compressed as Keats's *Odes*, and some as seemingly impenetrable as Joyce's *Finnegans Wake*. The differences in linguistic orientations were yet another reason that the shelter was not a place to make friends or to form political alliances. Some people got stuck in a certain plane of meaning. Some, like Richard and Peter, were known for speaking a certain way and so acquired identities founded on the way they spoke to others. Some shifted gears by chance, in accordance with how well they felt, with the force of their medications, with whom they were talking, or with the pragmatics and politics of a conversation. Often there were moments of miscomprehension, bewilderment, and isolation. Interruptions, false starts, deadends, abrupt departures, and other situational improprieties marked many exchanges. Conversations were difficult to follow through on; people had a tough time cueing into what others said. Sometimes it was simply not worth the effort, as when Simone said "Never mind" when Nancy falteringly asked her, "Who?—What's your name?"

"We're Losing Him, Sam"

As with my exchanges with Simone and Nancy, I found that I was often engaged in two or more conversations at once—for instance, talking to Richard, responding to Simone's request for change to buy a cup of coffee, and watching Helen show me what she bought at a store. People would vie for my attention. One day I found myself in the lobby conversing with Larry about the rules of the shelter, and at the same time with Stuart about where the best free meals in Boston could be found. "Stop interrupting," Larry said to Stuart. "*I'm* talking to him," Stuart countered. The conversations continued simultaneously, with each man trying to be "with" me, and me trying to respond to both. In general, when a staff person or I was present, conversations tended to involve several concurrent dialogues rather than a collaborative discussion: they were V-shaped rather than triangular. Residents often relied on members of the staff (or me) as communicant and translator because it was expedient to do so. A third often mediated between a first and a second.

At the various "placement group meetings" I attended, for instance, many were reluctant to speak on their own. Due to the lack of conversational patter, Lisa, the staff person who ran the meetings, needed to lead the way. Quite often there were several conversations going on at once, with her involved in each one, and no two residents talking together for any length of time. Helen regularly attended these meetings before she moved into an apartment of her own. At one meeting she sat next to Nhor, who, although he had moved into a group home some months before, disliked the place and wanted to get an apartment of his own. "Where's he living?" Helen asked Lisa of Nhor, even though she was sitting next to Nhor and could have asked him directly. "You see how they don't ask each other questions directly?" Lisa asked me afterward. Information sometimes had to flow through the circuitry of the staff.

In fact, many conversations between residents and staff (or me) involved only two people, even if there were three or more people present. Lisa would have one conversation with Helen while talking at the same time with Nhor. To fight this tendency, however, she and other staff members tried to create a more communal, interlocutionary space by getting people to join in on a shared and mutually understood conversation—particularly during group meetings, when different planes of meaning and lines of thought advanced simultaneously. They also tried to get people to speak more clearly as well as to avoid going on about things, carrying on in monologues with themselves, or speaking too quickly, too slowly, too loudly, or too softly. One day, for instance, Joanne, a recruiter for the housing project, gathered a few residents together to talk about the project. When Larry cut into the conversation, Joanne said, "Larry, you have to learn how to participate in a group. If someone else is talking, you don't. Okay?" On another occasion Lisa held a "housing meeting" to discuss potential options with several residents. Joey joined this meeting and soon began to talk about the kind of place he would like, but in a ragtime idiom that I found hard to follow. Lisa also appeared to have difficulty understanding because she said "I'm not following you" on several occasions; this had the effect of redirecting Joey's stream of words. Stuart, who sat and smoked a cigarette throughout the meeting, spoke about his concerns a few minutes later. He also relied on highly figurative speech. Lisa listened to him for a while, then turned to Sam, seated to her right, and said in a jovial way, "We're losing him, Sam." Sam nodded his head and Stuart rambled on, but now more clearly to himself, until someone else broached a new topic.

Lisa's statements reflected several concerns. Many social theorists, particularly those concerned with the methods of everyday life, have spoken of intersubjectivity—the plane of meaning or consciousness shared between separate minds—as the hallmark of human social life.[1] In the shelter, however, intersubjectivity was not an intrinsic aspect of social discourse but something that needed to be constantly striven for. It could not necessarily be counted on in the course of an interaction. People could speak, mean, listen, and interpret in "their own individual way," as Julie might say. Some held onto utterly private visions and spoke at times in unique, monologic languages comprehensible to themselves alone. In general, many residents lived in altogether subjective worlds that were noteworthy for their intense constancy of concerns and purposes. Nancy, for instance, spoke continuously of having lost her mind, Richard wanted to "touch" people as much as he could, Brian kept to a strict routine of pacing and tea-drinking, Sylvia found she was unable to touch or look at people without hurting them, and Anthony was forever bent on trying to make a few bucks.

These and other orientations to life involved distinct strands of space, time, and meaning, as well as disparate possibilities for interpersonal contact and understanding. People participating in the "same" social interaction thus often had different concerns, which made for diverse subjectivities and phenomenal worlds more than they did for a solid and lasting plane of intersubjectivity. Residents often adjusted their speech and social stances to repair rifts or gaps in understandings with others. As a rule, it was important to work in "international waters" and try to find some common ground when speaking with another. But just as often a mutual attunement failed to take form. As many of the conversations quoted above suggest, people were often at a loss to understand another's meaning, or they heard things differently than they were intended.

Staff members often acted in ways that promoted a world of socially shared meanings and understandings, as if there were too many disparate subjectivities and not enough intersubjectivity in the shelter. One way they tried to counteract the multiplicity of meanings and subjectivities was by establishing and encouraging the conscious awareness of a single time that residents and staff alike could share, understand, and abide by. The routines of the shelter helped to convey a sense of co-evality, of people living in the same age or time. The routines were something that could be counted on, in both senses of the word: people could count the different hours and times of a day, and they could rely on the steady and unchanging pacing of those times. The clocks and routines seemed objective: they meant the same thing to everyone (the shelter opened always and *for everyone* at 3:30 in the afternoon). The routines were also constructed interactively, with staff and residents doing things together (such as distributing and taking medications, or running the token store) or agreeing on the passage of time. Doing time together or collaborating on its reckoning implied a shared orientation to the world at large. In order to get on in the shelter, people needed to mind the clock. In minding the clock, they participated in a shared field of consciousness.

These efforts recall the "therapeutics of movement" employed by eighteenth-century French physicians, in which manics and melancholiacs were made to walk, exercise, and move about in order to fall in step with the workaday world. As Foucault notes, the regular movements appealed to the mad to "return to the world, to entrust oneself to its wisdom by returning to one's place in the general order of things, thus forgetting madness, which is the moment of pure subjectivity."[2] Building on similar assumptions, many modern therapies and "therapeutic environments" encourage the overly subjective to realign themselves with the timings and shared truths of others. In the shelter, one of the staff's main tasks was to keep people from going or remaining "crazy," a state of mind which, for staff and residents alike, often meant living in a world significantly and sometimes painfully at odds with the world of others.

Staff members tried to develop mutually shared meanings and understandings, as Lisa did at her housing meeting. By saying "I'm not following you" to people speaking at the meeting, Lisa made them think twice about how they were communicating. The implied message was that their words could not be understood; they were overly personal and insufficiently intersubjective in meaning. To be "followed," one needed to heed the rules of conversation and make oneself understood to one's audience. And by saying "We're losing him, Sam" when Stuart was speaking, Lisa indirectly told Stuart that he was drifting unmoored in a sea of meanings. Her statement thus announced the need to bring Stuart back into a more intersubjective plane of meaning; "he" had to be brought back into the orbit of "we." In addition, the statement, couched in the sense of a communal "we," probably carried a stronger moral import and sense of social regard than her earlier, more dyadic statement, "I'm not following you": his meaning was lost to more than one person; residents as well as staff could not follow him; communally shared, intersubjective meanings were worth striving for. As Lisa made clear, the "we" included Sam—and, by association, others at the meeting—who were also at risk of drifting away, especially if they could not follow Stuart's meanings. Yet by casting her observation in a gerundive present (saying "We're losing him" rather than "We've lost him"), her words suggested that there was still time for Stuart to mend his ways as well for the group to bring him back. At the same time, the focus on the present situation underscored the coevality implicit in mutual comprehension. Stuart was failing to make himself understood at that moment, a moment shared—Lisa implied—by her, Sam, and others. If he (or anyone else, for that matter) was to make more sense, he would need to be aware of a vivid present. The statements thus worked to anchor all involved in the same world of time and meaning, although in the end Stuart's speech became even more monological.

Reasonable Reasonableness

The efforts of Lisa and other staff members to get their guests to talk and act in certain ways, as well as the staff's approach to language, time, and action in general, reflected their professional responsibilities and approaches to care.

Staff members like Lisa, Bill, Peggy, and Ray needed to act on several fronts at once in order to carry out their duties and serve the best interests of their guests. In working for an agency of the state, they were responsible for the proper care of those staying in the shelter and so could be held accountable for any inappropriate handling of their responsibilities. This meant they had to work within the guidelines authorized by the Department of Mental Health, provide a safe and therapeutic environment for the shelter residents, and maintain accurate daily records of their guests' whereabouts, problems, and behaviors. The status of staff members' jobs (including promotions or raises) largely depended on their ability and willingness to carry out these responsibilities, which entailed several activities and understandings. The staff understood that the residents' main concerns were to keep off the streets, to keep their health problems to a minimum, and to stay in a place that made finding work and employment a feasible option. They tried in good faith to facilitate these efforts. They also understood that they were dealing with a population that was prone to poor mental health. To lessen any paranoia and nervousness, and to prevent episodes of psychosis or "decompensation" when a person's psychological integrity collapsed, they tried to instill an atmosphere of safety, trust, and stability by acting in consistent, sincere, and fair ways and by maintaining a smoothly running schedule of activities. The staff also found that if residents were to live safer, healthier, and more fulfilling lives they would need to learn a number of skills: to take a more active stance in life, to hold down a job, to manage money better, to find and keep a place to live, to conduct tasks such as cooking, cleaning, and shopping, to maintain lasting social ties with others, to stay clear of nonprescription drugs and the excessive use of alcohol, to prevent others from taking advantage of them (financially, sexually, or psychologically), and to be able to make their way about the city without undue fear or nervousness. To help residents achieve these goals, the staff advanced a therapeutic agenda that encouraged people to act and think in terms of self-industry, responsibility, sociability, and independence.

The agenda, which was realized through explicit protocols and everyday practices and interactions, drew from two moral domains integral to mainstream American culture. One was the culture of therapy, in which people tried to improve the physical, psychic, and social well-being of themselves or others both by creating a healthy environment and by changing the penchant to think or act in certain, usually ill-fated, ways.[1] The other was the culture of capitalism, in which individuals, families, or corporations tried to advance their economic and social status by increasing their capital and resources and by acting and thinking in ways that would ensure them a better economic future. The culture of therapy existed because of the understanding that the residents, like many people in psychiatric hospitals and out-patient mental health clinics, were in need of therapeutic care. The culture of capitalism was present because of the idea that those staying in the shelter needed to learn how to work, to hold down jobs, and to manage their finances better. The latter idea was a powerful one in the 1980s and early 1990s, when popular and political sentiment moved away from the Welfare State understanding that the down-and-out were entitled to health care, food and clothing, and decent housing, to the neo-Victorian assumption that poor folk were responsible for their poverty and were thus in dire need of moral "reform."[2] With this "remoralization of poverty," which focused more attention on changing the poor as individuals than on revamping the economic and political system that spawned impoverishment, social and governmental services like homeless shelters often entailed ideas of "rehabilitation" and spiritual and economic guidance.[3]

The two sets of concerns were not necessarily separate in spirit or practical implications, and so tended to blend into each other in the shelter, making for a kind of therapeutic capitalism. Both fed into general ideas of well-being and proper ways to live as well as culturally patterned assumptions that people could, in fact, improve themselves. As staff members saw it, a person's health and economic status were inherently interrelated. Since it was their job to improve the health and economic status of their guests, there was a strong therapeutic line inherent in many of their interactions with residents. "You don't run my life!" said a relatively new resident to Peggy, a psychiatric nurse on the staff, as I walked into the shelter one day. "We want you to live in such a way that you're not hurting yourself or others," the nurse replied. The idea that the staff wanted residents to "live in such a way that . . ." was ubiquitous, though often it was only implied. Staff members tried to improve the residents' welfare by fashioning new ways of acting and living, and so were constantly anticipating future possibilities and new, improved selves. Residents, who wanted most to feel "like their old selves" again, were inclined to locate models of well-being in the past, before they fell ill. Since they understood their problems to relate not to any ill-conceived orientations to time, labor, or money but to the ailments with which they were saddled, they were preoccupied more with lessening or exorcising those ailments than with heeding the staff's advice.

Staff members were comfortable telling their guests what to do—when and why they should take medications, for instance, or where they should look for housing. The staff also set the rules for the shelter autocratically in that they decided on new rules and then announced them at "mandatory" group meetings between staff and residents. Their authority sometimes irked residents. During one meeting, the manager introduced a new rule for cleaning up after oneself, saying that no one would be able to bring food into the shelter unless all the tables remained clean. "You ain't bringing it up diplomatically. You ain't asking us. You're telling us!" responded Ralph. After the meeting he told me, "The staff can say anything, but the so-called guests can't." Able to tell their guests what to do, members of the staff were secure in their power. One day Susanne responded to the staff's assertion of rules on some matter by saying, "There's an overload of authority here. None of you are qualified!" Her point, I took it, was that while no staff member was qualified on his or her own, together they formed a heavy burden of authority.[4]

Susanne's reading of the staff's power, in which the sum was greater than its parts, hinted at one of the linguistic dimensions of that power: the staff often spoke as a collective, parental "we." Peggy's use of "we" when talking with Jackson, even though she was the only staff member at the desk at that time, both pointed to and legitimated the authoritative stance of the shelter staff (residents in turn relied on the third person plural to refer to the staff). This stance was reinforced through the staff's actions. In the course of each month, the staff held meetings, wrote notes, had conversations, and drew up various "treatment plans" for the care and improvement of residents. Different opinions were voiced through these exchanges, and staff members would argue about how to proceed with a certain person or situation. Once they decided on a course of action, however, they worked together as a single, unified front, in part because they found it therapeutically and bureaucratically necessary to maintain and promote a climate of consistency, stability, and fairness. Most actions were systemic and rooted in collective agreements.

The "we-ness" that characterized the staff's actions was lacking for residents: I rarely heard staff members refer to shelter residents as "they"; each resident was indexed as a distinct person. Residents referred to themselves more in the first person singular than in the first person plural. A sense of a "we" pointed and contributed to the staff's systemic actions; a sense of an "I" pointed and contributed to an isolated agent that went his or her own way. The authority of "we" was thrown into relief when staff members assumed other stances in talking to their guests; at times, for example, they spoke in more personal terms about the weather or the kinds of food they preferred. But this amiable talk underscored the political thrust of other, more assertive phrasings, in which the staff encouraged residents to act in certain ways. A set of subtle linguistic and semantic markers (such as the explicit or implicit use of "we," certain tones of voice, and the act of standing with clipboard in hand or behind the staff desk) framed these wordings. Members of the staff, able to tell their guests what to do, were secure in their power and knowledgeable about what they could or could not do. They often spoke to their guests in commanding terms, as a few of the nurse's directives suggest:

"Lock up your cigarettes," Peggy told Brian when he arrived with a new carton of cigarettes. "When people see you carrying them around, they're all gonna want some."

"Is it time to eat?" Stuart asked Peggy just after five o'clock. "Yes, so put some socks on," she answered.

Simone walked up to the desk one day and said something in a loud voice, which I could not make out. "Simone," Peggy said, "count to ten and speak softer, so I can understand you."

"Stuart, will you stop mumbling?!" Peggy said when Stuart was talking to himself. "I really don't enjoy that. Stuart, you gotta learn to speak to people directly."

Staff often linked these statements (via an explicit or implicit conjunction such as "because") to an extrasituational logic that went beyond the immediate concerns at hand. It often entailed questions of principle, foresight, and reason rather than just the necessities of the moment:

put some socks on *because* it is time to eat; stop mumbling *because* you have to learn to speak to people directly; lock up your cigarettes *because* people will want some; take your time and speak softer so that, in general, people can understand you.

Elements of this extrasituational logic were played out one day when Wendy, Lisa, and I were sitting and talking at a table. Wendy picked up a half-smoked cigarette left by someone else in an ashtray and lit it with a match.

"You're not going to smoke that, are you?" Lisa asked in disbelief.

"Yeah, I am," Wendy said with a quick laugh.

"I really don't think you should smoke that. You don't know who's been smoking that before you. You could get sick or something."

"But it's just one cigarette."

"Am I making myself clear on how I feel about that?"

"Yeah," Wendy said, and puffed on the snipe.

We went on to discuss other topics.

In trying to prevent Wendy from smoking the cigarette, Lisa practiced the kind of "spontaneous philosophy" that, Antonio Gramsci noted, is regularly reflected in our language, "common sense," and "ways of seeing things and of acting."[5] Lisa wanted to make it clear, for the record, how she felt, which turned a single event into an exemplar with schematic connotations. She related the present to both the past ("You don't know who's been smoking that before you") and the future ("You could get sick or something") in order to spell out the reasons Wendy should not inhale.

Through the telos of this consequential temporality, in which a person's actions in the present were understood to bear consequences, the staff instructed and encouraged residents to anticipate and plan for the future. "You need to make plans, like a Christmas list," Jay, a staff member, said at a meeting of the men's health group in outlining how to improve their lives; he then added, "But you need to be realistic in your goals." For the staff, a focus on being methodical and "realistic" worked to counter the penchants of residents for minding the day at hand, spending their money all too quickly, drifting rudderlessly through time, and dreaming up unreachable goals. In general, they plotted temporal, narrative-like orientations that promoted ideas of causality, reliability, foresight, calculation, and responsibility.

These and other values colored the uses of language. In telling residents to speak clearly and directly, to lower their voices, or to make sure people were following them when they spoke, the staff advanced a way of thinking about language that came close to an ideology dominant in many contemporary English-speaking societies which gives priority to the referential, semantic, and propositional functions of language, with the primary purpose of language understood to be to mean or refer to something rather than, say, to work as a medium of social action.[6] In terms echoing the monoglot Standard English in North America, which, as Michael Silverstein observes, valorizes uniformity, clarity of expression, and supposedly truthful referentiality, the staff's state-driven aesthetics of speaking centered on the value of clarity, propriety, communication, and intersubjectivity.[7] One should speak clearly and quietly, the staff advised, preferably in straightforward terms, without being rude or loud or incomprehensible, and one should communicate to others rather than simply talk or mumble to oneself. Much of the staff's orientation to language related to the immediate and distant audiences of that language. Staff members usually had at least two groups in mind when they spoke: the residents of the shelter (who were often directly involved in the particular situation) and the decision makers in the mental health care system (who regularly assessed their work with the residents).[8] The referential aspect of language dominated in a world characterized by therapeutic mandates and bureaucratic concerns for accountability, efficacy, predictability, and reliability.[9]

A sense of sincerity came with these priorities. Shelter personnel and other DMH employees said that they as well as residents should "walk what they talk," that is, follow through on what they said. An effort to walk what one talked pointed to an important distinction between the two activities. Words alone could not do the work of actions; promising something did not necessarily mean following through on that promise. In the best of worlds there was a felicitous congruence between words and actions. Speech-acts on their own did not count for much. Words should indicate or lead to action rather than be taken simply as actions. Since direct and transparent communication made the staff's jobs easier (how could you monitor or care for someone whom you could not "follow"?), the residents were also expected to be sincere. "The more 'sincere' I am," Roland Barthes finds, "the more interpretable I am."[10] Please be sincere, please be interpretable, the message seemed to say, so that we can do our work well and so that you can be well as well.

In effect, the staff tried to launch a world ruled by thirdness. For Peirce, the category of thirdness, in contrast to those of firstness or secondness, is heavily concerned with habit and lawlike generalities. In consisting of the mediation of relations between firsts and seconds, thirdness implies a mix of habit, purpose, continuity, morality, and reasonableness; it involves a "directive tendency" that guides and influences habitual and lawlike (but flexible) modes of behavior. Thirdness integrates, synthesizes, moderates, anticipates, regulates, guides, and begets "sympathy."

Residents and staff alike acted in terms of habit, routine, and purposive action. But the nature of the thirdness was different for each, as if two distinct cultures were involved. Residents arranged their lives largely in terms of a thirdness of secondness, of struggling along, in which the principles of distraction, brute shocks and surprises, frail conversations, and hanging in there ruled the day. The staff, less encumbered with secondness and wedded to a philosophy of therapeutic care, advanced a thirdness of thirdness, in which the principles of habit, foresight, abstract calculation, and reasonableness reigned. Make it a habit to be habitual, the staff advised, and make it a rule to follow rules. For Peirce, "action is second, but conduct is third."[11] The residents faced a world of action and reaction, and occasionally sought refuge from this world in firstness. The staff, trying to remedy what ailed their guests, found that residents would be better served if they lived in a world of conduct wherein they were consistent, reliable, and purposeful for the sake of being consistent, reliable, and purposeful.

The staff's orientations to time tied into such thirdlike reasonableness. According to Peirce, firstness involves mere potentials and therefore is pretemporal; it is generative of time, but not, ideally, in time. Secondness, meanwhile, refers to interruptions, individual events, and actual facts in a rudimentary before and after, and thus is temporal in a binary sense. It is the predominant character of what *has been* done.[12] As Corrington puts it, "past and present obtain in the domain of secondness, but the future remains mute."[13] Thirdness, in turn, is the domain of genuine tridimensional temporality: "The full power of the future only emerges with thirdness. With the rise of thirdness, time becomes fully actualized."[14] Thirdness consists of mediated relations between first and seconds; with such mediation comes comparison, habit, generality, synthesis, purpose, and continuity. Thirdness, often involving for Peirce a "consciousness that binds our life together," "goes beyond actual instances, without which it would have no existence, to signify still other conceivable instances to which it may refer in the future."[15]

These themes coursed through the staff's arrangements of time, from the focus on habit and purpose in the shelter's shipboard beat of routine tasks to the narrative air of synthesis, purpose, and continuity in events past, present, and future. Lisa's response to the snipe that Wendy picked up and smoked reflected this synthetic air. While Wendy was conscious of the object in ad hoc, empirical terms as "just one cigarette," Lisa wanted to go beyond the actual instance of the cigarette in order to signify calmly and rationally other conceivable instances.

Peirce notes that "reasonable reasonableness is thirdness as thirdness."[16] In step with many other American citizens, institutions, and businesses, the staff's approach to thought and action was one of reasonable reasonableness. The orientations to time, language, knowledge, and money inherent in such reasonings bore more affinities with the institutional workings of City Hall or the Bank of Boston than with the residents' focus on barter, ragtime, and the day and cigarette at hand. Genuinely concerned with the residents' predicaments, staff members wanted their guests to live in such a way that they might leave the world of the latter and successfully join the world of the former. Since this other, more mainstream and dominant world was grounded in the kind of sober, methodical, instrumental rationality that Max Weber found to be integral to the capitalist, bureaucratic orders of the modern West, residents had to learn how to be more reasonable if they were to live more fully in it.[17] Any "rehabilitation" attempted came down to a dismissal of the resident's habitual routines and the inculcation of the staff's own brand of habits.

Tactics, Questions, Rhetoric

Like Wendy, who ignored Lisa and maintained the singular over the general ("It's just one cigarette"), residents did not always heed the staff's advice because it did not always ring true to them.[1] While the staff's views were quite potent, residents moved in different circles, primarily because they were in a position at odds with and defined in opposition to that of the staff. The kinds of words staff members and residents relied on, the way in which they used those words, and their reasons for doing so followed more often than not from the political exigencies of their lives.

A distinction Michel de Certeau draws between "strategies" and "tactics" helps to explain how and why residents tended to think, act, and talk in ways distinct from staff members. For de Certeau, the difference between strategies and tactics hinges on the spatial and organizational capacities of different social actors.[2] While strategies, which belong to the powerful, imply a proper and durable locus that enables a person, group, or institution to "keep to itself, at a distance, in a position of withdrawal, foresight, and self-collection," tactics are "an art of the weak."[3] A tactic is determined by the absence of power as much as a strategy is organized by the postulation of power. Without a proper locus that would provide the conditions necessary for autonomy and sustainable planning, tacticians must resort to isolated actions, various tricks and ruses, and the "good and bad tricks of rhetoric."[4]

The position of staff members in the shelter was defined by a proper locus in spatial and bureaucratic terms. Their relative political might, their mandate to house, feed, and protect the shelter's guests, and the fact that they could be held accountable for any inappropriate handling of their responsibilities occasioned a concerted, strategic orientation toward care—as suggested by their unified front, their aura of "we-ness," their focus on making "plans," and their systemic orientation toward time, space, language, and action. In contrast to what de Certeau's model would lead us to expect, however, the strategies did not involve a singular political status but rather an interlocking set of political, economic, and humanitarian concerns.

The political actions of residents, in contrast, were often tactical in nature. Lacking a proper locus, sufficient financial means, and any feasible place to stay outside of the shelter, they had little spatial, political, or economic ground on which to stand. They did not have the means to keep to themselves, to remain at a distance, or to maintain a position of withdrawal, foresight, or self-collection. To get something done they depended less on a concerted philosophy of action and knowledge than on timely opportunities, various tricks and ruses, and other nomadic actions. Since there was little opportunity for them to maintain a unified front—in fact, there was no tangible forum in which they could do so during my time at the shelter—the actions of shelter guests were less homogeneous and less systematic than the actions of staff members.

For the most part, shelter residents would have liked to have had what the staff wanted for each of them—a steady job, an apartment of their own, and a better life—and did make efforts toward these goals. But they often met with frustrating disappointments, finding that nothing much ever changed, or they lost their jobs and their places and ended up back on the street. Residents also had to contend with a gamut of more pressing concerns and thus devoted much of their energy to the practical affairs of shelter life. When staying in the shelter residents commonly wanted several things. They wanted enough cigarettes to last the day or at least to quench an hour's craving and they wanted enough money to last the week or month (until the next SSI check arrived), or at least to get them something to eat or drink. They preferred not to go hungry or to be without anything they really needed or desired. At times they desperately wanted someone with whom they could talk; at others they desired nothing more than to be alone. At times they wanted nothing to do with staff; they were bothered by the staff's constant requests and instructions and would have liked to do as they pleased. At others, they wanted the staff to attend to a problem or complaint. They also tried to stay clear of conflicts with staff or residents—unless they wanted to "mix things up a bit," as Richard once put it. Conflicts did arise when people wanted different things, and an undertow of tension marked many interactions. People traded what they had for what they wanted in an economy of needs and desires.

Rhetoric and indirection were integral to these efforts, for people tried to persuade others to do what they wanted them to do. Residents lacked the authority of their caretakers and so could not accomplish much through direct requests or commands.[5] They therefore relied on indirect, less declarative phrasings that often involved subtle or obvious rhetorical forms. Residents, unlike staff, found that talking *was* acting. To get things with words, residents would beg, plead, cajole, insult, insist, threaten, sweet talk, ask, or bemoan.

As for pleading, sometimes an air of desperation worked just as well as loftiness. For instance, whenever a resident like Simone walked by, Alice would ask, "Simone, give me a cigarette, please? Come on, come on!" She might get one or not, but since she appeared friendly and ineffective, she did not offend many of her patrons.

As for insisting, sometimes being more forceful could do the trick. "Irving owes me money," Debra told me just before Irving left the shelter, "but he's leaving tomorrow. And I haven't seen any money yet. He's doing it just because I'm a woman. Maybe if I was more insistent." She eventually got her money back, but only after several patient reminders.

As for insults, a few cross words were sometimes used in an attempt to "move" people, if that was the intention. "You smell," Susanne said to Anthony, who was sitting with her at a table. Susanne waited for a few seconds, got up, walked into the television room, came back, and sat down at another table.

Threats were sometimes worth a try, but often they did not do the trick, especially when directed toward staff. One day around six o'clock, Fred was banished to the lobby for an hour for "acting inappropriately." When Fred walked into the shelter around six-thirty, Bill, the staff member working the desk at that time, told him he had to stay out until seven. "Oh, knock it off," Fred said, "you don't want me to get like I was before, do you, or you'll be in trouble." He then left the shelter and did not return until after seven.

As for sweet talk, making "friends" could work, now or later, in one's favor. Billy, streetwise and new to the shelter, offered a cigarette to Sam, a gruff veteran of the place. "Here you go, my friend," Billy said. "Only if you can afford it," said Sam as he snatched the cigarette and walked off.

None of these actions were overly effective. Alice often failed to bum a cigarette, Debra could not be sure if her insistence would be successful, Susanne's insult did not get her very far, Fred's threat held little weight, Billy's friendly words had to be backed by a cigarette, and Sam's "friendship" wouldn't come cheap. Since a great deal depended on the situation at hand, the gambits were not certain to succeed. Nevertheless, a range of tactical abilities characterized the residents' willful actions.

Asking questions, for example, was a weak art, but it was often the only way to gain or to effect something. In contrast to staff, residents did more "asking" than "telling." Among residents, questions were a key stroke in the song and dance. The questions hinged on the dialogic, economic, and contractual dimensions of many exchanges (verbal or otherwise) and the lack of a solid political footing. Since residents were rarely in a position to demand anything or tell others what to do, they often asked indirectly.

"Is anybody leaving soon?" Eva, a veteran of the shelter system, asked one evening as she stepped into the television room, which was populated at that moment by five residents and me. The six of us who were sitting on the half-moon couch remained silent. I looked to the others to see if they might respond, then said, "I may be getting up in a few minutes, Eva." Eva ignored my response and repeated her question. "I know what she means! I know what she means!" Nina said in a spirited tone, then moved to her left a bit. "Here's a warm spot right here," she said and patted the cushion beside her.

During my stay in the shelter I lacked some of the finer skills that helped the residents to act, speak, and interpret appropriately; while I responded to the literal, surface claims of Eva's question, Nina quickly latched onto the language game that she was playing (which was not always an easy thing to do, given the multitude of semiotic registers in the shelter). As with many forms of rhetoric, the words had the effect of "moving" someone—in this case Nina, to make room for Eva.[6]

Other questions asked by residents carried less tangible motives. Ideally, they could invoke certain sentiments on the part of the audience; the movement in question was emotional. Early one evening Nina and I were talking to each other while seated on the benches in the lobby. Carla, who had been sitting in a corner for some time, came over and asked, "Where can we go to be by ourselves, to get away from other people's conversations? Is there a place we can go? Because there's no place to go where we can be alone. I don't want to keep hearing people's conversations. Like yous two, but I have to, and the noise from here to here." She gestured toward the lobby, and then toward the shelter, into which she walked.

I doubt that Carla was trying to get Nina and me to leave the lobby; we also had no other place to go. Nor do I think that she expected an easy answer to her questions. Asked so as to produce an effect, they had a rhetorical force but one that was less tangible than Eva's inquiry. With its invocation of pity, identification between speaker and audience, and call for an active response, Carla's oratory would surely have satisfied Aristotle's requirements for the *techne* of rhetorical persuasion.[7] Carla had no place to go to be alone and was forced to keep hearing people's conversations (in which, perhaps significantly, she was not a participant). Asking unanswerable questions hammered that discomforting point home.

That Carla laced many of her conversations with questions of this sort points to how rhetorical forms could entail a way of being in the world. It was as if this was Carla's approach to the world; she translated a lack of feasible options into a passively anxious linguistic stance. The best she could do was to ask questions that through their very form said something about why this was the best she could do. Sometimes the pitch of the rhetoric made so much sense and came so naturally that one asked rhetorical questions of oneself. One evening Sylvia told me about how she had spent much of her time before coming to the shelter walking around Boston, Cambridge, and Arlington. "I saw some beautiful houses then—I thought, oh my God, in this big wide world, isn't there a place for me? Could I find just a small corner, somewhere, even in Russia? I'm sorry to be so dramatic, but that's how I felt then."

Rhetorical phrasings were found throughout the conversations that residents had with themselves. Sylvia's words to herself one night and her later conversation with me hinted at the complex personal and temporal dimensions of the rhetoric. She felt "dramatic" then, even though she was the only one taking notice of her plight, and through her questions she had the potential to move herself as much as she would any future listener. The possibility that the questions worked just as well when Sylvia was alone (or with an audience a year later) suggests not simply that such phrasings enhanced her testimony but that rhetorical phrasings largely patterned how she felt and acted.

In the conversation-based reality of the shelter, speaking, listening, and acting were closely tied together, to the extent that what people heard or said shaped who they were. One afternoon Richard told me that the television was "putting ideas" into his head. "They tell you to have a good kind of life," he said. "I sleep right next to the television room, and I hear voices at night." "What do the voices say?" I asked. "They say that my life ain't that great."

Richard was probably not referring to the kinds of "voices" Julie and others heard since he never mentioned "hearing voices" on other occasions. He most likely had in mind the talking heads and commercial images that promoted the good life, a life which told him that his own left something to be desired. The inculcation of images here can serve as a model for how linguistic and imaginal phrasings congeal in a person's life. Even though the words and images came from the television, they were patterned by the shelter's dominant rhetorical frames. "They tell you to have a good kind of life" is not much different from Peggy telling a resident, "We want you to live in such a way that . . ."; the phrase "They tell you" is indicative of its overriding authority. The message of the medium—that Richard's life was not so great—carried forth the lamentations of hopeless lives and beautiful ruins. Two trajectories of language, what one heard and what one said, crystallized in an emergent rhetoric of selfhood. As with Sylvia's dramatics when she asked herself if she could find "just a small corner, somewhere, even in Russia," Richard's voices were heard late at night, when he was alone, but they had a rhetorical cast to them that made them effective later on, when spoken to me or others. This rhetorical cast was not added subsequently, as an afterthought or reworking of the past. It was built into the phrasing of the moment such that the moment itself was a rhetorical one. For those who spent much of their time in the shelter, rhetoric of this sort could become integral to the makings of personhood.

In the past few decades several lines of thought have worked toward the idea that human beings are not as autonomous, monadic, monologic, or self-constituting as many European and American philosophical and psychological accounts have made them out to be. According to thinkers like Mead, Bakhtin, Vygotsky, Burke, Bateson, Lacan, and Levinas, a person is, by the very nature of being a person, enmeshed in social, communicative, and moral relations with others.[8] This way of thinking about selfhood makes a great deal of sense in and around the shelter, but not because many residents "heard voices." Rather, the structures of language, thought, feeling, and action were inherently caught up in characteristic utterances and asides to and from others. People were far from self-made speakers and actors. Their senses of who they were, how they suffered, what they wanted, what they could get, and their general lot in life emerged out of, and was reinforced by, actual and imagined conversations, both verbal and gestural, with staff, family members, psychiatrists, friends, acquaintances, other residents, nameless pedestrians, bureaucratic decrees, and the distant voices of the media. It may in fact be that, given the grounds of the residents' lives, those lives were more profusely dialogic than others', such as the staff's.

As befits the spirit of dialogism, a dialogic view of the self has found its way into both psychology and anthropology. More often than not, however, writers, particularly those inspired by Bakhtin, have focused on how a speaker's "voice" is, like a text, fashioned by the voices of others. As Bakhtin might put it, words always have a "sidewards glance" toward other words and other contexts. While this focus on intertextuality has the important merit of underscoring the role of others in people's lives and thus getting away from ideas of self-constituting beings, it is, by its very design, geared more toward what a person says in life than to what he or she *hears*, and thus reflects an unfortunate tendency in mod-

ern Western thought to attend more to acts of discourse and speaking
than to the active reception of discourse in acts of listening.[9] An ear
toward the latter is important in terms of the shelter, for Richard, Sylvia,
and others were best thought of not only as interlocutors but as interauditors. They had to attend constantly to what others were saying (or
telling them to do) and crafted many of their own utterances in direct or
indirect response to what others said. The tenor and political underpinnings of conversations in the shelter were commonly such that residents,
in situating themselves pragmatically in the give and take of talking and
listening, would often rely on subtle rhetorical positionings to advance
their causes or respond to the actions of others. In time these pragmatic and rhetorical footings could contribute to enduring and usually
tacit stances toward the stances of others, like the rule to "stand away,"
the need to work in international waters, or the penchant for indirect
questions. The ways in which they heard or listened to others thus profoundly shaped how they thought, spoke, or acted.

Epistemologies of the Real

Questions such as Carla's and Sylvia's pointed to another side of many
utterances in the shelter. This was a tendency to bemoan some aspect of
one's life. The larger realities of many shelter lives, which were spent in
and out of hospitals, psychiatrists' offices, and halfway houses, help to
explain the use-value of complaints. Complaints typically rode on the
first person singular: the "I" was plaintive. They often alluded to some
private feeling or personal trouble, but primarily for practical reasons:
by noting a pain or oppression, the complaints could effect a reality
to which one's audience might feel compelled to respond. "You know,"
said Alice as she rushed up to me one day, "they put me into a hospital
and forced me to take drugs. They're just monsters." We went on to discuss her situation for several minutes and she asked, "Don't you think
I'd be a good candidate for welfare?"

Like the most rhetorical of questions, however, complaints were a
weak tactic. The complainer conveyed a sense of dependency that could,
in turn, encourage someone else to speak or to act. Agency was bestowed on others, particularly the listener, and sometimes was even sur-
rendered to them. Yet the surrender itself could be a powerful act if it
led to further, occasionally more significant, movement in a larger field
of action (as when the staff attended to a person's problem).

The way in which someone responded to a complaint could nevertheless be at odds with the complainer's intentions. One afternoon Peggy, the staff nurse, said to one of her co-workers, "Wendy told me she's going to kill herself, and I said, 'What kind of flowers would you like?' She said, 'You don't even care, do you?!'" Peggy's handling of Wendy, a durable resident, was not particularly mean-spirited. It was understood that it was in Wendy's nature "to talk a lot" about her illnesses—as Wendy herself said on occasion. Since the staff approached what Wendy said from a referential stance, in which words could and should refer to an authentic thought or feeling, they found little of substance in her threat. But the dominant force of her words was apparently to move someone into talking with her, even though complaints of this sort often had the opposite effect. Martin told me of a man who, the week before, was standing outside the building, "yelling at the top of his lungs for hours," saying that he had a knife and was going to cut people up. I asked how people responded. "They just ignored him," he said. "That happens a lot around here."

Other interactions flirted with a similar play between proclamation and listening. One evening the nurse called Richard to the staff desk to take a medication that he had been prescribed a few days earlier. "I don't want these lousy drugs," he said. "They make me feel lousy." "Then say you don't want to take them," the nurse said in a tired voice. "I *do* want to take them," Richard said resignedly. He then swallowed the pills with some juice and walked away.[1]

Richard apparently did not want to take the drugs but knew he had to; the stakes were too high if he did not. There was a difference between not wanting the drugs and not wanting to take them—that is, between expressing distaste for the medications and expressing a commitment to not taking them. Because the consequences of not taking them were worse, Richard could not *not* take his medications and so in effect did want to take them. Peggy was probably aware of the distinction. In order to do her job appropriately, however, she had to note any refused medications in the records and so needed a more definitive statement from him. She tried to get him to make his words congruent with his actions. Since Richard could not do that, she apparently took his declarations as tiresome complaints. The staff's governing ideology of language and referentiality led Peggy to discount or overlook any expressive or pragmatic value Richard's words might have possessed.

Other complaints elicited different responses. On Halloween, while Evelyn, an employee of the experimental housing project, was trying to drum up recruits, a few guests were invited to carve some pumpkins to put on display. While they were doing this, Richard said that his life was "hopeless anyways." Upon hearing this, Evelyn asked, "Do you really think that your life is hopeless, Richard?" "Yeah," Richard said with a nervous laugh. "Well, that must be a really terrible way to live," Evelyn said. "Have you ever thought of being involved in the project?" Richard listened to Evelyn and agreed to meet with her to discuss the possibility of finding a place to live.

Evelyn took Richard's words as sincere—or better yet, made it clear that she wanted to hear them as sincere—in the sense that there was a pure congruence between avowal and actual feeling, without any rhetorical adulteration.[2] Richard's laugh suggested he was unsure how seriously he wanted his words to be taken. In any event, his attitude invited a response distinct from Peggy's; the ensuing discourse spoke of action, responsibility, and personal agency. In general, the staff responded to complaints by tracking and evaluating their referential worth. If residents were to be taken seriously, they had to convey the sense that their words were from the heart rather than generic expressions of discontent. When they succeeded in so doing, the staff typically responded by prodding them to act on the situation in question.

"I feel wretched, I really do," Carla said at a staff-resident meeting one afternoon. "I just feel wretched—all this talk about money," she said, then added a minute later, "The state makes us all feel wretched. That's what it does."

"Do you think you can do something about that?" asked Bill, one of the staff members present at the meeting.

Carla appeared to be taken aback by the question, then replied, "Well, I try to go about my business and do my things, that's what we can do, I guess." She remained silent for a few minutes, until the staff began to discuss whether they needed to purchase any new supplies. She then asserted that she needed a new pillowcase because her current one was always dirty and the stains were "multiplying."

"You should wash it then," said Susan, one of the staff members.

"Why should I do that?" Carla asked.

"Because the stains might come off."

"But they don't come off."

"Sometimes," Susan said, "you can take them off with special detergents."

"I'm too tired of this. I really am," Carla scoffed, and stood up and left the shelter.

Two language games took place simultaneously here. Carla signaled a sense of passivity in an attempt, I believe, to get people to act on her behalf. To be taken seriously by the staff, however, she had to show that she was offering more than vacuous complaints; she therefore said she was "really" wretched and "really" tired, with the adverbs working as evidentials marking the epistemic status of her utterances.[3] Yet her fatalism and passivity were precisely the attitudes staff members were trying to combat. In fact, one of the staff's main goals was to make agents out of patients: that is, to get residents to do more on their own, to take more responsibility for their lives, and to realize that they could, in fact, attain power and agency in the world (even though this fact was sometimes antithetical to the residents' lives). Staff members therefore tried to use complaints as an opportunity to advance their therapeutic goals: Bill and Susan countered Carla's fatalism and so tried to create a sense of agency and responsibility. Carla apparently became thoroughly irritated by the resistance, as each of her grievances was being parried with a call for her to act in some way, and broke off the conversation with one last angry grievance: she was "really" tired of it all.

Veracity was important in other aspects of shelter life as well. In the course of a day or a week residents had to engage in a variety of tasks such as showering, cleaning their sleeping areas, doing laundry, and taking medications. The staff kept a written record of some of these activities and gave the residents "tokens" when they were completed. Although it was clear when residents did not make their beds or get up on time in the mornings, acts of showering and taking medications were not so obvious after the fact. So, when staff members asked or reminded their guests to take a shower, residents needed to make it clear that they had, in fact, bathed recently. One evening Louise came into the shelter and walked by the staff desk. "Louise, shower," a staff person said in a low, directive voice. "I took one yesterday," Louise said. "I did! I really did!"

While staff members accepted these claims at times, they were usually unwilling to give out tokens if there was no evidence to verify the claims. The best way to demonstrate that one had taken a shower, therefore, was to let the staff know immediately afterward, with the signs of showering (wet hair, towels, bathrobe, slippers) all solid evidence. If residents succeeded in proving their cases, the staff then noted what had happened in the records and gave out the appropriate number of tokens. The act of writing itself created a criterion of truth in that the items written down were what counted most in the guests' lives; psychological and characterological observations and other "progress notes" were the most noted and notable verities.

Residents had to verify other actions as well. One evening, for instance, the staff nurse handed Estelle a few pills, then went out to the lobby to track down someone else. Without anyone there to watch her, Estelle wanted to establish her imminent claim that she had taken her medication. Since I was sitting in a chair a few feet from the desk, she asked me to watch her take the pills. When the nurse came back she said, "I took my medication. Right, sir?" As with complaints, residents had to couch statements and actions within the register of the real—

and often through the observations and testimony of others. It took at least two to verify; truths needed to be intersubjective to be of any use. If words were to be worth anything, they had to be verified and accounted for, and they had to conform to the criteria of such accounting. They had to be factual; someone had to have "really" done something or "really" felt something. This was the staff's epistemology. Residents were required to work within it in order to be taken seriously.

Staff members focused on the potential authenticity of words and actions for several reasons. Concerned with people who might be "faking it" or who did not do what they said they did, they needed to verify truth-claims and note what "really" happened in the records and log books. They held themselves up to similar criteria; they needed to walk what they talked. They therefore emphasized through myriad acts and gestures the requisite congruence between words and actions. They were also called on to settle disputes between residents and so had to cut their way through films of words to find out what "really" happened when, say, one man accused another of stealing his radio. At the same time, they found themselves working with a population that, they believed, often had to be brought back into the fold of the real. One of the goals of the staff was to help guests realize that many of the voices they heard, the thoughts they thought, and the images they saw were illusory and so factually unfounded. The staff held that there was a valid basis to the perceptions. To understand this basis, however, the perceptions had to be read in metaphoric or symbolic terms: a fear of persecution, for instance, could reflect anxiety in one's life. The staff helped residents to understand these correspondences, usually as part of an ongoing strategy of care.

One day while taking a shower Sylvia Covert overheard a conversation that she thought might have been between a staff member and a doctor, in which they were talking about operations they might perform on her body. She went to the desk to report this conversation to Bill. "I don't know if I should report them to the Capitol Police," she said.

"What's going on?" Bill asked in a concerned voice. "You seem upset today."

"Well, I heard," Sylvia said, "I heard these two people talking and I don't know if I heard them right but they were saying they were going to do all these terrible things."

"But that doesn't sound very real," Bill said. "What's going on with you today?"

The conversation went on in this way, with Sylvia telling Bill what she had heard and Bill trying to figure out—and so help Sylvia to figure out—what was really going on with her.

The exchange tied into politically charged ways of hearing and assessing the voicings of others. Staff members approached talk as a means of understanding. They usually spoke with their guests in order to get something done: to "have a meeting" with someone, to tell a person that they had "a bone to pick" with him, to find out what really happened in someone's life, to advise someone on how to look for an apartment, or to assess another's state of mind. The main concept of language in all this was a textual one: staff members, anchored as they were in a space of writing, usually approached language in readerly, writerly ways, interpreting a few utterances, taking notes on an interaction, or trying to diagnose a malady based on its verbal expressions (affinities with the ethnographic process will not be lost on the reader). This sort of language was visual, referential, and monological in its epistemic underpinnings; one listened to what another was saying as if reading and thus interpreting a single speaker's monologue. The most significant criteria of such readerly assessments were those of lucidity, validity, accuracy, authenticity, and transparency of meaning. Is a person's talk lucid? Does it make sense? Is it truthful? Does it leave a lasting trace? Such questions, which tacitly framed how people were heard and thus sometimes spoke in turn, were rooted in administrative concerns for bureaucratic and personal accountability, legal concerns for the need to state something "for the record," and therapeutic concerns for deducing proper psychiatric diagnoses. More generally, this kind of language echoed the dominant focus in modern European and North American cultures on writing and interpretation. Language, for the staff, was purposeful. Similar to the way each space in the shelter had a purpose, talk usually had to have a point to it or be "about" something.

Residents, who lived in terms of a logic and language second to the dominant one of modern capitalism and psychiatry, were usually most concerned with "having a conversation." Their common understanding of language took form in a world of panhandling, of constant exchanges, of hearing voices—in a place, in short, where people were always talking and could not but hear the talk of others. Their utterances were thus often acoustic and dialogic in their epistemic underpinnings. Talk took form in terms of the logic and tempo of a conversation, of waiting and hanging out, and, more fundamentally, of the secondness of the streets and the lobby. Most residents valued conversations for the companionship they provided and for the ways in which they enabled one to make contact with others. While the tactical uses of rhetoric were crucial, it often came down to talking for the sake of talking. Problems arose when someone could not understand what another was saying or when an intended audience was not listening. Thus residents, like staff, valued understanding, and complained about talk that did not "make sense." But such talk was problematic chiefly because it made "having a decent conversation" difficult. For staff, talk facilitated understanding. For residents, understanding facilitated talk; it was more important to converse than to understand fully.

Understanding sometimes took a back seat to listening. One day I walked into the television room and found Larry and Susanne, seated on two chairs, talking to one another. Susanne would talk for a while about something of concern in her life while Larry listened. Then Larry would talk about something going on in his own life, but altogether unrelated to what Susanne spoke of, and Susanne would listen. While I found it difficult to follow either monologue very well and doubted that either of them understood well what the other was saying, they both appeared to be attending intently to each other's speech, as if serving as audience for the other's lament. The two apparently hit upon a reciprocating method of conversing that enabled both to talk and be heard without necessarily being understood fully.

Residents upheld an ethics of listening that often conflicted with the staff's ethics of understanding. The ethics related to, among other things, the call-and-response tempo of people's interactions with one another, the need to reciprocate and hold up one's end of the exchange, the important if thorny place of companionship in everyday life, the pleasures of conversing with others, the "rudeness" sometimes implied in not being acknowledged, and the extreme disregard people faced when on the street. People valued listening; they particularly liked it when others listened to them. To be appreciated a person did not necessarily need to respond verbally—nor even, at times, understand well what another was saying. He or she could reciprocate simply by listening. By listening, one enabled another to speak and be heard. There was little in the way of a "testimony" or "giving witness" in any of this. Residents just appreciated being heard.

Their gratitude was apparent at the end of several conversations that I had with them. "Thanks for talking with me. I feel better," Wendy said after a lengthy, tearful talk about the problems in her life. "It's good that you sit down and talk with us," Martin, in turn, said to me one afternoon, then added: "I wish the people here did that. It makes me wonder what they're here for." On another occasion Lisa and I sat at a table in the shelter and talked for a while with Larry and then with Bill. Both men said "Thanks for talking with me" before getting up from the table. When I noted this afterward, Lisa said, "They say that!" in an amazed voice that I took to mean, "How odd that they can be so grateful for something as simple as talking with them." The appreciation was understandable, however, once one realized that residents found it difficult to have a "decent conversation" with others, and this for two reasons: other residents were hard to follow at times, and staff members, as Martin noted, did not usually "sit down and talk" with them unless they had an overriding therapeutic, political, or bureaucratic goal in mind. "I'm not gonna stop and chat if you're gonna complain," a staff member said to Wendy one evening. Since there was no point in such idle talk, staff seldom stopped and chatted. In the course of things, staff wondered why residents spoke and acted as they did, while Martin wondered what purpose the staff served.

Such were the kinds of concerns at stake when Sylvia and Bill spoke with one another about the voices that Sylvia heard. Two methods of verification quickly took form. Sylvia, living more than others, because of problems with her eyes, in a world of acoustic presences, was concerned with the possible danger she overheard. Apparently assuming an ethics of listening, she wanted Bill to hear her out and to help her to understand what she had heard. Bill, suggesting that the overheard conversation did not "sound very real," sought instead to decipher its metaphoric or symbolic truthfulness. Serving as an auditor of a particular kind, his response fit in with the way in which the staff worked with her in general. She often overheard things (and often submitted reports to the police) and had to be encouraged to realize that the factual basis of these perceptions lay not in any real voices but in the psychological or familial tensions of her life. Whereas Sylvia wanted to know if what she heard was true or not, Bill wanted to figure out what the voices meant.

To interpret in this fashion was to draw on a certain kind of power—the power to assess, decipher, and redefine. In responding to Sylvia's words, staff members advanced an interpretation. More importantly, they advanced a distinct modality of interpretation, common to many modern psychiatric institutions, in which words and images referred to or stood for psychological or social realities; the interpretation was a "hermeneutic" one in the modernist sense that what Sylvia heard was "taken as a clue or a symptom for some vaster reality which replaces it as its ultimate truth." [4] Far removed from the covenants of hermeneutics in the human sciences, however, in which interpretation is taken to be an ethically ideal way to approach the meanings and realities of others, these acts of interpretation were deeply political. In assessing Sylvia's voices or deciphering someone's actions, the staff was able to set and reset the terms of the real, of what was authentic and truthful. If residents wanted to be heard, they had to work within these terms.

Reactivity

Residents also interpreted events and actions, and tried to recast them in their own image. But the force of the staff's modality of interpretation made it the more potent and lasting one. Matters were not one-sided, however. Residents did not necessarily follow the staff's advice or readily conform to their view of things, nor did they take everything at face value ("They tell me I have cancer," Barbara whispered to me one day, "but the Good Savior told me I don't, so who you gonna believe?!"). In general there were different wants and competing pragmatics. Staff members tried to advance their therapeutic agendas, and residents acted in a variety of ways.

One evening after dinner Roy, a staff member who generally worked day shifts (when the residents were away), walked through the shelter and said "Hello" to Alice, who was seated on a couch. "Hi Roy," Alice said, then quickly added, "You know, we haven't had a meeting in a while. Would you like to sit down?"

"Yeah, sure," Roy said, seating himself next to Alice. "So what's up?" he asked.

The two spoke for several minutes, but at cross-purposes. As she had at similar "meetings" with staff members, Alice spoke about religion and the passages in the Bible that she found most helpful, and asked numerous questions about Roy's own life. It struck me that she wanted to have a high-level conversation—between equals, as it were—and said several things, such as "We both have the same color eyes," that worked to create a bond. Roy, in turn, tried to maintain a safe distance and asked on several occasions what "problems" Alice was having at the shelter. "Nothing," she said at one point. "Everything's fine."

Alice and Roy were apparently aware of the other's orientation toward the encounter and relied on that orientation to further their own concerns. In order to have a conversation, Alice depended on Roy's willingness to meet with her to review her status. Roy distanced himself from Alice's intimacies but still relied on her desire to talk in order to meet his responsibility for finding out how things were going in her life and for helping her, if need be, to work out any problems. Roy could not simply have a conversation; he had to root his words in a therapeutic agenda. He was doing his job, but Alice wanted him to do more (or less) than that. The exchange seemed rather forced, with both parties trying to get what they were after.

Alice's conversation with Roy underscored the fact that to enter into a verbal exchange with a staff member was to enter into a therapeutic relation. Since the therapy itself implied a dynamic of change and the attribution of value to certain ways of being, speaking, and thinking, the relation was a political one. Indeed, the fact that even the most seemingly innocuous interaction had a political edge made some residents think twice about entering into such an exchange. Brian appeared to do just that one evening after he walked up to the staff desk in a bathrobe and with damp hair and stood there without speaking.

"How can I help you, Brian?" asked Dan, a staff member.

"Never mind," Brian said a few seconds later, then turned around and started toward the dorm area. "You don't have to be rude," he said out of earshot of Dan.

My guess is that Brian thought Dan was rude because Brian wanted to get tokens for taking a shower but did not want to have to ask for them. Brian's bathrobe and wet hair should have been sufficient clues for Dan. Dan, however, did not respond to the clues because it was the staff's aim to get people to be more active in life rather than keep silent. For Brian, however, it was insulting that Dan had asked how he might "help" him and so had unnecessarily made manifest the therapeutic mandate as well as the political cast of that mandate. By being forced to participate in a conversation, Brian would have been inculcated into the political determinants of that exchange.

One way to try to avoid staff members' inculcation was to refrain from interacting with them. This was Brian's solution. Another and perhaps more potent tactic was to try to buck their orders of meaning, conduct, and agency. One evening around six, Larry walked into the shelter and passed the staff desk, heading toward the dormitory area. Peggy, the staff nurse, called him from the desk. Larry kept walking and Peggy called him again: "Larry. . . Larry! . . . Larry!" On the third shout, Larry stopped, turned around, and said "What?!"

"Why didn't you answer me?" Peggy asked.

"I don't have to answer you," Larry said while taking a few steps toward the desk.

"Sure you do!" Peggy said.

"Not if you don't call me by my right name."

"Your name is not Larry?"

"Not the Larry that you're thinking of."

"What?! Which Larry are you, then?" Peggy asked in discomfort.

"Never mind," Larry said, smiling, and started to walk away from the desk.

"No, come on. I don't like this," Peggy said with a plaintive, frustrated tone.

"Never mind," Larry laughed, and walked up to the desk. "What do you want?"

"Aren't you going to take your meds?"

"What do you got for me?" Larry asked, and leaned over the counter. Peggy set out the medications and Larry downed them with a drink of water.

Larry's responses to the nurse's queries did not appear to be intentional in any deep-seated sense; there was no overarching strategy of resistance in his actions.[1] He did not have a set stance or "footing" in the exchange but rather relied on a series of tactics to keep shifting the grounds of the conversation.[2] Indeed, the abrupt change could itself be taken as tactical.

When Larry walked into the shelter and passed the staff desk, Peggy asked him a question (that she probably knew the answer to) to get him to take his medications. In much the same way that Brian walked away from Dan, Larry's first tactic was to ignore Peggy's summons. His second was to say he did not have to answer. When Peggy contradicted him on this claim, asserting that he must respond to any questions or summons made by the staff, he shifted his line of defense and questioned the factual accuracy of her summons ("Not if you don't call me by my right name"). His third act and his actions altogether thus involved a diagram of power common to the Center: that of obscuring. Peggy, perhaps worried about Larry's state of mind, then tried to pin him down on this with her question ("Your name is not Larry?"), which led to a fourth act on Larry's part: he was not the Larry of whom she was "thinking." Her frame of reference, which hinged on a split between thought and actuality, was confused and misguided. Peggy asked him to identify himself, but Larry dismissed the question. The fifth tactic, then, was to try to end the conversation without resolving Peggy's concerns. Peggy did not let him do this and called on her discomfort to keep him from walking away. In so doing, however, she relinquished some of her authority. Larry spoke summarily, telling her again to pay no attention. Perhaps finding, however, that the stakes would be too high if he just left her there, swirling in his semantic dust or worried about his psychological integrity, he ended the frame and began a new, more customary one ("What do you want?"), which, significantly, and in contrast to Brian's exchange with Dan, implied that the staff needed something from him. Peggy's final query ("Aren't you going to take your meds?") sounded off-balance and uncertain. With the tables turned and a trace of volition in his favor, Larry decided to take his medication.

The tricksterly ways in which Larry responded to Peggy's queries upended, at least for a moment, her orientation toward language and meaning. His words, which were as playful as they were counterhegemonic, pointed out the metaphysical grounds of her linguistic stance, the political assumptions motivating that stance, and the methods on which it rested. Implicit in Peggy's words were the contentions that

Larry needed to heed the staff's game of call and response, that he could not walk away from a conversation or dismiss a confusion, that he needed to be clear about what he was saying, that he should have a single identity, and that his conduct should be habitual, consistent, and knowable. Larry threw into question each of these assumptions while proposing more unfixed alternatives. In effect, he skewed and muddied the semantic and bureaucratic logic that underpinned the interaction. To do so, however, he had to cloak himself in confusion—much as people hid among the building's obscurities. He also had to forgo momentarily the sense of a stable identity. At the least, his actions hinted at the semantic and linguistic assumptions on which the staff's authority was based and so illustrated both the frailty and arbitrariness of the authority as well as its potency to influence how people acted.

The staff's potency was on display one summer evening when two police officers came to the shelter to take Jeff, a middle-aged man who had been in and out of psychiatric hospitals, to yet another hospital because he had performed a "disgusting" sexual act in the lobby (as a resident put it) and the staff had decided that he needed to leave the shelter to undergo psychiatric evaluation. When the police walked in, Bill and Dan, two members of the shelter staff, went over to the men's dorm to get Jeff. After a few argumentive words he came out of the dorm area and said in the direction of the police, "You must be looking for another Jeff. I haven't done anything wrong."

Bill and Dan explained that he had to leave the shelter.

"Am I coming back?" he asked.

"If the doctor says you can come back," Dan said, "then you can come back."

"Then can I get some of my things?"

"Sure."

Jeff went back to the dorm area and one of the police officers asked Walter, the shelter manager, "What's his claim to fame? He seems somewhat together."

Walter took the officer aside and quietly explained what had happened while the other officer called on his radio to find a hospital where they could take Jeff. They eventually found a free bed in a psych ward several towns away and told Jeff the name of the hospital when he returned with a bag of clothes.

"That's far away from here, isn't it, Sir?"

"It's not too far. We'll have you there in no time."

The officers escorted Jeff out of the building and strapped him into an ambulance, which then left for the hospital.

In being committed to a hospital, Jeff contested the displacement, suggested (much as Larry did) that they had the wrong man, denied that he had done anything wrong, and asked several questions about his fate. Jeff's acts of denial, negation, and questioning followed from what he was able to do, just as the staff's acts of judgment, displacement, care, and instruction followed from what they were able to do.

The different actions and capabilities of staff and residents prompt several concerns about the means and grounds of human agency. In *Oneself as Another* philosopher Paul Ricoeur points out that human action can be effectively studied by asking a chain of questions: "who did or is doing what, with what design, how, in what circumstances, with what means and what results?"[3] Of the specific questions entailed in this network of action—who? what? why? how? where? when?—Ricoeur takes up the question of "who" in order to develop a person-centered semantics of action that rectifies the limitations of the focus in analytic philosophy on the twin questions "what?" and "why?" Neglected in much of his thought and that of others, however, is the question of "how?" How do people act? What are the means of action specific to a person, a group, an institution, or a social setting, and how do these ways of acting differ from person to person, place to place, and time to time? What orientations to time, language, and social interaction accord with these ways of acting? What are the cultural, pragmatic, and political forces that tie into diverse forms of personal agency?

In anthropology a small but incisive body of recent work has attended to the questions "who?" "where?" and "when?," albeit more from the vantage of ethnography than from that of analytic philosophy. Much of this work tries to establish the role of human agency in the play of culture, structure, and history.[4] Other studies show that the locus, timing, and conditions of agency need not rest within a person but can in fact occur in the extrapersonal forces of a society.[5] In turn, research that is more linguistically attuned shows how the members of a society come to attribute agency to social actors in everyday interactions and formal political settings.[6] Throughout much of this work, however, the question of the specific and potentially divergent means and forms of personal agency in diverse societies remains unexamined. The "how?" of agency is typically answered with a vague call to practical reason or methodological individualism.[7] Ivan Karp's claim that Pierre Bourdieu's view of human agency lacks an understanding of "differences in personhood or ideas of being" applies to many ethnographic and theoretical perspectives.[8] Despite the wealth of studies showing that models of personhood take distinct forms throughout the world, the methods of agency are assumed, for the most part, to be much the same everywhere, as if agency was an essential, unchanging given and ontologically prior to the situations in which it arises.[9] Only with the burgeoning wealth of studies of "resistance," subaltern practices, and the various "arts of the weak" do we find extensive thought on the distinct forms that human doings can take.[10] Given the planned, strategic nature of many of these arts, however, this literature generally attends more to the means and conditions of skilled *practices* than those of distinct *actions* (as Ricoeur distinguishes the two in a hierarchy of praxis, with actions entailing basic first-order units and practices entailing integrative second-order ones).[11] In general, although many contemporary anthropologies draw on a concept of human agency, they often lack a thorough understanding of the cultural underpinnings of the concept as well as any theoretical specificity on what agency is, how it comes about, and how and why it varies from place to place.

Sherry Ortner addresses some of these issues in her 1984 review of anthropological theories of practice. In assessing the different theories of human action and motivation that theories of practice imply, she finds that a "strain theory" of motivation, which sees action in terms of long-term developmental "projects," is more judicious than the pervasive "interest theory," which sees action in terms of short-term tactical "moves."[12] "From a tactical point of view," she writes, "actors seek particular gains, whereas from a developmental point of view, actors are seen as involved in relatively far-reaching transformations of their states of being—of their relationships with things, persons, and self. We may say, in the spirit of Gramsci, that action in a developmental or 'projects' perspective is more a matter of 'becoming' than of 'getting.'"[13] She then concludes that we should build on the developmental point of view and dislodge interest theory.

Despite the corrective wisdom of Ortner's conclusions, her perspective on human action requires an either-or stance on the presumably generic nature of human agency. Yet the situation in the shelter, in which the residents had to contend repeatedly with issues of "getting" amidst the staff's calls for "becoming," points to the way in which distinct kinds and ideologies of motivation can take root in a specific locale. It also illustrates how agency arises out of a specific set of activities; how political, linguistic, and cultural forces give rise to certain perspectives on and forms of agency in an institutional setting; and how the complex, indirect folds of conversational and interpretive acts common to this setting form a distinct system of meaning and action. The situation also suggests the dangers of solidifying one's theoretical framework in advance and underscores the need for an anthropological approach that includes from the start the possibility of diverse motivations for human action and diverse grounds for, and forms of, personal agency.

Shelter staff members usually worked along lines of consensus, assertion, sincerity, and foresight. Their orientation prompted and promoted an active agency characterized by activity, autonomy, forthright-ness, consistency, and reliability; it was in the staff's character to act in these terms. The geometry of the actions was direct and lineal: there was, for most staff members, a straightness to time, meaning, action, and intentionality. The need to walk what one talked reflected a semi-otics of sincerity and transparency, and the therapeutic focus on goals, treatment plans, and the long-term consequences of actions implied a consequential rationality in which people acted in certain ways *because* those actions would bear consequences in the future. In 1887 Friedrich Nietzsche sketched a portrait of "the truthful man": "simple, transpar-ent, not in contradiction with himself, durable, remaining always the same, without wrinkle, volt, concealment, form." [14] The staff's professed means of action—directly capable, freely engaged, and temporally con-tinuous—mirrored these qualities.

They also reflected the features of agency commonly set forth by dic-tionaries, philosophers, and social theorists. Agency presently entails the idea of "being able to do something" or "being able to do other-wise" [15] over simply "doing something," as its etymology might suggest. The capability for motivated and consequential action thus ties into ideas of intentionality and free will.[16] Agency is also often sided with power and political might: Webster's New Collegiate Dictionary defines agency as "the capacity, condition, or state of acting or exerting power." Finally, agency often carries a sense of continuous, consistent action. Anthony Giddens holds, for example, that agency "does not refer to a series of discrete acts combined together, but to a *continuous flow of conduct.*" [17] Since, notably, the industrial revolution and the advent of capitalist economies, human action has generally and increasingly been characterized as being engaged freely, willfully, consistently, and con-tinuously by individuals, and as being indicative of those individuals' abilities to exert power in directly active ways.

Yet each of these tenets, which should be questioned through anthro-pological inquiry, went against the grain of actions commonly enacted by residents. In contrast to the staff, residents often proceeded crabwise. Given the politics and dialogic beat of their lives, they typically acted in terms of negation and opportunism. The orientation prompted a form of agency characterized by reactivity, indirection, contradiction, spon-taneity, and impermanence. The geometry of the actions was wrinkled, oblique, tropic: residents tended to rely on indirect uses of speech and to act in ways that responded to the abilities and authority of others. This was an agency of indirect footings, of singular phrasings, and of a practical temporality in which people acted in certain ways *in order to* achieve or gain something. At the same time, the tendencies in themselves were not durable, consistent, or predictable rules of behavior. As Larry's and Jeff's statements suggest, residents evaded steadfast identities on occasion.

While the residents' indirection related to their need to talk and act in oblique ways, their reactivity tied into the complex relations of power in which they were involved. In his exchange with Peggy, for instance, Larry responded to her ability to summon, to tell, and to name; in questioning the consequences of this ability but not the ability itself, he assumed an agentive stance founded on denial, negation, and transient subversion. The stance was commonplace. Faced with the staff's frames of meaning, intentionality, and therapeutic progress, residents could take one of several actions. They could adopt, borrow, mimic, or usurp those frames, as many did in getting along in shelter life. They could make use of them, as Alice did in her conversation with Roy. They could try to avoid them, as Brian did when he walked away from Dan's question. Or they could try to evade or upend them, as Larry did. They could rarely alter or rework them, however. Combined with the other elements of action in the shelter—including dyadic exchanges, a rhetoric of weakness, a plaintive "I," an unstable identity, and an occasional inability to act on one's own—the politics made for frailty and reaction.

The fact that the staff's understanding of agency meshed with themes central to the cultural values inspired by capitalism and the industrial revolution (autonomy, self-sufficiency, productivity, progress, reliability) raises important questions. Much as others celebrate the idea of human experience, some social theorists salute agency as the royal road either to human freedom or to our philosophical acumen on the nature of that freedom. In his 1992 study of the symbolic roots of Western bureaucracy, for example, Michael Herzfeld concludes that "restoring time and individuality to our analyses—the recognition of human agency—is the only viable defense against the reification of bureaucratic authority."[18] Yet the realities of the shelter, wherein an institutional authority promoted and at times enforced a direct and active agency among its wards (as when they advised Carla to wash her laundry), suggest that any call for direct, full-blown personal agency is more complicated than it might first appear.

In the shelter at least, agency was context-dependent, if we take context to mean both a specific "place" and the social, political, and cultural dynamics that give rise to that place. The idea and the reality of agency emerged out of a context and a set of practicalities; it was not ontologically prior to them. It also carried a great deal of ideologically weight, tethered as it was to ideas of production, autonomy, and responsibility. We therefore cannot talk about agency without taking into account the practical concerns that contribute to certain activities or lasting dispositions. Nor can we talk about the pragmatic or persuasive elements of personal agency without considering the political forces that create the conditions for these elements. Agency, poster-child of capitalism, is a political creature through and through.

The Office of Reason

So, too, is reason. In the shelter at least, ideas of truth, reason, sincerity, and responsibility were not foundational in any sense. They owed their strength to political concerns and pragmatic effects, and served as tropes in the lives of staff and residents alike. Paul Rabinow notes that sociologies of scientific practices "have sought (with some success) to lower-case the abstractions of Science, Reason, Truth and Society."[1] Reflections on a commonplace but perhaps less well understood kind of reasoning—reasoning that takes form in everyday life—might enable us to similarly lower-case reason, intimate its cultural and political features, and assess the role it played in a few lives.

"Social clubs are for the office of reason," said Catherine Mohr, a white woman in her early forties who had lived for more than three years in the shelter. She said this in the spring of 1992, when several residents and staff members gathered to discuss the news that the people who ran the Step by Step social club had decided to charge a dollar for each lunch served there, which in effect meant to Catherine that she and others would have to pay to attend the program. "Sociability is free," said Catherine, who was known for her idiosyncratic but apt use of arcane words. "I don't believe you should have to pay to communicate. Social clubs are for the office of reason." Her point, I took it, was that social clubs provided the conditions for the proper "office" or function of reason; a person should not have to pay to communicate or to achieve the faculties of reason gained through such communication.

Catherine's statement was noteworthy in part because it fit with a geography of language commonly advanced by residents. The streets, which lay at the furthest points of the linguistic geography, could entail months of living on the margins of communication and sociability. As noted above, one's very nature could change, particularly in terms of the capacity to talk with others. The longer one lived on the streets, the less language played a part in life; the closer people came to the shelter and other social institutions, the closer they came to rational and reasonable forms of language. Simply put, the shelter and other mental health services were known to encourage people to talk and act in direct and reasonable ways.

That Catherine and others had to go to a distinct place to cultivate the faculties of reason suggests that those faculties were context-dependent; they were born of specific social, linguistic, and political arrangements linked to some locales and situations but not to others. Her sentiment echoed the dominant understanding of space in the shelter, in which each locale served a precise function. In my estimation, the "reason" of which Catherine spoke, which usually manifested itself in particular acts and utterances, consisted of the elements of referentiality, realism, directedness, intersubjectivity, calculation, and consequential temporality encouraged by the staff; the social club and the shelter were the places where these elements were commonly found, encouraged, and engaged. If the psychiatric ward on the fourth floor of the building was where they made you "go crazy," the shelter and social club, with their air of reasonable reasonableness, was where they made you sane.

Economics and a pervasive cultural sensibility were implicit in this brand of sanity. As Max Weber pointed out years ago, ideas of autonomy, foresight, consequential rationality, and strategic calculation have been integral to modern bureaucracies and capitalist economies since at least the eighteenth century.[2] Since the city of Boston provided few exceptions to the dominance of instrumental rationality in the workings of that city, the ability to reason was essential equipment for living there. In order to make do in the markets, schools, and bureaucracies of metropolitan Boston—which usually had little time or room for magical, associative thinking or ragtime speech—people needed to be able to think and communicate rationally. The staff tried to get the residents to learn how to do this better and to grasp the merits of such an education.

The economic concerns went hand in hand with assessments of madness. As Foucault and others have noted, irrationality has been one of the main (but by no means the only) indications of madness or mental illness in Europe and North America since at least the Enlightenment.[3] Whereas the citizens of another age or place might understand madness to stand on divine inspiration, an excess of passion, or the humours of mania or melancholia, for those alive in the twentieth century it has often come down to an absence or derangement of reason. Most Americans today assume that people who are crazy cannot think rationally and do not make sense to others. Residents of the shelter themselves heeded this historically and culturally constituted understanding and often concluded that their neighbors were "crazy" or "sick in the head" because they spoke or acted in ways that did not make sense. Helen, for example, noted that Carla would put out her cigarettes on a bench even though an ashtray was on hand, and she complained that Rose would wear up to five hats at once in the summertime. "What reason could she possibly have [to wear all those hats at once]?!" Helen once asked me in exasperation. At the same time, residents also understood that both they and others made a great deal of sense much of the time. While most domains of life and thought were steadfastly rational, others could be tinged with madness. Helen herself could play a mean game of chess, even though by her own account the airless confines of her apartment were making her go "crazy" in a way that she herself knew was "illogical." Life for most involved a combination of reason and unreason in an ever-shifting ratio.

Staff members, for their part, tried to increase the balance of reason in this ratio as much as possible so that irrational acts or beliefs did not dominate people's lives. They therefore tried to work with people like Helen or Sylvia in such a way that they might realize the folly of their hallucinations and gain more insight into the psychological concerns that gave rise to them. But since so much value was placed on reason and reasonableness, and the residents were characterized in terms of their unreasonableness, a negative cloud was cast over many of their customary ways of thinking, talking, and acting. Residents of the shelter were made to understand that there was something wrong with them and that they needed to become more reasonable if they wanted to live a better life. One of the undercurrents of the dominance of reason was that it led to the devaluation of certain ways of being.

Many residents were therefore motivated—though in different ways— to seek out the office of reason during their stay in the shelter. Some, like Catherine, apparently wanted a modicum of reason in their lives, if only to make up for its absence on the street or elsewhere. Some simply took pleasure in thinking rationally. Some wanted to find jobs or intended to get a formal education and so wanted to adopt the ways of thinking prerequisite to such activities. Some were encouraged to spend more time around others in order to cultivate the social skills that might make them "feel better." Some hung out in the shelter or the social club to get things—food, coffee, shelter, card games, companionship—that coincided with the orders of language and being found there. Some, meanwhile, did not care much for the business at all and spent most of their time outside structured programs, hanging out on the streets or in the unused rooms of the building. Each of these motives shows how desires—what people wanted as well as the rhythm of that wanting—were entangled in the practices, conversations, and forms of life specific to a setting. Access to, the need for, and the price and advantages of reason varied from person to person, time to time, and place to place. The functions of reason took different forms in different lives.

Reason was often a practical affair. Residents relied on reason in their everyday lives because it was good to think with. As such, it was deeply enmeshed in the conversations and ways of acting peculiar to the bundle of practical concerns, subjective values, language games, and political forces known as the State Service Center. Catherine rightly declared that "sociability is free," but sociability came with strings attached. Since the reason that informed the communality desired by her and others involved the styles of thinking and talking intrinsic to the workings of the institution, to be sociable in this way usually meant that one was required to act in terms of those institutionally supported styles. In talking with others, residents could not but acquire a measure of reason and, consequently, contribute to the increasing tide of reason in their own and others' lives. "How did reason come into the world?" Nietzsche asks in *The Dawn*. "As is fitting, in an irrational manner, by accident. One will have to guess at it as at a riddle."[4] As in Nietzsche's world, reason took hold in the shelter through cultural happenstance: through the valuation of certain forms of talking and thinking and through the coupling of these forms with acts of pleasure, desire, utility, and power.[5]

At the same time, since being "mentally ill" was the main criteria for being able to stay in the shelter, some residents understood that they had to continue to act "crazy" in order to hold onto their beds—as when Peter worried that one day people might prematurely say to him, "You're not so crazy so you can't live here." While I doubt that people pretended to be crazy or played up their perceived illnesses in any significant ways, they still knew in the back of their minds that only crazy people could stay in the shelter. Portrayals of mental illness could thus draw on a rhetoric of authenticity. As one man explained to me, when street dwellers or others were admitted to a psychiatric hospital, they often encountered suspicion from the staff there. "They might think you're faking it, to get a warm place to sleep or something," he said. Those committed to a hospital were thus encouraged to act in credibly crazy ways (even though the act itself might be tactical in spirit) because it could secure them more lasting care and shelter.[6]

The staff, at least, took note of this possibility when reflecting on people who stayed in the shelter for months or years on end. They questioned whether or not some played up their illnesses in order to assure a bed in the shelter, and wondered if someone like Sylvia unconsciously set up her fears in such a way that the most sensible thing to do was to refrain from moving out until she got "better." Then again, one could argue that there was an institutional need for madness in that the mental health care system, an integral part of the growth industry of government, required a steady clientele of sick people in order to fulfill its mandate and pay its employees—as Richard suggested in the course of a conversation with Peter and me one day. "The staff here," he said, "need crazy people to stay in business, so they irritate the guests to make them act crazy." "You just might be on to something there," Peter replied. While both this proposition and the staff's concern that people might be "acting up" their illnesses were not confirmed facts, they often snuck themselves into the intimations and second-guesses of everyday converse. As with notions of reason, ideas of madness involved a set of countervailing functions, assessments, and positionings, making for a wealth of forces and inflections to be heard in an offhand statement like, "You're causing me to have a schizophrenic reaction!" which is what Susanne said to Peggy, the psychiatric nurse, one afternoon when Peggy repeatedly tried to get her to do something.

Figure, Character, Person

The doubly pragmatic approach to reason and madness sketched above, in which words did things on their own in the pragmatics of everyday discourse as much as practically minded people did things with words, applies equally to the makings of self and personhood in the shelter, for residents and staff alike drew on different genres of human identity and agency in their dealings with others.

Ideas of "personhood," for one, were powerfully at work. Whereas the streets often eroded a sense of personhood, the shelter worked in fundamental ways to reconstitute that sense. "The idea of a person," Amelie Rorty notes,

is the idea of a unified center of choice and action, the unit of legal and theological responsibility. Having chosen, a person acts, and so is actionable, liable. . . . Since they choose from their natures or are chosen by their stories, neither characters nor figures need to be equipped with a will, not to mention a free will. . . . Characters can be arranged along a continuum of powers and gifts, but personhood is an all-or-none attribution. It is the formation of intention rather than the habits of action which are crucial to the moral education of a person.[1]

The shelter, which implicitly took its guests as persons-in-the-making, was far from being the depersonalizing nightmare that many homeless shelters are made out to be. Yet, as Foucault hinted, sometimes the most humane forms of care are the ones most invested with power.[2]

The production of personhood entailed a great deal. The state wanted the residents to become unified centers of choice and action, intend-

TABLE 1. Worlds of the Street, the Residents, and the Staff

	"Street people"	*Residents*	*Staff*
Domain	street ("outside")	lobby (marginal-liminal)	shelter ("inside")
Economics	panhandling, bumming, scavenging	spending down of SSI & SSDI; loans at 100% interest; shadow work; reciprocal "give and take"; exchange	employment; savings and investment; rational calculation
Forms of agency	reactive, passive	tactical; dialogic; oblique, indirect	strategic; direct, active, autonomous
Forms of consciousness	subjective (selfhood); extreme secondness; a firstness of secondness	subjective and intersubjective; a thirdness of secondness, with pockets of firstness sought after	ideally: intersubjective (fully realized personhood); a thirdness of thirdness
Language	monologic; "talking to oneself"; can lose ability to talk with others	dialogic; rhetoric; conversational call & response; language of the marketplace; "ragtime"	direct, referential; language of the clinic; implies or calls for interpretive hermeneutic
Temporality	vague, dreamlike; no storylines; distinct incidents and generic facts	episodic; practical temporality of reciprocal exchanges; conversational give & take, call & response	consequential temporality of "making plans"; foresight, hindsight; narrational
Dominant morality	ethics of personal survival; "Street people are uncouth"; "Nobody gives a damn"	ethics of exchange, reciprocity, acquaintances, rhetorical persuasion; efforts to "treat each other right."	ethics of sincerity, responsibility, autonomy, foresight, rational calculation; reasonable reasonableness; Nietzsche's "truthful man"
Spatial-moral-therapeutic trajectory encouraged by the state	————>	————>	Housing

ing and acting in an autonomous, responsible manner. It wanted them to recover the sense of "wanting" to do things that Julie spoke of, and it wanted them to act independently, of their own volition, and in responsible, reasonable, and rational terms. The implied transformations, which entailed movements from the worlds of the street and the residents to the state-nurtured world of the staff, were as much moral and economic as they were medical or therapeutic (see Table 1). The ultimate success of this moral education—which would, in the best scenario, coincide with living successfully on one's own—was signaled by the complete internalization of these principles, such that the residents would become, despite their ailments, fully realized, undifferentiated, and economically self-sufficient persons in the society at large.[3] Given the state of things, the staff's humanitarianism was a bit behind the times. In fact, it's quite possible that a technology of care more sharply attuned to the continued presence of impoverished and troubled peoples will follow in its wake, with the Capitol Police's concern for the welfare of the Center over that of the people who sleep within it perhaps foretelling the shape of things to come.

Residents also drew on the stuff of personhood. They tended to adopt for practical and rhetorical reasons the ideas of responsibility, autonomy, accountability, rationality, and judgment that staff members encouraged in their person-making work. The process was complex and requires a bit of backtracking.

As we have seen, the shelter staff—who worked to create a sense of sincerity, consensus, and reason—promoted a referential, realist language in which a neat congruence ideally subsisted between words and actions and expressions and feelings. By contrast, residents of the shelter—who lacked the authority of their caretakers—often depended on a tactical form of language and action, in which questions, pleas, complaints, and entreaties worked largely *as* actions. But since members of the staff had the upper hand politically, their orientations toward shelter life had a central role in encouraging people to act in certain ways and positioned residents as people in need of linguistic and agentive reformation. An ideology of truth, sincerity, and responsibility thus reigned.

Residents, in advancing their concerns, also relied on ideas of sincerity and accountability, but in more makeshift ways, so that the ideas became caught up in a rhetoric of self-presentation. However much the staff tried to encourage a therapeutic orientation toward life, and however much the residents followed the staff's advice, residents tended to rely on tactics to get things done, primarily because they did not possess the political capabilities that gave rise to strategies or the phenomena that promoted a thirdness of thirdness. They therefore drew from the staff's repertoire of sincerities and interpretive modalities in ways distinct from how the staff themselves used that repertoire. They tended to act and interpret along certain lines not because it made sense in the long run but in order to achieve something.

The staff's understanding of personhood and advice about ways of thinking and acting had powerful effects because there were good and practical reasons for the residents to follow that advice. Acting in an "appropriate" manner kept one from getting thrown out of the shelter. Other ways of interpreting and phrasing things also had their rewards. As Richard put it, they would give you "strawberries" if you behaved: assessing random voices as personal conflicts spoke of progress, insight, and relief; conveying what one "really" felt got one farther than re-hashing a seemingly baseless complaint; and acting in credible ways was almost always helpful in affecting listeners. One consequence of this reality was that residents, in their dealings with staff, often did not do or feel something and then try to verify those actions or feelings; they came to act in ways that already carried an air of authenticity and truth-fulness—much as those committed to psychiatric hospitals tried to act in credible ways because it secured them more care and shelter. Indeed, the common focus on the authenticity and truthfulness of statements contributed to an orientation toward action that lent priority to the verifiability of those actions; the moment of acting itself was caught up in the rhetoric of verification. Residents thus came to act in perceivably authentic ways (a fact, incidentally, that renders suspect clinical studies of mental illness that ignore the social and political worlds in which people live and ailments take form).

In general, residents acted in autonomous, rational, responsible, and sincere ways—and thus assumed the garb of personhood—in order to achieve things. The inculcation of reason and personhood was neither direct nor incidental, neither hegemonic nor a front for resistance. It was practical and rhetorical. The pragmatics of agency were deeply caught up with the rhetoric of sincerity and responsibility in such a way that the rhetoric was entwined in the strands of personhood.

Residents also advanced the other main strand fused in the concept of person: the person as a bearer of inalienable legal and moral rights. They did so in order to be taken seriously, to be treated with respect, and to be heard out when the situation called for it. Staff members also took the concept of rights quite seriously (the shelter's DMH-designated "Human Rights Officer" considered any situations in which someone's rights might have been violated). Consequently, playing the "person" card could be very effective. In turn, some occasionally adopted the staff's emphasis on the person as a responsible and autonomous agent in order to invoke the idea of a person as a bearer of inalienable rights. If I act independently and responsibly in, say, getting an apartment, the argument went, then I, as a person with certain rights and privileges, should not be prevented from doing within reason as I please once I get that apartment. But since the one strand often implied the other, staff could throw the argument back at the residents: if you want to be treated like a person, then act like one.

A similar set of dynamics was involved when residents drew on ideas of figures, characters, and individuals. Figures most came into play when residents interacted with the public, particularly when those that panhandled did so on the city's streets. When asking for money, these folks took on the outward appearance of a homeless person, an itinerant vet, a needy but harmless and honorable crazy person, or an earnest woman down on her luck. Anthony tried to get Nancy—whom he described as "a mental patient, of course"—to sell flowers on his behalf. Helen, who said she panhandled because "we don't have enough to live on as it is," would try to find a busy place near the Center but would walk away when the police approached. "Can you help the homeless?" she would ask with her hand extended. She would make from two to five dollars a day this way, which was enough to buy a decent meal. One day she returned to the building to rest on a bench in the lobby after panhandling for an hour. She had earned three and a half dollars. "Here's a dollar. Take care of your baby," several people told her as they put money into her open hand.

As Helen's comments suggest, the arts of panhandling required a busy place, preferably by the exit to a convenience store, where people had change on hand and might feel bad about buying something when others went without. They required a quick eye to watch out for the police, who, if they did find someone bumming for money, usually made that person move on. They also required a presentation of self that built on the stigmata of poverty, need, and despondency, such as a sullen pitch, dirty skin and hair, ragged clothes, or a protruding stomach.[4] The rhetoric drew on the public side of abjection and echoed the imageries of homelessness present in many journalistic accounts.

The basic idea was to present the kind of "apt type" that overcame Wordsworth when he roamed the streets of London in his *Preludes* of 1950:

> . . . lost
> Amid the moving pageant, I was smitten
> Abruptly, with the view (a sight not rare)
> Of a blind Beggar, who, with upright face,
> Stood, propped against a wall, upon his chest
> Wearing a written paper, to explain
> His story, whence he came, and who he was.[5]

Similarly "full-formed" scenes worked on the streets of Boston because they could, as Wordsworth realized, "take, with small internal
help, possession of the faculties."[6] "Can you help a homeless vet?" someone asked me recently as I walked through Kendall Square. The timing
was crucial: in the seconds that it took a pedestrian to pass, there was
not enough time to present oneself as a distinct character—let alone as
a fully realized person. Tried and true allegorical figures, on the other
hand, could quickly effect sentiments of concern, pity, or moral obliga-
tion among passers-by. These sentiments could then induce ritualized,
archetypal scenes of almsgiving, comraderie, or redemption (thereby
triggering positive counterfigures of almsgiver, comrade, or redeemer).
Yet since the pitches could also effect feelings of fear or contempt, some
types (such as "mental patient" or pregnant woman) worked better than
others (such as degenerate drunk). The trick was to draw on the public
sides of abjection and intimate its heartfelt misfortunes without spark-
ing sentiments of disgust or horror.

People also tried to avoid association with anyone who might dispute
or complicate the steadfast idea of earnest need. One day, for instance,
while dressed in office clothes I ran into Jeff—the man mentioned above
who was sent to a psychiatric hospital because of certain sexual acts he
engaged in—as he was bumming for money in Harvard Square while
sitting on a concrete curb along the perimeter of a savings bank. He
jingled a few coins in a styrofoam cup as he asked passers-by for "spare
change." He spotted me walking up and said hello. I returned the greet-
ing and sat down next to him on the curb. "It's a small world. A small
world," he said, then looked at the space between us and said with a
wave of his hand: "Don't sit so close to me, okay? You can sit a bit further down, but not right here. Nobody's gonna give me money if they
see me sitting next to you!" I moved away a few feet and we spoke for a
few minutes. Throughout the conversation Jeff kept his eye on the passing crowd. Every so often he would pitch for "spare change," but had
no luck while I was there. When it came to the performance of homelessness, you had to mind the company you kept.

Characters mostly took form in the shelter and in the various clinical
offices that residents frequented. Some saw themselves in terms of a certain character because the traits associated with that character helped to
explain their actions or name what ailed them. Wendy's "mental illness,"
for instance, justified why she got angry so quickly, and Mitch said that
being "a bipolar manic" meant that his mind got "really high." Some relied on psychiatric characterizations for financial reasons. Anthony, for
instance, said he used the system: "The psychiatrist wants something
from me, and I get something out of him." He thus assumed the role
of a particular character—that of a paranoid schizophrenic—to receive

benefits and services that came with that identity. The language of characters also came up repeatedly but quietly in the residents' dealings with staff, for character traits helped to explain people's actions and dispositions, as when Lorraine told the nurse that she was making her have a "schizophrenic reaction." Drawing on the stuff of character could, ideally, get you things.

There was also a strong sense of individuality in the shelter. Indeed, many took the form of wholly unique "individuals." As Amelie Rorty notes, individuals, in contrast to figures or characters, actively resist typing: they often represent the "unique private voice."[7] Invented "as a preserve of integrity, an autonomous *ens*" that might resist and transcend what is binding and oppressive in society, individuals have in the twentieth century become the mark of extremely differentiated and isolated consciousnesses.

The rugged indomitable survivors of hardships, the upright representative of social equality against the viciousness of social selves, the members of the Kingdom of Ends, Daniel Boone and Thoreau, figures of moral endurance, have become Molloy and Malone, monologues describing the wintry ending, the fading of the northern light. . . . In the swirl of achieving individuality, the styles of speech flow loose, fall apart.[8]

In the shelter, both the earlier and later forms of individuality took root in many lives. Alice Weldman and others found themselves fighting a desperate battle against the encroachments of society and somehow managed to endure that battle. Yet some also held onto utterly private visions, went their own individual way, and spoke at times in a unique, monologic language comprehensible to the speaker alone. The individualism, while highly reflective of American mainstream culture, was so extreme as to be painful; it got people into trouble at times.

In all, residents drew on a host of ways of thinking about their lives—as figures, characters, individuals, and multifaceted persons—in their daily involvements with others. Rhetorical effectiveness was more important than consistency. People continuously shape-shifted in this untidy, post-institutional world of conversational pitches and counterpitches. Indeed, some deftly switched in the span of a conversation from one discourse to another and so from one orientation to time and agency to another. Alice, for example, advanced a libertarian discourse of individuality when she told me that the leviathan "monsters" put her into a hospital and forced her to take drugs. She then evoked a society-based discourse of personal rights and privileges in asking, "Don't you think I'd be a good candidate for welfare?"

Positionings of this kind speak to general musings on selfhood in anthropology and other disciplines. Ever since Descartes, who found that subjective consciousness was the "sticking point" of modern phi-losophy, psychologists, philosophers, and social theorists have tried to work out ways to think about the nature and construction of human subjectivity.[9] Anthropologists, as befits their tricksterly role in such dis-cussions, have consistently underscored the powerful role of culture. Thinkers as diverse as Mauss, Hallowell, and Geertz have posited that different cultural formations entail different conceptions of self and per-sonhood.[10] More recent ethnographies confirm such assessments. But many of these works also argue against the idea that a culture implies a single, dominant conception of selfhood (the Christian self, the Ojibwa self, the Moroccan self, and so on) in contending that we all invoke and apply to ourselves and others a range of different, culturally patterned conceptions of selfhood.

Katherine Ewing, for example, argues that "in all cultures people can be observed to project multiple, inconsistent self-representations that are context-dependent and may shift rapidly."[11] Her argument, which takes as its evidence the somewhat contradictory presentations of self-hood put forth by a young Pakistani woman (e.g., a dutiful daughter, a clever "politician"), has the important merit of getting beyond static, reductionistic portraits of a culture's characteristic concept of self by suggesting that people draw upon different cultural representations of selfhood when talking to themselves or to others. Such a perspective both fuels and follows from an emerging paradigm in psychological an-thropology and other disciplines that assumes, as Tanya Luhrmann puts it in conveying the gist of this perspective, "there is no unitary, simple, coherent, entity which is selfhood; there are persons purposefully act-ing according to various notions of their selves."[12]

The above reflections on the business of personhood in the shelter accord with such an understanding at the same time that they call for further considerations. The first of these relates to one of Amelie Rorty's points: that different genres of personal identity and agency (such as that of "character" or "figure" in American and European societies) are often subliminally at work.[13] Such genres can be invoked, agreed upon, disputed, or denied. It's not just a question of the kind of "person" one presents or sees oneself as being; ideas of "personhood" or "selfhood" themselves carry a great deal of social, psychological, and ideological weight. They must therefore come under question and be understood to result from a particular historical and cultural heritage.

As it is, one of the most significant but unstated aspects of a prag-maticist model of selfhood is that the model itself implies a set of cul-turally and ideologically patterned orientations to human agency and psychology. A statement like "there are persons purposefully acting," for example, connotes a great deal, including the capitalist-honed assumption, questioned above, that there are individuated "persons" who act purposefully and forthrightly. While it's clear that many people do act in purposeful or highly pragmatic ways, we need to bear in mind the possibility that it's not simply human nature or general psychological dynamics that leads them to do so but, rather, an interlocking set of social, cultural, political, and psychological forces.

Another, related feature of such a model is that it usually presumes that people act of their own accord: that self-made men and self-making women define and characterize themselves (and thus have the power to define and characterize) much more than others define and characterize them. This was far from the case in the shelter, however, for residents were personified in profound ways by various authorities. Many of their own presentations of self developed in tactical response to these identifications; complaints, declarations, and panhandling stints often employed the dominant imageries cultivated by others. Acts of this kind underscore the fact that representations of selfhood do not simply accord with or "depend" on a specific context. They can invoke a context, as when the figure of an earnest panhandler sets up a frame of interactions founded on an apt scene of beggar and almsgiver. The invocations, then, are often tied into pressing political concerns; politics is prior to and feeds into psychology. Such caveats call for a retuning of Ewing's universalist, "in all cultures" stand, for it is likely that some people (such as a young, politically marginal Pakistani woman) need to rely on multiple, shifting representations more than others.[14] In the shelter the tricksterly, seize-the-moment stances required of residents led them to present themselves in a myriad ways, whereas the staff could usually rely on strategies of consistency and sameness. Shape-shifting is a political endeavor.

How to Do Things with Feeling

In the State Service Center, feeling was ensconced in rhetoric. The shelter was a place for all things psychological. A great deal of talk involved comments on or indications of states of feeling—such as when Carla said, "I just feel wretched. I really do," at a group meeting. Although I did not keep count, overt references to feelings seemed more numerous in the shelter than in most other contexts. The high frequency of glossings had a lot to do with the fact that shelter life evolved around therapeutic care. Niko Besnier points out that "in probably all speech communities, emotions can be described (e.g., *I hate him*), although such overt avowals in the first person are likely to be associated with rather marked situations. More commonly, emotions are alluded to, and the decoding task is a process of 'reading off' complex covert messages."[1] One uncommonly marked situation, Besnier notes, is the therapeutic encounter, where feelings are often the focus of talk, and "emotion-labelling, emotion-term glossing, and negotiations of the meaning of emotion terms" are common activities.[2]

In the therapeutic surroundings of the mental health center, the staff encouraged talk about emotions and the vagaries of distress. Residents, in turn, commonly spoke of feeling depressed, nervous, anxious, fearful, moody, sad, wretched, hopeless, tired out, excited, hyper, hopped up, numb—or of not feeling anything at all. They also spoke in equally affective terms of desperate, rambling, lost minds or of the general quality of their lives. Feelings were also indicated through a range of semiotic actions and paralinguistic signals, such as a slow walk, a lowered heard, or words uttered slowly or without affect. Through these actions and utterances, ideas of "selfhood"—of a reflecting, feeling, thinking, doubting "I"—were invoked intentionally or unintentionally.[3] These ideas carried a different phenomenal and moral force than ideas of character, figure, or personhood did, for an embodied, possibly suffering subject was at stake.

Since it was difficult for anyone involved to ignore the presence of such subjects or the possibility of suffering, staff and residents often gave priority to states of feeling. This priority was evident when I posed to residents a question such as "How are you?", for they usually took the query to mean "How are you feeling?" Their responses often gauged fluctuating states of well-being: "How are you?" I asked Simone one evening; "Not as good [as how I felt in the afternoon]," she replied. To the same question Roy responded: "I'm good. I'm good. My spirits are up today." With these call-and-response sequences, the responses often signaled an affective or sensory state. In general, the shelter was primed for assessments of personal states of feeling and being.

In listening to the residents' responses and the understandings they implied, I soon gathered that the sensations in question usually involved consistent features and categories. People commonly spoke of "feelings," with the feelings involving a combination of psychological, physiological, and sensory features. The feelings often had the temporal and existential quality of "moods," which, according to Clifford Geertz, "vary only as to intensity: they go nowhere. They spring from certain circumstances but they are responsible to no ends. Like fogs, they just settle and lift; like scents, suffuse and evaporate. When present they are totalistic. . . . moods merely recur with greater or lesser frequency, coming and going for what are often quite unfathomable reasons."[4] The

feelings were more states than processes for they did not proceed to anything. Rather, they stayed the way they were until another state of mind
or feeling took form. This meant that the states were usually temporary;
a person feeling "lousy" or "depressed" could feel "good" an hour later.

The residents' feeling-states were unpredictable, "coming and going"
like the voices people heard. They could be sparked by a range of
forces: social events, "God's will," neurophysiological (mis)firings, the
side effects of medications. Or they could occur without any apparent
reason. They were understood to take root within a body and often had a
bodily or physiologic basis to them. Perhaps for this reason, the feelings
themselves were taken to be distinct and internal to the person feeling
them; they were more often subjective than intersubjective in nature. In
contrast to some cultural contexts, where, as Besnier notes, "Speakers
talk about emotion as organically inseparable from the social acts they
engender and situations in which they are found," feelings around the
shelter were usually thought to be distinct from the social situations
that might spark, enhance, or lessen them.[5] Despite the internal, indi-
vidualized air of feelings, however, residents drew on a common lexicon
and a mutually understood vocabulary of feeling: one felt lousy, sad,
depressed, angry, or the like. With this lexicon, states of feeling were semantically distinct: everyone knew that feeling lousy was different from
feeling depressed. In turn, most feelings came with a name; Helen's use
of "psssssshh" to describe the uncanny and so unnameable night scene
in the women's dorm was exceptional. The question Bill posed to Sylvia
when she reported hearing voices while taking a shower—"What's going
on with you today?"—cut to the heart of the matter. Staff and residents
alike understood feelings or moods to be specific, statelike, nameable
entities ("What is"), entailing temporally distinct and changeable dynamics ("going on today"), and rooted in the personal existence and
subjective field of awareness of an individual ("with you"). But whereas
the staff, suspicious hermeneuticists all, worked to underscore what they
took to be the causal links between behavior, mood, and life-events,
residents tended to focus on the mood at hand and usually took their
feelings as distinct episodes.

The general contours of feeling conformed to dominant understandings of emotion in the modern West: both residents and staff took
feelings as natural, involuntary, autonomous, uncontrollable, internal,
and physiologically grounded events lodged in the individual.[6] In general, these sentiments fit well with modernist models of selfhood, which,
according to Fredric Jameson, involve ideas of interiority, emotional
depth, and authenticity and are expressed negatively in the pathologies
of anxiety and alienation.[7] But there were also several specifics that related to the structures of time, agency, and personhood common to the

shelter. As noted above, the phenomena entailed bodily "feelings" as much as psychological "emotions," perhaps because of the priority of a medical model in people's lives. Such "feelings" were episodic in nature. They appeared to be activities or "ingings" on a par with acts of smoking or eating or talking. Perhaps for this reason, they were taken as discrete, all-encompassing states of being or action. I rarely heard people refer to themselves as the bearers of two feelings at the same time and people often did not do much of anything else when they were "feeling lousy." Feelings were hyper-individualized in the shelter: much as several languages could be heard at any one time, different feelings took form in different people. Moments of intersubjective sorrow or effervescence common to many Western social settings, in which people participating in a group activity or shared social frame feel much the same way, rarely occurred. Each person felt in his or her own way. In turn, the lexicons of feelings often had a symptomatic, hermeneutic air, with staff and residents working to discover or reveal what was "really going on."

The revelations could carry a great deal of rhetorical force, in large part because of their almost unquestionable nature. In an essay, "Glossing Emotions," Vincent Crapanzano distinguishes between the experience of emotions (a sensation of pain or joy), the expression of emotions (a laugh, a shrug, a cry), and the glossing of emotions ("I am angry at you").[8] In considering the rhetorical use of glossings, he finds, "From the point of view of our dominant linguistic ideology, words and propositions that gloss emotions derive their rhetorical force from their putative referentiality. They are thought to refer to, denote, describe, and signify a particular state of affairs: the emotion being experienced. It is the existence of this state of affairs, this emotion, their truth value, as it were, that gives such words their rhetorical power."[9] Although glossings are referential or symbolic of emotions, they are often imbued with an immediate indexicality. Much as smoke unarbitrarily points to fire, so first-person declarations of feeling point unquestionably to felt emotions.[10] It is therefore difficult to question the truth and sincerity of such glossings.

Crapanzano does not really go into why glossings of emotion so often go unquestioned. There is undoubtedly a lot involved, including the assumed sincerity of first-person testimonies and the pragmatic import of emotional revelations in the modern West. One reason they tended to go unquestioned in the shelter was that bodily and psychological states and processes carried a great deal of moral, ontic, and epistemic weight. Given the understood reality of the body and the significance and diagnostic value of sensorial or affective states, it was difficult to ignore or deny glossings of such states. Indeed, I believe residents said "I feel sad" more often than "I am sad" because the former phrasing underscored the felt, sensorial qualities of the matter at hand (and because, as with certain aspects of illness, "feeling" something carried a visceral and moral tone distinct from "being" something).

Whatever the reason for the efficacy of first-person glossings of feeling, residents often drew on them to great effect in talking to others or to themselves. "I'm nervous. [So] I need a smoke," Eva said to herself one day. The logic, because it involved the justifying force of a self-felt sensation, was indisputable—at least to her. The use of an implicit conjunction like "so" or "therefore" followed other glosses. The perlocutionary grammar often went, "I feel x now [so do or do not y]," with x being a certain idiom of feeling, and y a type of activity: "I feel lousy [so do not talk to me]"; "I feel wretched [so please do not talk about money]." While there were variations on the theme—as when Amy said, "You're nervous, Tommy," and then held his hands, or when Richard said to me, "Stop writing, you're making me nervous"—the moment-based temporality of the logic was distinct from that evoked in the staff's reasonings, which usually involved an extended, if-then consequential logic.[11]

The rhetoric of feeling, which typically held sway over any moral, religious, or economic rationales, tied into the nature of agency in the shelter: residents got things done through indirect, left-handed means. Indeed, the glossings were valuable and valid tools for people with little power. They were effective, perhaps the most effective, ways to explain or justify certain actions or to persuade others to act (or not to act) in certain ways. Sometimes residents alluded to how they felt to evoke sympathy or concern, to get someone to tend to their problems, or simply to get someone to listen to them. Sometimes they did so in order not to talk to people: "I'm in a bad mood, okay?" Sam said in an implied attempt to get me to stand away, much as Brian once told me that he could not "talk now" because his lithium level was not balanced. Most often the glossings involved pragmatically complex and hard-to-categorize pitches, as when Richard said he did not want his medications because they made him feel "lousy."

Residents would often approach the staff and report on how they were feeling. The interactions that followed from these reports tied into the modalities of care and exchange central to life in the shelter. The staff was on guard for signs of undue pain, distress, or trouble. Residents made use of this vigilance, for they found they could get things (including comfort, attention, care, and a measure of safety) through the display of fear, pain, nervousness, distress, and ailments. Yet staff and residents tended to approach the interactions through different models of action and meaning. Residents, drawing on their arts of exchange, barter, and persuasion, understood such interactions in terms of the language of the marketplace. In general, they relied on a model of exchange when presenting feelings to staff. For them, feelings often had the air of commodities, which could be had for something else in turn.[12] Staff members did not necessarily think of such encounters as exchanges, however. Drawing on the arts of diagnosis and therapy, they usually understood such interactions in terms of the language of the clinic. Attentive to the veracity of residents' expressions of distress, and mindful of the best therapeutic tack to take, they sought to evaluate the authenticity and existential depth of any distress reported, interpret its psychological and social bases, and outline steps that residents could take to ameliorate it. Despite the different assumptions, methods, and goals involved, both parties usually got something out of the transactions; staff got residents to listen to their advice, and residents—if the staff took them seriously—often effected some change in their situation through the expression of distress.

Day by day, then, feelings and sensations were constantly being produced, listened to, acknowledged or denied in the shelter. The focus on feelings led, I believe, to a general intensification and hyper-realization of acts of feeling and subjective states among residents. Much as one side of a Möbius strip becomes the other, the realm of discourse, of rhetorical glossings on feelings, melded with the phenomenal realm of feeling, of the feeling of feeling. Residents felt rhetorically. This is not to say that people did not feel what they said they felt, nor does it mean that they simply felt something and then drew on that feeling for rhetorical effect. Rather, it was in the nature of the game—of being alive in the shelter—to realize and intensify one's feelings. Feelings of "nervousness" and the like were often politically motivated; they had a rhetorical air to them from the start. An implicit irony, then, was that, while the displays were effective largely because they pointed to conditions understood to be truly personal, the grounds for those sentiments were, in fact, often profoundly social and transactional in nature.

The idea that there is a rhetorical and political edge to how people feel circles back on, and perhaps even short-circuits, the data presented in these pages. How can one effectively study the nature of people's subjectivities when the nature and intensity of those subjectivities are fused with numerous political, cultural, and discursive forces? Surely not by taking things at their face value, attending only to the referential content of people's words, or by treating "feeling," "bodiliness," "experience," or "suffering" as primal realities more authentic or essential than other cultural formations. Nor can one simply try to describe the phenomenal contours of a person's life without taking into account the makings of those contours.

I tried something of the latter approach early in my research, when

Nancy Ange joined me late one afternoon on a bench in the lobby. "Can you talk to me?" she asked.

"Sure," I said. "What's up?"

"I lost my mind."

"How, how did that happen?"

"Because I put down the Government Center. I didn't like my counselors. They made me worse. They put a voice into me."

I went on to ask what kind of voices they were ("Of movie stars and actors"), what kinds of things they told her ("Nice things, not bad things"), and what it felt like to lose her mind ("I feel numb"). Yet through questions bent on grasping the nature of Nancy's mind, I took the conversation into a different pragmatic zone than she might have desired. In fact, the more referentially minded I became, the less inclined she was to talk. Just one more professional poking about her head, perhaps. My sense is that Nancy's question ("Can you talk to me?") and lament ("I lost my mind") carried more tactical than descriptive weight. The description itself was a practical one: she might have wanted help, sympathy, or simply someone to hear her out. In focusing on what her words might "mean," however, I neglected a great deal.

When it comes to the study of feeling and subjectivity, ethnographic situations like this call for a mode of anthropological inquiry that attends at once to the felt immediacies of people's lives and the pragmatic, social, and cultural makings of those immediacies.

The situations are double-edged, however. Since those who speak with anthropologists can find that conversations are best built upon an ethics of "talking with" and "listening to," the interpretive zeal of anthropological research can, like psychiatric probings, be at odds with the needs and values motivating such conversationalists. It may be, then, that there are times when ethnographers should put aside their notebooks and simply listen to, and not overly analyze, another person's words.

Architectures of Sense

The rhetoric of feeling seeped into the building itself. Richard held that "when people breath onto [the building], when they look at it, or touch it, then what they're feeling goes into it, like that." People apparently breathed and touched a lot, for by all accounts the ecology of the building was a richly sensate one. Yet different areas of the building entailed different sensibilities. As we have seen, Catherine sited the faculty of reason in particular rooms and social arrangements. Other residents also found that distinct places familiar to and frequented by them tended to involve *different* patterns of sensation and distinct ways of thinking about and attending to sensations. In scanning through my field notes, I was surprised to find a close yet inexact correlation between the domains of the street, the lobby, and the shelter and the sensory modalities common to those domains.

As noted earlier, most of those who lived for a spell on the street found that its constant exposure and brutal harshness led to nonreflective states. Losing everything but a sense of survival, people had to take it as it came. There was little "peace around the ears," as Thelonious put it. Street dwellers risked being engulfed by the elements. Responses to the world were reactive, almost tropic. In trying to survive people hid, kept mute, or got off the street altogether. Their ability to sense or make sense of the world was often overwhelmed by the harshness of physical and social environments. For many, life on the street involved a corporeal existence in which the senses were dulled or stripped bare in response to the brutal demands made on those senses.

Frequenters of the State Service Center sensed the world differently from those who lived on the street. Their sensations were less reactive and implied a more reflexive and more mindful consciousness. Yet both the form and the content of sensings varied depending on where people stood in the building. The ecology of the shelter set up ways of being founded on interiors, psychological intensities, a hermeneutics of feeling, and mindful, reflective engagements with the world. The main forms of engagement in the outer chambers of the building, in contrast, were auditory, tactile, or visual, making for direct, continuous, and sometimes unnerving contact between an environment and an organism. Thus, whereas people recalled comfort or bouts of pain on the streets and spoke of "feelings" when in the shelter, they usually spoke of "sensations" in the lobby. These modalities of sensing implied different orientations to an environment and, thus, different forms of selfhood. By definition, the lobby's sensations took place between subject and object, between a body and an environment.[1] Figuratively speaking, one's existence was spotted on the ears, the eyes, and the fingertips. Where the shelter effected a mix of Cartesian and Freudian sentiments, with people thinking and feeling as individuated subjects, the lobby often involved multiple sensations: if the eighteenth-century British philosopher David Hume were to hang out in the lobby, he would probably find robust evidence for his theory that, except for a few metaphysicians, mankind is "nothing but a bundle or collection of different perceptions, which succeed each other with an inconceivable rapidity, and are in a perpetual flux and movement."[2]

Given the different sensorial environments of lobby and shelter, it's not surprising that they tended to spawn two distinct problems: feeling "tense" or "nervous" in the shelter, and being "distracted" in the lobby and outer cavities of the building. There were "fifty tensions" in the shelter, Helen noted, one for each person living there. Her assessment encourages us to think of the shelter residents as bothered with a "tension" that dominated any time spent in the shelter as well as any interactions with other, similarly tensed persons. While bodies could easily feel the effects of such tension, this was primarily the domain of the psychological. Nervousness and tension spoke of mental or social strains spawned by anxiety, stress, need, conflict, or disequilibrium. Both states were intensive, tempting one to invoke the etymological roots of "nerve" in the Latin *nervus*, "sinew, bowstring": living in the shelter could make a person feel high-strung. One way to relieve tension was to pace or go for walks outside the shelter. Kevin, who spoke of "feeling tight inside, constricted," found that pacing helped him to soothe his worries and burn off excess energy; William Fordham, who found that "tension builds if you stay in one place all day, whether you're mentally ill or not," went for long walks through Boston. The movements helped people to unwind taut thoughts.

In the lobby, meanwhile, people mostly complained of being "distracted"; they were forced to deal with sights and sounds that disturbed their ability to stay calm or focused. Feeling "distracted" and feeling "nervous" were both subjectively based sensorial matters, with either state easily acerbated by stimulants like coffee or medications. Yet while nervousness usually entailed indigenous psychic energies — rooted at least metaphorically in one's nerves — that emanated from and hovered about the body-self, being distracted implied external or otherly events or circumstances that diverted one's sense. In general, the sensate grounds of the building smacked of the discontinuities, discordant stimuli, and tactility and distraction noted by observers of big city life.[3] Finding a modicum of "quiet" in less hectic parts of the building was a good antidote to such distractions. "Playing dead" was another. In response to sensing too much, people tried to hear, see, or touch less of the world. There was little interiority to speak of in these ways of being. It was a question of exteriors, of extensities, of having to overhear "the noise from here to here," as if people at times could get overly extended into the building's sights and sounds and then need to draw back into the shelter of their bodies. Since the noises, distractions, and states of quiet or disquiet were understood as more environmental than psychological in cause and nature, and since psychological dispositions, not environmental conditions, were assumed to be most subject to interpretation, such phenomena called more for a comment or note-taking than for an active interpretation of feeling or selfhood. Much as Roy said to me when he had the Haldol shakes, "You might have noticed that I'm shuffling around a bit," people would often simply take note of a sensation or event rather than try to assess its psychic or social underpinnings.

The distinct sensoriums of the street, the lobby, and the shelter imply a great deal. "The sense of place: the idiom is so pervasive that the word 'sense' is almost completely transparent," writes Steven Feld. "But how is place actually sensed? How are the perceptual engagements we call sensing critical to conceptual constructions of place?"[4] These questions are especially thorny ones when applied to the environs of the State Service Center, for there was not one, culturally honed way of sensing place. Rather, different places—and different positionings within those places—implied different sensory engagements. In a discussion of the forms through which people relate to one another through their bodies, M. L. Lyon and J. M. Barbalet propose that "it is possible to characterize particular social institutions in terms of the forms of bodily relations which they entail and which in turn make them possible."[5] It makes just as much sense to contend that particular social institutions entail and invoke distinct kinds of sensory relations. Consequently, movements from one locale or social world to another imply a transformation in sensibilities and subjective consciousness. These movements can take form in the span of an afternoon or they can involve a long-term change in a person's way of being in the world, as when Carla Bataille took shelter from the streets beneath the lobby stairwell and then, after staying in the psychiatric hospital upstairs, settled into the shelter. In the Center, movement from street and lobby to shelter implied the potential conversion of consciousnesses mostly concerned with bodily pains, comforts, and distractions to ones occupied with psychologically intensive thoughts and feelings. Inversely, many took a return to the street to imply a less refined, more corporeal existence. These different forms of consciousness implied different kinds of selfhood, with the lobby involving Humean bundles of sensations that took form between body and environment, and the shelter involving more bounded, interiorized, interpretative, Cartesian selves. The state encouraged such changes in consciousness, hoping that homeless individuals would move from the worlds of the street and the lobby to the shelter and then, ideally and without excessive delay, to the world of apartments, employment, and personal and financial security and order.

To be sure, this was not an all-or-nothing situation. People were, at times, sensorially oriented toward distractions in the shelter and psychologically mindful of tension in the lobby. Yet each domain appeared to have a distinct "feel" to it. Architectural form surely had something to do with the differences between the areas: the lobby had corduroy walls, irregular forms, sliding glass doors, and acoustic echoes; the shelter contained straighter, smoother surfaces, longer lines of sight, and relatively muted acoustics. Much as the sea of tranquility could convey a mood of relaxation and a carefree gait, the bureaucratically aligned spaces of the shelter could contribute to forms of consciousness that were distinct from those common to the lobby. In turn, the understanding that the shelter was a place "inside" and the street "outside," and that the lobby was a site betwixt and between the shelter and the street, led people to associate the shelter with interiority, the streets with exteriority, and the lobby with a liminal mix of the two. At the same time, activities that commonly took place in these areas contributed to different sensory orientations: the lobby's bazaar-like hustle and bustle affected the senses in ways distinct from the shelter's more muted, rational activities and discourses. These discourses also played a role, for the staff's therapeutic focus on inner psychological states and the residents' tactical invocation of such states contributed to a focus on inner feelings in the shelter.

Finally, these and other discourses involved ideologies of consciousness subtly associated with different, politically charged ways of being. In a recent study of colonialism and consciousness in South Africa, Jean and John Comaroff note that a set of European lay and scientific understandings of human biology in the nineteenth century gave legitimacy to an idealized image of rational man. Unlike women and non-Europeans, such a man "was a self-contained individual and was driven by inner reason, not by sensory stimuli from the social and material environment."[6] Despite the fact that, by anyone's count, European men have always been in the minority, the ideal of personhood invested in such an outlook has carried a great deal of social force for over a century. In fact, shelter staff and residents alike (and perhaps the ethnographer) appeared at times to mind a similar idea, with the streets presumably belonging to "uncouth," corporeal creatures, the lobby frequented by people saddled with distractions, and the shelter inhabited by more bounded, reasonable, inwardly attuned people.

The sensory makings of different domains thus involved semi-systemic amalgams of social, discursive, and architectural factors. Out of a crowd of sounds, voices, sensibilities, and reciprocal glances emerged particular formations of sense and selfhood. While the Center presents a dramatically tangible situation, unlikely to be found in such clear-cut terms in many other places, the fact that distinct kinds of emotions, senses, and forms of bodiliness and suffering took form in different locales suggests that the way in which we sense or use our bodies is not fixed in any biologically predetermined or culturally set mix of physiological or psychological faculties. Rather, it is caught up in and forms but one part of a complex ecology of forces. To be a sensorially minded creature or a psychologically minded one is to inhabit a certain kind world.

We might conclude, in following Richard, that when people feel, when they "look, touch, or breathe" in life, the political relations and discursive stances that make up their lives "go into" how and what they feel—and so reciprocally shape and are shaped by the phenomenal world. I hear Nadia Seremetakis saying much the same as Richard (yet in a heavier language) when she asserts that "perceptual memory, as a cultural form, is not to be found in the psychic apparatus of a monadic, pre-cultural and ahistorical seer, but is encased and embodied out there in a dispersed surround of created things, surfaces, depths and densities that give back refractions of our own sensory biographies." [7] In other words, both the form and content of perception is rooted as much, if not more, in a culturally meaningful material environment as it is in the psychic dispositions of any perceivers of that environment. We need to bear in mind, however, that it is not just a question of whether sensing is more "mind" or "matter." Sensory processes and memories, as well as the stuff of mind and matter, are situated, often in very practical ways, in pervasive political arrangements, language games, modalities of interpretation, and bodily sensibilities. As Seremetakis notes, people have their own sensory biographies. Residents and staff sometimes developed quite individual takes on perception: Sylvia worried over her throbbing eyes and hands, Richard could not refrain from touching people and things, and staff members were displeased by the residents' odors. There was no bottom line, no true core of authentic feeling. The palpable sensateness to be found in the building's walls, in the balancing acts of medicating, or in the livening feel of a razor blade was rooted in complex circuits of meaning and action.

Bodies with Organs

Shelter residents suffered from assorted pains, wounds, and afflictions. "Mental illnesses" commonly fused and overlapped with "physical" ailments, to the point where the line between the two domains was unclear. The ailments were palpable, nameable, and often rooted in specific organs or bodily processes: headaches, crushed brains, upset stomachs, pinched nerves, sore arms, cancerous cells, and pained and problematic eyes, ears, toes, glands, and fingers.

"A nervous breakdown," Eva explained, "is like feeling your brain fall down to your knees, fall down on the ground, and get crushed." She said that she had "psychosomatic pains" and sometimes got an upset stomach; she found that worries about her family caused both pains.

"I'm kinda hurting pretty bad right now," Warren told me as he stood in a stairwell. "My brain feels crushed in back."

"Every time I lie down," Louise said in a dreamy voice, "it feels like someone's sticking a needle in my eye, letting the air out. And then I go down, down, down, down."

Martin had boils on his thigh and a toothache. "I don't think anybody would want to be me right now," he said. "There's just too much going wrong."

"It's a fine place but I'm paranoid," Sylvia said of the shelter. "I hear that they're performing operations. They take my body at night downstairs." "There's a cockroach round in my ear," she said a few minutes later. "I'm worried that at night they're taking my body, changing parts. . . . I've had different people's eyes for four days now."

Evonne, who had her own place but left it because of poor health, suffered from a tumor, had problems with her fingers, was nagged by a pinched nerve, and was allergic to smoke; the ailments made her keep away from "social areas." "But I can walk again," she noted at a meeting, "my toes are okay."

"I'm suffering, for thirty years, from an overactive thyroid, mental exhaustion, and an upset stomach," said Simone. Later she told me that she was losing her voice because of a thyroid problem.

The phrase "I'm suffering . . ." was crucial. People's words indicated the brute facts of suffering, of "hurting pretty bad right now." Words like "right now" marked the felt presence of the pains in the here and now, even though that presence was sometimes chronic, as when Simone said "I'm suffering, for thirty years." The pains and ailments involved a world of dense matters and tangible frailties; a body's organs, flows, and linkages often went wrong.

This consciousness of organs was not something I usually heard articulated so directly outside the shelter. Except in hospitals and morgues, most Americans usually do not talk about their innards in such tangible terms. The kinds of bodies felt and imagined in the shelter were also quite distinct from the corporealities of "the street," which typically involved a more gestaltlike, less internalized sense of the body, with physical harms and violations affecting its surfaces and limbs. The extreme focus on the physical, palpable matter of pain or misery did remind me of something, however, and that was the writings of Antonin Artaud, the quasi-surrealist French writer who was confined to a psychiatric hospital for several years and who wrote of mind and body in such terms as sclerotic thoughts, tensed nerves, monstrous sexes, words rotting at the base of the brain, and a slender belly exploded by a grenade. "Description of a Physical State," for instance, details "a painful exacerbation of the skull, a sharp pressure of the nerves, the nape of the neck straining after its pain, temples turning to glass or marble, a head trampled by horses."[1] Hobbled by "the menacing, never tiring presence" of his body and the numbing constraints of his "unusable" body on his ability to speak, think, and feel, Artaud spoke in many poems of his revulsion of the body's sexual and biological functions and his desire to break free of an "ill-assembled heap of organs":

For you can tie me up if you wish,
but there is nothing more useless than an organ.

When you will have made him a body without organs,
then you will have delivered him from all his automatic reactions
    and restored him to his true freedom.[2]

In their two-volume *Capitalism and Schizophrenia*, Gilles Deleuze and Félix Guattari build on Artaud's idea of a "body without organs" in order to propose the experimental enactment of an undifferentiated, imageless, organless body wherein intensities of pain, joy, and desire pass through a consistent, egglike field of immanence and becoming.[3] For them, this abstract ideal transcends the idea of a socially organized and interpreted organism subject to political and psychosexual orders.

There was, I think, something similar going on in the residents' search for firstness in that they sought to be free of the constant seconds of the street and the lobby while also trying to avoid or rework the staff's commands of language and interpretation. Yet an organless plenum of firstness was not easily attained, as evident in the nagging pains from which many suffered, and residents sometimes found themselves with splintered, fragmented bodies reminiscent of what Deleuze and Guattari call "organs without the body."[4] To invoke or reinvoke a sense of unity, people would try to get "glued" back together again. Others would try to "smooth out the joints" through pharmaceuticals. More rarely, some would try to achieve a field of joy or immanence by smoking crack. (Rarer still, a few would try to invoke an intensity of pure feeling by "cutting" themselves.) For the most part, people existed not in a fragmented state of organs without a body, nor in terms of a purely intensive body without organs, but with semi-organized, patched-up, and easily bruised bodies with organs. With this play between fragmentation and coherence, daily struggles often centered on getting one's organs to work effectively together.

Psychiatrists report that schizophrenic delusions are often somatic in nature: one person afflicted with schizophrenia understands that ants are crawling on his skin; another, that her brain is rotting; yet another, that an "influencing machine" controls all of her bodily movements and functions. Others find that their bodies have been transformed into mules' hoofs, or that, as with Sylvia, their organs have been removed and replaced by someone else's.[5] However, given the penchant of psychiatrists to spot everything associated with schizophrenia within the disease itself and so ignore the social contexts of meaning, it's difficult to grasp the communicative grounds of such statements or to know whether they are to be taken literally or metaphorically. In the shelter, there were good reasons for most bodily ailments. Far more complicated than anything "delusional," "psychosomatic," or "hypochondriacal," the aches and pains were often a testament to the brute force of living on the streets or hopping from shelter to shelter; the organs indexed the bruising secondness of being homeless, poor, and often without consistent medical care. Despite the lack of such care, the culture of medicine and medication in which residents circulated undoubtedly added to the sense that bodily and psychic pains were a question of internal medicine and thus to be found in distinct and internal organs. Residents thus heeded and invoked a state-managed medical "gaze" whose first incarnation came to life in Europe in the eighteenth century with the medical exploration of the body's interiors.[6] At times acutely aware of their bodies' workings, they often felt their bodies to be assemblages of distinct but interconnected parts and functions that could fragment from one another.

At the same time, the focus in the shelter on psychological "thoughts" and "feelings" prompted a situation in which some residents, already primed for a corporeal and sensate existence by the worlds of the street and lobby, couched their modalities of sensing within the frame of the staff's concern for interior states and processes. A hybrid consciousness could thus take form in which some residents felt their insides in highly palpable ways: a nervous breakdown could *feel* as if your brain had fallen to your knees and gotten crushed. Talking and thinking about the body's innards might have also related to larger structural positionings, in which the residents' bodies were construed, to use Bakhtin's terms, as torn, exposed, "rent" forms in contrast to the relatively bounded, impenetrable facades of staff and others.[7] Finally, siting pain in the organs and interstices of the body had an important truth value. Given that the staff tended to be skeptical of the residents' claims and residents needed to convince the staff that their pains were real and significant (the cycle was vicious at times), rooting pain in the tissues of the body was a good way to make such pain palpable and knowable to others. Even more than feelings of distress or nervousness, which had the air of being psychological and so possibly imagined, toothaches and pinched nerves could carry an indisputable, self-felt presence that was usually hard to deny. Another possibility is that, since people felt pains that were not readily apparent or visible to others, one way to account for such pains was to know them to occur inside their bodies. In all, the talk of organs stemmed from the facts of hardship and fragmentation, an incisive medical gaze, an active imagining of torn, exposed bodies, the palpable feel of bodily functions and ailments, and the knowledge and truth implied in organic pains.

Despite the implied veracity of such pains, comments about them could still be heard as just talk. Perhaps because of this, some men and women, apparently finding that talking about psychic or physical ailments was not good enough, would occasionally situate the reality of pain on the surfaces of their bodies. One day Simone Jacobs, sufferer of numerous ailments for thirty years, lay in the grass behind the northern side of the building while sporting a necklace, an ankle bracelet, and a wrist bracelet, each made of interlocking safety pins. When she returned to the shelter I complemented her on the bracelets. "Thank you," she said with a smile, then added: "I thought I would adorn my tortured body." She went on to say that "blacks and women are *killing* me inside." She then pulled down her lower eyelid, held her exposed eye close to me as if to show me the veracity of her claim, released her eyelid, and nodded her head in confirmation.

I took the latter demonstration, which she had relied on in "proving" similar claims during other conversations, as Simone's way of verifying what was going on in her life or "inside" her. The knowledge was optical: a witness to her suffering saw with and through an instrument of seeing. The eye was a window onto the soul, making accessible what would otherwise remain out of sight and thus out of mind. Simone communicated by means of an adornment of bodily surfaces (the bracelets) and through the circumvention of that surface (the exposed eye). Along with tying into a focus in American culture on insignias, cosmetic adornment, and superficial meanings, the logic of surface knowledge—in which visible surfaces either hid or embodied the truth—fit well with the focus in the shelter on knowing others first through their physical appearance. The metallic sharpness marked her body as a tortured one; the public, horrific side of distress matched up with and confirmed its intimate, painful side (the interlocking pins might have also worked to defend or integrate her body). We could say, as anthropologists and others have argued, that her body worked along symbolic or metaphoric lines to convey social, political, or psychological dynamics.[8] But it would be better to stress her body's rhetorical cast. Both the adornments and the exposed eye worked to verify and hence to persuade Simone's audience of the force and reality of her distress.

Fred Wiessner, a shelter regular, relied on a similar rhetoric in the spring of 1991, a time of severe government cutbacks in social services. A large, imposing man who, depending on his mood and pressures imposed upon him, tended to act in either childlike or menacing ways, Fred often got into trouble for threatening the staff with violence. When this happened he was usually sent to the psychiatric ward upstairs until the staff found he could control his passions again. Once, while staying in the shelter, he upended the medicine tray and threatened the staff, and was sent to the psychiatric ward. A couple of weeks into his stay he was able to take leaves from the ward and began to spend much of his time around the lobby. One afternoon I found myself sitting with him on a bench. "Look what I did to my arm, Bob," he said, and rolled up his sleeve to show his left forearm. There were cuts all along the forearm. Some fresh cuts, laced with black stitches, crossed over older and apparently more severe scars.

"Why did you do that?" I asked.

"To *prove*," he said slowly, and with an angry edge, "that *I'm* sick, the *government* is sick, the *state* is sick, and *you* are sick."

"I guess I was feeling kinda sad," he said a minute later, and went on to say that his case manager was leaving her job and moving to California.

Fred's cuts had an air of ragtime to them in that they involved a disquieting semi-private system of meaning that most onlookers would find difficult to grasp at first. Yet his actions made a lot of sense once the grounds of communication and meaning were understood. While other factors were likely involved in Fred's actions, his cuts took the staff's epistemology of the real to an extreme in "proving" his distress as well as the madness around him.[9] Just as people needed to show the physical signs of having showered in order to be rewarded for showering, the intuitive logic went here, so one needed to signal distress on the body, rather than with words thrown into the air.[10] As Judith Irvine notes, different societies acknowledge different modalities for the expression of affect; "some communicative channels may be privileged over others as more likely to convey 'true' information about affect."[11] In the shelter the body was at times the most evidential and most undeniable plane of existence—and, at times, of pain. Bodiliness and pain implied one another.

Wittgenstein found this to be the case in general. In *Philosophical Investigations* he refuted Descartes's idea that body must be differentiated from mind by showing that we understand sensations of pain to occur only in living bodies:

Look at a stone and imagine it having sensations—One says to oneself: How could one so much as get the idea of ascribing a *sensation* to a *thing*? One might as well ascribe it to a number!—And now look at a wriggling fly and at once these difficulties vanish and pain seems able to get a foothold here, where before everything was, so to speak, too smooth for it.[12]

Fred apparently minded a similar practice in cutting his arms: one may listen to his words and question their veracity; but now look at his cuts and scars and at once these doubts vanish and pain gets a foothold. There was something profoundly cultural in all this. The act took form in the same universe of meanings that renders not only imaginable but sensible tattoos, body piercings, cosmetic surgery, slit wrists, Jesus's lacerations, and the "apparatus" of Kafka's *In the Penal Colony*, which painfully inscribes into the body of a condemned prisoner that man's sentence in a "labyrinth of lines crossing and recrossing each other."[13] Yet there was also something peculiar to the shelter in Fred's act: a hybrid logic took form in which a man tried to be heard by couching his concerns in an idiom understandable to those empowered to evaluate his concerns—by making lasting, readable incisions on his forearms. The proof of sickness lay in part in how far he went to prove the sickness. Fred's reliance on this vehicle of communication was not due to any language-shattering inexpressibility inherent in the agony of pain or distress. It related, rather, to questions of acknowledgment and recognition.[14] In fact, it's quite possible that Fred showed me his arm in order to get me to recognize and so validate and share in his misery.

As such, Fred's actions tied into local and sometimes problematic modes of listening and truth making. A few years ago, Gregory Bateson pointed out that some personal, social, or cultural ways of knowing (such as those invested in alcoholism or a nuclear arms race) can be troublesome, if not downright pathological.[15] Fred put forth a similar claim in diagnosing and documenting a sickness common to himself and those empowered to manage his life. He was apparently onto something. A state government decreed that he and others be locked up, doped up, and psyched up by technicians of the mind, only to curtail such care when state funds ran dry. And while an ethnographer scribbled away, hashing out yet another interpretation, a therapeutic and bureaucratic agenda, promoted by the technicians and characterized by ideas of reading, reference, and truthfulness, encouraged those who received care to draw on those ideas in order to make known what ailed them. The agenda was of such lasting potency that its means of assessment could become ingrained in a person's actions and etched on the surfaces of his body.

With Your Head Tilted to the Side

When you're homeless, Richard explained, you end up with just your body because you don't own anything else. He and others made good use of what they had. From the rites of pacing to ingestions of caffeine and nicotine to occasional adornments of bodily surfaces, slight but consequential uses of bodies helped shape the phenomenal and social worlds in which people lived. General bodily comportments, in turn, were often the vehicle of rhetorical pitches in the State Service Center, for residents came to embody certain physical stances that helped them to present certain identities or to persuade others. During my fieldwork I came to realize that many of those who stayed in the shelter or in the psychiatric ward walked with slumping shoulders and downcast heads and eyes, as if they had come to incarnate their roles as supplicants and subalterns. I wanted to find out what Richard would think of my observations and so noted them to him as we sat in the lobby watching people step toward the cafeteria in search of dinner. Ever mindful of bodies, Richard responded quickly. "They force you to walk like that," he said. "Yeah, you walk around with your head tilted to the side so that people driving by think about what they're doing."

Inherent in his explanation—far subtler than my own at the time—was a complex loop of actions, reactions, and rhetorical messages. The stance implied a communicative act, and hence an audience: uses of a body could be geared toward how others might understand those uses. As he put it at first, these others "force" a person to walk "like that" (note that residents "walk" whereas others "drive," and it's quite possible that Richard was thinking not of people in cars but of the goal-driven bureaucrats who sped through the building). If he had stopped with this statement, it might lead us to conclude, as I had then thought, that the line of action was a direct and obvious one: that certain abuses and humiliations made people bend their heads and cast their eyes downward—much as "the hapless" in the biblical Psalm quoted by Alice "are crushed, sink down." But Richard went on to finesse his view (with the fine-tuning signaled through the use of "Yeah") in saying that the imposition of such a stance was an indirect, dialogic one, set to a reactive rhetoric: they force you—there appears to be no choice or direct agency in the matter—to assume a humble bodily stance, which in turn makes the drivers think about what they have done (or failed to do) to make you walk that way and, by extension, live within the shabby confines of a place like the mental health center. A phrase like "so that" echoed the grammar and logic of many glossings on feelings in and around the shelter: people stood and walked in a certain way *in order to* get something done. The footing was conversational in nature and relational in form. Much as phonemes acquire significance in systemic contrast with other phonemes, a titled, slow-moving body gained meaning through its counterpoint in more upright, straightlaced physiques. Although the communication involved a nonverbal vehicle of meaning, this was appropriate, given the fast-paced, vision-skewed attentiveness of its audience, so that the stance might settle in the unconscious optics of the building and its users.[1]

Bodies could thus serve, for Richard at least but most likely for others as well, as rhetorical devices, with the angle of communication (dialogic, indirect, rhetorical) oddly mirroring the nature of the stance (bowed, concave, with head tilted to the side). There was a certain technique to these positionings of the body, as there was in pacing. But while its mechanics were just as habitual and effective as pacing, they did not involve the kind of conscious deliberations that pacing did. Its workings were more reflexive, more subliminal, arising out of the give and take between people. The stance was social where pacing was psychological. While pacing was successful if it helped people to settle their nerves, the gist of walking around with your head tilted to the side was often communicative. The effectiveness of the technique depended on how persuasive it was. Its logic built on themes both cultural and discursive. If Aristotle was correct in arguing that a highly effective way to persuade others is to present a "character" suited to the interests of one's audience, then what better, more mimetic way to convey the nature of one's life or concerns in American society than through a body's look and gait?[2] And while the communication had the tone of a pragmatic move that might occur in the beat of a conversation, it could congeal in a lasting and tacit bodily stance—in part because of the routine, habitual nature of such conversations in people's lives.[3]

Other bodily, emotional, sensorial, and verbal stances took root in similar ways. Built into the idea of struggling along, for instance, were the kind of call-and-response sequences that structured many exchanges in the shelter and, by extension, many conversations about how people were feeling. "How you doing?" Louise Colbate or I would ask Alice, to which she would reply "Oh, struggling along." While others did not put it in so many words, struggling along carried an implicit sense of responding to a query or reacting to a situation. As noted above, this kind of language game was common to many interactions, with a question like "How are you doing?" often taken to mean, "How are you feeling?" As with other responses to this question, such as "Pretty lousy" or "Not so good today," struggling along implied an affective or sensory state. Launching a response with a sighing phrase like "Oh" or ending it in silence (as Alice did when Louise followed with "Yeah?") could help to underscore the tone. Ultimately it was a question of suffering through something.

Yet that question often played itself out in terms of a larger set of social and political concerns, with people signaling their distress possibly in order to get something done, be it to effect some change in their world, get someone to listen to them, or bum a few cigarettes. As with other stances in and around the building, struggling along had its rhetoric. The rhetoric related to the basic conditions that led to the sense of struggling, for both the rhetoric and the struggles took hold in a world of secondness, reaction, dialogues, tactics, and marginality. In fact, the nature of the struggle and the politics involved meant that "lower-enders" like Alice needed to assume a rhetorical stance. Much as life in the Center could lead someone to adopt a particular, habitual way of walking or talking, struggling along could entail a general, overriding stance toward the world. This meta-stance suggested how that world was to be sensed, thought of, and spoken to. The world helped to set up the stance, and the stance helped to mold the features of that world as understood by those embodying the stance.

Since there was no bottom line to these ways of being and talking, there could be no simple understanding of the question of subjectivity. While "struggling along," "hanging in there," or "the shelter blues" involved singular consciousnesses, these and other subjective processes were also irrevocably caught up in the doings and subjectivities of others. Contrary to what many psychologies and philosophies of selfhood imply, people did not act on their own. Yet with their grounds more dialogic than monologic, the processes were intersubjective not in the customary, sociological sense of a single, shared group consciousness (we saw how difficult that was to maintain in the shelter), but in the sense of emerging out of conversational exchanges between different consciousnesses. Tilting one's head to the side or adopting a certain tack in life resulted from a broader, unspoken conversation of motives and perceptions.

Pacing the Labyrinth

The short of it was that, the more people settled into the routines of the shelter, the more rhetorical their lives were, not the least because many of the daily routines evolved around rhetorical moves and counter-moves. Rhetoric was built into the voicing and feeling of things—in much the same way as it was a "rule" in the shelter to "stand away" when asking for something.

Residents minded other "rules" as well. From what people told me and from what I gathered, these precepts, which stood in counterpoint to the staff's posted mandates, included more or less implied, more or less shared, and occasionally contrary stances, sensibilities, and methods of everyday life:

- Steer clear of the assaults, reductions, and muting isolation of the streets.
- Avoid places or activities that invoke fear, distraction, or worries.
- Try to keep "voices" and "nervousness" to a minimum; if necessary, use alcohol, medications, or other drugs.
- Seek out a sense of calm, stasis, or timelessness when the distractions get to be too much. "Play dead" if need be.
- Try to hold yourself together. Try not to lose control or act in anger.
- Pace when you need to think or when you have energy to burn.
- Try to hang in there. As Kevin Halpern put it, "Live one day at a time, don't get of yourself, and don't get too worried."
- Establish routines of smoking and eating and talking. Drink coffee to keep up with the routines.
- Be wary of falling into a "rut," feeling depressed, or not feeling at all.
- Try to stay hopeful and spirited.
- When out of money, "just be broke," or panhandle, collect cans, work odd jobs, or bum or borrow from others.
- When giving to or taking from others, treat others "right"; work in international waters and give some room in between.
- "Walk away" or "take some space" when feuding with others.
- "Stand away" when interacting with others; in general, go your own, individual way.
- Seek distanced companionship in the company of others.
- Avoid "social areas" or interactions with others if they involve too much pain, discomfort, or unwanted intimacy.
- Seek obscurity or visibility when helpful.
- Try not to get displaced. If displaced, try not to be moved too far away.
- Abide by the staff's rules and heed instructions for practical reasons rather than for reasons of principle; as Roy Lerner advised, "blend in" if need be.
- Be wary of the stigmas associated with being mentally ill. Try to be "almost normal" from time to time.

- "Use" the health system and draw from the imageries of illness, when convenient.
- Rely on ideas of figure, character, person, self, or individual when need be.
- Try out or resort to other precepts or expediencies when the need arises. Ignore those which are no longer useful.

An angular, zigzagging geometry of action prevailed. Responsive to, but quite distinct from, the dominant bureaucratic orders—which tended by design to churn out a line of rational, methodical consistency—the precepts involved offbeat, ragtag ways of acting and knowing that were situational and practical in nature. Often reactive and indirect, more conversational than narrational in their trajectories, the precepts were inconstant and unheroic and sometimes dispiriting. They were, nonetheless, driven by concerns for well-being and treating each other right. While this local world was unique, its general bent recalled other, like-minded worlds and concerns; the kinds of powers entailed probably bore close affinity with the tactics of street urchins, gypsies, prison inmates, guerilla fighters, and other relatively powerless peoples.

Those who bed down in other homeless shelters in North America might very well think, act, and know in similar ways. But given the absence of extensive research on the subject, it remains to be seen how closely political realities and modes of action compare in different shelters. One aspect of shelter life that seems quite common, however, is the way in which people get "settled in." Indeed, the way the residents' precepts and sensibilities were geared predominantly toward life in the building, with people most concerned with the day at hand and caught up in routines of calm and stasis, recalls the process of shelter dependency or "shelterization" that researchers have documented among residents of other shelters. These researchers find that, similar to the "institutionalization" that has been known to occur among inmates of prisons and psychiatric hospitals, shelter residents gradually give up their ambitions, become involved with shelter activities at the expense of contact with the outside world, lose track of time, and focus more on immediate, tangible affairs than on any distant plans for finding a home.[1]

No single, all-defining phenomenon or pathology occurs in the institutional structure of a shelter. Rather, pervasive practices, perspectives, and a diverse set of social and environmental forces common to living on the street or in shelters work in complex ways in people's lives. Still, there is something in the idea of "shelterization" that helps to account for why Julie Mason and others found they did "good at first" when arriving at the shelter but soon got so "settled in" that they found it difficult to "get going." Those staying for a time in the Station Street shelter rooted themselves in everyday routines, came to live within a repetitive temporal cycle, usually resisted in ways that in the long run fueled their dependency, and learned to focus more attention and effort on immediate, tangible gains than on plans for leaving the shelter. In fact, more than a few grew quite fond of their lives in the shelter and were afraid or reluctant to move on to other, more "permanent" living arrangements, such as apartments of their own. Staff and other service providers thus faced an uphill battle in trying to get people to take the steps necessary to move out. The ground floor of the State Service Center was a no-man's limbo for the displaced, with residents trying to root themselves to a certain way of life and staff members trying to move people along. The dispositions were not necessarily indelible ones, however. It appears that once people moved on to other locations they soon got involved in new social and political relations and could come to incarnate ways of talking and thinking distinct from those common to the culture of the shelter—just as their lives had changed when they arrived from the streets or psychiatric hospitals.[2]

Public policy advisor is not a comfortable role for many anthropologists, including the present author, who finds that we must think very carefully before we begin to tinker with any social world. Given the hardships and suffering involved, however, it seems important to offer a few thoughts and exhortations based on the vantage point provided by conversations and observations conducted for the purpose of learning about life in a shelter. In general, it is not surprising that some settle into shelters for extended stays. These people cannot be faulted, especially since those outside of shelters grow just as attached to their homes and daily routines. For many residents, in fact, the routines and stasis were necessary equipment for well-being. Nor can the staff be blamed, since they worked in good faith to improve the guests' lives. Indeed, staff members were largely the conduit for larger structural and political forces—which, in the final analysis, were the primary agents at work. But given the force of the stasis and the meager living conditions of most shelters, it's clear that these machines for living are not the solution to homelessness.[3] At best, they entail stopgap measures to provide beds for increasing numbers of homeless people. At worst, they are part of the problem and add to people's impoverishment and despair. As things stand, the shelter industry has become part of the status quo. It has fueled the idea that shelters and shelter-goers are natural, unchangeable elements of urban landscapes, and it has contributed to a situation in which the homeless are gated, removed from public view, and given mythic, stigmatizing form through media portraits of underground creatures. Shelters often entail a publicly condoned and now quite enduring social institution through which local and national governments segregate and monitor undesirable peoples in a state of despondency and complacency. While communities still need to make shelters available to people in need of a place to stay, their energies and finances would be better served if they were directed primarily toward programs that make available safe and lasting housing. As others have noted, the development of affordable housing, stable living environments, meaningful, well-paying jobs, and sufficient incomes for those who cannot work are the best ways to address the problem of homelessness.[4]

The catch here, however, is that the goals many would wish onto those considered mentally ill—from productive, full-time jobs to strong friendships and richly experienced lives—are not necessarily possible for, or wanted by, those under consideration. There were very good reasons for Louise, Julie, and Kevin to look for "smooth days," to "stand away" from others, or to not get ahead of themselves. These efforts often enabled them to live in the best terms possible, given their concerns and circumstances. More durable labors or more intensive involvement in the lives of others could have invited additional distress and worries and thus destroyed the intricate, homeostatic balance that many took great pains to establish. Unfortunately, there are such strong positive moral connotations assigned to action, productivity, experience, intersubjectivity, and deep and lasting intimacy in mainstream American society that it can be difficult to fathom that these ideals are not the best medicine for some. It is all too easy, in turn, to condemn those who do not live up to these proposed ideals, or to devise therapeutic agendas that work to mold people into sociable and productive members of an intersubjectively shared world. But since these agendas can be at odds with what keeps people relatively sane and out of hospitals, engineers of mental health care and public policy would be wise to bracket their values and assumptions and try to understand, in good phenomenological fashion, the time-tested sensibilities and precepts of those they are authorized to care for. If they were to take such a phenomenology far enough, they would probably find that the circumstances of life can lead people to live, talk, think, and use money in terms of a logic and an ethics different from their own. They might also hit upon the discomforting idea—as I have through this inquiry—that a society's provision for rationality, truth, sincerity, responsibility, and agency can be rooted in political concerns.

This does not mean that those deemed homeless mentally ill should simply be left to their own devices or told to make do with what they can on the streets or in shelters—as if the different orientations called for a laissez-faire division of peoples. In general, conditions of poverty and distress lead to the lifestyles that the down and out assume in life;

the lifestyles do not promote or reinforce the conditions, as some "culture of poverty" theorists have argued. Alice and others struggled along not because they wanted to, but because they had to. Any mandate for change should therefore focus on the conditions, not the lifestyles. For reasons both logical and ethical, then, the makings and material consequences of poverty and misfortune must be addressed. Carla put it well when she said that nobody should have to be on the streets.

Ultimately, I think, there should be a two-fold strategy of providing shelter and a decent standard of living for people, and permitting those people their differentness. While the political climate in years to come might not make either of these possibilities—let alone the two together—all that feasible, the strategy can be effectively implemented if there is the political will to do so. The solution, however, is not to shunt people into single-room occupancy apartments, where they would be cut off and isolated from others. As many people who lived in apartments before or after staying in the shelter told me, living on one's own can bring its own problems: there can be no one to talk to, which means not only that one can get downright lonely but that any delusions or hallucinations cannot be checked by the realities of others. People spoke often of the need for community and companionship, as well as of the kind of states that Julie found herself in when she moved into an apartment of her own, in which she felt safer staying "inside" but ended up watching flames flare out of electrical sockets. (Julie's hallucinations point to the fact that some interventions are called for when people cannot care for their basic living needs or are at risk of committing violence against themselves or others.)

The best housing arrangements for most, then, would be those in which people lived in privacy within communities of others. Some might be comfortable on the sidelines of social life, some might prefer the center at times; arrangements must be flexible enough to allow for both options. Any therapeutic or social services should generally be made available to people rather than forced upon them. Providers of those services should not try to make people conform to capitalist values so much as allow them their differentness while also being attentive to their concerns and ailments. This kind of attentiveness, in which assistance rather than change is the priority, would probably imply an ethics of listening and acceptance over one of speaking and analytic interpretation.

Such a reorientation could also promote movements away from identifying people primarily through the all-defining characterizations of psychiatric diagnoses toward a situation in which we heed the subtle, multiplex, pragmatically attuned, and occasionally contradictory dimensions of people's lives, minds, and actions. If any socially or existentially salient echoes of the residents' lives are to be found in other documents on madness, they are best located, I think, not in the listings of DSM or the tables of epidemiological studies so much as in the pages of a book like *Oscar*, Peter Wilson's anthropological portrait of Oscar Bryan, a resident of the Caribbean island of Providencia.[5] Thought to be "mad" but accepted nonetheless by other islanders, Oscar spent much of his time by himself, only to arrive suddenly at his neighbors' homes, talk up a storm, comment on the foibles of others, demand food or companionship, and sometimes devastate or "sanitate" people's backyards if they did not yield to those demands. Like Oscar, those staying in the shelter were eccentrics—by and large intelligent, socially astute, ethically motivated, and usually lucid, but often tormented and opaque—who vexed and were vexed by those around them. Identities never fused completely with diagnoses; ailments were only one strand in very complicated lives. Any future policies toward those considered mentally ill need to take into account crucially different ways of thinking about personhood.

All this is easier said than done, of course, and it looks as if institutionally based, psychiatrically oriented shelters will be the rule for years to come. One need only consider the ever-increasing multitude of refugee camps, squatter settlements, and poorhouses throughout the world, or note the "cage"-like cubicles in places like Hong Kong, which reportedly house up to five thousand of the city's elderly, sick, and disabled, to gather that these kinds of social housing arrangements are more a thing of the future than of the past.[6] Given this forecast, an imminent task is to map and act on the powerful regional and global forces that determine the living arrangements of poor or marginal peoples.

Another task, with which this book has been most concerned, is to consider how these arrangements shape the lives and consciousnesses of those who live within them. This question itself ties into matters of human subjectivity. The climate-controlled, hermetic inclusiveness of the State Service Center, in which people minded much the same routines and struggles day after day, had several inadvertent consequences. One was that its all-inclusiveness could lead some to feel that they had "dissolved" into or become "part" of the building. Another was that the predilections of many to hang around the confines of the Center led to a compilation of ethnographic data focused primarily on life within the building (making me wonder on occasion if the data was leading to a palimpsest of one of Beckett's "closed space" tales, in which voices embodied or disembodied putter about a bound area). This institutionally dependent concentration of knowledge has its limitations, for I cannot speak with great certainty about many residents' lives outside the orbit of the shelter. Nevertheless, the inclusive and relatively knowable

parameters of many shelter lives readily lend themselves to reflections on the nature of selfhood within a particular cultural setting and how one might best think of self and subjectivity in general.

As for such reflections, a sentence penned by Georges Bataille in 1936 is germane: "One need only follow, for a short time, the traces of the repeated circuits of words to discover, in a disconcerting vision, the labyrinthine structure of the human being."[7] This thought reverberates for several reasons. One of them relates to my motives for and methods of research in the Center. Troubled by media accounts of the homeless and interested in advancing an anthropology of subjectivity, I tried to trace the repeated circuits of words spoken and shared in the shelter and sought to understand how these circuits tied into the lives of those who lived there. The idea of a labyrinth is fitting. Similar to the formations in a painting by Escher or in the Center itself, different aspects of knowing, feeling, listening, and acting circled back on other aspects, with no pure spaces, no straight lines, no clear inside or outside, and no true entry or exit points in sight. Bataille's focus on words in the makings of being human is also appreciated. In the Center, the musculature of language and silences, in conjunction with the broader concerns and powers in the lives of the residents, helped to form the stuff of personhood. Living on the streets or in the shelter led people to assume an existence founded on, among other things, conversational, call-and-response social interactions; reactive, rhetorical pitches implicit in many of these interactions; and a practical, shape-shifting approach to reason, feeling, and personhood. The nature of the residents' phrasings, as they took form in conversations with the staff, with other residents, or with themselves helps to confirm the insights of Nietzsche, Bakhtin, Lacan, and others that the set of processes we readily call the "self" is founded largely on poetic, dialogic, and rhetorical turns of language. It also leads me, in thinking about such processes, to agree with Benjamin Lee that the analysis of self and subjectivity requires an anthropology of discursive practices more than it does a psychology of consciousness—or rather, that a psychology of consciousness must first and foremost be grounded in a study of social uses of meaning and language.[8]

Yet an anthropology of language and meaning is not enough. Like Emmanuel Levinas, who has trouble accepting Heidegger's concept of *dasein* or "being-there" because *dasein* is never hungry, I find it problematic to frame a study of subjectivity on an account of discourse alone because people's lives involve so much more than indexes and icons.[9] One could not get very far in the shelter without heeding the pressing need for food, sleep, comfort, privacy, or nicotine. Nor could one step far into the Center without noticing the noises, smells, surfaces, distractions, worries, aches, pleasures, and desires common to each acutely public day. In studying actual, flesh-and-blood subjectivities, then, we also need to rely on phenomenological methods, however frail these methods might be, to get at the sensate and psychological dimensions of people's lives.

The grounds of feeling and desire are always semiotically mediated, of course, but they still entail something more than bundles of words and signs. At the same time, sensations of pain, joy, or nervousness are always already at least once removed from a pristine state. Every sensation occurs in a context of social and political relations. The claims of many anthropologists of experience to the contrary, there is no such thing as a pure, unmediated "lived experience." The only time a sense of authenticity comes into play is when it is effected pragmatically or evoked rhetorically—when, say, someone's words (such as an anthropologist's) suggest the idea that an emotion or sensation is an authentic or deeply felt one. These invocations are important not only because they often carry a great deal of rhetorical force, but because they point to the complex and often indeterminate linkages between meaning and sensation. As I have tried to show, it's not just a question of people having emotions and then expressing or reporting on those emotions. But neither, usually, is it a question of someone simply saying that he or she is feeling pain or struggling along without actually doing so. Discourse and sensation are forever intertwined. Acts of feeling are, from the start, immersed in rhetorical stances, pragmatic situations, and political relationships. We are often faced with a situation, as in the State Service Center, where both the force and the matter of feeling are caught up in complex patterns of speaking, listening, writing, and truth telling. Such situations make it difficult for us to stick with anthropologies of "emotion" or "the body" that try to describe in cultural terms what people feel without situating from the start moments of feeling or bodiliness within a more comprehensive set of social, linguistic, and political forces. Our lives, our subjectivities, are not only culturally and historically constituted, as a great deal of literature now suggests; they are intensely pragmatic and political in their makings.

Issues of power are all-important here. All too often approaches in psychological anthropology neglect serious discussions of the ways in which people think, sense, and know are embedded in pervasive and often quite pressing economic and political arrangements.[10] The realities of the Center suggest how myopic such approaches can be. A world of displacements, makeshift economies, bureaucratic careers, insufficient housing, and government cutbacks set up tactical and reactive ways of acting; ways of relating founded on the give and take of exchange; forms of sensing built of hyper-individualized states, sensations, and rhetorical stances; methods of reckoning time centered on generally unconnected episodes and distinct "doings"; and ways of knowing predicated on obscurities, surface knowledge, and disparate planes of meaning. These and other orientations, in tandem with other cultural, discursive, and political forces, patterned the grounds for what was possible in peoples' lives. They shaped what residents could do, what powers they could claim, how they spoke, knew, felt, and thought—their personal "psychologies," as it were—and how they lived as subjects. In turn, since healing involves the transformation of one way of being into another, it always implies politics: the therapeutic agendas advanced by the state encouraged residents to adopt new ways of speaking and knowing, to undertake different orientations to time, and, in the long run, to assume forms of consciousness distinct from those common to life on the street or in the lobby. Since each of these subjective orientations implies political forces, any discussions of the psychology of residents (or of anyone else, for that matter) must take into account the politics motivating particular lives.

These explorations must also take into account the modalities of meaning and interpretation that underpin minds and feelings. Different ways of making and heeding words took hold in the shelter: while staff members chiefly aligned themselves in writing, narrative, representation, and interpretive understanding, residents tended to live in terms of talking, listening, and rhetoric. As detailed above, these different orientations, rooted in the political exigencies of people's lives, led to conflicts, misunderstandings, and complex, hybrid forms of speaking, feeling, and being. So often these days we hear someone or other pushing a new academic trope—"interpretation," "textuality," "writing," "narrative," or "dialogue"—as the be-all of human communication, as if the concept might capture the essence of being human. One thing we can take home from the shelter, however, is the idea that all methods of meaning (including those common to ethnographic efforts) are enmeshed in a sea of forces. The distinguishing spirit of a narrative, readerly, or conversational approach to life has a great deal to do with fundamental, politically mediated understandings of time, meaning, truth, and knowledge.

The frames of meaning and assessment that coursed through residents' lives were not static, all-defining structures. They were always situated in and contingent on certain concerns that came to life in particular interactions. Yet those who lived for a time in the shelter tended to fall into routines, pick up habits, and develop certain bodily and subjective stances toward the world. Life thus often involved a mix of lasting stances toward the contingencies of life. The routines and stances involved a wealth of concerns, some economic in nature, some political, some social, some biological, and others psychological. All of these concerns implied various moral sensibilities—but again, not in any stead-fast way.

Residents, then, were culturally constituted, semiotically mediated, and institutionally stamped human beings who, primed for conversational, rhetorical stances toward the world, thought, felt, and reacted in creative, tactical, shape-shifting ways. Interauditors as well as interlocutors, assemblages of voices responsive to the voicings of others, people were complex, changeable, and contradictory. Yet there were limits to what they could change; many continued to hear voices and live in poverty. The coefficients of this book—conversation, rhetoric, power, obscurity, uncertainty, and differentness—were the uneven constants of their lives. The sense of selfhood that comes through all this is a decidedly pragmatic, worldly, rhetorical one. It is quite suited to the makeshift margins of a capitalist state. While some might detect similar themes in their own lives or want to apply this sketch of subjectivity in places like Nepal, Kansas, or New Guinea, we can do so only with caution. Other political economies and other realities imply other ways of being and forms of consciousness—as evident in the staff's and residents' different orientations to life. Yet the method of inquiry outlined in these pages—an admittedly integrative, pragmatic approach that takes into account the necessarily related, intersecting dimensions of being human—might help us to account for the constitution of subjects in other places.

This gets us back to the idea of experience. In and around the shelter, acts of experiencing, like those of struggling along, were the product of several interdependent forces. As suggested earlier, certain structural, social, and semiotic conditions could contribute to a sense of privacy, movement, travel, storytelling, and transcendence, which, in turn, could lead to culturally patterned modalities of being that can best be identified as "experience." At the same time, different engagements in or perspectives on much the same social scene could involve different forms of consciousness; one man's misery could be another's experience, or that misery could become an experience through later retellings. In turn, a person or group could try to get another to experience. Staff members, for instance, encouraged their guests to venture out into the world, to reflect deeply on the psychological makeup of their lives, to think and feel intensely, to look toward and plan for the future, to talk and reflect in terms of a consequential, if-then, narrative logic, to set up their lives in a way that promoted the possibility of a cumulative transcendence, and to adopt forms of consciousness common not to the streets or the lobby but to the shelter. In effect, and though it was not put in so many words, they encouraged and helped their wards to live within the arc of experience.

Yet, as with the makings of reason and personhood in the shelter, nothing was straightforward, and it often made sense for many residents to stick with the routines required of them. Indeed, the broader structural and phenomenal conditions of their lives often made this a necessity. The dimensions of their lives were usually not cut out for experiencing. At other times, experiencing could be an unwelcome activity. "Too much movement" a man diagnosed as schizophrenic said of a visit from his mother; "too much experience" could easily have been the comparable lament of many residents in regard to what they took to be overly active or interactive modes of being.[11] Most continued to struggle along. But there were also many forays into experience, as when William went on his walks through the city or Alvin tried to get a job and planned on writing his novel. It's also likely that some indexed or participated in the modalities of experience for much the same reasons that they assumed the role of specific characters or called on sensations of pain: because doing so helped them to get what they needed and wanted. Given the ideological weight ascribed to ideas of depth, narrativity, and transcendence these days, it would make sense that intimations of experiencing would carry a great deal of pragmatic and political force in either the split-second turn of a conversation or in recurrent responses to a therapeutic agenda.

Reflections on the everyday can get very messy indeed. The category of experience is riddled by structural forces, cultural sensibilities, subjective vicissitudes, political tensions, pragmatic moves, and rhetorical pitches. The ordinary-language notion of experience as the felt sense of life will probably thrive in anthropology for as long as we find uses for the metaphysic that propels that notion—as long, that is, as states of feeling are held to be more authentic than social or political processes. But for those who want to try to figure out what human subjectivities involve, how they come about, and what forces underpin them, a revaluation of methods and motives is called for. Rather than take ideas of "experience," "personhood," or "the body" as intensely human, existential givens that reappear in their empty sameness from culture to culture, we need to bracket the categories. We need to question the assumptions that shadow our understandings of human sentience. We need to ask how intimations of "experience" or "feeling" serve and respond to rhetorical and political needs that help establish certain ways of approaching the world. We need to reflect on the pragmatic consequences of intimations of feeling, bodiliness, psychological states, or the phenomenal more generally. We need to bear in mind that acts of reasoning, narration, and feeling are political through and through. We need to consider very carefully how the everyday is put together.

It's also worth the effort to situate particular manifestations of the everyday in their broader historical contexts. For the residents of the shelter, a set of circumstances contributed to certain worries and stances in life. Others alive today, from migrant farm workers and inner city youths to prisoners and overburdened homemakers, might very well face similar concerns. Indeed, some of the most fundamental constellations of time, space, and consciousness appear to be changing in the late twentieth century. In the modern industrial era, many took "experience" for an essential part of human nature because its defining features—reflexive depth, temporal integration, and a cumulative transcendence—blended so well with the reigning actions and sensibilities of that age. But the poverty and transience that are increasingly coming to characterize life on the fringes of many societies today suggest that experience might become, at least in some circles, a relic of the past.

Appendix: List of Shelter Residents

All names listed in the table are pseudonyms.

Name, age, race-ethnicity	Length of stay in shelter as of 1992	Moving from	To
Women			
Alice Weldman, 39, W	2 years	streets	streets
Barbara Harpham, 61, W	2	½ years +	shelters
Carla Bataille, 58, W	1 ½ years +	government center	
Catherine Mohr, 41, W	3 years +	?	
Debra Joyce, 42, AA	1 year	shelters	project housing
Estelle Trevor, 65, W	8 years +	shelters	
Eva Winfield, 35, AA	1 ½ years +	shelters	
Evonne Vinge, 34, W	1 year +	shelter	
Helen Kessler, 47, KA	3 ½ years	group home, psychiatric hospital	project housing
Julie Mason, 33, AA	1 year	streets, shelters	project housing
Louise Colbate, 32, AA	6 months	shelters	project housing
Nancy Ange, 30, White	1 year +	hospital	
Nina Anderson, 28, AA	6 months +	shelters	
Rose Crecco, 56, W	6 years +	apartment, streets	
Simone Jacobs, 62, W	6 months +	streets	
Susanne Kernan, 48, W	2 years +	streets, shelters	
Sylvia Covert, 36, W	8 years +	streets	
Wendy Dyer, 38, W	1 year	shelters	apartment
Men			
Anthony Scola, 52, W	1 year	makeshift accommodations	makeshift accommodations
Brian O'Grady, 33, W	5 ½ years +	?	
Bruce Baker, 34, W	7 years	streets, shelter	project housing
Colin Malory, 55, W	2 years +	streets	

Name, age, race-ethnicity	Length of stay in shelter as of 1992	Moving from	To
Fred Wiessner, 37, W	1 year, with intermittent stays in hospitals	hospital	hospital
Greg Bagnel, 31, W	5 months	streets	project housing
Hector Ortiz, 38, W	2 years +	streets	
Henry Williamson, 42, W	1 year	hospital	project housing
Ian Greene, 29, W	8 months +	shelters, different cities	
Irving Jackson, 49, AA	7 years	streets, shelters	project housing
Jeff Proulx, 48, W	3 months	hospital	hospital
Joey Austen, 36, W	4 months	hospital	hospital
Kevin Halpern, 36, W	2 years	streets, shelters	project housing
Larry Parker, 39, AA	8 years +	streets	
Logan Persain, 45, W	1 year +	streets	
Martin Aaron, 22, W	5 months	shelters	apartment
Mitch Anderson, 44, W	7 months	abandoned warehouse	project housing
Nathan Ellison, 28, AA	9 months	other cities, shelters	project housing
Peter Vaughn, 53, W	6 years	streets	project housing
Ralph Powell, 48, W	3 months	streets, different cities	another city
Richard Groton, 31, W	2 years +	mother's house, shelters	
Roger Minuchin, 47, W	1 ½ years +	streets	
Roy Lerner, 35, W	2 years +, with intermittent stays in hospitals	streets, shelters	
Sam Kinch, 57, W	4 years	shelters	hospital
Stuart Coopan, 34, W	1 ½ years	shelters	apartment
Ted Scranton, 64, W	3 years +	streets, shelters	
Tommy Frank, 30, W	6 months	streets	project housing
William Fordham, 51, W	7 months	shelters, streets	project housing

Others who frequented the building	Living arrangements
Amy Crenitz, 44, W	previous stay in shelter; had her own apartment in 1991–92
April Berreman, 34, W	had her own apartment
Eric Oberg, 39, W	previous stay in shelter; had his own apartment in 1991–92
Thelonious, 36, AA	slept on benches outside building
Walter Rech, 57, W	reportedly lived in psychiatric hospital for 10 years
Warren Nations, 32, W	lived in an apartment on the outskirts of Boston

Note: W = "white"; AA = African American; KA = Korean American.

Acknowledgments

The ethnographic research on which this book is based, conducted in 1991 and 1992 while I was a National Institute of Mental Health post-doctoral research fellow in the Department of Social Medicine, Harvard Medical School (Grant #MH1–8006), was linked to the McKinney Research Demonstration Project at Boston, directed by Stephen Goldfinger. My research and writing benefited greatly in its early stages from conversations with the project's ethnographic team—Norma Ware, Joshua Breslau, and Tara AvRuskin—as well as from feedback on presentations to the seminar in clinically relevant anthropology at Harvard University. Byron Good, Mary-Jo DelVecchio Good, and Arthur Kleinman advised me in my work in countless ways. John G. Kennedy continued to inspire. Theresa O'Nell read the entire manuscript and offered astute and probing musings on the material. Others who have given valuable feedback along the way include Anne Becker, Donald Brenneis, Lindsay French, Kostas Gounis, Paul Grifhorst, Anne Lovell, Dan Rose, Jamie Saris, Toni Tugenberg, Mirjam Von Ewik, Unni Wikan, and James Wilce. Vincent Crapanzano, Michael Herzfeld, Kim Hopper, Donald Pollack, Barbara Tedlock, Dennis Tedlock, and several other, anonymous reviewers fruitfully assessed several journal articles. Allen Feldman and Arthur Kleinman read a penultimate draft; many of their comments and suggestions have been incorporated into the present text. Michael Desjarlais helped to prepare the cover photograph. Patricia Smith and Paul Stoller have once again served admirably as editors.

At Sarah Lawrence College, support for research from the Marilyn Simpson Fund for Junior Faculty Development enabled me to complete the final draft. The intellectual and creative energies of that school have been a great boon to this work. David Castriota, Paul Josephson, Musifiky Mwanasali, Chi Ogunyemi, Elfie Raymond, Sandra Robinson, Lyde Sizer, and Komozi Woodard read portions of the manuscript and offered extremely instructive comments. Mary Porter and Peter Whiteley did so as well, while also offering the kind of collegiality that makes for good living. Conversations with Nancy Baker and Margery Franklin helped me to further my ideas and to understand better how they related to concerns in philosophy and psychology. The staff of the Sarah Lawrence Library assisted in many crucial ways. Thanks as well to my students at Sarah Lawrence, especially Anya Klyotsina, Marka Knight, Eliza Miller, and Robert Rauschenberger, for attending in generously critical ways to my thoughts as they developed in the classroom and on paper.

Early versions of some portions of this work were presented at the annual meetings of the American Anthropological Association in 1993 and 1994, where they received instructive criticism from Ansley Hamid, Lorna Rhodes, Dan Rose, Margaret Lock, Kim Hopper, and Mariella Pandolfi. I also presented portions of this work to the Department of Anthropology at the University of California, Santa Cruz, in 1994, and to the participants in the faculty symposium Perspectives on Body and Mind at Sarah Lawrence College in 1996.

As always, my family has been a fount of support. Tracy McGarry, who read all too many drafts, encouraged and suffered through this work for several years.

Lastly I want to thank the shelter's staff, who assisted me in numerous ways, and the residents, especially those who go here by the names of Alice, Helen, Richard, Carla, Eva, Anthony, Peter, Julie, Jean, Irving, Martin, Simone, and Fred. I hope that these people, who attend to difficult circumstances with remarkable grace, intelligence, and good humor, find something of value in this book, which is dedicated to them.

*   *   *

Portions of this work draw from revised versions of two published essays of mine: "Struggling Along: The Possibilities for Experience Among the Homeless Mentally Ill," *American Anthropologist* 96 (December 1994): 886–901; and "The Office of Reason: On the Politics of Language and Agency in a Shelter for the 'Homeless Mentally Ill,'" *American Ethnologist* 23 (November 1996): 880–900. The former essay also appears in a slightly different form in *Things as They Are: New Directions in Phenomenological Anthropology*, edited by Michael Jackson (Bloomington: Indiana University Press, 1996). I am grateful to the editors and publisher of *American Anthropologist* and *American Ethnologist* (American Anthropological Association) for their permission to draw from this work.

Excerpt from Samuel Beckett, *Endgame* (New York: Grove Weidenfeld, 1958). Copyright © 1958 by Grove Press, Inc. Reprinted by permission of Grove/Atlantic, Inc.

Excerpts from Amelie Rorty, "A Literary Postscript: Characters, Persons, Selves, Individuals," in *Identities of Persons*, edited by Amelie Rorty

(Berkeley: University of California Press, 1976). Copyright © 1976 by University of California Press. Reprinted by permission of University of California Press.

Excerpts from Art Jahnke, "Madhouse," *Boston Magazine*, September 1987. Copyright © 1987 by Boston Magazine. Reprinted by permission of Boston Magazine.

Excerpt from Mark Leibovich, "Compassion Fatigue," *Boston Phoenix*, March 13, 1992. Copyright ©1992 by Boston Phoenix. Reprinted by permission of Boston Phoenix.

Excerpts from Royal Ford, "A Novel Kind of Shelter," *Boston Globe*, December 9, 1991; Jordana Hart, "On Bitter Night, Boston Counts Its Homeless," *Boston Globe*, December 2, 1992; and Michael Blowen, "Beauty and the Street," *Boston Globe*, December 16, 1993. Copyright © 1991, 1992, 1993 by The Boston Globe. Reprinted courtesy of the Boston Globe.

Excerpts from "Koch, the 'Entertainer', Gets Mixed Review," *New York Times*, May 19, 1988; "Preferring the Cold Shelter of the Streets," *New York Times*, December 29, 1993; and Maureen Dowd "America's Front Lawn," *New York Times Magazine*, 1995. Copyright © 1988, 1993, 1995 by The New York Times. Reprinted by permission of the New York Times.

Photo excerpt from *The Architecture of Paul Rudolph*, edited by Gerhard Schwab (New York: Praeger Publishers, 1970). Copyright © 1970 by Verlag Gerd Hatje. Reprinted by permission of Verlag Gerd Hatje and Paul Rudolph.

Notes

"Beauty and the Street"

1. Leibovich 1992.
2. Mills 1992.
3. Dowd 1995.
4. *New York Times* 1993.
5. *Boston Globe* 1991.
6. *Boston Globe* 1993.
7. *New York Times* 1987.
8. *New York Times* 1988.
9. Bakhtin 1984.
10. *Boston Globe* 1992.
11. Jahnke 1987:132.
12. Rorty 1976.
13. Ibid.: 302.
14. Ibid.: 307.
15. Ibid.
16. As portrayed, for example, in the hagiographic diaries of Che Guevara (Rorty 1976:307–9).
17. *New York Times* 1994.
18. As cited in Mathieu 1993:179.
19. Noted in Mathieu 1993:173.
20. *New York Times* 1995.
21. National Law Center on Homelessness and Poverty 1996.

Alice Weldman's Concerns

1. Kristeva 1982:140.
2. Rorty 1976:315–18.
3. See, for instance, Wagner 1993; Snow and Anderson 1993; Liebow 1993; and Timmer, Eitzen, and Talley 1994.
4. See Tessler and Dennis 1989 and Dennis et al. 1991 for reviews of epidemiological surveys of psychiatric disability among the homeless mentally ill.
5. Mathieu 1993 documents the ways in which the New York City government publicly and politically linked homelessness with mental illness in the 1980s in

order to divert attention from the socioeconomic roots of the problem and to justify the removal of homeless people from public spaces.

6. Koegel 1992.

7. See, for instance, the articles by Lovell 1992 and Gounis 1992a.

8. Hopper 1991b:127.

9. See Kleinman 1988; Corin 1990; Hopper 1991a; Good 1992; Kleinman and Kleinman 1995; and Desjarlais et al. 1995, for instance.

10. See Turner and Bruner 1986; Comaroff and Comaroff 1991; Scheper-Hughes and Lock 1987; Csordas, 1994a,b; Howes 1991; Seremetakis 1991, 1994; Cohen and Rapport 1995; and Jackson 1996.

11. See Feldman 1991; Seremetakis 1991; Farmer 1992; Scheper-Hughes 1992; and Bourgois 1995, for instance.

12. Haraway 1991:172.

13. Ibid.: 173.

Rethinking Experience

1. Thompson 1978:170.

2. See Kleinman and Kleinman 1995, for instance.

3. See Stoller 1989; Howes 1991.

4. See Jackson 1989; Wikan 1991.

5. Kleinman and Kleinman 1995.

6. Boas 1940[1887]:644–45. See Stocking 1989.

7. Taylor 1989:469. See also Gadamer 1975:63.

8. See, for example, E. Bruner 1986; Jackson 1989; Wikan 1991; DelVecchio Good et al. 1992:199; and Kleinman and Kleinman 1995.

9. As E. Bruner (1986:4–5) puts it.

10. As Jackson (1989:133) puts it.

11. Kleinman and Kleinman 1995:117.

12. Jackson 1989:1.

13. In works of this kind, experience is sometimes encountered as a verb—one can be led "to experience" something (Wikan 1991:295)—but is most often used as a noun, particularly as something one "has" (E. Bruner 1986:5). The focus is on experience as a commodity-like entity because many scholars are interested in experience as primary data.

The partiality has a history. For William James (1912:10), experience was a "double-barred" word that included both *what* men did and suffered and *how* men acted and were acted upon. Working in the wake of James, philosophers like John Dewey (1926) and Michael Oakshott stressed the integral nature of this duality, but at a certain expense. Writing in 1933, Oakshott finds that " 'Experience' stands for the concrete whole which analysis divides into 'experiencing' and 'what is experienced.' . . . the character of what is experienced is, in the strictest sense, correlative to the manner in which it is experienced" (1985[1933]:9). Given this, he deduces that "it would, then, be possible to build up one's views of the character of experience either from the side of experiencing, or from the side of what is experienced; and it would be superfluous to do both, for whatever is true of the one side will be true of the other."

One consequence of this outlook is that one can remain content with studying "what is experienced" without questioning how "experiencing" comes about. The word can thus soon become one of James's "single-barred words," like "thing" or "thought," as it generally has been in American anthropology. Indeed, the tendency to reify experience might itself be rooted in Anglo-Saxon language and culture: Norwegian anthropologist Unni Wikan tells me that her native languages hold no ready equivalents for the English *noun* "experience."

14. See Williams 1979:164–70; Scott 1991.

15. Geertz 1986:374. See also Scott 1991.

16. Heidegger 1962:2.

17. Ayto 1990 reports that "experience," like "experiment" and "expert," comes from the Latin *experiri,* a compound verb, formed from the prefix *ex-* "out" and a prehistoric base **per-* denoting "attempt, trial" that meant "to try, test." Turner (1982:17) notes that **per-* also relates to the Latin *periculum,* "peril, trial, danger," through the suffixed extended form **peri-tlo.*

18. Ayto 1990.

19. Barnhart 1988:357.

20. Taylor 1989.

21. Lévy-Bruhl 1938:8–9.

22. See Lévy-Bruhl 1938; Leenhardt 1979[1947]; Hallowell 1955; Lienhardt 1961; Crapanzano 1977; and Kleinman and Kleinman 1995.

23. Taylor 1989.

24. As the Oxford English Dictionary defines it in this context.

25. Williams 1983:128.

26. See Geertz 1986:373, for instance. The private aspects of experience make some, like Geertz, wary of experiential approaches in anthropology. Those critical of such approaches tend to question the legitimacy of the research more than the universality and relevance of the concept. Yet, in finding that experience denotes a subjective realm that can only be poorly comprehended, they uphold the view that experience is interior, private, and ubiquitous.

27. As Good puts it (1993:139). Desjarlais 1992 is responsible for the "marrow" image.

28. Auerbach 1953:3–23.

29. See Shore 1982; Ochs 1988; and Duranti 1994.

30. Taylor 1989:289.

31. Taylor 1989:465. As Gadamer (1975:67) describes the philosophy of Dilthey and Husserl, "essential to an experience [*erlebnis*] is that it cannot be exhausted in what can be said of it or grasped as its meaning. . . . What we call an *erlebnis* in this emphatic sense thus means something unforgettable and irreplaceable, something whose meaning cannot be exhausted by conceptual determination."

32. See Ricouer 1970, for instance.

33. See DelVecchio Good et al. 1992:200; Jackson 1989; E. Bruner 1986.

34. Geertz 1986:373.

35. Faulkner 1986[1936]:54.

36. Dewey 1926; Oakshott 1985[1933].

37. Heidegger 1971[1959]:57.

38. Ibid.: 66.

39. Gadamer 1975:100.

40. Heidegger 1971[1959]:61. Needham (1972:171) notes the etymology.

41. Carr 1986:30–31.

42. Charles Taylor (1989:47) holds that a narrative orientation to life is "inescapable." But since a narrative orientation entails a quite specific understanding of time and meaning, it might be safer to say that a *temporal* orientation is in-

escapable. See Becker 1979, R. Rosaldo 1986, and Good 1993 for three studies that systematically inquire into the forms of and conditions for narrativity in, respectively, Javanese, Ilongot, and Turkish societies.

43. See Foucault 1978.

Struggling Along

1. See, for instance, Mattingly 1989; J. Bruner 1990; and DelVecchio Good et al. 1992.

2. Gadamer 1975:69; citing Simmel 1922:13. In his 1911 essay "The Adventurer" (1971a[1911]), Simmel finds that, for European men, an adventure has close affinities with a "love affair."

3. Others have noted the link between journeying and storytelling. Walter Benjamin, for instance, writes in his essay "The Storyteller," in which he equates the nearly lost art of storytelling with the exchange of experiences: " 'When someone goes on a trip, he has something to tell about,' goes the German saying, and people imagine a storyteller as someone who has come from afar" (1968a:84). Michel de Certeau, in turn, contends that "narrative structures have the status of spatial syntaxes. . . . Every story is a travel story—a spatial practice" (1984:115).

If the link between journeying and storytelling is a close one, as I think it is in the history of Europe, then any ways of being not predicated on traveling—real or metaphoric—could involve a nonnarrative orientation to language, time, and meaning. This appears to be one of the factors that went into the conversational tenor of the shelter. De Certeau favorably cites Pierre Janet, who says that "Narration created humanity" (1928:261). It would be better to say that narration, which emerges out of a particular constellation of forces, creates a certain kind of humanity.

4. De Certeau 1984:91–102. Although the differences here do not necessarily hinge on any simple contrast between inside and outside, or between pacing and going for a walk, these themes perhaps exemplify the principles of movement, thought, and meaning involved in the subjective folds of many, perhaps less clear-cut lives.

5. Orwell 1961[1933]:20.

6. Eighner 1993:xi.

7. Ibid.: 96–97.

8. I find that acts of struggling along have more to do with environmental and political forces than with the vagaries of "mental illness" because I know of other people who must contend with similar afflictions (including the "deinstitutionalized" residents of a halfway house where I worked in the mid-1980s) yet whose lives are organized much more along the lines of "experience." To hear voices, feel paranoid, and think and act differently than others can have a tremendous and often disabling effect on a person's life, but the environment in which one lives determines so much more.

A Critical Phenomenology

1. See Husserl 1931:110–11, for instance. See Corin 1990, Csordas 1994a and Jackson 1995, 1996 for exemplary phenomenological approaches in anthropology.
2. Derrida 1973:3–6.
3. See, for instance, Feldman 1991; Seremetakis 1991; Scheper-Hughes 1992; Kleinman 1995; Das 1995; and O'Nell 1996.
4. See Hanks 1996:122, for instance.
5. Foucault 1980:116–17.
6. See Bateson 1972:315–20.
7. Deleuze 1988:114–15.
8. Ibid.: 114. Or, as Foucault puts it in a 1983 interview: "Three domains of genealogy are possible. First, an historical ontology of ourselves in relation to truth through which we constitute ourselves as subjects of knowledge; second, an historical ontology of ourselves in relation to a field of power through which we constitute ourselves as subjects acting on others; third, an historical ontology in relation to ethics through which we constitute ourselves as moral agents" (1983:237).
9. All this raises a final question. How can one conduct a phenomenology of a group, particularly one composed of persons of diverse backgrounds, concerns, and futures? One possible, somewhat unsatisfactory answer is to attend to the dominant concerns of the group, while bearing in mind its diversity and heterogeneity. As it was, the ubiquity of regulations, the constancy of routines, and the commonality of afflictions (fear, hearing voices) encouraged people to lead quite similar lives while staying in the shelter.

To develop a phenomenology of that world, including the forms of action and meaning intrinsic to it, we need to infer two or three things about what is going on in specific encounters, including the motives and intentions of local actors. Although alternative interpretations of the situations, actions, and utterances noted throughout this book are of course possible, I think my reading of events and utterances are accurate, in part because they accorded with the ways in which other participants in the shelter's social world generally made sense of words and events. Yet they are interpretations nonetheless. In turn, several scholars writing in the wake of speech-act theory, which at times rests heavily on ideas of personal motivation, have rightly pointed out that intentionality itself is a cultural construct that cannot be assumed in the study of language (see M. Rosaldo 1982; Du Bois 1987; and Graham 1993). While I agree with this position, the idea of individual intentionality was so built into the ways that staff and residents made sense of actions in the shelter that, in order to make secondary sense of those actions, their pragmatic force, and how people accounted for and responded to them, I have to base my own interpretations on that same idea, however provincial it might be.

Questions of Shelter

1. For these reasons, I use the past tense in describing what took place in the shelter. Since Malinowski, anthropologists have written ethnographies in the present tense in order to give a "you-are-there" feel to the descriptions, underscore the generality of the writer's findings, and integrate the tense of ethno-

graphic observations with the wording of theoretical statements. But I find that the present tense poorly fits the situation of the shelter because of the unique confluence of different forces, activities, and personalities involved. Since much of what I observed occurred during a specific stretch of time, and the nature of life in the shelter might be quite different today or tomorrow, what took place in 1991 and 1992 is best heard as a thing of the past.

The following also makes no claims to being an account of homeless people generally. As Rosenthal (1991:117) points out, data culled from shelters must be understood to reflect only a subgroup of the total homeless population. Indeed, the following is a study of a particular set of people living in a unique bureaucratic and architectural setting. The study is also slanted toward residents who came to live in the shelter for at least several months and who tended to spend much of their time in the building—inadvertently making for a kind of "in vivo," climate-controlled account of the effects of a specific political and cultural environment on a set of lives.

2. See Jencks 1994 and Timmer, Eitzen, and Talley 1994 for recent accounts of the causes of contemporary homelessness in the United States.

3. Gounis 1992b; Gounis and Susser 1990.

4. Jencks 1994:103.

5. Link et al. 1993; cited in Jencks 1994:106.

6. Gounis and Susser 1990:223.

7. By 1989, there were 130 state-funded shelters for homeless people in the state of Massachusetts, compared to only 2 in 1983 (Tiernan 1992:648). In 1991, there were 3,422 shelter beds in Boston (more than half in shelters for single adults), compared to 972 in 1983 (Argeriou 1992:459). See Bassuk and Lauriat 1986 for an account of the proliferation of shelters in Boston in the early 1980s.

8. As Hopper (1988:165) notes. Gounis (1992a,b, 1993) has written several insightful ethnographic essays on shelters in New York City, and Liebow (1993) writes of the women who live in shelters in the Washington, D.C., area.

9. Hopper 1990a.

10. Ibid.: 14–15.

11. See Gounis 1992b; Timmer, Eitzen, and Talley 1994.

12. See Klerman 1977 and Lamb 1984, for example.

13. Jencks 1994:21–24.

14. See Sclar 1990; Timmer, Eitzen, and Talley 1994:30.

15. Dennis et al. 1991:1129; Hitov 1992:600.

16. Tessler and Dennis 1989.

17. Stephens and Hodgkin 1992:441.

18. For details see Hirsch 1989; Kaufman 1992; and Argeriou 1992.

19. See Schutt and Goldfinger 1992.

20. See ibid.: 409.

21. See Davis 1990; Gounis 1993; Lash and Urry 1994:145–70; and Mitchell 1995; and Bourgois 1996:250.

22. Gounis (1992a:135–36) makes this point as well.

23. See Foucault 1965:3–37. Hopper (1987:97–98) notes that shelters in New York have often been set up in isolated, marginal, liminal places, such as on islands in surrounding waters.

24. Foucault 1991.

25. Ibid.: 100.

26. See Castel, Castel, and Lovell 1982.

27. See Rothman 1971 on the discovery of the asylum; Castel, Castel, and

Lovell 1982 and Grob 1994 for comprehensive histories of mental health care in the United States; and Katz (1986:99–103) on the mentally ill and the centralization of state power.

28. See Shatan 1969; Castel, Castel, and Lovell 1982:134. Twenty years later, advocates of the mentally ill were still critical of the Department of Mental Health's "hospital-centered, doctor-driven approach" (Hitov 1992:601).

29. See Lovell 1996 for a discussion of this new wave of triage-like psychiatric services as they have taken form among the roadside "interstices" of public space in the United States.

30. See Goffman 1961.

31. See ibid.: 14.

32. Saris 1995 develops such an approach to psychiatric institutions more generally.

33. Hirsch 1989:198.

34. Bill, a staff member, told me once that the shelter housed two "specific kinds" of people: people in "a crisis situation," who were homeless and had a psychiatric diagnosis; and people who might not have had a psychiatric diagnosis, but were already "in the system."

35. Schutt and Goldfinger 1992:410.

36. On "the drama of difference" regularly staged in total institutions see Goffman (1961:111), who found that the most salient social distinction in mental asylums was that between "staff" and "patients."

37. Schutt and Goldfinger 1992:412.

38. One reason that the staff did not want to make the shelter a permanent home for people is that they saw it as an undignified way to live. "It's a basketball court with some partitions thrown up," one staff member told me. "It's a question of human dignity not to make it permanent. It's a temporary shelter for people until they find housing." There were other people who could have benefited from the shelter's services as well, had there been room.

Five Coefficients

1. See Ware et al. 1992 and Dickey et al. 1996, for instance. One practical effect of the research project was that the number of people leaving the shelter for a spot in one of the project's houses or apartments significantly increased the shelter's rate of turnover for a few months. From January 1 to February 18, 1992, for example, twenty-two people left the shelter and an equal number took their places (in contrast to forty in all of 1991).

2. I spent time in each of the three DMH shelters, but focused on the Station Street shelter. Although I worked alone, the fieldwork coincided with ethnographic research conducted by several other anthropologists in the different houses and apartments monitored by the research project. To discuss our findings and perspectives, we met regularly for over a year, often with the director of the project, a psychiatrist employed by Massachusetts Mental Health Hospital, in active attendance.

3. The present study, along with Estroff's 1981 account of the concerns of patrons of a mental health system in the midwest United States, thus complements exemplary studies by Rhodes 1991, Young 1995, and Barrett 1996 on the cultural worlds and therapeutic logics of psychiatric staff and counselors in North America and Australia.

4. Liebow (1993:322) found in his study of a homeless shelter for women in Washington, D.C., in which he also tried to record conversations verbatim after the fact, that "with practice, one does this pretty well." Although I have come to a similar conclusion, readers should be warned that these methods of data collection might have subtly influenced my understandings. For instance, I note below that, due to the local politics of language, the nature of socioeconomic exchanges, and the difficulties that many residents faced in communicating with others, the conversations to be found in the shelter were often brief, awkward ones—"like something out of the plays of Harold Pinter," a reader once remarked. But the perceived brevity might also relate to the fact that I could not ably record longer conversations, since my memory of such exchanges faded over time. Nevertheless I think that my observations are accurate in part because they were borne out by what residents themselves reported hearing.

5. See Rosenthal 1991 and Koegel 1992 on the advantages of participant observation over survey interviews or epidemiological surveys in research on the homeless.

6. Basso 1990:172.

7. While recent work in anthropology has rightly stressed the fundamentally "dialogic" nature of human social life as well as of anthropological inquiry (see Tedlock and Mannheim 1995, for instance), I prefer the idea of "conversation" over that of "dialogue" for several reasons. Dialogue conveys ideas of egalitarian communication between two speakers on an equal political footing with one another. Yet, humanitarian ideals aside, few interactions in the world exhibit such an equality of voices. In turn, as the advocates of "conversation analysis" continue to point out, conversation, unlike dialogue, patently consists of sequentially situated utterances, adjacency pairs, and the like that imply the sequencing of meaning, knowledge, and agency in time (see C. Goodwin 1990; M. Goodwin 1990). Finally, "conversation" was the word that residents themselves regularly used in talking about their talk.

8. As Seremetakis (1991:10) found to be the case during fieldwork in her native home in Inner Mani.

9. At the same time, I refrain from writing of many of the more personal dimensions of people's lives, such as their family backgrounds and details of their afflictions. As a general principle I try to portray their lives in a way that anyone unfamiliar with them would be unable to locate and identify them (though anyone who knows Alice will probably recognize who I am talking about, given how distinctive her life is). I have therefore altered names, exact ages, the name of the shelter, and the precise location of people's previous and future dwellings.

10. K. Burke 1950:43.

11. Yet despite the commendable focus in current linguistic anthropology on the pragmatic and indexical aspects of language (how words do things on their own) over its rhetorical uses (how people do things with words), residents in particular were set up to be rhetorical speakers and their words were consequently often rhetorical in nature. They therefore need to be considered as such.

12. The differences here lead me to rely on a language of "most," "many," "some," "similarly," "only," "usually," "at times," or "tends to." This language is often an inadequate, ambiguous one, for it tries both to embrace the variant and to get at something definitive. Kenneth Burke once noted that "the social sciences would be cramped fatally" if forced to forgo the use of the term "tendency" or its equivalent (1959:256). A similar frailty applies here.

13. Cutting and Dunne 1989:222.
14. Malinowski 1935:218–23.

"A Crazy Place to Put Crazy People"

1. This blurb, cited by Conzen and Lewis (1976:70), can be compared to a subway placard posted in June 1992: "If you were homeless you would be home by now." See Gans 1962 and Fried 1963 on the details and impact of the West End redevelopment project.
2. Herrera 1964:91.
3. Cited in Venturi 1966:41.
4. Banham 1966:71.
5. As Norman Mailer dubbed them; cited in Scully 1989:50.
6. Jacobs 1961:10.
7. Ibid.: 372.
8. As recounted in Herrera 1964.
9. Le Corbusier 1928:211; Rudolph 1956:184.
10. *Progressive Architecture* 1964:64.
11. Rudolph 1977:319.
12. "From a distance," Rudolph (1977:319) observes, "all floors are seen and the true height of the building is revealed, but close at hand the top, receding floors disappear behind the first floor, so that now one reads the building as a single floor. The building's scale has been reduced."
13. Rudolph 1977:317. Early in his career Rudolph found that the experience of space was "wanting" in his early houses, which were built in Florida according to the dictums of the International Style. He consequently began to renew the "almost lost art" of exterior space by attending to the "psychological impact of space," cultivating its rich textures, reflected light, and complex, flowing spaces (1977). By 1963 his style owed less to the functional purity of the International Style and more to the American Naturalism of Frank Lloyd Wright—to the extent that some consider the "radical" State Service Center a "head-on collision" between these two sensibilities (as described in *Progressive Architecture* 1964:64).
14. Arnason 1986:206.
15. Rudolph 1977:320.
16. Ibid.: 320.
17. Ibid.
18. Ibid.
19. To quote Banham (1966:66).
20. *Time Magazine* 1963.
21. Rudolph 1977:317.
22. Jahnke 1987.
23. As described by Southworth and Southworth (1991:32).
24. Quoted by Jahnke 1987:134.
25. Robert Twombly sums up the sentiments of many in describing Rudolph's Art and Architecture Building at Yale, which students tried to burn down in 1969: "As realized in New Haven, brutalism is an architecture of rejection and impenetrability. Entries are tucked under downward-bearing cantilevers or at the rear of slots cut into the building. Enter at your peril, it seems to say. . . . Its chunky blocklike forms in rough concrete and its jagged profile turreted against

the sky suggest a bunker. Inside, its staggering levels and complicated spaces flow into each other vertically and horizontally, making visual surveillance easy but circulation confusing. . . . Physical and aural privacy are in short supply but not skin abrasions from too intimate contact with the walls" (1995:99).

26. Jahnke 1987:132.

27. To use Pevsner's words (1960[1936]:17).

28. Rudolph 1977.

29. Ibid.: 320.

30. Many residents had thoughts on the tower when I showed them a photocopy of Rudolph's original model of the Center and asked them how they would find the building if the tower was actually built. "That would be too aggressive," Stuart told me. "It wouldn't fit with the spirit of the North End. You would need something low-profile. . . . I wouldn't want to see the tower. It could block out the sun and stuff." "There's too much emphasis on sex," Richard added. "It'll have guys and girls screwing in the city. It's too cumbersome." A friend of Stuart's walked up, took a look at the photocopy, and said: "I wouldn't build that. It would cause a lot of complications. There could be fires and such." "You just don't put a tower in the center of a mental institution," Stuart said. "People could commit suicide very easily, jumping off the fifteenth floor, you know." On another occasion Brian said of the original plans, "That has power. They didn't want it built."

31. *Progressive Architecture* 1964.

"Too Much"

1. E. Burke 1958[1759].

2. Crowther 1989:67.

3. Kant 1914[1790]:112.

4. Ibid.: 112.

5. E. Burke 1958[1759]:62.

6. Weiskel 1976. In my mind, Weiskel's innovations mark a distinctive turn in the slow history of Western concepts of the sublime: while Burke found the sublime in nature, and Kant tied it to the perceptual and imaginative faculties of the mind, more recent authors such as Weiskel (1976) and Hertz (1978) hold that the sublime arises out of specific orientations to language and meaning.

7. Weiskel 1976:26–7.

8. Ibid.: 26.

9. Hertz 1978.

10. Weiskel 1976:27–28.

11. Siegel 1981:74.

12. Jahnke 1987.

Beautiful Ruins

1. E. Burke 1958[1759]:136.

2. Jahnke 1987:133, 136.

3. Walter Benjamin alludes to such a sensibility in the final words of his prescient 1936 essay "The Work of Art in the Age of Mechanical Reproduction": "Mankind, which in Homer's time was an object of contemplation for the

Olympian gods, now is one for itself. Its self-alienation has reached such a degree that it can experience its own destruction as an aesthetic pleasure of the first order. This is the situation of politics which Fascism is rendering aesthetic. Communism responds by politicizing art" (1968b[1936]:242). Modern architecture, too, has rendered the ruin an aesthetic pleasure. The question is whether we can respond by revealing the relations of power invested in such ruins.

4. Quoted in Kern 1983:40.
5. Harvey 1989:272.

Framing the Homeless

1. See page 1; Leibovich 1992.
2. Derrida 1987.
3. Carroll 1987:141.
4. Derrida 1987:127–28.
5. Kant 1974[1796]:111.
6. Bernstein 1992:173; Derrida 1987:128.
7. Auden 1976:134.
8. On this see Vidler 1992.

Sensory (Dis)Orientations

1. Others advanced similar sentiments. "It reminds me of a bomb shelter," Sylvia said. "Well, I guess we'll be safe if anyone ever bombs us." "The walls in this place are still pretty strong," Brian said. "They would hold up well during an air-raid."

2. "This place has an expansiveness, you know," Henry told me, "so you don't always feel so hedged in, and the cafeteria is nice. It's a unique building, but it could be dangerous." "It sort of seems human," Stuart said. "It gives you a lot of space. . . . I feel that there's a lot of space here. I don't feel claustrophobic at all."

3. The tendency to both enchant and confuse was common to several of Paul Rudolph's larger buildings built in the 1960s. In a 1973 interview with Rudolph, Heinrich Klotz offered his thoughts on the Yale Art and Architecture building: "In that space it is exciting to discover the many possibilities to move around. It becomes an adventure to explore the space. But, on the other hand, a stranger can get completely lost. It can be very confusing." Rudolph responded: "But it's *not* a *public* building! When that building first opened, there were literally thousands of people who came to see it, but it was never intended for that. It was intended for a few students who, presumably, soon learn the purposely secret, labyrinthlike circulation system" (Cook and Klotz 1973:98). Frequenters of the Mental Health Center needed to undergo a similar education.

4. Feldman 1991.
5. Ibid.: 126–27.
6. See Taussig 1992:11–35; Suárez-Orozco 1990, 1992.
7. Dumézil 1958; see also Tyler 1987:182.
8. See Tyler 1987:149–70; Ong 1977.

The Walls

1. Bachelard 1964.

Roots to Earth

1. Alice's intuition is supported by several studies that have found links between childhood physical and sexual abuse and the development of mental illness, as well as high rates of childhood abuse and domestic violence in groups of homeless adults (see Fischer 1992 for a review).

2. As of 1992 the territory outside the State Service Center offered several places to sleep. The benches on the upper, open-air plaza presented places to lie down during the night. One could also sleep along the edges of this area or atop one of the irregular surfaces or within the cavities that accompanied the staircase as it wound down from the piazza to the sea of tranquility. This was where Richard preferred to stay on the nights when he was kicked out of the shelter. There was also an offshoot stairwell, with a solid corduroy bannister that stood about three feet high on each side, that rose up to, and ended at, a glass door. The door, which was usually locked, led to the offices on the fifth floor of the building. "This is where the bums sleep," Richard said of the small covelike space that topped the stairwell and offered some protection from the elements.

3. The practices were similar to those described by Erving Goffman in *Asylums*, in which patients in a psychiatric hospital cultivated "personal territories"—ranging from veritable homes or "nests" to refuge sites "in which the individual feels as protected and satisfied as is possible in the setting" (1961:243–48). Yet the residents' nests and refuges were less personal, less steadfast, and more mobile than the ones occupied by the inmates studied by Goffman. More nomadic than sedentary, residents occupied temporary sites. They did not store their possessions in their territories or mark them in any way that I could see, and others could readily occupy them on a "first come, first served" basis.

4. I felt a similar inappropriateness in the lobby one afternoon when Ted, an aged man who lived in the shelter, asked me with a look of confusion and anger, "What are you doing here?"

"What?" I mumbled.

"You look like somebody who works inside."

"No. I'm not a staff member. I'm here doing research, to see what it's like to live around here," I explained. He continued to stare at me in displeasure.

5. Goffman 1961:230.

6. Bakhtin 1984[1965]:145–85.

7. See Mitchell (1995) for a discussion of some of these tensions and contradictions, particularly as they apply to the uses of People's Park in Berkeley, California.

On the Basketball Court

1. Later, this rule was changed to "[There is to be no] smoking in the shelter."

2. Kafka 1956[1925]. Gounis (1992a:135) discusses the way in which shelters in New York city serve as collective "community bedrooms."

3. See Baker, Llewelyn Davies, and Sivadon (1959:25–6) and Good, Siegel,

and Bay (1965:18), for instance. It was the absence of such a therapeutic environment in the building at large that led many to think that it was a terrible place for crazy people to inhabit.

4. See Daniel 1984:61–104.

Smoking and Eating and Talking

1. Bakhtin 1981.

2. See Gounis 1992a:137.

3. See Goffman 1961; Thompson 1967; Foucault 1977; Zerubavel 1981; and Rothman 1987.

4. See Rothman 1971:130–54. As one of the era's leading medical superintendents put it, "Quiet, silence, regular routine would take the place of restlessness, noise and fitful activity" (quoted in Rothman 1971:138). Rothman (1971:265–70) notes that, in the period following the Civil War, when those in charge became less hopeful that many of the insane could be cured, everyday care in asylums became more custodial, and the regimens often became more rigid and repressive.

5. Staff members occasionally tried to get Richard out of such ruts by encouraging him to do things. One day, for instance, Bill walked by Richard with a clipboard and said quietly, "Richard. Laundry day."

"So what," Richard said quietly.

"So what!?" Bill said. "What's wrong? You sound a little depressed."

"Bill," Richard said, "you're always trying to get on my nerves. I already take medication."

"You sound a little down. Maybe you should do something. Usually, if you do something, you feel better."

Bill walked off with his clipboard, only to return a few minutes later to ask Richard if he wanted to play a game of checkers. Richard shook his head no.

Whereas Richard tried to get out of a rut by "mixing things up," staff tried to alleviate any perceived depression on his part by getting him to undertake constructive activities.

6. Goffman 1961:69.

7. Ibid.: 69–70.

8. See Munn 1992:94.

9. I define episodic time much as Aristotle defines episodic tragedies in his *Poetics* (1987, 3.3.1), as a plot or stretch of time "in which there is neither probability nor necessity that the episodes follow one another."

Murray (1986) and Gounis (1992a), who write insightfully about the institutional routines of several "homeless" shelters in the United States, come to similar conclusions.

Displacement and Obscurity

1. Richard, for instance, was constantly being told that he was "out for an hour" for swearing, touching people "inappropriately" and so forth. The discipline was part of the staff's attempt to help Richard to act in more commendable ways. One day he was talking in a rather loud voice. "Richard, be quiet!" Roy, a staff member, told him. He then started to sing off-key until Roy yelled, "You're

outside for an hour!" Richard left the shelter but later stood by the entrance, then took a few steps inside. Finally a staff member said, "If you're not out that door in two seconds, you're out for the night." He then danced around the entrance, waved his arms across an imaginary border, and shimmied out into the lobby.

2. Foucault 1980:154.
3. Foucault 1977:202,207.
4. Ibid.: 141.
5. Ibid.: 197.
6. Deleuze 1988:28.
7. Ibid.
8. Foucault 1977:200.
9. Augé 1995.
10. Foucault 1977:200.
11. Ibid.: 218.
12. Ibid.: 154.
13. See Lovell 1992.

A Physics of Homelessness

1. See, for instance, Jencks 1994; Timmer, Eitzen, and Talley 1994; and the special issues of *American Psychologist* (1991, vol. 46, no. 11) and *New England Journal of Public Policy* (1992, vol. 8, no. 1).
2. See Bourdieu et al. 1993; Wacquant 1989.
3. Foucault 1977:200.
4. As quoted in Salerno, Hopper, and Baxter 1984.
5. Foucault 1977.

Hearing Voices

1. Rorty 1976:303–7.
2. American Psychiatric Association 1987, 1994.
3. See Kleinman 1988:121, for instance.
4. See Estroff et al. 1991; Estroff 1993.
5. Goffman 1963:3. Some residents were keenly and ambivalently aware of the "stigma symbols" that marked them as different from others. Being mentally ill—and hence living in the shelter—was known to bring an appearance of difference, dishevelment, and awkwardness. "You gonna go eat with us?" Mitch asked me one night. "Yeah, just put on a raggedy shirt, take off your glasses, and mess your hair a bit." He contorted his face and uttered a few syllables. "You'll fit right in. You could say that you're Richard's brother."
6. See Ewald 1991, who refers to this kind of configuration as the "normative society."

Holding It Together

1. See Desjarlais 1992 for a discussion of everyday aesthetic sensibilities in the context of questions of illness, health, and healing in Nepal.

2. See, for instance, Waxler 1974; Leff et. al. 1992; Estroff 1989, 1993; and Hopper 1991a.

3. Estroff 1989:194.

4. See, for instance, Waxler 1974; Harding et al. 1987; Estroff 1993; and Desjarlais et al. 1995:42–44.

5. As Estroff (1993:251) glosses the idea of chronicity.

6. Barthes 1972:75.

Taking Meds

1. See Castel, Castel, and Lovell 1982:86; Grob 1994:228–30.

2. As Deleuze 1992 calls them.

3. These ways of talking about the effects of medications were similar to those articulated by a set of psychiatric patients in the United States, as observed by Rhodes 1984. The patients commonly drew on metaphors that referred to modalities of blockage/release, fogging/clearance, breakage/remediation, and immobility/mobility. The staff who cared for these patients, in contrast, drew more on images that implied the filtering of excessive mental stimuli, the diminishment of symptoms, and the control of unmanageable actions.

4. Estroff 1981:87–109.

5. Ibid.: 109–17.

The Street

1. See, for instance, Fischer 1992:234–38; Lovell 1992; Wagner 1993; Eighner 1993; and Snow and Anderson 1993.

2. As Snow and Anderson (1993:194) conclude for homeless people living on the streets of Austin, Texas.

3. See Snow and Anderson 1993:193, 346; Segal and Baumohl 1980:361; and Lipton, Sabatini, and Katz 1983, for instance.

4. See Segal and Baumohl 1980; Fischer 1992:236–37.

5. Welsh 1993:326.

6. The isolation of street dwellers is analogous to that recalled by the unnamed narrator of Beckett's *The End* (1995[1946]:97), who comes to dwell alone for days on end in a boat lodged in a shed on the shore of an abandoned riverfront estate: "You become unsociable, it's inevitable. It's enough to make you wonder sometimes if you are on the right planet. Even the words desert you, it's as bad as that."

7. On "avolition" and the "disappearance of voluntary activity" among schizophrenics, see Kraepelin (1921:226) and American Psychiatric Association (1994: 275–77).

8. The demeanors mentioned also reminded me of the "presences" that Amelie Rorty writes of at the close of her essay on the different forms that ideas of personhood have taken in Western societies and literature.

And all along this while there has been The Russian Novel. Novels of a person tell a tale of development, of discovered responsibility, fulfilled or failed. A person's life has a form: it is continuous and unified. Myshkin or Alyosha are not persons: they are presences, the return of the unchartable soul. . . . They

are a mode of attending, being present to their experiences, without domi-
nating or controlling them. . . . It is precisely the absence of willfulness, or
choice of roles, of grace or enactment, swirl of action that make an Alyosha
present, with immense gravity and density, to his experiences. . . . Though
others respond strongly to the quality of their presence, to something of the
mood they induce, they are not agents (Rorty 1976:318–19).

Greg, Tommy, and Roy were similarly present in their worlds, innocent, and
living without strong willfulness or action. Roy, a quiet, spirited, and religious
white man in his mid thirties who said he last had a home in 1978, reminded me
in particular of Myshkin, the preternatural subject of Dostoevsky's *The Idiot.* Like
Myshkin, he was troubled by ill health and was spiritually good and intensely
"observant" (as he once described himself) though inactively and unwillfully so.

9. Harris 1989:604.

10. Geertz 1973:412.

11. To quote "Margaret Mullins," a woman in her sixties who had been homeless for twenty-two years. In telling Melissa Shook (1992) something of her life,
she mentioned that among other things she had "been harassed by punks,
beaten by the police, and humiliated—a person of no existence."

12. Anne Lovell writes of the "permanent temporal dislocation" found among
New York City's homeless street people. "I feel dead," one man told her, "'cause
that's what dead people do. They never change. . . . It's all been like one god
damn long humble day." "It's a one-day-at-a-time-Sweet-Jesus kind of thing,"
said another (1992:98, 94).

13. Sass 1992:156.

14. Cited in ibid.

15. Simmel 1971b[1911]:325.

16. Musil 1995[1952]:4.

17. It could be, in following Simmel's logic that "the metropolitan type . . . creates a protective organ for itself against the profound disruption with which the
fluctuations and discontinuities of the external milieu threaten it" (1971b:326),
that people simply got used to or adapted themselves to the stimuli of the street
and thus did not recall the street in those terms. Yet it appears more likely that
an extended stay on the streets, without recourse to the homes that other metro-
politans could take refuge in, minimized such protection or rendered it useless.

18. Eighner 1993:96–97.

19. Given these differences, it makes sense that much more than psychogenic factors associated with schizophrenia influenced how people remembered
either the shelter or the street.

Secondness to Firstness

1. Peirce 1931–35: vol. 1, para. 356.

2. Ibid.: 1.353.

3. Ibid.: 5.44.

4. Ibid.: 1.302.

5. Ibid.: 1.322.

6. Ibid.: 1.358.

7. Ibid.: 1.457; see Stearns 1952:201.

8. Corrington 1993:125.

9. Peirce 1931–35: 5.121.
10. Stearns 1952:203.
11. Ibid.
12. Corrington 1993:128.
13. Peirce 1931–35: 1.324.
14. Ibid.: 1.358.
15. Corrington 1993:138.
16. Peirce 1931–35: 7.543.
17. Liebow 1993:115.
18. Peirce 1931–35: 1.530.
19. Ibid.: 1.531.
20. Ibid.: 1.336.
21. Minkowski 1970:26.
22. Peirce 1931:35: 1.304.
23. Ibid.: 1.318.
24. Ibid.
25. Ibid.: 1.343.
26. Corrington 1993:130–31.
27. Beckett 1958:69. See the epigraph to the present book. As for the relevance of Peirce's categories of firstness, secondness, and thirdness for non-Western peoples, Daniel (1984, 1989, 1996) has put them to effective use in studies of Tamil culture in India and Sri Lanka.
28. Jaspers, 1963[1923]:111.

Pacing My Mind

1. Mauss 1973[1935].
2. Deleuze and Guattari 1987:381. Emphasis in original.
3. De Certeau 1984:91–102.

The Give and Take

1. Anthony and Dion 1986.
2. See Carling 1992:283.
3. Link 1982; Black 1988.
4. Estroff et al. 1997:60.
5. Ibid.: 61.
6. Schutt and Goldfinger 1992:410.
7. Ibid.: 410.
8. Grob 1983; Estroff et al. 1997:58.
9. See Estroff et al. 1997:63. A 1991 national study, using the federal Department of Housing and Urban Development's (HUD) standard of affordability, found that there was not a single county in the United States where individuals on SSI could afford either an efficiency or a one-bedroom apartment (McCabe et al. 1991).
10. Baxter and Hopper 1982; Calsyn, Kohfeld, and Roades 1993.
11. Some people held that the shelter's benefits were relatively luxurious. One day in the lobby I spoke with a woman who told me she was about to lose her housing and did not know how she could come up with the rent and security

deposit for another place. "These people," she said, pointing to the shelter, "go through four hundred dollars a month, and they don't have to worry about housing. Me, I'm just trying to keep from getting evicted." In fact, one of the main reasons that people stayed in the shelter was because it was an inexpensive way to live.

12. See Snow and Anderson 1993 on the role of "shadow work" in the lives of Austin's homeless, and Hopper, Susser, and Conover 1986 on the existence of "makeshift economies" in New York and elsewhere.

13. A few residents regularly scavenged and collected. "I'm sorry. I'm collecting bottles. That's what I do," said one man after brushing the "sore arm" of a woman sitting next to a trash can. He stayed in the psychiatric ward on the fourth floor and routinely scoured the building for empty cans. Others were similarly occupied. Ted always seemed to have a bag stuffed with, among other things, *Popular Mechanic* magazines and a package of envelopes. Rose was known to wear up to five hats, even in the summer, a fact that drove Helen "crazy" ("What reason could she possibly have?" she implored one day). Susanne walked by a table, noticed the *Boston Globe*, looked at an ad for Jordan Marsh, tore it off the page, and carried the clipping to her locker. From time to time, the staff told her that she could not keep the items she brought into the shelter because she had "too much stuff already."

The occasional penchants to collect or to hoard related, as did many aspects of shelter life, to the economics of homelessness. Rose, for instance, spoke of how she lost her apartment, her library, and her record collection when she fell ill. "It's all gone now," she said. Without a home to keep things ("Home is the place where you keep all your stuff," the comedian George Carlin once quipped), possessions soon filled bags and lockers. "It's not right to take all the things we have," Eva said on hearing that the staff was going to limit the articles residents could keep in their bed areas. "We don't have enough money for a place. That's why we have all our things here, and we can't even keep our own things or our own children." Collecting also arose from marginal shares of Boston's makeshift economies. Residents could earn pocket money by collecting bottles or selling the few quality items they could find in the trash, although Richard advised that "you can find blankets and clothes but not much else" in the trash bins downtown.

14. Irvine 1989.

15. As Appadurai (1986:14–15) uses the term, the commodity candidacy of an object refers to the way an object can be conceived, at certain times, as a commodity.

The street value of words was brought home to me one balmy October evening when I was in Harvard Square, talking with someone who frequented the State Service Center. He was selling flowers that he found in a trash bin behind a florist's shop for twenty-five cents each. He said he could offer people bits of his poetry or translations of Chinese characters he wrote on a piece of cardboard, but they might steal his words. "How do I know," he asked, "that if I put my words on this cardboard, or put them into the air, you or someone else won't take my words and sell them somewhere else? No, you gotta be more careful than that these days."

16. This situation accorded with some of the social relations that Humphrey and Hugh-Jones (1992:8) find to be integral to barter exchanges. They note that, because a barter exchange consists of mutual payment, "the relationships created by simultaneous barter are in themselves discontinuous and unstable. It is

possible to call quits and turn aside never to see the partner again." At the same time, "People may often wish, or need, to repeat a transaction at a later date. . . . There is therefore an in-built tendency to act fairly, that is, in a way which will satisfy the other partner such that the exchange may be repeated in the future."

17. "I like to give people food," Helen said. "It makes me feel good. I remember when I was homeless, and people gave me food." She and others would not give food to those who were not "really broke." Louise, for example, asked Barbara if she could have a cigarette. "No," Barbara said. "You spend all your money on tickets. You're not really broke." Barbara later told me that Tommy was broke: "He never has money. He goes out, gets cigarettes for people and gets two to four in return. But other people aren't really broke." For her and others, only the truly needy deserved handouts.

18. Parry and Bloch 1989.

19. See Appadurai (1986:15) on the idea of "regimes of value."

20. As quoted in Ware et al. (1992:309), where the provisional explanation for "spending down" noted in the following paragraph is also found. Gounis came to a similar conclusion in his study of a homeless shelter in New York City: "Money in the shelter does not last long—it is either consumed fast, or else it marks its possessor as a target. The pressure for immediate consumption is understandable, even rational, under these circumstances" (1992a:138).

21. Several colleagues and I also advance these observations in Ware et al. (1992). Murray (1986:83) comes to similar conclusions in his study of "time on the street."

22. See Simmel 1990[1907].

23. Schudson 1984.

Stand Away

1. Similarly, when Stuart told me that he was mad that he had to take his medications, I asked what he did when he got angry at staff. "Well," he said, "I tell them that I'm angry. I yell at them, and then I go for walks." Wendy, in turn, told me, "Sometimes, I tell people 'I am angry' or say 'You're making me angry.' If I'm angry, I need to take a time out in the lobby." It is noteworthy that many American parents nowadays tell their children to take a "time out" when they are acting inappropriately.

2. Sometimes the companionship did indeed appear to be constant. "It's a place where everybody's together. You have to be together," Carla once said. Her view was supported by something that Irving said when he joined Susanne at a table in the shelter's common area. "I'd like to be alone, if you don't mind," Susanne said when he sat down. "Alone?!" Irving said in disbelief. "How can you be alone here? Everybody's together. You could be off somewhere by yourself." He then got up and walked into the television room.

3. Corin 1990.

4. See Corin 1990; Hopper 1991a:319.

5. In turn, one of the main concerns of those who left the shelter for an apartment of their own was whether or not they would be able to maintain the same degree of contact with people as they did in the shelter. People often spoke of the loneliness that could come with living alone.

Ragtime

1. See Goldstein and Scheerer 1941, for instance.
2. Rochester and Martin 1979:91. Others speak of the "concretistic mentality" known of many schizophrenics, which is said to involve, as Louis Sass (1992:157) puts it, "an inability to transcend the literal, physical presence of a stimulus-object by perceiving it as representative of some meaning or some hypothetical world existing beyond itself."
3. Foucault 1970.
4. As defined in Webster's Ninth New Collegiate Dictionary.
5. Aristotle 1987; 1459 a 3–8; cited and translated in Ricouer 1977:23.
6. See Aristotle 1987; 4.5.4; and chapter 3.3 of section 9, on "style," in *The Art of Rhetoric* (Aristotle 1991).
7. Bleuler 1950:14.
8. See, for instance, Arieti 1974; Rochester and Martin 1979; and Wrobel 1990.
9. Kaysen 1993:75–8.
10. The "Combat Zone" is a red-light section of downtown Boston known for its strip joints and curbside prostitutes.
11. See Rieber and Vetter (1994) for a review.
12. Kernan and Sabsay 1989:229.

"Who?—What's Your Name?"

1. See Goffman 1971:19–21.
2. As Grice outlines them in his seminal 1975 paper "Logic and Conversation." In a 1989 paper, Keith Kernan and Karen Sabsay detail how mildly retarded speakers often fail to communicate effectively because they violate these maxims in similar ways: "Many of the mildly retarded individuals we work with have a tendency to provide information piecemeal, to omit necessary information, to include irrelevant or unnecessary details, to voice incomplete thoughts and to run unconnected thoughts together in the same utterance, with the result that their interlocutors find their accounts, explanations and descriptions difficult to understand" (1989:231). Whereas the difficulties of mildly retarded speakers in communicative interactions stems largely from their inability to provide, organize, and "package" or "design" information adequately in extended discourse (1989:231), the difficulties of many living in the shelter related more to their use of obscure or ambiguous meanings, lexically cohesive but incoherent discourse, and lengthy, hard-to-follow digressions. Swartz 1994, one of the few studies that attends to the pragmatic and conversational dimensions of "psychotic speakers," comes to similar conclusions.
3. Schutz 1977[1951].

"We're Losing Him, Sam"

1. See Schutz 1977[1951]; Jackson 1996:23–29.
2. Foucault 1965:175.

Reasonable Reasonableness

1. On the cultural themes and ideals implicit in American therapeutic perspectives, see, among others, Broverman, Broverman, and Clarkson 1970.

2. See Hopper 1991b; Gounis 1993:109–10.

3. Hopper 1991b.

4. As with all of the residents' statements, we must consider Susanne's indictment for its pragmatic force as well as for its semantic content. Indeed, the very power and purpose of the words, when heard in context, underscored the "overload of authority." That is, the excess of authority called for a weak, rhetorical assessment of that authority. The statement also worked to cut at the power of the staff: although Susanne might not have been able to conquer, she could at least try to divide. One could also hear a Hegelian, "master-slave" inflection in Susanne's words, in which the staff was burdened by its own authority.

5. Gramsci 1971:323.

6. See Silverstein 1979; Crapanzano 1992; and others (as noted in Woolard and Schieffelin 1994:71) for discussions of the nature and implications of this dominant ideology.

7. Silverstein 1996.

8. See Brenneis 1994 for a germane discussion of the way in which similar concerns for accountability and social norms influence the grant evaluation process in several federal agencies in the United States.

9. See Jakobson 1987[1960] on the way in which the referential aspect of language can dominate in a communicative context.

10. Barthes 1977:120.

11. Peirce 1931–35: 1.337.

12. Ibid.: 1.343.

13. Corrington 1993:132.

14. Ibid.

15. Peirce 1931–35: 1.382; Stearns 1952:203.

16. Peirce, 1931–35: 5.121.

17. See Weber 1930, 1978.

Tactics, Questions, Rhetoric

1. Peirce might account for this by drawing on his idea of a "degenerate" form of thirdness, which he calls "accidental thirdness," in which "there is an external compulsion upon us to think things together." As he notes, "it would be putting the cart before the horse to say that we are compelled to think certain things together because they are together in time and space; the true way of stating it is that there is an exterior compulsion upon us to put them together in our construction of time and space, in our perspective" (Peirce 1931–35: 1.383). The staff encouraged residents to inhabit a world of conduct, foresight, and rational calculation. But since the relation between past, present, and future struck residents as false, they often continued to act in terms of the principles and habits cultured through life on the street, in hospitals, and in the shelter. They often took the staff's mandates as an exterior compulsion to think otherwise than they usually would.

2. De Certeau 1984.

3. Ibid.: 35–37.

4. The difference between the substance of strategies and tactics is nicely conveyed in a common slave saying from South Carolina, which James Scott cites (1990:163) as a motto of the trickster hero: "De bukrah [whites] hab scheme, en de nigger hab trick, en ebery time de bukrah scheme once, de nigger trick twice." Strategists scheme. Tacticians trick.

5. Although residents tried to be authoritative at times, it seldom got them very far. Susanne sat at a table in the shelter with a cigarette in one hand and a cup of coffee in the other. Greg, another resident, sat down across from her. "I'd like to sit alone, please," she said. Greg remained seated. Susanne picked up her coffee, her cigarette, and her cigarette lighter and left the room.

Fred was singing out loud in the lobby in a deliberate, testing-the-rules kind of way. Joseph, a staff member who worked in the manager's office on the third floor of the building, came out of the shelter and walked toward the stairs. "Joseph," Fred said in an authoritative voice. "Come here for a second." "I can't, Freddy," Joseph said. "I have to go talk to someone." "Well, FUCK YOU!" Fred shouted. "FUCK YOU."

In contrast to the staff's commands, Fred's and Susanne's words had little power to move someone else to another location. Fred became hostile and Susanne moved on.

6. See K. Burke (1950) for a history of rhetoric in Western literature. Several anthropologists have noted that indirection—in which there is more than meets the eye in a verbal message—is common in societies in which it is important to get on tactfully and equivocally with one's peers. Michelle Rosaldo 1973, for instance, notes that "crooked language," rich in art, wit, and indirection, is valued among the Illongots of the Philippines, and Donald Brenneis 1987 points out that indirection is common to local-level egalitarian groups in Fiji and the Caribbean. Both authors find that the egalitarian ethos of these three groups promotes a preference for indirect speech, in large part because there is a pressing need to convey meaning and effect change through oblique, persuasive means rather than directly confrontational ones. As Rosaldo explains, "Elaborate, 'crooked' language belongs to a world in which none can offend, command or give orders, and speakers must negotiate the agreement and understanding of their opposites, through an aesthetically attractive and politically non-directive style" (1973:221).

Shelter residents relied on comparable forms of indirection. Unlike the Illongots or Fiji Indians, however, who prefer not to speak in direct, declarative terms because it is inappropriate and sometimes dangerous to do so, residents did not command because it would have been futile to do so: it was unlikely that anyone in the television room would have paid any attention to Eva if she had directly demanded that others make room for her. There was an art to being oblique, but since indirection was at some times the only feasible option, with the staff or with one's peers, it was motivated from the start by practical rather than by aesthetic concerns. There was not much choice in the matter.

7. Aristotle 1991.

8. See, for instance, Mead 1934; Bakhtin 1981; Vygotsky 1986[1934]; K. Burke 1950, 1959; Bateson 1972; Lacan 1966; and Levinas 1981. Such an understanding is commonplace in many non-European societies, however. As Margaret Trawick observes of the Tamil of South India, "As we speak of 'intertextuality' among poems or myths in South India, so we may speak of 'interpersonality' among human beings there. Considered in himself, a lone man has no meaning. He is suffused with the feelings, the spirits and substances, of those who live

near him, and they are suffused with his" (1990:252; see also works like Leen-hardt 1979[1947]; Shore 1982; Daniel 1984; and Comaroff and Comaroff 1991 for similar accounts of peoples in other parts of the world).

9. See Ihde (1976), however, for a phenomenology of listening, and Corradi Fiumara (1990) for a critique of contemporary philosophy's dominant consider-ation of ideas of discourse and talking, over those of listening.

Epistemologies of the Real

1. Henry similarly rushed into the shelter one day and walked up to the staff desk. "I'm sick of these meds," he said. "They're terrible! They're making my hair fall out and my tongue gets dry. I'm not gonna take them anymore!" He then walked out of the shelter. As far as I know, he continued to take his medi-cations regularly.

The similarity between Henry's and Richard's actions made me wonder if Richard overheard and then mimicked Henry's complaint.

2. See Trilling 1972:2, 12.

3. See Besnier 1990:424.

4. As Jameson (1991:8) describes the gist of a hermeneutic approach to mean-ing. Gadamer outlines the "proximity" of hermeneutics to psychiatry more gen-erally: both involve an attempt to understand the incomprehensible (1996:163–73).

See Friedrich (1989:304) on modalities of interpretation.

The appearance of this sensibility was not always directly functional or inten-tional; the uses of certain words as well as the way of saying those words pointed to, lent value to, and rendered commonplace certain exemplars of talk and action (Silverstein 1976; Hanks 1990). The sensibility thus resulted more from the staff's political positioning than from any overt ideology, with this position-ing taking form through specific pragmatic effects. To use Michael Silverstein's terms (1985), they stemmed more from the indexical function of talk than from its purposive function, which is to say that the staff's utterances effected quietly and without intention certain valuations of the world.

Reactivity

1. Larry's skewing was more trick than scheme. It would therefore be incor-rect to attribute an art of "resistance" to Larry's actions, at least as the word is now commonly used—as a concertedly intentional act of or "consistent pattern" of negation or opposition (see James Scott 1990, for example). Larry was not trying to negate, subvert, or deconstruct the metaphysic itself. He was simply trying to get out of Peggy's grasp, and the most effective way to do so was to eschew or cloud the semantic waters in which that grasp lay.

2. See Goffman 1981 on the concept of "footing."

3. Ricoeur 1992:58.

4. See, for instance, Giddens 1979; Ortner 1984; Sahlins 1985; and Herzfeld 1992.

5. See, for instance, Feldman 1991; Battaglia 1995; Marcus 1995; and Daniel 1996:189–92. As I read it, much of this work, which draws from semiotic, cyber-netic, or Nietzschean influences, tries to undo Aristotle's positioning of action

within the self (*en auto*) of a person, as set forth in his *Nichomachean Ethics* (1941; see Ricoeur 1992:89–90). Yet this work tends to be concerned more with the question of agency in the sense of "what sets something into motion" than in the sense of actions—such as speaking, acting, or moving about—that a socially recognized agent undertakes. Here I am concerned more with forms of *personal* agency than with the general and often extrapersonal forms of action justly considered by the scholars noted above.

6. Duranti 1994.

7. See Sahlins 1976; Karp 1986.

8. Karp 1986:133; Bourdieu 1977.

9. However, see Witherspoon 1977; Gardner 1987; Clay 1992; and Drewal 1992.

10. See, for instance, Guha 1983; de Certeau 1984; James Scott 1990; Kondo 1990; and Bhabha 1994.

11. Ricoeur 1992:152–53.

12. Ortner 1984:151–52.

13. Ibid.: 152, citing Gramsci 1957.

14. Nietzsche 1967[1901]:292.

15. See Giddens 1979:92, for instance.

16. See Moya 1990, for instance.

17. Giddens 1979:55.

18. Herzfeld 1992:157.

The Office of Reason

1. Rabinow 1992:7.

2. Weber 1930, 1978.

3. Foucault 1965; Scheper-Hughes and Lovell 1987.

4. Nietzsche 1954[1881]:81.

5. Given this, I am skeptical, as others are, of the projects of some philosophers and anthropologists who try to deduce a universally valid concept of rationality based on rules of logic and inference and then rely on that concept in making comparative, transcultural judgments as to the degree of rationality or irrationality manifest in certain beliefs or actions. (See for instance, the essays in Hollis and Lukes 1982 and in Overing 1985, as well as Tambiah's 1990 summary of the debate and its implications). To begin with, the cultural, institutional, and situational embeddedness of acts of reasoning underscores the extent to which those acts (including those of philosophers and anthropologists) adhere to a particular cultural history and "form of life," as Wittgenstein (1953) might say. As others have pointed out, it is futile to try to wrench those acts and the logic they imply out of their workaday contexts and then apply them as the ideal in other contexts. Secondly, ideas of reason and rationality always involve a local "color" or patterning, making for different kinds of rationality, one brand of which we have just detailed; the assumed universally valid concept of rationality is usually found only in the notebooks of logicians, mathematicians, and philosophers. Finally, something the rationalists tend to neglect but the workings of the shelter make clear is that acts of reasoning always imply political forces. To act or think in reasonable terms or to apply the criteria of rationality to other people's lives leads to the valuation of some ways of thinking, talking, and being over others. All told, the projects of the rationalists are, like the agendas of the

shelter staff, rooted in broader historical and political projects; when applied to other peoples, they contribute to "the process of rationalization as a world historical project" of which Weber spoke and that the residents, among others, felt the consequences of every day.

6. See Estroff 1981 for a nuanced discussion of the ways in which clients of a mental health care system in an American city learn how to manipulate and maneuver as well as suffer while "making it crazy" in a paradoxical, doubled-edge cultural system that at once stigmatizes, rewards, and reinforces the identity of a "full-time crazy person."

Figure, Character, Person

1. Rorty 1976:309–11. See also Rorty 1987.

2. Foucault 1965, 1977.

3. Robert Barrett similarly finds that the central objective of treatment in a psychiatric hospital in Australia "was to transform a case of schizophrenia into a person who could be held responsible for his or her actions" (1996:144). Personhood in that context chiefly involved the idea of a self-contained moral being invested with volition, responsibility, self-control, and unity of consciousness (1996:272–307).

4. See Goffman 1963:41–50.

5. Wordsworth 1979[1799–1850]:261.

6. Ibid.

7. Rorty 1976:315.

8. Ibid.: 315–18.

9. Descartes 1984[1641]:16.

10. Mauss 1985[1938]; Hallowell 1955; Geertz 1973.

11. Ewing 1990:251.

12. Lurhmann 1996:209. Lurhmann herself observes that the "route to authenticity" adopted by a young Parsi woman attending school at Harvard (as well as other elite South Asians living in a postcolonial world) is "to continually reinvent herself through sequentially identifying with contradictory narrative self-descriptions, while simultaneously learning to treat them as just that: narratives to be manipulated" (1996:203). Robert Jay Lifton 1993, in turn, finds that the modern self is a "protean" one that is fluid, resilient, and multifaceted, while Kenneth Gergen 1991 concludes that contemporary, Western selves are "saturated" with a multiplicity of expectations, roles, points of view, and lines of communication.

13. Rorty 1976, 1987.

14. Ashis Nandy gets at a similar idea in suggesting that the "strategy of survival" of Indians in the face of British colonialism partly lies in their culture's demand "that a certain permeability of boundaries be maintained in one's self-image and that the self be not defined too tightly or separated mechanically from the not-self" (1983:107).

How to Do Things with Feeling

1. Besnier 1990:428.

2. Ibid.: 432.

3. In order to maintain consistency with indications of selfhood in this book as well as anthropological understandings of selfhood in general, my definition differs from the one advanced by Amelie Rorty (1976), who sees "selves" as "possessors of their properties."

4. Geertz 1973:97.

5. Besnier 1990.

6. See Lutz 1986; Besnier 1990:433; Crapanzano 1992:231. As Crapanzano notes, emotions understood as such "conform to, indeed confirm, our non-transactional, essentialistic notions of self and personhood. They attest to the self's independence, uniqueness, individuality, facticity—its personality and character—and its duration" (1992:231).

7. Jameson 1991.

8. Crapanzano 1992.

9. Ibid.: 232.

10. Ibid.: 235.

11. Yet staff members also indexed states of feeling at times, as when Peggy said in distress, "No. Come on, I don't like this," when Larry was trying to evade her directives.

12. It is important to note that the grounds for these proposed exchanges linked up to a more general theater of the senses: cults of sensation thrived in American cities, the television piped in sensational talk shows every afternoon, and panhandlers could be heard pitching to prospective patrons, "Com'on big man, it's freezin' out here!" (as I overheard an apparently homeless African American man say to an apparently well-employed white man in Harvard Square one chilly November afternoon). Residents lived in a society in which the articulation of feelings or sensations could have great rhetorical effect.

Architectures of Sense

1. My understanding of "sensation," and I think that of residents, is similar to that advanced by Deleuze in a discussion of Cezanne's use of the term: "One face of sensation is turned toward the subject (the nervous system, vital movement, 'instinct,' 'temperament,' an entire vocabulary which is common to both naturalism and Cezanne); the other face is turned toward the object ('the fact,' the place, the event). Or rather, sensation has no faces at all, it is indissolubly both things" (1993:187).

2. Hume 1961[1740]:229.

3. "Hundreds of noises wove themselves into a wiry texture of sound with barbs protruding here and there," Musil (1995:3) wrote of Vienna, "smart edges running along it and subsiding again, with clear notes splintering off and dissipating." Residents tended to hear the acoustics of the lobby and its surroundings in similar ways.

4. Feld 1996:91.

5. Lyon and Barbalet 1994:56.

6. Comaroff and Comaroff 1991:107.

7. Seremetakis 1994:129.

Bodies with Organs

1. Artaud 1976:65.
2. Ibid.: 571.
3. Deleuze and Guattari 1983, 1987.
4. Deleuze and Guattari 1987:164.
5. See, for instance, Kraepelin 1921:219–75; Jaspers 1963 [1923]:90–92; Cameron and Rychlak 1985:411–54; Sass 1992.
6. See Foucault 1973; Martensen 1995.
7. Bakhtin 1984[1965]:197.
8. See Scheper-Hughes and Lock 1987; Low 1994.
9. For example, of the many "current factors" that Favazza (1992:202) finds increase the probability of "deviant self-mutilation" among people considered mentally ill, two appear quite relevant in Fred's case: "residence in a restrictive environment such as a prison or mental hospital" and "real or perceived rejection by a therapist or other significant person." Favazza also notes that the most common precipitants of "repetitive self-mutilation" are "real or perceived rejection and situations that produce feelings of helplessness, anger, or guilt" (1992:xviii).
Acts of this sort did not happen every day. When they did happen, they were usually taken by residents and staff alike as bizarre, as signs of madness per se, or as incomprehensible actions akin to the ragtimes of speech. It made sense to see them in terms of the latter because, like so much talk in the shelter, they had the air of a private system of meaning and reference. In general, they were not fussed over; they were ignored, much like the man's performance with the knife outside the building, which Martin witnessed. But as distinct as these actions were, like-minded ways of knowing and proving states of mind were the rule in the shelter. People tried to persuade others of pain or distress by making the signs of distress appear not only evident but very real to others.
10. Martin followed a similar logic when he noted that if he went back on "dope" to calm himself down, he would have to wear his jacket all the time because any needle marks on his skin would signal his reliance on heroin.
11. Irving 1982:35.
12. Wittgenstein 1953:98, sec. 284.
13. Kafka 1971[1919]:148.
14. Veena Das 1996 makes this point in a study of violence and bodily pain in India. Critiquing the idea, found in the work of Elaine Scarry 1985 and others, that pain is above all a question of the inexpressible, she notes, "pain, in this rendering, is not that inexpressible something that destroys communication or marks an exit from one's existence in language. Instead, it makes a claim asking for acknowledgement, which may be given or denied" (1996:70).
15. Bateson 1972.

With Your Head Tilted to the Side

1. The concept of "unconscious optics" comes from Benjamin (1968b[1936]: 237).
2. See Aristotle 1991.
3. Such an assessment might help to resolve the debate between those who find that the stuff of selfhood and personality is relatively unchanging and per-

manent and those who contend that it is inherently situation-dependent, changing, and ephemeral (see Block 1981 and Spiro 1987 for proponents of the first position; Gergen 1991, Shweder 1991, and Crapanzano 1992 for proponents of the second; and Ingham 1996:113–14 for a discussion). The pragmatics of social discourse are such that people apply or index aspects of selfhood and character in shifting, fluid, and multiform ways, but the habitual social, cultural, and political underpinnings of such discourse can often lead to lasting dispositions and stances.

Pacing the Labyrinth

1. See Gounis and Susser 1990; and Gounis 1992b. The term was probably first used by Edwin Sutherland and Harvey Locke, two sociologists who studied twenty government-run shelters in Chicago during the depression. "After a period of time," they observed, "a man becomes less sensitive. . . . He shows a tendency to lose all sense of personal responsibility for getting out of the shelter; to become insensible to the element of time; to lose ambitions, pride, self-respect and confidence; to avoid former friends and to identify himself with the shelter group" (1936:146). Goffman writes similarly of "colonization" as a standard alignment in asylums: "The sampling of the outside world provided by the establishment is taken by the inmate as the whole, and a stable, relatively contented existence is built up out of the maximum satisfactions procurable within the institution" (1961:62).

2. See Ware et al. 1992. In discussing the work of Anderson and Sutherland and Locke, Hopper (1990b:1357) notes that "lasting damage [from shelterization] was never documented. Indeed, cohorts in both instances proved remarkably resilient when the American war machine cranked up at the end of each decade. Shelterized men apparently had little trouble acquitting themselves as soldiers or factory hands."

3. Researchers and advocates for the homeless have already made this point. See, for instance, Bassuk and Lauriat 1986; and Timmer, Eizten, and Talley 1994:183–88.

4. See, among others, Rossi 1989; Snow and Anderson 1993; Timmer, Eitzen, and Talley 1994; and Jencks 1994.

5. Wilson 1974. Hopper (1991a:321) draws the same conclusion.

6. See Terrill (1991:112) and Glasser (1994:25) on Hong Kong; Glasser (1994) for a global perspective on homelessness; and Desjarlais et al. (1995:136–54) on the features and consequences of dislocation in various parts of the world.

7. Bataille 1985[1936]:174.

8. Lee 1992:368.

9. Levinas 1969:134.

10. The field of psychological anthropology stresses, by definition, the cultural dimensions of psychological functioning. To date, however, it rarely considers seriously the political and economic underpinnings of human thinking, feeling, and knowing (see Suárez-Orozco 1994:22; Scheper-Hughes 1992, 1994; White 1992:38; and Ingham 1996:8).

11. Minkowski 1970:26.

Bibliography

American Psychiatric Association. 1987. *Diagnostic and Statistical Manual of Mental Disorders.* 3rd edition, revised. Washington, DC: American Psychiatric Association.

———. 1994. *Diagnostic and Statistical Manual of Mental Disorders.* 4th edition. Washington, DC: American Psychiatric Association.

Anthony, William A., and G. Dion. 1986. *A Review of Psychiatric Rehabilitation Research.* Washington, DC: National Rehabilitation Information Center.

Appadurai, Arjun. 1986. Introduction: Commodities and the Politics of Value. In *The Social Life of Things: Commodities in Cultural Perspective,* edited by A. Appadurai, pp. 3–63. Cambridge: Cambridge University Press.

Argeriou, Milton. 1992. Homelessness in Massachusetts: Perception, Policy, and Progress. *New England Journal of Public Policy* 8:455–70.

Arieti, Silvano. 1974. *Interpretation of Schizophrenia.* New York: Basic Books.

Aristotle. 1941. *The Basic Works of Aristotle,* edited by R. McKeon. New York: Random House.

———. 1987. *Poetics.* Indianapolis: Hackett Publishing Company.

———. 1991. *The Art of Rhetoric.* London: Penguin Books.

Arnason, H. Harvard. 1986 [1968]. *History of Modern Art: Painting, Sculpture, Architecture.* Englewood Cliff, NJ: Prentice-Hall.

Artaud, Antonin. 1976. *Selected Writings,* edited by S. Sontag, translated by H. Weaver. New York: Farrar, Straus and Giroux.

Auden, W. H. 1976. *Collected Poems,* edited by E. Mendelson. New York: Vintage.

Auerbach, Erich. 1953. *Mimesis: The Representation of Reality in Western Literature.* Princeton, NJ: Princeton University Press.

Augé, Marc. 1995. *Non-Places: Introduction to an Anthropology of Supermodernity,* translated by J. Howe. London: Verso.

Ayto, John. 1990. *Bloomsbury Dictionary of Word Origins.* London: Bloomsbury.

Bachelard, Gaston. 1964. *The Poetics of Space,* translated by M. Jolas. Boston: Beacon.

Baker, A., R. Llewelyn Davies, and P. Sivadon. 1959. *Psychiatric Services and Architecture.* Geneva: World Health Organization.

Bakhtin, Mikhail. 1981. *The Dialogic Imagination,* edited by M. Holquist, translated by C. Emerson and M. Holquist. Austin: University of Texas Press.

———. 1984 [1965]. *Rabelais and His World,* translated by H. Iswolsky. Bloomington: Indiana University Press.

Banham, Reyner. 1966. *Theory and Design in the First Machine Age.* New York: Praeger.

Barnhart, Robert. 1988. *The Barnhart Dictionary of Etymology*. New York: H. W. Wilson.

Barrett, Robert. 1996. *The Psychiatric Team and the Social Definition of Schizophrenia: An Anthropological Study of Person and Illness*. Cambridge: Cambridge University Press.

Barthes, Roland. 1972. *Mythologies*, translated by A. Laven. New York: Hill and Wang.

———. 1977. *Roland Barthes*. Berkeley: University of California Press.

Basso, Keith. 1990. *Western Apache Language and Culture*. Tucson: University of Arizona Press.

Bassuk, Ellen, and Alison Lauriat. 1986. Are Emergency Shelters the Solution? *International Journal of Mental Health* 14:125–36.

Bataille, Georges. 1985 [1936]. The Labyrinth. In *Visions of Excess: Selected Writings, 1927–1939*, edited by A. Stoekl, translated by A. Stoekl, with C. R. Lovitts and D. Leslie, Jr., pp. 171–77. Minneapolis: University of Minnesota Press.

Bateson, Gregory. 1972. *Steps to an Ecology of the Mind*. New York: Ballantine.

Battaglia, Deborah, ed. 1995. *Rhetorics of Self-Making*. Berkeley: University of California Press.

Baxter, Ellen, and Kim Hopper. 1982. The New Mendicancy: Homelessness in New York City. *American Journal of Orthopsychiatry* 52:393–408.

Becker, A. L. 1979. Text-Building, Epistemology, and Aesthetics in Javanese Shadow Theatre. In *The Imagination of Reality*, edited by A. L. Becker and A. A. Yengoyan, pp. 211–43. Norwood, NJ: Ablex.

Beckett, Samuel. 1958. *Endgame*. New York: Grove Weidenfeld.

———. 1995 [1946]. The End. In *Samuel Beckett: The Complete Shorter Prose, 1929–1989*, edited by S. E. Gontarksi, pp. 78–99. New York: Grove Press.

Benjamin, Walter. 1968a [1936]. The Storyteller. In *Illuminations*, edited by H. Arendt, pp. 83–109. New York: Harcourt, Brace and World.

———. 1968b [1936]. The Work of Art in the Age of Mechanical Reproduction. In *Illuminations*, edited by H. Arendt, pp. 217–51. New York: Harcourt, Brace and World.

Bernstein, J. M. 1992. *The Fate of Art: Aesthetic Alienation from Kant to Derrida to Adorno*. Cambridge: Polity Press.

Besnier, Niko. 1990. Language and Affect. *Annual Review of Anthropology* 19:419–51.

Bhabha, Homi. 1994. The Postcolonial and the Postmodern: The Question of Agency. In *The Location of Culture*, pp. 171–97. New York: Routledge.

Black, Bertram. 1988. *Work and Mental Illness*. Baltimore: Johns Hopkins University Press.

Bleuler, Eugen. 1950. *Dementia Praecox, or the Group of Schizophrenias*. New York: International Universities Press.

Block, Jack. 1981. Some Enduring and Consequential Structures of Personality. In *Further Explorations in Personality*, edited by A. I. Rabin, J. Arnoff, A. M. Barclay, and R. A. Zucker, pp. 27–43. New York: Wiley.

Blowen, Michael. 1993. "Beauty and the Street," *Boston Globe*. December 16, p. 74.

Boas, Franz. 1940 [1887]. The Study of Geography. In *Race, Language, and Culture*, pp. 639–47. New York: Macmillan.

Bourdieu, Pierre. 1977. *Outline of a Theory of Practice*, translated by R. Nice. Cambridge: Cambridge University Press.

Bourdieu, Pierre et al. 1993. *La Misère du monde*. Paris: Editions du Seuil.

Bourgois, Philippe. 1995. *In Search of Respect: Selling Crack in El Barrio.* New York: Cambridge University Press.
———. 1996. Confronting Anthropology, Education, and Inner-City Apartheid. *American Anthropologist* 98:249–57.
Brenneis, Donald. 1987. Talk and Transformation. *Man* 22:499–510.
———. 1994. Discourse and Discipline at the National Research Council: A Bureaucratic *Bildungsroman. Cultural Anthropology* 9:23–36.
Broverman, Inge, Donald Broverman, and Frank Clarkson. 1970. Sex-Role Stereotypes and Clinical Judgements of Mental Health. *Journal of Consulting and Clinical Psychology* 34:1–7.
Bruner, Edward. 1986. Experience and its Expressions. In *The Anthropology of Experience,* edited by V. Turner and E. Bruner, pp. 3–32. Urbana: University of Illinois Press.
Bruner, Jerome. 1990. *Acts of Meaning.* Cambridge, MA: Harvard University Press.
Burke, Edmund. 1958 [1759]. *A Philosophical Enquiry into the Origin of Our Ideas of the Sublime and Beautiful.* Notre Dame, IN: University of Notre Dame Press.
Burke, Kenneth. 1950. *A Rhetoric of Motives.* Berkeley: University of California Press.
———. 1959. *A Grammar of Motives.* Berkeley: University of California Press.
Calsyn, Robert, Carol Kohfeld, and Laurie Roades. 1993. Urban Homeless People and Welfare: Who Receives Benefits? *American Journal of Community Psychology* 21:95–112.
Cameron, Norman, and Joseph Rychlak. 1985. *Personality and Development and Psychopathology: A Dynamic Approach.* 2nd edition. Boston: Houghton Mifflin.
Carling, Paul. 1992. Housing, Community Support, and Homelessness: Emerging Policy in Mental Health Systems. *New England Journal of Public Policy* 8:281–95.
Carr, David. 1986. *Time, Narrative, and History.* Bloomington: Indiana University Press.
Carroll, David. 1987. *Paraesthetics: Foucault, Lyotard, Derrida.* New York: Methuen.
Castel, Robert, Françoise Castel, and Anne Lovell. 1982. *The Psychiatric Society.* New York: Columbia University Press.
Clay, Brenda. 1992. Other Times, Other Places: Agency and the Big Man in Central New Ireland. *Man* 27:719–33.
Cohen, Anthony, and Nigel Rapport, eds. 1995. *Questions of Consciousness.* London: Routledge.
Comaroff, Jean, and John Comaroff. 1991. *Of Revelation and Revolution: Christianity, Colonialism, and Consciousness in South Africa.* Chicago: University of Chicago Press.
Conzen, Michael, and George Lewis. 1976. *Boston: A Geographical Portrait.* Cambridge, MA: Ballinger.
Cook, John, and Heinrich Klotz. 1973. Paul Rudolph. In *Conversations with Architects,* pp. 90–121. New York: Praeger.
Corin, Ellen. 1990. Facts and Meaning in Psychiatry: An Anthropological Approach to the Lifeworld of Schizophrenics. *Culture, Medicine and Psychiatry* 14:153–88.
Corradi Fiumara, Gemma. 1990. *The Other Side of Language: A Philosophy of Listening.* New York: Routledge.
Corrington, Robert S. 1993. *An Introduction to C. S. Peirce: Philosopher, Semiotician, and Ecstatic Naturalist.* Lanham, MD: Rowman and Littlefield.

Crapanzano, Vincent. 1977. Introduction to *Case Studies in Spirit Possession*, edited by V. Crapanzano and V. Garrison, pp. 1–40. New York: John Wiley.

———. 1992. *Hermes' Dilemma and Hamlet's Desire: On the Epistemology of Interpretation*. Cambridge, MA: Harvard University Press.

Crowther, Paul. 1989. The Kantian Sublime, the Avant-Garde, and the Postmodern: A Critique of Lyotard. *New Formations* 7:67–76.

Csordas, Thomas. 1994a. *The Sacred Self: A Cultural Phenomenology of Charismatic Healing*. Berkeley: University of California Press.

———, ed. 1994b. *Embodiment and Experience: The Existential Ground of Culture and Self*. Cambridge: Cambridge University Press.

Cutting, John, and Francis Dunne. 1989. Subjective Experience of Schizophrenia. *Schizophrenia Bulletin* 15:217–31.

Daniel, E. Valentine. 1984. *Fluid Signs: Being a Person the Tamil Way*. Berkeley: University of California Press.

———. 1989. The Semeiosis of Suicide in Sri Lanka. In *Semiotics, Self, and Society*, edited by B. Lee and G. Urban, pp. 69–100. Berlin: Mouton de Gruyter.

———. 1996. *Charred Lullabies: Chapters in an Anthropography of Violence*. Princeton: Princeton University Press.

Das, Veena. 1995. *Critical Events: An Anthropological Perspective on Contemporary India*. Delhi: Oxford University Press.

———. 1996. Language and Body: Transactions in the Construction of Pain. *Daedalus* 125:67–92.

Davis, Mike. 1990. *City of Quartz*. New York: Vintage.

De Certeau, Michel. 1984. *The Practice of Everyday Life*. Berkeley: University of California Press.

Deleuze, Gilles. 1988. *Foucault*, translated and edited by S. Hand. Minneapolis: University of Minnesota Press.

———. 1992. Postscript on the Societies of Control. *October* 59:3–7.

———. 1993. Painting and Sensation. In *The Deleuze Reader*, edited by C. Boundas, pp. 187–92. New York: Columbia University Press.

Deleuze, Gilles, and Félix Guattari. 1983. *Anti-Oedipus: Capitalism and Schizophrenia*, translated by R. Hurley, M. Seem, and H. Lane. Minneapolis: University of Minnesota Press.

———. 1987. *A Thousand Plateaus: Capitalism and Schizophrenia*, translated by B. Massumi. Minneapolis: University of Minnesota Press.

DelVecchio Good, Mary-Jo, Paul Brodwin, Byron Good, and Arthur Kleinman. 1992. Epilogue. In *Pain as Human Experience: An Anthropological Perspective*, edited by M-J. DelVecchio Good, P. Brodwin, B. Good, and A. Kleinman, pp. 198–207. Berkeley: University of California Press.

Dennis, Deborah, John Buckner, Frank Lipton, and Irene Levine. 1991. A Decade of Research and Services for Homeless Mentally Ill Persons: Where Do We Stand? *American Psychologist* 46:1129–38.

Derrida, Jacques. 1973. *Speech and Phenomena, and Other Essays on Husserl's Theory of Signs*, translated by D. Allison. Evanston, IL: Northwestern University Press.

———. 1987. *The Truth in Painting*, translated by G. Bennington and I. Mcleod. Chicago: University of Chicago Press.

Descartes, René. 1984 [1641]. Meditations on First Philosophy. In *The Philosophical Writings of Descartes*, vol. 2, translated by J. Cottingham, R. Stoothoff, and D. Murdoch, pp. 3–62. Cambridge: Cambridge University Press.

Desjarlais, Robert. 1992. *Body and Emotion: The Aesthetics of Illness and Healing in the Nepal Himalayas*. Philadelphia: University of Pennsylvania Press.

Desjarlais, Robert, Leon Eisenberg, Byron Good, and Arthur Kleinman. 1995. *World Mental Health: Priorities and Responses in Low-Income Countries*. Oxford: Oxford University Press.

Dewey, John. 1926. *Experience and Nature*. Chicago: Open Court Publishing Company.

Dickey, Barbara, Olinda Gonzalez, Eric Latimer, Karen Powers, Russell Schutt, and Stephen Goldfinger. 1996. Use of Mental Health Services by Formerly Homeless Adults Residing in Group and Independent Housing. *Psychiatric Services* 47:152–58.

Dowd, Maureen. 1995. America's Front Lawn. *New York Times Magazine*. January 15, p. 18.

Drewal, Margaret Thompson. 1992. *Yoruba Ritual: Performers, Plays, Agency*. Bloomington: Indiana University Press.

Du Bois, John. 1987. Meaning Without Intention: Lessons from Divination. *Papers in Pragmatics* 1:80–122.

Dumézil, Georges. 1958. Métiers et classes fonctionnelles chez divers peuples indo-européens. *Annals, Economies, Sociétés, Civilisation* 13:716–24.

Duranti, Alessandro. 1994. *From Grammar to Politics: Linguistic Anthropology in a Western Samoan Village*. Berkeley: University of California Press.

Eighner, Lars. 1993. *Travels with Lisbeth*. New York: St. Martin's Press.

Estroff, Sue. 1981. *Making It Crazy*. Berkeley: University of California Press.

———. 1989. Self, Identity, and Schizophrenia: In Search of the Subject. *Schizophrenia Bulletin* 15(4):189–96.

———. 1993. Identity, Disability, and Schizophrenia: The Problem of Chronicity. In *Knowledge, Power, and Practice: The Anthropology of Medicine and Everyday Life*, edited by S. Lindenbaum and M. Lock, pp. 247–86. Berkeley: University of California Press.

Estroff, Sue, William Lachicotte, Linda Illingworth, and Anna Johnston. 1991. Everybody's Got a Little Mental Illness: Accounts of Illness and Self among People with Severe, Persistent Mental Illness. *Medical Anthropology Quarterly* 5:331–69.

Estroff, Sue, Catherine Zimmer, William Lachicotte, Julia Benoit, and Donald Patrick. 1997. "No Other Way to Go": Pathways to Disability Income Application Among Persons with Severe Persistent Mental Illness. In *Mental Disorder, Work Disability, and the Law*, edited by R. Bonnie and J. Monahan, pps. 55–104. Chicago: University of Chicago Press.

Ewald, François. 1991. Norms, Discipline, and the Law. *Law and the Order of Culture*, edited by R. Post, pp. 138–61. Berkeley: University of California Press.

Ewing, Katherine. 1990. The Illusion of Wholeness: Culture, Self, and the Experience of Inconsistency. *Ethos* 18:251–78.

Farmer, Paul. 1992. *AIDS and Accusation: Haiti and the Geography of Blame*. Berkeley: University of California Press.

Faulkner, William. 1986 [1936]. *Absalom, Absalom!* New York: Vintage.

Favazza, Armando. 1992 [1987]. *Bodies Under Siege: Self-Mutilation in Culture and Psychiatry*. Baltimore: Johns Hopkins University Press.

Feld, Steven. 1996. Waterfalls of Song: An Acoustemology of Place Resounding in Bosavi, Papua New Guinea. In *Senses of Place*, edited by S. Feld and K. Basso, pp. 91–135. Santa Fe: School of American Research.

Feldman, Allen. 1991. *Formations of Violence*. Chicago: University of Chicago Press.

Fischer, Pamela. 1992. Victimization and Homelessness: Cause and Effect. *New England Journal of Public Policy* 8:229–46.

Ford, Royal. 1991. "A Novel Kind of Shelter." *Boston Globe.* December 9, pp. 1, 9.

Foucault, Michel. 1965. *Madness and Civilization: A History of Insanity in the Age of Reason*, translated by R. Howard. New York: Vintage.

———. 1970. *The Order of Things: An Archaeology of the Human Sciences.* New York: Vintage.

———. 1973. *The Birth of the Clinic: An Archaeology of Human Perception*, translated by A. M. Sheridan Smith. New York: Vintage.

———. 1977. *Discipline and Punish: The Birth of the Prison*, translated by A. Sheridan. New York: Vintage.

———. 1978. *The History of Sexuality. Vol. 1; An Introduction*, translated by R. Hurley. New York: Pantheon.

———. 1980. *Power/Knowledge: Selected Interviews and Other Writings*, edited and translated by C. Gordon. New York: Pantheon.

———. 1983. On the Genealogy of Ethics: An Overview of Work in Progress. In *Michel Foucault: Beyond Structuralism and Hermeneutics*, Hubert Dreyfus and Paul Rabinow, pp. 229–52. Chicago: University of Chicago Press.

———. 1991. Governmentality. In *The Foucault Effect: Studies in Governmentality*, edited by G. Burchell, C. Gordon, and P. Miller, pp. 87–104. Chicago: University of Chicago Press.

Fried, Marc. 1963. Grieving for a Lost Home. In *The Urban Condition: People and Policy in the Metropolis*, edited by L. Duhl, pp. 151–71. New York: Basic Books.

Friedrich, Paul. 1989. Language, Ideology, and Political Economy. *American Anthropologist* 91:295–313.

Gadamer, Hans-Georg. 1975. *Truth and Method*, translated by G. Barden and J. Cumming. New York: Crossroad Publishing Corporation.

———. 1996. *The Enigma of Health: The Art of Healing in a Scientific Age*, translated by J. Gaiger and N. Walker. Stanford, CA: Stanford University Press.

Gans, Herbert. 1962. *The Urban Villagers: Group and Class in the Life of Italian-Americans.* New York: Free Press.

Gardner, D. S. 1987. Spirits and Conceptions of Agency Among the Mianmin of Papua New Guinea. *Oceania* 57:161–77.

Geertz, Clifford. 1973. *The Interpretation of Cultures.* New York: Basic Books.

———. 1986. Making Experience, Authoring Selves. In *The Anthropology of Experience*, edited by V. Turner and E. Bruner, pp. 373–80. Urbana: University of Illinois Press.

Gergen, Kenneth. 1991. *The Saturated Self: Dilemmas of Identity in Contemporary Life.* New York: Basic Books.

Giddens, Anthony. 1979. *Central Problems in Social Theory.* Berkeley: University of California Press.

Glasser, Irene. 1994. *Homelessness in Global Perspective.* New York: G. K. Hall.

Goffman, Erving. 1961. *Asylums: Essays on the Social Situation of Mental Patients and Other Inmates.* New York: Anchor Books.

———. 1963. *Stigma.* Englewood Cliffs, NJ: Prentice-Hall.

———. 1971. *Relations in Public: Microstudies of the Public Order.* New York: Basic Books.

———. 1981. *Forms of Talk.* Philadelphia: University of Pennsylvania Press.

Goldstein, Kurt, and Martin Scheerer. 1941. Abstract and Concrete Behavior: an Experimental Study with Special Tests. *Psychological Monographs* 53(2):1–151.

Good, Byron. 1992. Culture and Psychopathology: Directions for Psychiatric Anthropology. In *New Directions in Psychological Anthropology*, edited by T. Schwartz, G. White, and C. Lutz, pp. 181–205. Cambridge: Cambridge University Press.

——. 1993. *Medicine, Rationality, and Experience*. Cambridge: Cambridge University Press.

Good, Lawrence, Siegel, Saul, and Alfred Bay. 1965. *Therapy by Design: Implications of Architecture for Human Behavior*. Springfield, IL: Charles C. Thomas.

Goodwin, Charles. 1990. Conversation Analysis. *Annual Review of Anthropology* 19:283–307.

Goodwin, Marjorie Harness. 1990. *He-Said-She-Said: Talk as Social Organization Among Black Children*. Bloomington: Indiana University Press.

Gounis, Kostas. 1992a. Temporality and the Domestication of Homelessness. In *The Politics of Time*, edited by H. Rutz, pp. 127–49. American Ethnological Society Monograph Series, Number 4. Washington, DC: American Anthropological Society.

——. 1992b. The Manufacture of Dependency: Shelterization Revisited. *New England Journal of Health Policy* 8:685–93.

——. 1993. The Domestication of Homelessness: The Politics of Space and Time in New York City Shelters. Ph.D. Dissertation, Columbia University.

Gounis, Kostas, and Ezra Susser. 1990. Shelterization and Its Implications for Mental Health Services. In *Psychiatry Takes to the Streets*, edited by N. Cohen, pp. 231–55. New York: Guilford Press.

Graham, Laura. 1993. A Public Sphere in Amazonia? The Depersonalized Collaborative Construction of Discourse in Axavante. *American Ethnologist* 20:717–41.

Gramsci, Antonio. 1957. *The Modern Prince and Other Writings*. New York: International Publishers.

——. 1971. *Prison Notebooks*. New York: International Publishers.

Grice, H. P. 1975. Logic and Conversation. In *Speech Acts*, edited by P. Cole and J. Morgan, pp. 41–58. Syntax and Semantics 3. New York: Academic Press.

Grob, Gerald. 1983. *Mental Illness and American Society: 1875–1940*. Princeton, NJ: Princeton University Press.

——. 1994. *The Mad Among Us: A History of the Care of America's Mentally Ill*. Cambridge, MA: Harvard University Press.

Guha, Ranajit. 1983. *Elementary Aspects of Peasant Insurgency in Colonial India*. Oxford: Oxford University Press.

Hallowell, A. Irving. 1955. The Self and Its Behavioral Environment. In *Culture and Experience*, pp. 172–83. Philadelphia: University of Pennsylvania Press.

Hanks, William. 1990. *Referential Practice*. Chicago: University of Chicago Press.

——. 1996. *Language and Communicative Practices*. Boulder, CO: Westview Press.

Haraway, Donna. 1991. *Simians, Cyborgs, and Women: The Reinvention of Nature*. New York: Routledge Press.

Harding, C. M., Joseph Zubin, and John Strauss. 1987. Chronicity in Schizophrenia: Fact, Partial Fact, or Artifact? *Hospital and Community Psychiatry* 38:477–86.

Harris, Grace. 1989. Concepts of Individual, Self, and Person in Description and Analysis. *American Anthropologist* 59:1046–66.

Hart, Jordana. 1992. "On Bitter Night, Boston Counts Its Homeless." *Boston Globe*. December 2, pp. 31, 36.

Harvey, David. 1989. *The Condition of Postmodernity*. New York: Blackwell.

Heidegger, Martin. 1962. *Being and Time*. New York: Harper Collins.

——. 1971 [1959]. *On the Way to Language*. New York: Harper and Row.

Herrera, Philip. 1964. Government Center: Symbolic Showpiece of a New Boston. *Architectural Forum.* June, pp. 88–93.

Hertz, Neil. 1978. The Notion of the Blockage in the Literature of the Sublime. In *Psychoanalysis and the Question of the Text,* edited by G. Hartman, pp. 62–85. Baltimore: John Hopkins University Press.

Herzfeld, Michael. 1992. *The Social Production of Indifference.* Chicago: University of Chicago Press.

Hirsch, Kathleen. 1989. *Songs from the Alley.* New York: Ticknor and Fields.

Hitov, Steven. 1992. Ending Homelessness Among Mentally Disabled People. *New England Journal of Public Policy* 8:599–612.

Hollis, Martin and Steven Lukes. 1982. *Rationality and Relativism.* Oxford: Basil Blackwell.

Hopper, Kim. 1987. The Public Response to Homelessness in New York City—The Last Hundred Years. In *On Being Homeless: Historical Perspectives,* edited by R. Beard, pp. 89–101. New York: Museum of the City of New York.

———. 1988. More Than Passing Strange: Homelessness and Mental Illness in New York City. *American Ethnologist* 15:155–67.

———. 1990a. Public Shelter as a "Hybrid Institution": Homeless Men in Historical Perspective. *Journal of Social Issues* 46:13–29.

———. 1990b. Shelterization. Letter to the Editor. *Hospital and Community Psychiatry* 41:1357.

———. 1991a. Some Old Questions for the New Cross-Cultural Psychiatry. *Medical Anthropology Quarterly* 5:299–330.

———. 1991b. A Poor Apart: The Distancing of Homeless Men in New York's History. *Social Research* 58:107–32.

Hopper, Kim, Ezra Susser, and Sarah Conover. 1986. Economies of Makeshift: Deindustrialization and Homelessness in New York City. *Urban Anthropology* 14:183–236.

Howes, David, ed. 1991. *The Varieties of Sensory Experience: A Sourcebook in the Anthropology of the Senses.* Toronto: University of Toronto Press.

Hume, David. 1961 [1740]. *A Treatise of Human Nature.* New York: Doubleday.

Humphrey, Caroline, and Stephen Hugh-Jones. 1992. Introduction: Barter, Exchange and Value. In *Barter, Exchange and Value: An Anthropological Approach,* edited by C. Humphrey and S. Hugh-Jones, pp. 1–20. Cambridge: Cambridge University Press.

Husserl, Edmund. 1931. *Ideas: General Introduction to Pure Phenomenology,* translated by W. R. Boyce Gibson. New York: Macmillan.

Ihde, Don. 1976. *Listening and Voice: A Phenomenology of Sound.* Athens, OH:Ohio University Press.

Ingham, John. 1996. *Psychological Anthropology Reconsidered.* Cambridge: Cambridge University Press.

Irvine, Judith. 1982. Language and Affect: Some Cross-Cultural Issues. In *Contemporary Perceptions of Language: Interdisciplinary Dimensions,* edited by H. Byrnes, pp. 31–47. Washington, DC: Georgetown University Press.

———. 1989. When Talk Isn't Cheap: Language and Political Economy. *American Ethnologist* 15:248–67.

Jackson, Michael. 1989. *Paths Toward a Clearing: Radical Empiricism and Ethnographic Inquiry.* Bloomington: Indiana University Press.

———. 1995. *At Home in the World.* Durham, NC: Duke University Press.

———. 1996. Phenomenology, Radical Empiricism, and Anthropological Critique. Introduction to *Things as They Are: New Directions in Phenomenological*

Anthropology, edited by M. Jackson, pp. 1–50. Bloomington: Indiana University Press.

Jacobs, Jean. 1961. *The Death and Life of Great American Cities.* New York: Vintage.

Jahnke, Art. 1987. Madhouse. *Boston Magazine.* September, pp. 132–37.

Jakobson, Roman. 1987 [1960]. Linguistics and Poetics. In *Language in Literature*, pp. 62–94. Cambridge, MA: Harvard University Press.

James, William. 1912. *Essays in Radical Empiricism.* New York: Longmans, Green.

Jameson, Fredric. 1991. *Postmodernism, or, The Cultural Logic of Late Capitalism.* Durham, NC: Duke University Press.

Janet, Pierre. 1928. *L'Évolution de la mémoire et de la notion du temps: comte-rendu intégral des conférences d'après les notes sténographiques.* Paris: A. Chahine.

Jaspers, Karl. 1963 [1923]. *General Psychopathology*, translated by J. Hoenig and M. Hamilton. Chicago: University of Chicago Press.

Jencks, Christopher. 1994. *The Homeless.* Cambridge, MA: Harvard University Press.

Kafka, Franz. 1956 [1925]. *The Trial.* New York: Schocken Books.

———. 1971 [1919]. In the Penal Colony. In *Franz Kafka: The Complete Stories*, edited by N. Glatzer, pp. 140–67. New York: Schocken Books.

Kant, Immanuel. 1914 [1790]. *Critique of Judgement*, translated by J. H. Bernard. London: Macmillan.

———. 1974 [1796]. *Anthropology from a Pragmatic Point of View*, translated by M. J. Gregor. The Hague: Martinus Nijhoff.

Karp, Ivan. 1986. Agency and Social Theory: A Review of Anthony Giddens. *American Ethnologist* 13:131–37.

Katz, Michael. 1986. *In the Shadow of the Poorhouse.* New York: Basic Books.

Kaufman, Nancy. 1992. State Government's Response to Homelessness: The Massachusetts Experience, 1983–1990. *New England Journal of Public Policy* 8:471–82.

Kaysen, Susanna. 1993. *Girl, Interrupted.* New York: Turtle Bay Books.

Kern, Stephen. 1983. *The Culture of Time and Space, 1880–1918.* Cambridge, MA: Harvard University Press.

Kernan, Keith, and Sharon Sabsay. 1989. Communication in Social Interactions: Aspects of an Ethnography of Communication of Mildly Mentally Handicapped Adults. In *Language and Communication in Mentally Handicapped People*, edited by M. Beveridge, G. Cont-Ramsden, and I. Leudar, pp. 229–53. London: Chapman and Hall.

Kleinman, Arthur. 1988. *Rethinking Psychiatry.* New York: Free Press.

———. 1995. *Writing at the Margins: Discourse Between Anthropology and Medicine.* Berkeley: University of California Press.

Kleinman, Arthur, and Joan Kleinman. 1995. Suffering and Its Professional Transformation: Toward an Ethnography of Interpersonal Experience. In *Writing at the Margins: Discourse Between Anthropology and Medicine*, pp. 95–119. Berkeley: University of California Press.

Klerman, Gerald. 1977. Better but Not Well: Social and Ethical Issues in the Deinstitutionalization of the Mentally Ill. *Schizophrenia Bulletin* 3:617–31.

Koegel, Paul. 1992. Through a Different Lens: An Anthropological Perspective on the Homeless Mentally Ill. *Culture, Medicine, and Psychiatry* 16:1–22.

Kondo, Dorinne. 1990. *Crafting Selves: Power, Gender, and Discourses of Identity in a Japanese Workplace.* Chicago: University of Chicago Press.

Kraepelin, Emil. 1921. *Clinical Psychiatry: A Textbook for Students and Physicians*, edited by A. R. Dienfendorf. New York: Macmillan.

Kristeva, Julia. 1982. *Powers of Horror: An Essay on Abjection*, translated by L. S. Roudiez. New York: Columbia University Press.

Lacan, Jacques. 1966. *Écrits*. Paris: Seuil.

Lamb, H. Richard. 1984. Deinstitutionalization and the Homeless Mentally Ill. *Hospital and Community Psychiatry* 35:899–907.

Lash, Scott, and John Urry. 1994. *Economies of Signs and Space*. London: Sage.

Le Corbusier. 1928. *Towards a New Architecture*, translated by F. Etchells. New York: Payson and Clarke.

Lee, Benjamin. 1992. Metalanguages and Subjectivities. In *Reflexive Language: Reported Speech and Metapragmatics*, edited by J. Lucy. pp. 365–89. Cambridge: Cambridge University Press.

Leenhardt, Maurice. 1979 [1947]. *Do Kamo: Person and Myth in the Melanesian World*, translated by B. Miller Gulati. Chicago: University of Chicago Press.

Leff, Julian, Norman Sartorius, Aaron Jablensky, A. Korten, and G. Ernberg. 1992. The International Pilot Study of Schizophrenia: Five Year Follow-up Findings. *Psychological Medicine* 22:131–45.

Leibovich, Mark. 1992. Compassion Fatigue. *Boston Phoenix*. March 13, sec. 2, pp. 4–5.

Levinas, Emmanuel. 1969. *Totality and Infinity: An Essay on Exteriority*, translated by A. Lingis. Pittsburgh: Duquesne University Press.

———. 1981. *Otherwise than Being; or, Beyond Essence*, translated by A. Lingis. The Hague: Martinus Nijhoff.

Lévy-Bruhl, Lucien. 1938. *L'Expérience mystique et les symboles chez les primitifs*. Paris: Alcan.

Liebow, Elliot. 1993. *Tell Them Who I Am: The Lives of Homeless Women*. New York: Free Press.

Lienhardt, Godfrey. 1961. *Divinity and Experience: The Religion of the Dinka*. Oxford: Clarendon.

Lifton, Robert Jay. 1993. *The Protean Self: Human Resilience in an Age of Fragmentation*. New York: Basic.

Link, Bruce. 1982. Mental Patient Status, Work, and Income: An Examination of the Effect of a Psychiatric Label. *American Sociological Review* 47:202–15.

Link, Bruce, Ezra Susser, Robert Moore, Sharon Schwartz, Elmer Struening, and Ann Stueve. 1993. Reconsidering the Debate About the Size of the Homeless Population. Paper presented at the Annual Meetings of the American Public Health Association, October.

Lipton, Frank, Albert Sabatini, and Steven Katz. 1983. Down and Out in the City: The Homeless Mentally Ill. *Hospital and Community Psychiatry* 34:817–21.

Lovell, Anne. 1992. Seizing the Moment: Power, Contingency, and Temporality in Street Life. In *The Politics of Time*, edited by H. Rutz, pp. 86–107. American Ethnological Society Monograph Series, 4. Washington, DC: American Anthropological Association.

———. 1996. Mobilité des cadres et psychiatrie "hors les murs." In *La Folie dans la place*, edited by I. Joseph and J. Proust, pp. 59–85. Paris: Éditions de l'École des Hautes Études en Sciences Sociales.

Low, Setha. 1994. Embodied Metaphors: Nerves as Lived Experience. In *Embodiment and Experience: The Existential Ground of Culture and Self*, edited by T. Csordas, pp. 139–62. Cambridge: Cambridge University Press.

Lurhmann, Tanya. 1996. *The Good Parsi: The Fate of a Colonial Elite in a Postcolonial Society*. Cambridge, MA: Harvard University Press.

Lutz, Catherine. 1986. Emotion, Thought, and Estrangement: Emotion as a Cultural Category. *Cultural Anthropology* 1:287–309.

Lyon, M. L., and J. M. Barbalet. 1994. Society's Body: Emotion and the "Somatization" of Social Theory. In *Embodiment and Experience: The Existential Ground of Culture and Self,* edited by T. Csordas, pp. 48–69. Cambridge: Cambridge University Press.

Malinowski, Bronislaw. 1935. *Coral Gardens and Their Magic.* Vol. 2, *The Language of Magic and Gardening.* New York: American Book Club.

Marcus, George. 1995. On Eccentricity. In *Rhetorics of Self-Making,* edited by D. Battaglia, pp. 43–58. Berkeley: University of California Press.

Martensen, Robert. 1995. Alienation and the Production of Strangers: Western Medical Epistemology and the Architectectonics of the Body: A Historical Perspective. *Culture, Medicine, and Psychiatry* 19:141–82.

Mathieu, Arline. 1993. The Medicalization of Homelessness and the Theatre of Repression. *Medical Anthropology Quarterly* 7:170–84.

Mattingly, Cheryl. 1989. Thinking with Stories: Story and Experience in a Clinical Practice. Ph.D. Dissertation, Massachusetts Institute of Technology.

Mauss, Marcel. 1973 [1935]. Techniques of the Body. *Economy and Society* 2:70–88.

———. 1985 [1938]. A Category of the Human Mind: The Notion of Person; the Notion of Self. In *The Category of the Person: Anthropology, Philosophy, History,* edited by M. Carrithers, S. Collins, and S. Lukes, pp. 1–25. Cambridge: Cambridge University Press.

McCabe, S. S., E. R. Edgar, D. A. King, L. Mancuso, and B. Emery. 1991. *Holes in the Housing Safety Net . . . Why SSI Is Not Enough: A National Comparison Study of Supplemental Security Income and HUD Fair Market Rents.* Burlington: University of Vermont, Center for Community Change Through Housing and Support.

Mead, George Herbert. 1934. *Mind, Self, and Society from the Standpoint of a Social Behavioralist.* Chicago: University of Chicago Press.

Mills, David. 1992. Hear the Homeless—It's an Art Thing. *San Francisco Chronicle.* February 15, C3.

Minkowski, Eugene. 1970. *Lived Time: Phenomenological and Psychopathological Studies,* translated by N. Metzel. Evanston, IL: Northwestern University Press.

Mitchell, Don. 1995. The End of Public Space? People's Park, Definitions of the Public, and Democracy. *Annals of the Association of American Geographers* 85:108–33.

Moya, Carlos. 1990. *The Philosophy of Action: An Introduction.* Cambridge: Polity Press.

Munn, Nancy. 1992. The Cultural Anthropology of Time: A Critical Essay. *Annual Review of Anthropology* 21:93–123.

Murray, Harry. 1986. Time in the Streets. In *Housing the Homeless,* edited by J. Erickson and C. Wilhelm, pp. 53–69. New Brunswick, NJ: Rutgers University Press.

Musil, Robert. 1995 [1952]. *The Man Without Qualities,* Vol. 1. Translated by S. Wilkins. New York: Vintage.

Nandy, Ashis. 1983. *The Intimate Enemy: Loss and Recovery of Self Under Colonialism.* Delhi: Oxford University Press.

National Law Center on Homelessness and Poverty. 1996. *Mean Sweeps.* Washington, DC: National Law Center on Homelessness and Poverty.

Needham, Rodney. 1972. *Belief, Language, and Experience.* Chicago: University of Chicago Press.

New York Times. 1987. Grand Central May Bid Homeless to Travel On. March 22, B6.

————. 1988. Koch, the "Entertainer," Gets Mixed Review. May 19, B4.

————. 1993. Preferring the Cold Shelter of the Streets. December 29, A1, D18.

————. 1994. Vigilantes in Colombia Kill Hundreds in a "Social Cleansing." October 31.

————. 1995. Ex-Outreach Workers Say They Assaulted Homeless. April 14, B1, B8.

Nietzsche, Friedrich. 1954. *The Portable Nietzsche.* Edited and translated by W. Kaufmann. New York: Viking Press.

————. 1967 [1901]. *The Will to Power.* Edited and translated by W. Kaufmann. New York: Vintage.

Oakshott, Michael. 1985 [1933]. *Experience and Its Modes.* Cambridge: Cambridge University Press.

Ochs, Elinor. 1988. *Culture and Language Development: Language Acquisition and Language Socialization in a Samoan Village.* Cambridge: Cambridge University Press.

O'Nell, Theresa. 1996. *Disciplined Hearts: History, Identity, and Depression in an American Indian Community.* Berkeley: University of California Press.

Ong, Walter. 1977. *Interfaces of the Word: Studies in the Evolution of Consciousness and Culture.* Ithaca, NY: Cornell University Press.

Ortner, Sherry. 1984. Theory in Anthropology Since the Sixties. *Comparative Studies in Society and History* 26:126–66.

Orwell, George. 1961 [1933]. *Down and Out in Paris and London.* New York: Harcourt Brace Jovanovich.

Overing, Joanna, ed. 1985. *Reason and Morality.* London: Tavistock Publications.

Parry, Jonathan, and Maurice Bloch, eds. 1989. *Money and the Morality of Exchange.* Cambridge: Cambridge University Press.

Peirce, Charles S. 1931–35, 1938. *The Collected Papers of Charles Sanders Peirce,* vols. 1–8. Edited by C. Hartshorne and P. Weiss. Cambridge, MA: Harvard University Press.

Pevsner, Nikolaus. 1960 [1936]. *Pioneers of Modern Design.* Harmondsworth: Penguin.

Progressive Architecture. 1964. Another Major Project for Boston. Vol. 45: 62–64.

Rabinow, Paul. 1992. Studies in the Anthropology of Reason. *Anthropology Today* 8:7–10.

Rhodes, Lorna. 1984. "This Will Clear Your Mind": The Use of Metaphors for Medication in Psychiatric Settings. *Culture, Medicine and Psychiatry* 8:49–70.

————. 1991. *Emptying Beds: The Work of an Emergency Psychiatric Unit.* Berkeley: University of California Press.

Ricoeur, Paul. 1970. *Freud and Philosophy: An Essay on Interpretation,* translated by D. Savage. New Haven, CT: Yale University Press.

————. 1977. *The Rule of Metaphor: Multi-Disciplinary Studies of the Creation of Meaning in Language,* translated by R. Czerny. Toronto: University of Toronto Press.

————. 1992. *Oneself as Another,* translated by K. Blamey. Chicago: University of Chicago Press.

Rieber, Robert, and Harold Vetter. 1994. The Problem of Language and Thought in Schizophrenia: A Review. *Journal of Psycholinguistic Research* 23:149–95.

Rochester, Sherry, and J. R. Martin. 1979. *Crazy Talk: A Study of the Discourse of Schizophrenic Speakers.* New York: Plenum Press.

Rorty, Amelie. 1976. A Literary Postscript: Characters, Persons, Selves, Individuals. In *The Identities of Persons,* edited by A. Rorty, pp. 301–23. Berkeley: University of California Press.

———. 1987. Persons as Rhetorical Categories. *Social Research* 54:55–72.

Rosaldo, Michelle Z. 1973. "I Have Nothing to Hide": The Language of Ilongot Oratory. *Language in Society* 2:193–223.

———. 1982. The Things We Do with Words: Ilongot Speech Acts and Speech Act Theory in Philosophy. *Language in Society* 11:203–37.

Rosaldo, Renato. 1986. Ilongot Hunting as Story and Experience. In *The Anthropology of Experience,* edited by V. Turner and E. Bruner, pp. 97–138. University of Illinois Press.

Rosenthal, Rob. 1991. Straighter from the Source: Alternative Methods of Researching Homelessness. *Urban Anthropology* 20:109–26.

Rossi, Peter. 1989. *Down and Out in America: The Origins of Homelessness.* Chicago: University of Chicago Press.

Rothman, David. 1971. *The Discovery of the Asylum: Social Order and Disorder in the New Republic.* Boston: Little, Brown.

———. 1987. The First Shelters: The Contemporary Relevance of the Almshouse. In *On Being Homeless: Historical Perspectives,* edited by R. Beard, pp. 11–19. New York: Museum of the City of New York.

Rudolph, Paul. 1956. The Six Determinants of Architectural Form. *Architectural Record* (October):183–88.

———. 1977. Enigmas of Architecture. In *Paul Rudolph: 1946–74, 100 by Paul Rudolph,* pp. 317–21. Tokyo: A and U Publishing.

———. *The Architecture of Paul Rudolph.* Edited by G. Schwab, introduction by S. Moholy-Nagy. New York: Praeger, 1970.

Sahlins, Marshall. 1976. *Culture and Practical Reason.* Chicago: University of Chicago Press.

———. 1985. *Islands of History.* Chicago: University of Chicago Press.

Salerno, Dan, Kim Hopper, and Ellen Baxter. 1984. *Hardship in the Heartland: Homeless in Eight U.S. Cities.* New York: Community Service Society of New York, Institute for Social Welfare Research.

Saris, A. Jamie. 1995. Telling Stories: Life Histories, Illness Narratives, and Institutional Landscapes. *Culture, Medicine, and Psychiatry* 18:39–72.

Sass, Louis. 1992. *Madness and Modernism: Insanity in the Light of Modern Art, Literature, and Thought.* New York: Basic Books.

Scarry, Elaine. 1985. *The Body in Pain.* New York: Oxford University Press.

Scheper-Hughes, Nancy. 1992. *Death Without Weeping: The Violence of Everyday Life in Brazil.* Berkeley: University of California Press.

———. 1994. The Violence of Everyday Life. In *The Making of Psychological Anthropology II,* edited by M. M. Suárez-Orozco, G. Spindler, and L. Spindler, pp. 135–57. Fort Worth, TX: Harcourt Brace.

Scheper-Hughes, Nancy, and Margaret Lock. 1987. The Mindful Body: A Prolegomenon to Future Work in Medical Anthropology. *Medical Anthropology Quarterly* 1:6–41.

Scheper-Hughes, Nancy, and Anne Lovell, eds. 1987. *Psychiatry Inside Out: Selected Writings of Franco Basaglia.* New York: Columbia University Press.

Schudson, Michael. 1984. *Advertising, the Uneasy Persuasion: Its Dubious Impact on American Society.* New York: Basic Books.

Schutt, Russell, and Stephen Goldfinger. 1992. Mentally Ill Persons in Emergency and Specialized Shelters: Satisfaction and Distress. *New England Journal of Public Policy* 8:407–18.

Schutz, Alfred. 1977 [1951]. Making Music Together: A Study of Social Rela-
tionships. In *Symbolic Anthropology*, edited by J. Dolgin, D. Kemnitzer, and
D. Schneider, pp. 106–19. New York: Columbia University Press.
Schwab, Gerhard, ed. 1970. *The Architecture of Paul Rudolph.* New York: Praeger
Publishers.
Sclar, Elliot. 1990. Homelessness and Housing Policy: A Game of Musical Chairs.
American Journal of Public Health 80:1039–40.
Scott, James C. 1990. *Domination and the Arts of Resistance: Hidden Transcripts.* New
Haven, CT: Yale University Press.
Scott, Joan. 1991. The Evidence of Experience. *Critical Inquiry* 17:773–95.
Scully, Vincent. 1989. *Modern Architecture.* New York: George Braziller.
Segal, Steven, and Jim Baumohl. 1980. Engaging the Disengaged: Proposals on
Madness and Vagrancy. *Social Work* 25:358–65.
Seremetakis, Nadia. 1991. *The Last Word: Women, Death, and Divination in Inner
Mani.* Chicago: University of Chicago Press.
———, ed. 1994. *The Senses Still: Perception and Memory as Material Culture in
Modernity.* Boulder, CO: Westview Press.
Shatan, Chaim. 1969. Community Psychiatry—Stretcher Bearer of the Social
Order? *International Journal of Psychiatry* 7:318.
Shook, Melissa. 1992. Streets Are for Nobody: Margaret Mullins. *New England
Journal of Public Policy* 8:453–54.
Shore, Brad. 1982. *Sala'ilua: A Samoan Mystery.* New York: Columbia University
Press.
Shweder, Richard. 1991. *Thinking Through Cultures: Expeditions in Cultural Psychol-
ogy.* Cambridge, MA: Harvard University Press.
Siegel, James. 1981. Academic Work: The View from Cornell. *Diacritics* 11:68–83.
Silverstein, Michael. 1976. Shifters, Linguistic Categories, and Cultural Descrip-
tion. In *Meaning in Anthropology*, edited by K. Basso and H. Selby, pp. 11–55.
Albuquerque: University of New Mexico Press.
———. 1979. Language Structure and Linguistic Ideology. In *The Elements: A
Parasession on Linguistic Units and Levels*, edited by R. Cylne, W. Hanks, and
C. Hofbauer, pp. 193–247. Chicago: Chicago Linguistic Society.
———. 1985. Language and Gender: At the Intersection of Structure, Usage,
and Ideology. In *Semiotic Mediation: Sociocultural and Psychological Perspectives*,
edited by E. Mertz and R. Parmentier, pp. 219–59. Orlando, FL: Academic
Press.
———. 1996. Monoglot "Standard" in America: Standardization and Metaphors
of Linguistic Hegemony. In *The Matrix of Language: Contemporary Linguistic Anthropology*, edited by D. Brenneis and R. Macaulay, pp. 284–306. Boulder, CO:
Westview Press.
Simmel, Georg. 1922. *Lebensanschauung; Vier Metaphysische Kapitel*, 2nd edition.
Munich: Dunker and Humblot.
———. 1971a [1911]. The Adventurer. In *On Individuality and Social Forms: Selected
Writings*, edited by D. Levine, pp. 187–98. Chicago: University of Chicago
Press.
———. 1971b [1911]. Metropolis and Mental Life. In *On Individuality and Social
Forms: Selected Writings*, edited by D. Levine, pp. 324–39. Chicago: University
of Chicago Press.
———. 1990 [1907]. *The Philosophy of Money*, translated by T. Bottomore and
D. Frisby. New York: Routledge.

Snow, David, and Leon Anderson. 1993. *Down on Their Luck: A Study of Homeless Street People*. Berkeley: University of California Press.

Southworth, Susan, and Michael Southworth. 1991. *A. I. A. Guide to Boston*. Chester, CT: Globe Pequot.

Spiro, Melford. 1987. *Culture and Human Nature: Theoretical Papers of Melford Spiro*, edited by B. Kilborne and L. L. Langness. Chicago: University of Chicago Press.

Stearns, Isabel. 1952. Firstness, Secondness, Thirdness. In *Studies in the Philosophy of Charles Sanders Peirce*, edited by P. Wiener and F. Young, pp. 195–208. Cambridge: Harvard University Press.

Stephens, Margaret, and Dominic Hodgkin. 1992. Financing Mental Health Services for the Homeless Mentally Ill in New England. *New England Journal of Public Policy* 8:435–52.

Stocking, George, ed. 1989. *Romantic Motives: Essays on Anthropological Sensibility*. Madison: University of Wisconsin Press.

Stoller, Paul. 1989. *The Taste of Ethnographic Things: The Senses in Anthropology*. Philadelphia: University of Pennsylvania Press.

Suárez-Orozco, Marcelo. 1990. Speaking of the Unspeakable: Toward a Psychosocial Understanding of Responses to Terror. *Ethos* 18:353–83.

———. 1992. A Grammar of Terror: Psychocultural Responses to the State Terrorism in Dirty War and Post-Dirty War Argentina. In *The Paths to Domination, Resistance, and Terror*, edited by C. Nordstrom and J. Martin, pp. 219–59. Berkeley: University of California Press.

———. 1994. Remaking Psychological Anthropology. In *The Making of Psychological Anthropology II*, edited by M. M. Suárez-Orozco, G. Spindler, and L. Spindler, pp. 10–59. Fort Worth, TX: Harcourt Brace.

Sutherland, Edwin, and Harvey Locke. 1936. *Twenty Thousand Homeless Men*. Chicago: Lippincott.

Swartz, Sally. 1994. Issues in the Analysis of Psychotic Speech. *Journal of Psycholinguistic Research* 23:29–44.

Tambiah, Stanley. 1990. *Magic, Science, Religion, and the Scope of Rationality*. Cambridge: Cambridge University Press.

Taussig, Michael. 1992. Terror as Usual: Walter Benjamin's Theory of History as State of Siege. In *The Nervous System*, pp. 11–36. New York: Routledge.

Taylor, Charles. 1989. *Sources of the Self: The Making of the Modern Identity*. Cambridge, MA: Harvard University Press.

Tedlock, Dennis, and Bruce Mannheim, eds. 1995. *The Dialogic Emergence of Culture*. Urbana: University of Illinois Press.

Terrill, Ross. 1991. Hong Kong. *National Geographic* 179:103–38.

Tessler, R. C., and D.L. Dennis. 1989. *A Synthesis of NIMH-funded Research Concerning Persons Who Are Homeless and Mentally Ill*. Rockville, MD: National Institute of Mental Health.

Thompson, E. P. 1967. Time, Work-Discipline, and Industrial Capitalism. *Past and Present* 38:56–97.

———. 1978. The Poverty of Theory or an Orrery of Errors. In *The Poverty of Theory and Other Essays*. New York: Monthly Review Press.

Tiernan, Kip. 1992. Homelessness: The Politics of Accommodation. *New England Journal of Public Policy* 8:647–67.

Time Magazine. 1963. Death of the Gargoyle. November 15, pp. 80, 85.

Timmer, Doug, D. Stanley Eitzen, and Kathryn Talley. 1994. *Paths to Homelessness: Extreme Poverty and the Urban Housing Crisis*. Boulder, CO: Westview Press.

Trawick, Margaret. 1990. *Notes on Love in a Tamil Family.* Berkeley: University of California Press.

Trilling, Lionel. 1972. *Sincerity and Authenticity.* Cambridge, MA: Harvard University Press.

Turner, Victor. 1982. *From Ritual to Theatre.* New York: Performing Arts Journal Press.

Turner, Victor, and Edward Bruner, eds. 1986. *The Anthropology of Experience.* Bloomington: Indiana University Press.

Twombly, Robert. 1995. *Power and Style: A Critique of Twentieth-Century Architecture in the United States.* New York: Hill and Wang.

Tyler, Stephen. 1987. *The Unspeakable: Discourse, Dialogue, and Rhetoric in the Postmodern World.* Madison: University of Wisconsin Press.

Venturi, Robert. 1966. *Complexity and Contradiction in Architecture.* New York: Museum of Modern Art.

Vidler, Anthony. 1992. *The Architectural Uncanny: Essays in the Modern Unhomely.* Cambridge, MA: MIT Press.

Vygotsky, Lev. 1986 [1934]. *Thought and Language,* edited and translated by A. Kozulin. Cambridge, MA: The MIT Press.

Wacquant, Loic. 1989. The Ghetto, the State, and the New Capitalist Economy. *Dissent* (Fall): 508–20.

Wagner, David. 1993. *Checkerboard Square: Culture and Resistance in a Homeless Community.* Boulder, CO: Westview Press.

Ware, Norma, Robert Desjarlais, Tara AvRuskin, Joshua Breslau, Byron Good, and Stephen Goldfinger. 1992. Empowerment and the Transition to Housing for the Homeless Mentally Ill: An Anthropological Perspective. *New England Journal of Health Policy.* 8:297–314.

Waxler, Nancy. 1974. Culture and Mental Illness: A Social Labeling Perspective. *Journal of Nervous and Mental Disease* 159:379–95.

Weber, Max. 1930. *The Protestant Ethic and the Spirit of Capitalism,* translated by T. Parsons. New York: Charles Scribner's Sons.

———. 1978. *Economy and Society.* Edited by G. Roth and C. Wittich, translated by E. Fischoff et al. 2 vols. Berkeley: University of California Press.

Weiskel, Thomas. 1976. *The Romantic Sublime: Studies in the Structure and Psychology of Transcendence.* Baltimore: John Hopkins University Press.

Welsh, Irvine. 1993. *Trainspotting.* London: Martin Secker and Warburg.

White, Geoffrey. 1992. Ethnopsychology. In *New Directions in Psychological Anthropology,* edited by T. Schwartz, G. White, and C. Lutz, pp. 21–46. Cambridge: Cambridge University Press.

Wikan, Unni. 1991. Toward an Experience-Near Anthropology. *Cultural Anthropology* 6:285–305.

Williams, Raymond. 1979. *Politics and Letters.* London: New Left Books.

——— 1983. *Keywords: A Vocabulary of Culture and Society.* Oxford: Oxford University Press.

Wilson, Peter. 1974. *Oscar: An Inquiry into the Nature of Sanity.* New York: Random House.

Witherspoon, Gary. 1977. *Language and Art in the Navajo Universe.* Ann Arbor: University of Michigan Press.

Wittgenstein, Ludwig. 1953. *Philosophical Investigations.* New York: Macmillan.

Woolard, Kathryn, and Bambi Schieffelin. 1994. Language Ideology. *Annual Review of Anthropology* 23:55–82.

Wordsworth, William. 1979 [1799–1850]. *The Prelude 1799, 1805, 1850.* Edited by J. Wordsworth, M. H. Abrams, and S. Gill. New York: Norton.

Wrobel, Janusz. 1990. *Language and Schizophrenia.* Amsterdam: John Benjamins.

Young, Allan. 1995. *The Harmony of Illusions: Inventing Post-Traumatic Stress Disorder.* Princeton, NJ: Princeton University Press.

Zerubavel, Eviatar. 1981. *Hidden Rhythms: Schedules and Calendars in Social Life.* Berkeley: University of California Press.

Index

Aesthetics: of the everyday, 22, 114, 119; and representations of homelessness, 2, 65–68; of urban planning, 45, 48, 64
Agency: anthropological understandings of, 24, 28, 71, 201–5, 216–17, 241; among residents, 26–27, 71, 123–24, 128, 189, 191–92, 197–201, 203–4, 212, 221, 239; among staff, 191–92, 197–203
Appadurai, Arjun, 274 n.15
Aristotle, 17, 162, 186–87, 236, 269 n.9, 279–80 n.5
Artaud, Antonin, 229–30
Auden, W. H., 67
Auerbach, Erich, 14–15
Augustine, 13, 15
Ayto, John, 259 n.17

Bachelard, Gaston, 93
Bakhtin, Mikhail, 3, 79, 87, 188, 231, 244
Barrett, Robert, 281 n.3
Barthes, Roland, 117, 181
Basso, Keith, 41
Bataille, Georges, 244
Bateson, Gregory, 26, 188, 234
Baudelaire, Charles, 126
Beckett, Samuel, 94, 136, 166, 243, 271 n.6
Benjamin, Walter, 126, 260 n.3, 266–67 n.3
Bentham, Jeremy, 96, 98, 99, 102, 104
Bernstein, J. M., 67
Besnier, Niko, 217, 219
Boas, Franz, 11
Bodies, 3, 16, 96, 127; anthropological research on, 222, 226, 227–28, 232, 237, 245, 248; epistemology of, 220, 231–34; and mental illness, 228–34; of residents, 22, 72–74, 75, 86–87, 112–14, 117–20,

127, 158, 164, 166, 193, 219, 224–27, 228–37; rhetorical uses of, 232–37; techniques of, 139, 236. *See also* Feeling; Sensory orientations
Bourdieu, Pierre, 201
Brand, Bill, 5
Brenneis, Donald, 277 n.8, 278 n.6
Brutalism, 47, 48, 73
Burke, Edmund, 59, 62, 63
Burke, Kenneth, 188, 264 n.12, 278 n.6

Capitol Police, the, 77, 80, 97, 99–100, 104, 193, 211
Carr, David, 17
Character(s), ideas of, 4, 107–10, 117, 192, 209, 214–15, 236, 239
Chronicity, 116–17
Coleridge, Samuel Taylor, 67
Collins, John, 45
Comaroff, Jean, and John Comaroff, 227
Conversation: and economics, 146–48; ethics of, 194–96, 223; and ethnographic research, 6, 28, 41–42, 223, 240, 264 n.4, 264 n.7; among residents, 41–42, 63, 77, 157, 159, 160–61, 167, 168–76, 182, 186–89, 194–96, 197–98, 207–9, 215, 236–37, 239, 244, 247, 248. *See also* Language; Ragtime; Rhetoric
Corin, Ellen, 156
Corrington, Robert S., 130, 131, 182
Crapanzano, Vincent, 220, 282 n.6

Daniel, E. Valentine, 273 n.27
Das, Veena, 283 n.14
De Certeau, Michel, 21, 140, 183, 189, 260 n.3